COMPUTER CONCEPTS BASICS

Second Edition

Dr. Dolores Wells
Ann Ambrose

THOMSON ™
COURSE TECHNOLOGY

Australia • Canada • Mexico • Singapore • Spain • United Kingdom • United States

Computer Concepts BASICS, Second Edition
by Dr. Dolores Wells and Ann Ambrose

Senior Vice President
Chris Elkhill

Managing Editor
Chris Katsaropoulos

Senior Product Manager
Dave Lafferty

Product Marketing Manager
Kim Ryttel

Associate Product Manager
Jodi Dreissig

Development Editor
Jean Findley
Custom Editorial Productions

Production Editor
Anne Chimenti
Custom Editorial Productions

Compositor
GEX Publishing Services

COPYRIGHT © 2004 Course Technology, a division of Thomson Learning, Inc. Thomson Learning™ is a trademark used herein under license.

Printed in the United States of America

2 3 4 5 6 7 8 9 BM 06 05 04 03

For more information, contact Course Technology, 25 Thomson Place, Boston, Massachusetts, 02210.

Or find us on the World Wide Web at: www.course.com

ALL RIGHTS RESERVED. No part of this work covered by the copyright hereon may be reproduced or used in any form or by any means—graphic, electronic, or mechanical, including photocopying, recording, taping, Web distribution, or information storage and retrieval systems—without the written permission of the publisher.

For permission to use material from this text or product, contact us by
Tel (800) 730-2214
Fax (800) 730-2215
www.thomsonrights.com

Disclaimer
Course Technology reserves the right to revise this publication and make changes from time to time in its content without notice.

ISBN 0-619-05578-2
ISBN 0-619-18295-4

Get Back to the Basics...
With these *exciting new products*

Our exciting new series of short concepts and application suite books will provide everything needed to learn this software. Other books include:

NEW! Computer Concepts BASICS by Wells and Ambrose
35+ hours of instruction for additional projects on computer concepts

0-619-05578-2	Textbook, Hard Spiral Bound Cover
0-619-18295-4	Textbook, Soft Perfect Bound Cover
0-619-05581-2	Activities Workbook
0-619-05579-0	Instructor Resource Kit
0-619-05580-4	Review Pack (Data CD)

NEW! Computer Projects BASICS by Korb
35+ hours of instruction for additional projects on all software applications

0-619-05987-7	Textbook, Soft Spiral Bound Cover
0-619-05988-5	Instructor Resource Kit

NEW! Internet BASICS by Barksdale, Rutter, & Teeter
35+ hours of instruction for beginning through intermediate features

0-619-05905-2	Textbook, Soft Spiral Bound Cover
0-619-05906-0	Instructor Resource Kit
0-619-05907-9	Review Pack (Data CD)

NEW! Microsoft Office XP BASICS by Morrison
35+ hours of instruction for beginning through intermediate features

0-619-05908-7	Textbook, Hard Spiral Bound Cover
0-619-05906-0	Instructor Resource Kit
0-619-05909-5	Activities Workbook
0-619-05911-7	Review Pack (Data CD)

NEW! Microsoft Office v.X Macintosh BASICS by Melton and Walls
35+ hours of instruction for beginning through intermediate features

0-619-05563-4	Textbook, Hard Spiral Bound Cover
0-619-05568-5	Activities Workbook
0-619-05566-9	Instructor Resource Kit
0-619-05567-7	Review Pack (Data CD)

Join Us On the Internet **http://www.course.com**

How to Use This Book

What makes a good text about Computer Concepts? Sound instruction and hands-on skill-building and reinforcement. That is what you will find in *Computer Concepts BASICS*. Not only will you find a colorful and inviting layout, but also many features to enhance learning.

Objectives—Objectives are listed at the beginning of each lesson, along with a suggested time for completion of the lesson. This allows you to look ahead to what you will be learning and to pace your work.

Step-by-Step Exercises—Preceded by a short topic discussion, these exercises are the "hands-on practice" part of the lesson. Simply follow the steps, either using a data file or creating a file from scratch. Each lesson is a series of these step-by-step exercises.

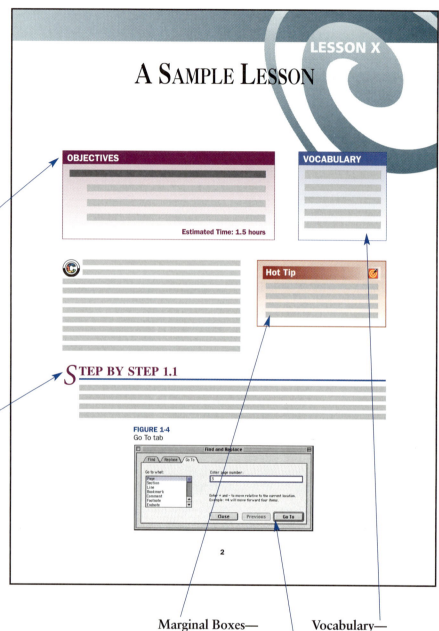

Marginal Boxes—These boxes provide additional information about the topic of the lesson.

Vocabulary—Terms identified in boldface/italic throughout the lesson and summarized at the end.

Enhanced Screen Shots—Screen shots come to life on the pages with color and depth.

How to Use This Book

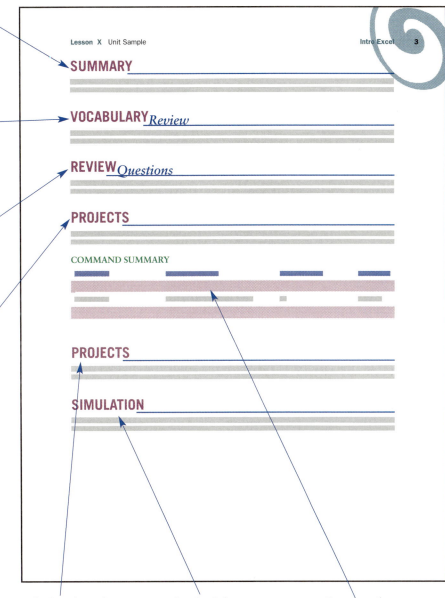

Summary—At the end of each lesson, you will find a summary to prepare you to complete the end-of-lesson activities.

Vocabulary Review— Review of important terms defined in the lesson reinforce the concepts learned.

Review Questions—Review material at the end of each lesson and each unit enables you to prepare for assessment of the content presented.

Lesson Projects—End-of-lesson hands-on application of what has been learned in the lesson allows you to actually apply the techniques covered.

End-of-Unit Projects—End-of-unit hands-on application of the concepts learned in the unit provides opportunity for a comprehensive review.

On-the-Job-Simulation—A realistic simulation at the end of most units reinforces the material covered in the unit.

Command Summary—At the end of some units, a command summary is provided for quick reference.

PREFACE

Computer Concepts BASICS, Second Edition, is a brief introduction to computers. This text covers computer hardware, software, application skills, keyboarding skills, the Internet and Internet searching, Web page creation, networking, careers, and computer ethics. It can be used in any class on business applications, technology, or computer applications. This textbook, along with the Instructor's Resource CD-ROM and Activities Workbook, is all that is needed for a brief course on computer concepts and the Internet and can be used for 35 or more hours of instruction. After completing these materials, the student should have an understanding of the basics of computers, how technology is changing the world in which we live, and the importance of the Internet.

Partnered with a tutorial on a software application, such as Microsoft Office, Microsoft Works, or ClarisWorks, this text provides a complete course on computer concepts—with hands-on applications. It is assumed in this course that students have no prior experience with computer concepts. Other possible applications include supplementing a mathematics, science, language arts, or social studies class through the integrated end-of-lesson and workbook activities and exercises. The lessons within the textbook are built around a company called Vista Multimedia. Relating lesson information to this company provides the student a link to the real world.

About the Materials

The full materials for this course include the textbook, the workbook, and the Instructor's Resource CD-ROM. Although advanced students may complete the course successfully in a self-guided manner, it is recommended that the course be taken in an instructor-guided, hands-on environment, especially for beginning or intermediate students.

Features of the Text

Sixteen lessons gradually introduce the skills necessary to learn the fundamentals of what computers are and how they can be used, including how to access and use the Internet and World Wide Web. Step-by-step exercises divide each lesson into conceptual blocks and are accompanied by integrated hands-on exercises that reinforce the presented information. At the end of each lesson is a summary, review questions, including multiple choice, true/false, and short answer; Web projects, team projects, and cross-curricular projects. Other features include margin notes on topics such as Did You Know?, Internet Tips, and Hot Tips.

Included within each lesson are objectives, vocabulary lists, estimated completion times, screen illustrations for visual reinforcement, and photos and illustrations to provide interest and clarity. Special sections on ethics and careers are included.

Activities Workbook

The student workbook contains additional exercises and additional review questions. Definitions, short answer, fill in the blank, and true/false questions are provided in the activities workbook as a basis for study, lesson review, or test preparation.

Instructor's Resource and Review Pack CD-ROMs

All data files necessary for the Step-by-Step exercises, end-of-lesson Projects, and end-of-unit Projects and simulations are located on the *Review Pack* CD-ROM.

The *Instructor's Resource* CD-ROM contains a wealth of instructional material you can use to prepare for teaching this course. The CD-ROM stores the following information:

- ExamView® tests for each lesson. ExamView is a powerful testing software package that allows instructors to create and administer printed, computer (LAN-based), and Internet exams. ExamView includes hundreds of questions that correspond to the topics covered in this text, enabling learners to generate detailed study guides that include page references for further review. The computer-based and Internet testing components allow learners to take exams at their computers, and also save the instructor time by grading each exam automatically.

- Electronic *Instructor Manual* that includes lesson plans, answers to the lesson and unit review questions, and suggested/sample solutions for Step-by-Step exercises, end-of-lesson activities, and Unit Review projects.

- Copies of the figures that appear in the learner text, which can be used to prepare transparencies.

- Suggested schedules for teaching the lessons in this course.

- PowerPoint presentations that illustrate objectives for each lesson in the text.

START-UP CHECKLIST

HARDWARE

- ✓ IBM or IBM-compatible PC
- ✓ 233-MHz or higher Pentium-compatible processor (600-MHz or faster is preferred)
- ✓ 64 MB of RAM (256 MB of RAM is preferred)
- ✓ One hard disk (2 GB) with at least 650 MB of free hard disk space
- ✓ CD-ROM drive
- ✓ SVGA-capable video adapter and monitor (SVGA resolution of a minimum of 800 x 600 pixels with 256 or more colors)
- ✓ Enhanced keyboard
- ✓ Mouse or pen pointer
- ✓ 14,000 or higher baud modem (56,000 is preferred)
- ✓ Printer

SOFTWARE

- ✓ Windows 95 or later version
- ✓ Microsoft Office
- ✓ Web browser

Macintosh users can open Word, Excel and PowerPoint files using Microsoft Office for the Macintosh.

Photo Credits

Lesson 1

1-1	Rapid Rental Software (1.800.263.0000)
1-2	© PhotoDisc
1-4	© PhotoDisc
1-5	Introduction to Computers and Technology
1-7	© PhotoDisc
1-8	Courtesy of International Business Machines Corporation. Unauthorized use not permitted.
1-11	Arc map created by visualization researchers at Bell Laboratories-Lucent Technologies © Stephen Eick, Bell Labs / Visual Insight
1-12	© PhotoDisc

Lesson 3

3-3	© PhotoDisc
3-4	© PhotoDisc
3-7	© PhotoDisc

Lesson 4

4-2	© PhotoDisc
4-4	GEX Publishing Services

Lesson 5

5-1	© PhotoDisc
5-2	© PhotoDisc
5-3	© PhotoDisc
5-4	© PhotoDisc
5-5	Lernout & Hauspie Speech Technology Products & Services
5-6	© PhotoDisc
5-7	© PhotoDisc
5-8	© PhotoDisc
5-13	© PhotoDisc
5-17	© PhotoDisc

Lesson 10

10-1	© PhotoDisc

Lesson 12

12-1	© PhotoDisc

Lesson 16

16-6	© PhotoDisc
16-10	© PhotoDisc
16-16	Courtesy of IriScan; IriScan's iris recognition technology identifies people by the patterns in the iris of the eye

Table of Contents

iv How to Use This Book
vi Preface

UNIT 1 COMPUTER BASICS

3	**Lesson 1: Understanding Computers and Computer Literacy**
4	What Is a Computer?
4	A Computer System
6	What Makes a Computer So Powerful?
7	Computer Literacy
7	A Brief History of the Computer
9	How Computers Are Used
9	Categories of Computers
11	Communications and the Beginning of the Internet
13	The Internet
13	How Vista Multimedia Uses Computers
14	Computers in Our Future
15	Summary
21	**Lesson 2: The Internet and the World Wide Web**
22	Evolution of the Internet
23	How Does the Internet Work?
24	Major Features of the Internet
27	Accessing the Internet—Dial-in or Direct Connection
29	What Is a Browser?
46	Summary
51	**Lesson 3: How a Computer Processes Data**
51	Computer System Components
53	System Components
59	Data Representation
60	Summary
65	**Lesson 4: Keyboarding**
66	The Keyboard Layout
68	The Display Computer Screen
69	Correct Keyboarding Techniques
72	Developing Beginning Keyboarding Skills
74	Saving Your Practice Work
74	Printing a File
74	Exiting the Program
75	Retrieving a File
75	Additional Concepts
79	Summary

Table of Contents

83	**Lesson 5: Input, Output, Storage, and Networks**
84	Input Devices
89	Output Devices
93	Connecting Input/Output Devices to the Computer
93	Storage Devices
97	Caring for Removable Storage Media
97	Introducing Networks
99	Communications Media
105	Types of Networks
107	Network Topologies
108	Communications Protocols
109	Network Operating Systems Software
109	Summary
117	**Lesson 6: Operating Systems and Software**
117	Hardware vs. Software
118	Types of Software
120	Microcomputer Operating Systems Interfaces
122	Microcomputer Operating Systems
128	Summary
133	Unit Review

UNIT 2 SOFTWARE

141	**Lesson 7: Word Processing**
142	What Is Word-Processing Software?
151	Formatting Text
172	Creating a Simple Table
175	Summary
179	**Lesson 8: Spreadsheets**
180	What Is the Purpose of Spreadsheets?
180	The Anatomy of a Spreadsheet
181	Moving Around in a Spreadsheet
182	Entering Data into a Spreadsheet
183	Entering Formulas and Functions
185	Copying Data
187	Printing the Spreadsheet
189	Formatting a Spreadsheet
195	Workbooks
195	Hiding Data
196	Headers and Footers
197	Adding Objects in a Spreadsheet
198	Creating Charts
199	Using a Spreadsheet
199	Summary

205	**Lesson 9: Databases**
205	What Is Database Software?
206	Creating a Database
211	Modifying the Table Structure
212	Entering Data into a Table
213	Printing a Table
213	Sorting a Table
214	Querying a Database
220	Creating and Using Forms
223	Creating and Using a Report
228	Summary

233	**Lesson 10: Presentation Graphics and Multimedia**
234	Using Visuals in a Presentation
234	Overview
235	Creating a Presentation
240	Working in Different Views
241	Add Clip Art to Your Presentation
242	Adding a Chart to Your Presentation
244	Adding WordArt to a Presentation
247	Playing Your Presentation
247	Printing Your Presentation
248	Preparing an Effective Presentation
249	Delivering a Presentation
250	Using Multimedia
253	Creating a Multimedia Presentation
255	Summary

259	**Lesson 11: Integration**
259	Software Integration
260	Creating a Form Letter
265	Creating Mailing Labels
269	Importing Files
275	Summary
279	Unit Review

UNIT 3 ADVANCED COMPUTER CONCEPTS

289	**Lesson 12: The Internet and Research**
290	The Key to a Successful Search
290	Why Search the Internet?
291	Search Engines
296	Specialty Search Engines
299	Subject Directory Searching
303	Tools and Techniques for Searching the Web
307	Summary

Table of Contents

313   **Lesson 13: Evaluating Electronic Information**

313	Evaluating Information Found on the Internet
314	Viewing a Page
317	Types of Internet Resources
317	Understanding Rules of Copyright
319	Internet Detective
319	Evaluation Survey
320	Other Legal and Ethical Issues
321	Summary

325   **Lesson 14: Desktop Publishing**

326	What Is Desktop Publishing?
327	Stages in the Desktop Publishing Process
329	Layout and Design
330	Using Graphics
332	Using Color
332	Using Lines
333	Using Other Elements
334	Using Microsoft Publisher
337	Desktop Publishing Tips
338	Summary

343   **Lesson 15: Creating a Web Page**

343	How a Web Page Works
344	Plan a Document
345	A Basic Page
349	Page Formatting
359	Links
364	Images
368	Backgrounds
370	Publishing Your Web Page
372	Summary

377   **Lesson 16: How Technology is Changing the Workplace and Society**

378	Education
384	Scientific Discovery and Technological Innovations
387	Work and Play
392	Technological Issues
395	Risks of Using Computer Hardware and Software
399	Summary
403	Unit Review

409	**Glossary**
417	**Index**

COMPUTER BASICS

Unit 1

Lesson 1 — 1.5 hrs.
Understanding Computers and Computer Literacy

Lesson 2 — 1.5 hrs.
The Internet and the World Wide Web

Lesson 3 — 1.5 hrs.
How a Computer Processes Data

Lesson 4 — 1.5 hrs.
Keyboarding

Lesson 5 — 3 hrs.
Input, Output, Storage and Networks

Lesson 6 — 1.5 hrs.
Operating Systems and Software

🕐 Estimated Time for Unit: 10.5 hours

LESSON 1

Understanding Computers and Computer Literacy

OBJECTIVES

Upon completion of this lesson, you should be able to:

- Define the term *computer*.
- Describe a computer system.
- Explain the importance of computer literacy.
- Discuss the history of computers.
- Identify how computers and technology are used in our daily lives.
- List the categories of computers and their uses.
- Describe communications.
- Define networks, intranets, and extranets.
- Discuss the use of the Internet and the World Wide Web.

Estimated Time: 1.5 hours

VOCABULARY

Clients
Computer
Data
Desktop computer
Electronic communication
Extranet
Handheld or palmtop computer
Hardware
Information
Internet
Intranet
Mainframe computer
Mid-range server
Network
Nodes
Notebook computer
Personal computer
Servers
Software
Supercomputer
Users

Congratulations on your new job at Vista Multimedia (VM)! VM is a multifaceted business representing today's information society. Customers can rent CDs, DVDs, games, and videos. CD and DVD duplicators are available to transfer video data and create multimedia discs. Customers can rent time in the Internet Café to surf the Web, chat with friends, and play online games.

As part of your job as a sales assistant, you will use a computer to perform many of your duties. In fact, the computer appears to be the most important piece of equipment in the store. Some of its uses include recording sales, maintaining employee and customer records, managing inventory, and communicating with suppliers of goods and equipment.

The importance of the computer in this business or any business is not surprising. Many individuals consider the computer as the single most important invention of the twentieth century! This technology affects all aspects of our daily lives. Computers are no longer only the personal computers that sit on our desktops. They come in every shape and size and are found everywhere.

Computers and computer technology are pervasive throughout our society—from businesses and financial organizations, to home electronics and appliances, and even in your favorite electronic toy. As more powerful and special-purpose computers become available, society will find more ways to use this technology to enhance our lives. See Figure 1-1.

> **Extra for Experts**
> Supercomputers often are used to test medical experiments.

FIGURE 1-1
A customer checks the availibility of a video at a video store

What Is a Computer?

Throughout a normal workday, millions of people interact globally with computers, often without even knowing it. Doctors, lawyers, warehouse workers, store clerks, homemakers, musicians, and students, to name a few examples, constantly depend on computers to perform part of their daily duties.

So, what is a *computer*? Modern computers are electronic and digital devices that:

- Respond to a specific set of instructions or a program.
- Execute the prerecorded list of instructions.

A Computer System

A *computer system* includes hardware, software, data, and people. The actual machine, wires, transistors, and circuits, are called *hardware*. Peripheral devices such as printers and monitors are also hardware. The instructions, or programs, for controlling the computer are called *software*. *Data* is text, numbers, sound, images, or video. The computer receives data through an

input device, processes the data, stores the data on a storage device, and produces output or *information*. The *users*, the people who use computers, are also part of the system. See Figure 1-2.

FIGURE 1-2
Using a computer to process data into information

Compare the description of a computer system with examples of ways the computer at VM is used.

- *Receives data:* A customer's name and the title of a rented DVD are entered into the computer through an input device, such as the keyboard.

- *Processes data:* The computer uses stored instructions to process the data into information.

- *Stores data:* The data and information are stored in temporary memory and on a permanent storage device, such as a hard disk drive.

- *Outputs information*: Information is displayed on an output device such as a monitor and/or a printer. See Figure 1-3.

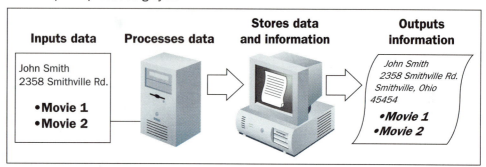

FIGURE 1-3
The computer processing cycle

This short overview of a computer and the listing of some of the tasks you can accomplish with a computer may appear to imply that the computer is a very complicated device. A computer, however, performs only two operations:

- Arithmetic operations (adding, subtracting, multiplying, and dividing)
- Logical/Comparison operations (greater than, less than, equal to)

You will learn more about these operations, how a computer works, and how data is transformed into information in Lesson 3.

> **Did You Know?**
> A computer won a World Chess Championship game against a human.

What Makes a Computer So Powerful?

Computers are not intelligent. They will do only what we ask them to do. If this is so, then what are the advantages of using a computer?

- *Speed*—A computer can perform billions of calculations per second.
- *Reliability*—The electronic components are dependable.
- *Accuracy*—If data is entered correctly, computers generate error-free results.
- *Storage*—Computers can store and retrieve unlimited amounts of data and information.
- *Communications*—Computers can communicate and share resources with other computers.

> **Net Tip**
> Visit The Journey Inside Intel Web site at *www97.intel.com/ scripts-tji/* and discover how a microprocessor works.

Computer Literacy

Many definitions of computer literacy exist today. *Webster's New College Dictionary* defines computer literacy as "the ability to use a computer and its software to accomplish practical tasks." As technology advances, computer literacy will likely mean something very different in the future than it does today. See Figure 1-4.

FIGURE 1-4
Student using handheld computer

A Brief History of the Computer

Computers have been around for more than 50 years. The first computers were developed in the late 1940s and early 1950s. They were giants with names like UNIVAC and ENIAC. These massive, special-purpose machines were designed initially for use by the military and government. These early computers had less processing power than today's pocket calculators, occupied small buildings or entire city blocks, and cost millions of dollars. Computers in the mid-1950s through

> **Extra for Experts**
>
> Explore the geography of the Ecuadorian Amazon through online simulation games and activities. The Web site for this fun and adventure is *www.eduweb.com/amazon.html*.

early 1970s were somewhat smaller and more powerful, but were still limited in what they could do. They remained expensive, so only major companies could afford these systems. See Figure 1-5.

FIGURE 1-5
Early computers

In 1971, Dr. Ted Hoff developed the microprocessor. It took visionaries like Steve Jobs and Steve Wozniak to see a future for the microprocessor and its application to personal computers. Jobs and Wozniak built the first Apple computer in 1976. Shortly thereafter, a second version, the Apple II, was released. It became an immediate success, especially in schools. In 1980, Bill Gates worked with IBM to develop the operating system for the IBM PC. This computer, introduced in 1981, quickly became the PC of choice in business. See Figure 1-6.

> **Did You Know?**
>
> In 1937, Dr. John Atanasoff and Clifford Berry designed and built the first electronic digital computer.

FIGURE 1-6
The Apple II and IBM PC

How Computers Are Used

Computers have affected our lives vastly and have changed dramatically the way in which we live. Without computers, the world as we know it today would come to a sudden halt. Think of the many ways computers affect you every day. They have become necessary tools in almost every type of activity and in almost every type of business. For example:

- In school, instruction is enhanced and information is accessible from anywhere in the world.
- Obtaining a high school or college degree via distance learning is possible.
- Electronic security systems protect our homes and work places.
- In game rooms, simulations transport you to an imaginary world.
- In government research operations, computer systems guide satellites through space.
- At home, our appliances are computerized.
- On television, we can watch an instant replay of a tackle in a football game.

In most everyday activities in which you participate, you benefit from the variety of applications and ways in which computers are used. See Figure 1-7.

FIGURE 1-7
Computers are everywhere

Categories of Computers

Computers today come in all shapes and sizes, with specific types being especially suited for specific tasks. Computers are considered special purpose or general purpose. Special-purpose computers are used mostly to control something else. Tiny chips are embedded in devices such as a dishwasher, bathroom scale, or airport radar system; and these chips control these particular devices.

> **Net Tip**
>
> Visit NASA's site, www.*nasa.gov*, to learn how computers and computer-related technologies are used in space exploration.

General-purpose computers are divided into five categories, based on their physical size, function, cost, and performance.

- Desktop and notebook computers are today's most widely used *personal computers* (PCs). A *desktop computer* is designed so that all components fit on or under a desk. A *notebook computer* is a lightweight PC that can fit easily into a briefcase.
- The *handheld* or *palmtop computer* is designed to fit into the palm of your hand and is used primarily for functions such as phone books and calendars.
- The *mid-range server* is used by small to medium-size companies and generally supports hundreds of users.
- The modern *mainframe computer* is a large, expensive computer, capable of supporting hundreds or even thousands of users.
- A *supercomputer* is the fastest type of computer and is used for specialized applications requiring immense amounts of mathematical calculations.

The small personal and handheld computers are more powerful than the mainframes and supercomputers of yesteryear. See Figure 1-8.

FIGURE 1-8
1. Desktop computer and Notebook computer 2. Palmtop computer 3. Mid-range server 4. Mainframe 5. Supercomputer

1.

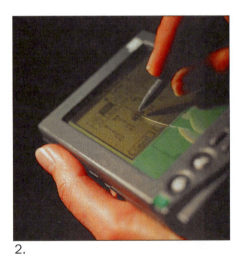

2.

FIGURE 1-8
(continued)

3.   4.   5.

Table 1-1 contains a list of the five categories of computers.

TABLE 1-1
Categories of computers

CATEGORY	SIZE	NUMBER OF USERS	PRICE RANGE	USES
Desktop or notebook	Fits on a desk or on a lap	One	$500–$3,000	Personal use or on desktops within businesses
Handheld or palmtop	Fits in your hand	One	$50–$500	Personal assistant
Mid-range server	Small cabinet	Two to thousands	$3,000–$750,000	Medium to large businesses
Mainframe	Partial to full room size	Hundreds to thousands	$200,000–millions	Large businesses
Supercomputer	Full room	Hundreds to thousands	$1 million and up	Universities and research institutions

Communications and the Beginning of the Internet

Electronic communication is the technology that enables computers to communicate with each other and other devices. It is the transmission of text, numbers, voice, and video from one computer or device to another. Communication has changed the way the world does business and the way we live our lives.

When computers were developed in the 1950s, they did not communicate with each other. This all changed in 1969. ARPANET was established and served as a testing ground for new networking technologies. ARPANET was a large wide-area network created by the United States Defense

Advanced Research Project Agency (ARPA). On Labor Day in 1969, the first message was sent via telephone lines from a computer at UCLA to another computer at Stanford Research Institute. This was the beginning of the Internet and electronic communication as we know it today.

Electronic communication requires four components:

- *Sender:* The computer that is sending the message
- *Receiver:* The computer receiving the message
- *Channel:* The media that carries or transports the message; this could be telephone wire, coaxial cable, microwave signal, or fiber optic
- *Protocol:* The rules that govern the transfer of data

This technology has made it possible to communicate around the globe using such tools as the Internet, electronic mail (e-mail), faxes, e-commerce, and electronic banking. See Figure 1-9.

FIGURE 1-9
Transmitting a message from sender to receiver

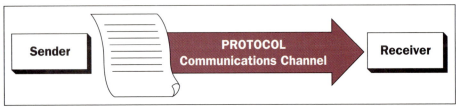

Networks

A *network* is a group of two or more computer systems linked together via communication devices. This connection enables the computers to share resources such as printers, data, information, and programs. A network can consist of two computers or millions and can connect all categories of computers, including handheld computers, microcomputers, mid-range servers, mainframes, and even supercomputers.

Computers on a network are called *nodes* or *clients*. Computers that allocate resources are called *servers*. See Figure 1-10. Networks are covered in detail in Lesson 5.

FIGURE 1-10
A network connecting users through various communication devices

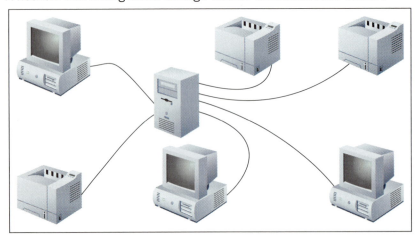

Intranets and Extranets

Many companies have implemented intranets within their organizations. An *intranet* is a network for the exclusive use of workers within the organization and contains company information. Company manuals, handbooks, and newsletters are just a few of the types of documents distributed via an intranet. Online forms are also a popular intranet feature. The major advantage of using an intranet is reliability and security—possible because the organization controls access.

Extranets are systems that allow outside organizations to access a company's internal information system. Access is tightly controlled and usually reserved for suppliers and customers.

The Internet

The *Internet*, the world's largest network, evolved from ARPANET. Following the first historic message between two computers in 1969, ARPANET grew quickly into a global network consisting of hundreds of military and university sites. In 1990, ARPANET was disbanded and the Internet was born. Today, millions of users surf the Internet and the World Wide Web, one of the more popular segments of the Internet. Other Internet services are e-mail, chat rooms, instant messaging, mailing lists, and newsgroups. See Figure 1-11. The Internet and World Wide Web are covered in detail in Lesson 2.

FIGURE 1-11
A graphical representation of the Internet

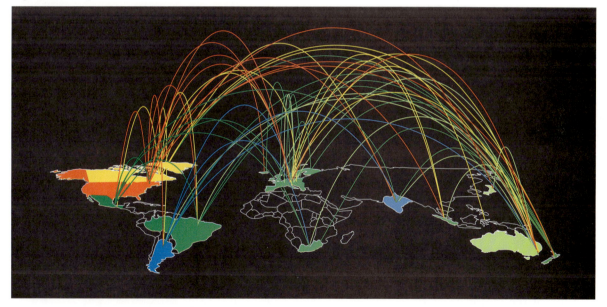

How Vista Multimedia Uses Computers

In your job as sales assistant at VM, you have learned much about the computer. You originally assumed it was used primarily as a cash register and to enter customers' data when they rented an item. You have been astonished to learn, however, of the many different ways in which the computer is used at VM. Some examples of computer usage are:

- Maintaining inventory of item rental and returns
- Maintaining records of all customers
- Maintaining personnel records
- Maintaining the store's budget and other financial records
- Recording sales figures
- Interacting with the computers at VM's main office
- Ordering inventory and supplies
- Engaging in e-commerce on the Internet
- Communicating with other stores, suppliers, and customers

Computers in Our Future

It is a fair assumption that computers of the future will be more powerful and less expensive. It is also a fair assumption that almost every type of job will somehow involve a computer. With long-distance connectivity, more people will work full-time or part-time from home. See Figure 1-12.

FIGURE 1-12
Working from home

One of the major areas of change in the evolution of computers will be connectivity, or the ability to connect with other computers. Wireless and mobile devices will become the norm.

> **Net Tip**
>
> Visit Intel's The Journey Inside Web site at *www97.intel.com/ scripts-tji/* and learn which is smarter—you or a computer.

SUMMARY

In this lesson, you learned:

- A computer is an electronic device that receives data, processes data, produces information, and stores the data and information.
- A computer derives its power from its speed, reliability, accuracy, storage, and communications capability.
- Computer literacy is the ability to use a computer and its software to accomplish practical tasks.
- Computers have been around for more than fifty years.
- Computers and technology affect almost every facet of our daily lives.
- Categories of computers include personal computers (desktop and notebook), palmtops or handhelds, mid-range servers, mainframes, and supercomputers.
- Electronic communication enable computers to communicate with each other and other devices.
- A network is a group of two or more computers, an intranet is a closed network within an organization, and an extranet is a closed network for an organization and its customers and suppliers.
- The Internet is the world's largest network.
- Computers in our future will be more powerful and less expensive.

Unit 1 Computer Basics

VOCABULARY Review

Define the following terms:

Clients	Hardware	Nodes
Computer	Information	Notebook computer
Data	Internet	Personal computer
Desktop computer	Intranet	Servers
Electronic communication	Mainframe computer	Software
Extranet	Mid-range server	Supercomputer
Handheld or palmtop computer	Network	Users

REVIEW Questions

MULTIPLE CHOICE

Select the best response for the following statements.

1. _____ is text, numbers, sound, images, or video.
   A. Software
   B. Information
   C. Hardware
   D. Data

2. Computers have been around for more than _____ years.
   A. 20
   B. 30
   C. 40
   D. 50

3. A(n) _____ is designed so all components fit on or under a desk.
   A. desktop computer
   B. mid-range server
   C. mainframe computer
   D. supercomputer

4. A(n) _____ is the fastest type of computer.
   A. mainframe computer
   B. handheld computer
   C. notebook computer
   D. supercomputer

5. _____ is the technology that enables computers to communicate with each other.
   A. Channels
   B. Protocols
   C. Communications
   D. Mainframe

6. The rules that govern the transfer of data are called _____.
   A. protocols
   B. networks
   C. channels
   D. receivers

7. The world's largest network is _____.
   A. an extranet
   B. an intranet
   C. the Internet
   D. the World Wide Web

8. Computers on a network are called _____.
   A. nodes
   B. servers
   C. extranets
   D. channels

9. The Internet evolved from _____.
   A. ARPANET
   B. clients
   C. supercomputers
   D. mid-range servers

10. A(n) _____ is an electronic and digital device.
    A. client
    B. node
    C. server
    D. computer

TRUE / FALSE

Circle T if the statement is true or F if the statement is false.

T F 1. Millions of people use computers every day.

T F 2. The instructions for controlling the computer are called hardware.

T F 3. Information is processed data.

T F 4. Computers are intelligent.

T F 5. Most computers are not very reliable.

T F 6. The first computers were small in size.

T F 7. Steve Jobs developed the operating system for the IBM PC.

Unit 1 Computer Basics

T F 8. A notebook computer is a lightweight computer that can fit into a briefcase.

T F 9. A network is a group of two or more computers linked together.

T F 10. The Internet is considered to be an extranet.

MATCHING

Match the correct term in Column 1 to its description in Column 2.

Column 1	Column 2
___ 1. Clients	A. text, numbers, sound, images, or video
___ 2. Information	B. processed data
___ 3. Data	C. people who use computers
___ 4. Network	D. a computer that will fit into a briefcase
___ 5. Notebook computer	E. technology that enables computers to talk with each other
___ 6. Intranet	
___ 7. Users	F. a group of two or more computers
___ 8. Communications	G. the computer and peripheral devices
___ 9. Software	H. another term for program
___ 10. Hardware	I. a network for the exclusive use of users within an organization
	J. computers on a network

PROJECTS

CROSS-CURRICULAR—MATHEMATICS

Select a career in the field of mathematics, such as a teacher or statistician. Use the Internet or other resources to search for information explaining how computers are used in a specific mathematics career. Use the keywords *mathematics careers* with one or two search engines, such as *www.google.com*, *www.yahoo.com*, or *www.askjeeves.com*. Prepare a two-page report on what you discover.

CROSS-CURRICULAR—SCIENCE

Use the Internet and other resources to find information about computers and the future. One example is robotics. These computerized helpers perform activities that can be dangerous or unpleasant. Prepare a two-page report describing what you found. Use *www.askjeeves.com* to locate resources for this report.

CROSS-CURRICULAR—SOCIAL STUDIES

Use the Internet or other resources to locate information on computer history. Prepare a one- or two-page report on computers developed in the early 1950s and 1960s. Include the specific uses of these early computers. Use *www.looksmart.com* to find information about early computers. Try *computer history* for your keyword search.

CROSS-CURRICULAR—LANGUAGE ARTS

The computer has influenced the way in which we communicate. Use the Internet and other resources to find information on different methods of communications. Prepare a two-page report on your findings.

WEB PROJECT

You are a member of a special group exploring the history of computers. Your teacher has asked you to investigate the history of computing and report your findings to the class. You are to research and report on significant contributors/contributions to the evolution of computing, using the Internet and other resources.

TEAMWORK PROJECT

Your supervisor at VM is considering putting a computer in her office and one in the office used by the part-time supervisor and other employees. She asks that you research the possibilities of networking these two computers with the existing computer located in the store.

She would like answers to the following questions: Is there a minimum number of computers required for a network? What information and resources can be shared? What special hardware is required? Prepare a report on your findings. Include any other information about networks you think will be helpful. Use *www.about.com* or *www.smartcomputing.com* and search for *networks*.

LESSON 2

THE INTERNET AND THE WORLD WIDE WEB

OBJECTIVES

Upon completion of this lesson, you should be able to:

- Describe the origin of the Internet.
- Describe how the Internet works.
- Describe the major features of the Internet.
- Explain the difference between the World Wide Web and the Internet.
- Explain how to connect to the Internet.
- Describe a browser.
- Understand browser terminology.
- Understand and use browser features.

Estimated Time: 1.5 hours

VOCABULARY

Address bar
AutoSearch
Bookmark
Browser
Content Advisor
Disk cache
Domain name
Favorites
Home page
Host computer
Host node
Hypertext markup language (HTML)
Hypertext transfer protocol (HTTP)
Internet Keywords
Internet service provider (ISP)
Interoperability
Location bar
NetWatch
Online service provider (OSP)
Protocol
Transmission control protocol and Internet protocol (TCP/IP)
Uniform Resource Locator (URL)
Web page
World Wide Web

Ms. Perez, your supervisor at Vista Multimedia, is interested in learning more about the Internet and how she can use it to promote Vista Multimedia. She has asked you to explain how the Internet can help her personally and within the business. You explain that the Internet is all about information and that each day millions of people "surf"—or search and use—the Internet, which often is referred to as the "information superhighway." It is compared to a highway system because it functions much like a network of interstate highways. Businesses use the Internet to provide information and to sell their products and services; this is called *e-commerce*. People use the Internet to research information, shop, take classes, communicate with family and friends, read the daily paper, make airplane reservations, and much more. They use the Internet at work and at home. Internet connections are available at public libraries and cyber-cafés. Anyone with access to the Internet can connect with and communicate with anyone else in the world who also has access.

Evolution of the Internet

Even though no one person or organization can claim credit for creating the Internet, its early origins can be traced to the 1960s and the United States Department of Defense. The birth of the Internet is tied closely to a computer-networking project started by a governmental division called the Advanced Research Projects Agency (ARPA). The goal was to create a network that would allow scientists to share information on military and scientific research.

The original name for the Internet was ARPANET. In 1969, ARPANET was a wide area network with four main host node computers. A *host node* is any computer directly connected to the network. These computers were located at the University of California at Santa Barbara, the University of California at Los Angeles, the Stanford Research Institute, and the University of Utah.

Over the next several years, the Internet grew steadily but quietly. Some interesting details are as follows:

- The addition of e-mail in 1972 spurred some growth.
- By 1989, more than 100,000 host computers were linked to ARPANET.
- In 1990, ARPANET ceased to exist, but few noticed because its functions continued.
- The thousands of interconnected networks were called an Inter-Net-Network and became known as the Internet, or, a network of networks.
- The real growth began when the World Wide Web came into being in 1992.
- In 1993, the world's first browser, Mosaic, was released. A *browser* is a software program that provides a graphical interface for the Internet. Mosaic made it so easy to access the Internet that there was a 340 percent growth in the number of Internet users in this one year.
- The Internet is still growing at an unprecedented rate. See Figure 2-1.

FIGURE 2-1
Global Internet map

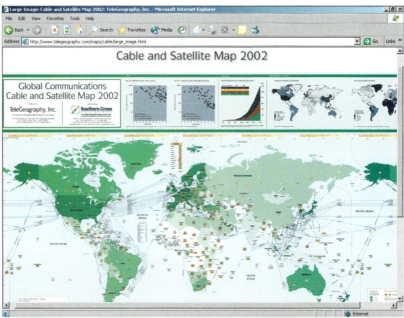

How Does the Internet Work?

The Internet is a loose association of thousands of networks and millions of computers across the world that all work together to share information. It is transitory, constantly changing, reshaping, and remolding itself. The beauty of this network of networks is that all brands, models, and makes of computers can communicate with each other. This is called *interoperability*.

So how do we communicate across the Internet? Consider our postal service. If you want to send someone a letter anywhere in the world, you can do that—as long as you know the address. The Internet works in a similar fashion. From your computer, you can connect with any other networked computer anywhere in the world—as long as you know the address or know how to find the address.

Computers on the Internet communicate with each other using a set of protocols known as *TCP/IP* or *Transmission Control Protocol and Internet Protocol*. A *protocol* is a standard format for transferring data between two devices. TCP/IP is the agreed upon international standard for transmitting data. It is considered the language of the Internet and supports nearly all Internet applications. The TCP protocol enables two host computers to establish a connection and exchange data. A *host computer* is a computer that you access remotely from your computer. The IP protocol works with the addressing scheme. It allows you to enter an address and sends it to another computer; from there the TCP protocol takes over and establishes a connection between the two computers. Returning to the postal service analogy, this is similar to what happens when you take a letter to the post office. You deliver the letter to the post office and then the post office takes over and delivers the letter to the recipient. See Figure 2-2.

FIGURE 2-2
Data travels the Internet using TCP/IP

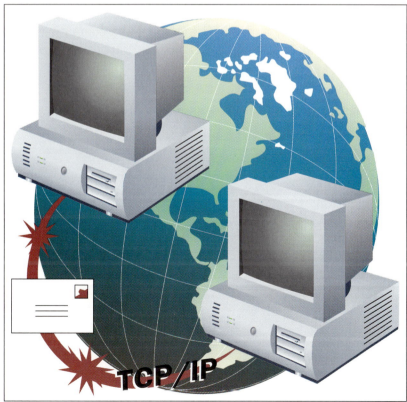

Postal addresses usually contain numbers and street names. Likewise, when we access another computer on the Internet, we are accessing it via a number. We do not need to remember or type the number. Instead, we can type in the domain name. The domain name identifies a site on the Internet. An example domain name is *www.disney.com*. If we want to access the Microsoft Corporation's computers that are connected to the Internet, we start our Web browser and type the domain name into the browser's Address box. Browsers are discussed later in this lesson.

Major Features of the Internet

The Internet is made up of many services. Some of the more popular of these services include e-mail, chat rooms, mailing lists, FTP (file transfer protocol), and newsgroups. Another popular Internet service is the World Wide Web.

The World Wide Web

Many people use the terms *World Wide Web*, or *Web* for short, and *Internet* interchangeably. In reality, they are two different things. The Web is a subset or an application that makes use of the Internet. The Internet can exist without the Web, but the Web cannot exist without the Internet. The Web actually began in March 1989, when Dr. Tim Berners-Lee, who works with a European organization known as CERN, wrote a small computer program for his own personal use. This text-based program permitted pages to be linked through a formatting process known as *hypertext markup language (HTML)*. Clicking a linked word or image transfers you from one Web page to another or to another part of the same Web page. You do not have to type the Web page address. HTML was a step forward, but it was not the catalyst that made the Web what it is today.

The number of people using the Web greatly increased in 1993. This increase occurred when Marc Andreessen, working for the National Center for Supercomputing Applications at the University of Illinois, released Mosaic. Mosaic was the first graphical browser. See Figure 2-3.

FIGURE 2-3
Mosaic Web page

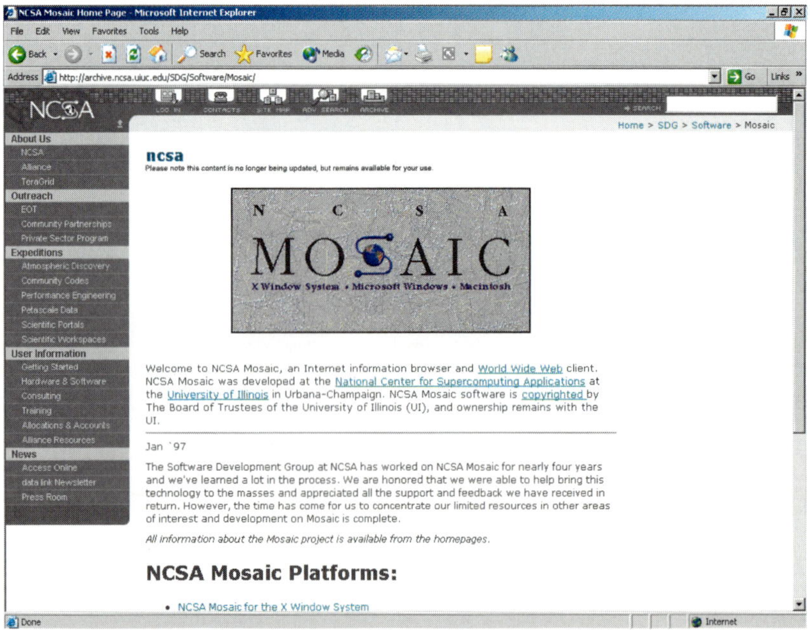

In 1994, Andreessen cofounded Netscape Communications. With the introduction of Mosaic and the Web browsers that followed, the Web became a communication tool for a much wider audience. Currently, two of the most popular Web browsers are Internet Explorer and Netscape Navigator; other browsers also exist. Because of these enhancements, the Web is one of the most widely used services on the Internet.

Web Protocols—HTTP

The Web has its own underlying protocols. One protocol is known as *HTTP* or *hypertext transfer protocol.* This protocol or standard defines how pages are transmitted. On the Web, you can send and receive Web pages over the Internet because Web servers and Web browsers both understand HTTP. When you enter a Web site address in your browser, for instance, this sends an HTTP command to the Web server to tell it to locate and transmit the requested Web page. A *Web server* is a computer that delivers, or serves up, Web pages. By installing special software, any computer can become a Web server. Every Web server has its own IP address and most have a *domain name*. The domain name identifies the IP address.

> **Did You Know?**
>
> Many people create a personal home page. If you have access to the Internet and can upload your own Web page, you may want to include frequently visited Web sites.

The Web page address often is referred to as the *URL* or *Uniform Resource Locator.* Every Web page on the Internet has its own unique address. The first part of the address indicates what protocol to use, and the second part specifies the IP address or the domain name where the resource is located. For example, in the URL *http://www.si.edu/*, the *http* protocol indicates this is a Web page and that the domain name is *si*. See Figure 2-4. The *.edu* at the end of the name indicates that this is an educational site. See Table 2-1 for other domain abbreviations.

FIGURE 2-4
Smithsonian Institute Web page

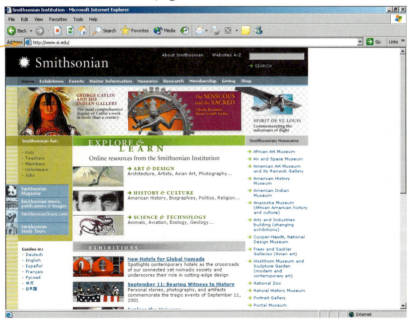

TABLE 2-1
Domain name abbreviations

TOP-LEVEL DOMAIN ABBREVIATIONS	TYPE OF ORGANIZATION
edu	Educational institutions
com	Commercial businesses, companies, and organizations
gov	Government institutions, such as the IRS
mil	Military organizations, such as the Army
net	Network provider
org	Associations and organizations
NEW DOMAIN ABBREVIATIONS	**TYPE OF ORGANIZATION**
aero	Air transport company
biz	Business
coop	Business cooperative
info	Information services
museum	Accredited museum
name	Individuals or families
pro	Professional such as a doctor or lawyer

Web Protocols—HTML

A second protocol or standard that controls how the World Wide Web works is HTML or hypertext markup language. This computer language determines how Web pages are formatted and displayed and allows the users to exchange text, images, sound, video, and multimedia files. *Hypertext* is a link to another location, often referred to as a *hyperlink*. The location can be within the same document, in another document on the same Web server, or on a Web server on the other side of the world. You click on the link and are transported to the Web page.

A **Web page** is nothing more than an ordinary text page that is coded with HTML markup tags and then displayed within a browser. Markup tags consist of a set of text commands that are interpreted by the browser. Different browsers may interpret HTML tags differently or may not support all HTML tags. Thus, the same Web page can display differently when viewed in Internet Explorer or Netscape. Altogether, three items determine how a Web page displays:

- The type and version of the browser displaying the Web page.
- The HTML markup tags used to code the page.
- The user's monitor and monitor resolution.

Hundreds of markup tags exist that can be used within a document. All Web pages, however, have a minimum basic requirement. See Figure 2-5. You will learn how to create a Web page in Lesson 15.

FIGURE 2-5
Required HTML tags

```
<HTML>
<Head>
<Title>My First Web Page</Title>
</Head>
<Body>
   <H1>Hello World!</H1>
</Body>
</HTML>
```

Accessing the Internet—Dial-in or Direct Connection

Before you can begin to "surf the net," you have to be connected and become part of the network. If you connect to the Internet from your school, you are probably connecting through a local area network. A *local area network (LAN)* connects computers and devices within a limited geographical area. You connect to the Internet using a *network interface card (NIC)*. This is a special card inside your computer that allows the computer to be networked. A direct connection is made from the local area network to a high-speed connection line, most likely leased from the local telephone company.

> **Extra for Experts**
>
> When surfing the Web, at one time or another you are going to receive a "401 – Unauthorized" message. This means that you are trying to access a Web site that is protected.

Home users generally connect to the Internet using one of the following three methods: a modem and a telephone line, a cable modem, or a digital subscriber line.

The slowest type of connection is the dial-up modem and telephone line. Signals that are transmitted across a normal telephone line are analog or continuous. A dial-up modem is a device that converts the computer's digital signal into an analog signal, therefore allowing data to be sent from one computer to another over telephone lines. A receiving modem at the other end changes the analog signal back to digital. See Figure 2-6.

FIGURE 2-6
Modem and telephone line connection

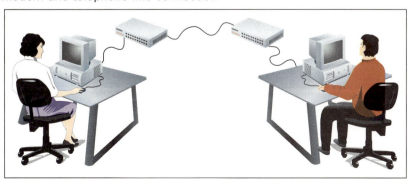

Some people are happy with their Internet telephone connection, but many want more speed and are willing to pay for it. They may choose to use high-speed options such as DSL (digital subscriber lines) or cable modems. *DSL (digitalsubscriber line)* is a service that offers a faster Internet connection than a standard dial-up connection. With DSL, special hardware is used that allows data transmission at far greater speeds than the standard phone wiring.

A cable modem also connects to your computer, but it uses a network interface card like the one that is probably used at your school instead of using a telephone line as a transmission media to connect to the service provider. This is the same type of cable as that used for cable TV.

Large corporations and research universities require even faster connections. They may use transmission lines called T1 or T3 lines to obtain more speed.

Data transmission is measured in Kbps (thousands of bits per second) and Mbps (millions of bits per second). Table 2-2 provides an overview of the more popular types of Internet connections and the speed at which they transmit data.

TABLE 2-2
Internet connections

TYPE OF SERVICE	SPEED	DESCRIPTION
Telephone line	28.8 Kbps to 56 Kbps	Normal telephone line service; used by individuals and small businesses
Digital subscriber lines (DSL)	Up to 9 Mbps	A high-speed connection across regular telephone wires; used by individuals and businesses
Cable modem	Up to 2.5 Mbps	Uses television cable to connect to the Internet; used by individuals and businesses
T1 line	Up to 1.5 Mbps	A high-speed digital cable; used by small- and medium-size companies
T3 line	Up to 45 Mbps	A super high-speed connection; used by large corporations and universities with high volumes of traffic

Getting Connected

Connecting to the Internet is a simple process, but there are a few steps you need to take.

- **Step 1:** The first step is to locate an *Internet service provider (ISP)* or an *online service provider (OSP)*. There are thousands of Internet Service Providers (ISPs). Most are small local companies. Their service is primarily an Internet connection. OSPs are large national and international companies. Two of the largest online service providers are America Online and MSN. Generally, the local ISP is less expensive than the OSP, but many people use the online services because of the additional information and services that they offer.

- **Step 2:** Once you decide which service provider to use, you must install some type of communication software. This software enables your computer to connect to another computer. Most likely, your ISP or OSP will provide this software.

- **Step 3:** You will need to install a Web browser in order to use the Web. Two of the most popular browsers are Netscape Navigator and Microsoft Internet Explorer. Some OSPs provide their own version of browsers.

You have contracted with your ISP, and you have installed your software. It is now time to connect to the Internet. This is the easy part. If you are using a dial-in modem, you give instructions to your computer to dial a local telephone number. This number connects you to your ISP's computer, which is in turn connected to the Internet, and you are online with the world. If you are using a cable modem or DSL, you are connected when you turn on your computer. The next step is learning how to use the Web browser.

What Is a Browser?

A browser is the software program you use to retrieve documents from the WWW and to display them in a readable format. The Web is the graphical portion of the Internet. The browser functions as an interface between you and the Web. Using a browser, you can display both text and images. Newer versions of most browsers also support multimedia information,

> **Extra for Experts**
>
> A common error message you may receive when surfing the Internet is "404 - Not found." This indicates that the server that hosts the site cannot find the HTML document. This could mean several things: You may have mistyped the URL; the Web page no longer exists; or the Web page could have moved. When this happens, try going up one level by deleting the last part of the URL to the nearest slash. This will give you an indication if the Web site still exists. If this does not work, you can try to delete the last slash and key **.html** or **.htm**. One more option is to try again later—the Web site could be down temporarily.

including sound, animation, and video. Browsers are constantly being updated to support the latest information the Web has to offer. It is important to keep your browser software updated to the most recent version your computer can handle.

You navigate through the Web by using your mouse to point and click on hyperlinked words and images displayed in the browser window. The two most popular browsers are shown in Figures 2-7 and 2-8.

FIGURE 2-7
Internet Explorer

FIGURE 2-8
Netscape Navigator

Both of these browsers have very similar features, but the menu options to select these features are somewhat different.

Browser Terminology and Browser Basics

Understanding browser terminology is the key to using a browser effectively. See Figure 2-9. Table 2-3 contains a definition of each part of the screen.

FIGURE 2-9
Internet Explorer browser window terminology

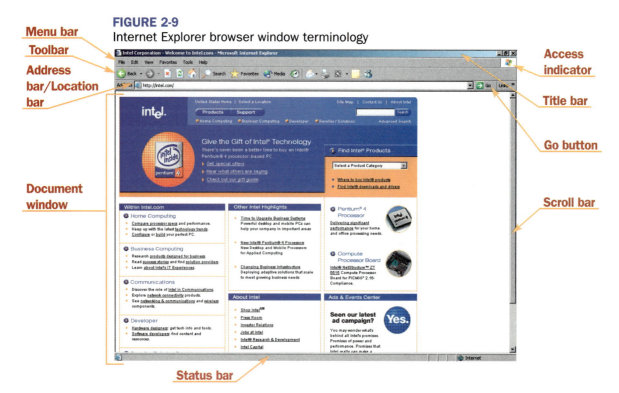

TABLE 2-3
Browser terminology definitions

FEATURE	DEFINITIONS
Title bar	The bar on top of the window that contains the name of the document
Menu bar	A horizontal menu that appears at top of the program window; provides a selection of options related to the Web page
Toolbar	Icons for single-click access to most commonly used menu commands
Address bar/ Location bar	Contains the URL or address of the active Web page; also where you type the location for the Web page you want to visit
Go button	Connects you to the address displayed in the Address bar
Document window	Displays the active Web page
Status bar	Located at the bottom of the browser; shows the progress of Web page transactions
Access indicator	A small picture in the upper-right corner of the browser; when animated, it means that your browser is accessing data from a remote computer
Scroll bars	Vertical and horizontal scroll bars let you scroll vertically and horizontally if the Web page is too long or wide to fit within one screen

In this lesson, it is assumed you have an Internet connection—either dial-in or direct connection. To connect to the Internet, you first launch your Web browser. In most instances, you can double-click the browser icon located on your desktop. If the icon is not available, click the Start button, select Programs or All Programs, and then click the browser name.

> **Net Tip**
>
> Visit Learn the Net at *http://www.learnthenet.com/ english/html/12browser.htm* to learn about the history of browsers.

Your Home Page

When your browser is installed, a default home page is selected. The *home page* is the first page that is displayed when you launch your browser. You can easily change your home page. Most people choose a home page they want to view frequently. To change your default home page, complete the following activity.

STEP-BY-STEP 2.1

Change your default page in Internet Explorer:

1. Start your browser, and then go to the page you want to appear when you first start your browser.

2. Click **Tools** on the menu bar, and then click **Internet Options**. The Internet Options dialog box is displayed.

3. Click the **General** tab, if necessary.

STEP-BY-STEP 2.1 Continued

4. In the home page area, click **Use Current** and click **OK**. See Figure 2-10. Close your browser.

5. Repeat steps 1 through 3, but return the default page to its original settings by clicking **Use Default**.

FIGURE 2-10
Internet Explorer Internet Options dialog box

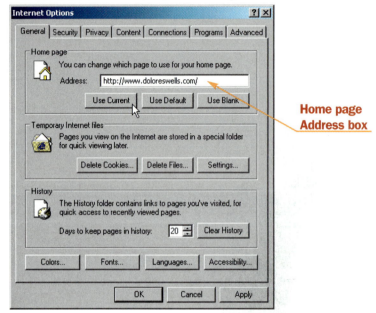

6. Click the **OK** button to close the Internet Options dialog box. Leave your browser open for the next Step-by-Step.

STEP-BY-STEP 2.2

Change your default page in Netscape Navigator:

1. Start your browser, and then go to the page you want to appear when you first start your browser.

2. Click **Edit** on the menu bar, and then click **Preferences**.

3. Click the **Navigator** category, if necessary.

STEP-BY-STEP 2.2 Continued

4. Click the **Use Current Page** button, and then click the **OK** button. See Figure 2-11.

5. Leave your browser open for the next Step-by-Step.

FIGURE 2-11
Navigator Preferences dialog box

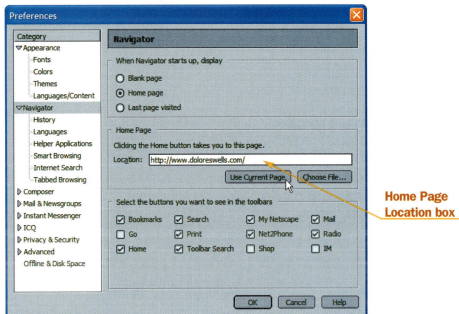

The Address Bar

The *Address bar* (Internet Explorer) or *Location bar* (Navigator) is situated near the top of the browser window. This bar contains the address of the current page. This address is called the Uniform Resource Locator (URL). The URL tells the browser where to locate the page. A unique URL identifies each Web page. The first part of the URL indicates the protocol and the second part specifies the domain name. If you want to visit a specific Web site, you must know the URL or the Web page address. Then, in the Address bar (Internet Explorer) or the Location bar (Navigator) you type the address of the Web site you wish to visit in place of the current page address that already appears there. Press Enter after typing the address to link to and display the Web page.

These Address/Location bar features may be similar, but not necessarily identical:

- **AutoComplete:** Keeps track of and provides a list of sites you have already visited or fills out forms automatically.

- **AutoCorrect:** Corrects typos as you type, especially those errors made on common URL conventions, such as *http://* or *www*.

> **Net Tip**
>
> The University of Albany features several Internet tutorials, research guides, and links and hints on how to use Netscape Navigator and Communicator. You can find this Web site at *http://library.albany.edu/internet/*.

Unit 1 Computer Basics

- **AutoSearch:** Helps you find a Web page quickly and easily by giving you Web search results when you type part of a URL in the address bar.

- **Address List:** Remembers the URLs you type; click the Address bar list arrow to view these. See Figure 2-12.

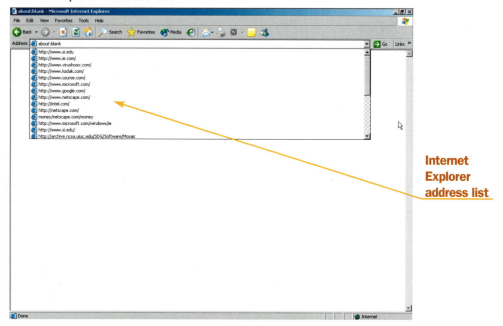

FIGURE 2-12
Internet Explorer Address list

Complete the following Step-by-Step to display the Intel Education Web site and to use Search.

STEP-BY-STEP 2.3

To find a Web page:

1. Start your browser.

2. In the Address bar or Location bar, type the following URL (Web site address):
   http://www97.intel.com/education/index.asp

3. Press **Enter** to display the Intel Education Web page.

4. Leave your browser open for the next Step-by-Step.

Toolbar and Menu Bar

The menu and toolbar are located at the top of your browser window. The toolbars for Internet Explorer (Figure 2-13) and Navigator (Figure 2-14) are quite different. The menus are similar. The following is an overview of the toolbar buttons:

- **Back**: Returns you to the previous page.
- **Forward**: Takes you to the page you viewed before clicking the Back button.
- **Home**: Takes you to your home page.
- **Refresh or Reload**: Refreshes or reloads the current Web page.
- **Stop**: Stops the current page from loading.
- **Print**: Prints the current document. In Navigator click the File menu and then click the Print command.
- **Search**: Connects you to the Microsoft or Netscape Internet search sites.
- **Favorites or Bookmarks**: Opens the Favorites or Bookmarks bar where you can store shortcuts to your most frequently visited Web sites.
- **History**: Opens the History bar, displaying a record of all the sites you have visited in the last 20 days. In Navigator, click Go on the menu bar, and then click History.

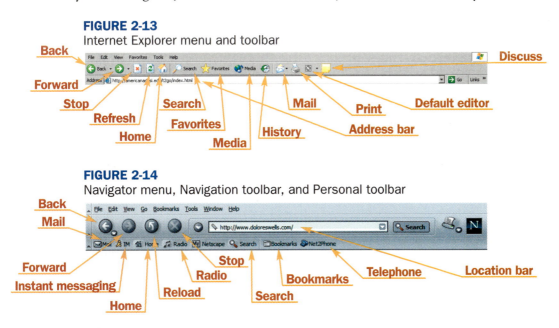

FIGURE 2-13
Internet Explorer menu and toolbar

FIGURE 2-14
Navigator menu, Navigation toolbar, and Personal toolbar

Searching

Both Internet Explorer and Navigator have a special search feature that makes it easy for you to locate quickly your desired information. Internet Explorer calls this *AutoSearch*, and Navigator calls it *Internet Keywords*. Type a common term in the Address or Location bar and press Enter. For example, imagine that you are saving your money for a new car, and you would like to have additional information about a Chevrolet Corvette. Launch your browser, type *Chevrolet Corvette*, and press Enter. Both Internet Explorer and Navigator display the Chevrolet Corvette Web page.

If the AutoSearch or Internet Keywords feature does not provide the information needed or these settings are turned off within the browser you are using, click the Search button.

Clicking Navigator's Search button takes you to the Net Search page where you can search with several different search engines. See Figure 2-15. Choose a search engine, type the words you are looking for in the text box, and click the button to get a list of matching sites.

FIGURE 2-15
Netscape Navigator's Net Search Web page

Clicking the Internet Explorer Search button opens the Search Companion. This is a separate pane on the left side of the window. Type the words you are searching for and then click the Search button. The MSN Search page is displayed with a list of selected Web sites. Searching will be covered in detail in Lesson 12.

History

The Back and Forward buttons take you to sites you have visited in your current session. However, what if you want to return to that Web page you found last week and you cannot remember the URL? Then the History button is for you.

Internet Explorer—History

In Internet Explorer, click the History button on the toolbar. The History window opens in the left pane and displays a record of all the sites you have visited in the last 20 days. The number of days (20) is the default. You can change the number of days through the Tools menu. To make it easier to find the site you are searching for, you can sort the list by date, by site, by most visited, and by order visited today. You also can search the list for a keyword in a site name.

To clear the History list, click Tools on the menu bar, and then click Internet Options to display the Internet Options dialog box. Click the General tab and then click the Clear History button.

Navigator—History

To access History in Navigator, click Go on the menu bar and then click History to display the History list. From the History list window, you can click the View menu and then sort by title, location, last visited, first visited, host name, and number of visits. When you have completed sorting, close the History window. To clear the History list, click Edit on the menu bar, and then click the Preferences command. In the Preferences dialog box, click Navigator, then click History, and then click the Clear History button.

Favorites and Bookmarks

The Web has so much to offer that it is very likely you are going to find some Web sites you really like and want to return to often. It is easy to keep these sites just a mouse click away by adding them to your *Favorites* (Internet Explorer) or *Bookmark* (Navigator) list.

To add a site to your list of sites:

- Go to the site you want to add.
- For Internet Explorer, click Favorites on the menu bar and then click Add.... For Navigator, click Bookmarks on the menu bar, and then click Add Bookmark.
- To revisit any of the Favorites or Bookmarks, just click the Favorites or Bookmarks button, and then select the shortcut to the site.

As your list begins to grow, you can organize it by creating folders. You can organize by topics in much the same way you would organize files in a file drawer.

STEP-BY-STEP 2.4

To create a folder in Internet Explorer Favorites (verify with your teacher before completing this exercise that it is OK to create the folder):

1. Click **Favorites** on the menu bar, and then click **Organize Favorites**.

Ethics in Technology

INTERNET SECURITY

If you have surfed the Internet recently, you know that you can purchase just about any item you want, from a Mercedes Benz to Uncle Bill's Jam and Jellies. You can have your purchase shipped to you and pay for it when it arrives, or you can use a credit card. The question is how safe would you feel about transmitting credit card and other financial information over the Internet?

When you provide your credit card number, it travels through several computers before it reaches its final destination. To ensure that your credit card number is not easily stolen, companies use a technology called *encryption*. Encryption software acts somewhat similar to the cable converter box on your television. The data is scrambled with a secret code so that no one can interpret it while it is being transmitted. When the data reaches its destination, the same software unscrambles the information.

Not all Web sites use security measures. One way to identify a secure site is to check the status bar at the bottom of your Web browser. There you will see a small icon—usually a lock. When the lock is closed, it indicates that the site is using security technology.

38 Unit 1 Computer Basics

STEP-BY-STEP 2.5 Continued

2. The Organize Favorites dialog box displays. See Figure 2-16.

FIGURE 2-16
Organize Favorites dialog box

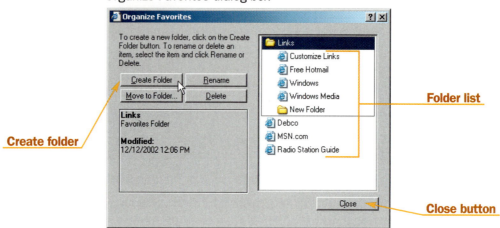

3. Click the **Create Folder** button, type a name for the folder, and then click the **Close** button. Leave your browser open for the next Step-by-Step.

STEP-BY-STEP 2.5

To create a folder in Navigator Bookmarks (verify with your teacher before completing this exercise that it is OK to create the folder):

1. Click **Bookmarks** on the menu bar, and then click **Manage Bookmarks** to display the Bookmarks for default window.

2. Click the **New Folder** button. See Figure 2-17. The Create New Folder dialog box displays.

FIGURE 2-17
Bookmarks for default window

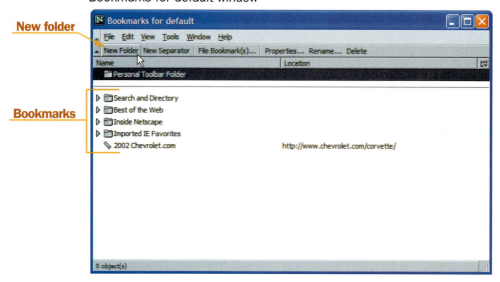

STEP-BY-STEP 2.5 Continued

3. Type a name for the folder and then click the **OK** button.

4. Close the Bookmarks for default window. Leave your browser open for the next Step-by-Step.

Controlling Access

The *Content Advisor* in Internet Explorer and *NetWatch* in Navigator provide some control over what content can be viewed on the Internet. With these two tools, you can:

- Control access to settings through a password.
- View and adjust the ratings settings to reflect what you think is appropriate content.
- Adjust what types of content other people can view with or without your permission.
- Set up a list of Web sites that other people can never view and a list of Web sites other people can always view.
- Set up a list of Web sites that other people can always view, regardless of how the sites' contents are rated.

Web site publishers voluntarily rate their pages. The Internet rating standard is known as PICS: Platform for Internet Content Selection. The Content Advisor and NetWatch use two independent PICS-compliant ratings systems—RSACi and SafeSurf. Each system uses a different method to describe in as much detail as possible the levels of offensive content on Web pages.

Ethics in Technology

HACKERS

Computer security violation is one of the biggest problems experienced on computer networks. People who break into computer systems are called hackers. The reasons why they do this are many and varied. Some of more common reasons are as follows:

- Theft of services—AOL, Prodigy, and other password-protected services charge a fee for usage. A hacker finds a way to bypass the password and uses the service without paying for it.
- Theft of information—A hacker may break into a system to steal credit card numbers, test data, or even national security data.
- Hatred and vengeance—Many people have groups or companies that they don't like. They may hack into the system to destroy files or to steal information to sell to opposing groups.
- For the thrill of it—Some hackers break into sites just to see if they can do it. The thrill for them is in breaking the code.

Cleanup Time

When you explore the Web, your browser keeps a record of the sites you visit. The pages are stored in temporary folders on your hard drive in your *disk cache* (pronounced *cash*). This process enables you to view the saved pages offline or without being connected to the Internet.

If you return to a cached Web page, that page will load faster because it is loading from cache. This can sometimes be a problem because the page may have changed since you were last at the site. The Refresh and/or Reload buttons were discussed earlier in this lesson. Clicking the Refresh or Reload button will load the current page from the server. Another option is to change the "Checking for newer versions of stored pages" setting.

STEP-BY-STEP 2.6

In Internet Explorer:

1. Click **Tools** on the menu bar, and then click **Internet Options**. The Internet Options dialog box is displayed.

2. Click the **General** tab and then click the **Settings** button to display the Settings dialog box. (See Figure 2-18.) You have four options:
   - Every visit to the page
   - Every time you start Internet Explorer
   - Automatically
   - Never

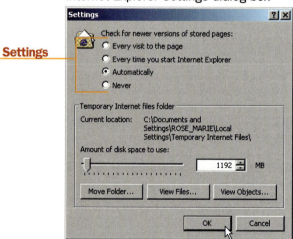

FIGURE 2-18
Internet Explorer Settings dialog box

3. Select the option that is best for you and your individual requirements. The first option, *Every visit to the page*, can considerably slow down browsing time between pages. *Never* provides the fastest browsing time.

4. Click **OK** and then click **OK** again to return to Internet Explorer. Leave your browser open for the next Step-by-Step.

STEP-BY-STEP 2.7

In Navigator:

1. Click **Edit** on the menu bar, and then click the **Preferences** command. The Preferences dialog box is displayed. See Figure 2-19.

FIGURE 2-19
Navigator Preferences dialog box

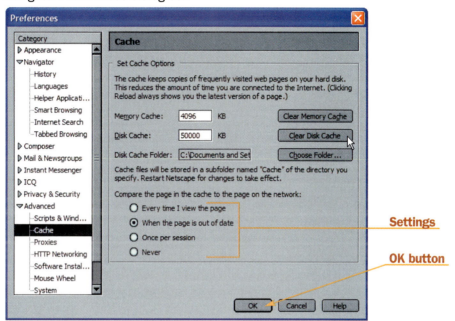

2. Open the **Advanced** category and then click **Cache**.

3. You have four options:
   - Every time I view the page
   - When the page is out of date
   - Once per session
   - Never

4. Select the option that is best for you and your individual requirements. *Every time I view the page* is the slowest and *Never* is the fastest. Keep in mind, however, that with *Never*, the page may be out of date. Even so, you can click the Reload button to access the latest version.

5. Click the **OK** button to return to Navigator. Leave your browser open for the next Step-by-Step.

As you browse the Internet, the disk cache can fill up. When this happens, pages do not load as quickly. You can speed things up by cleaning the cache. When you do this, you delete all of the Web pages stored in cache.

To empty the cache in Internet Explorer, click Tools on the menu, and then click Internet Options to display the Internet Options dialog box. Click the General tab. In the Temporary Internet Files section, click the Delete Files button to display the Delete Files dialog box. Click the OK button.

To empty the cache in Navigator, click Edit on the menu bar, and then click Preferences. The Preferences dialog box is displayed. Click the Advanced category and then click Cache. Click the Clear Disk Cache button and then click OK. See Figure 2-20.

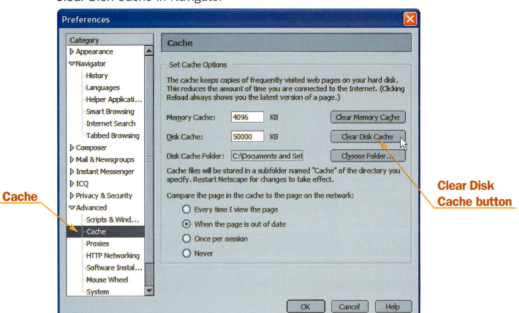

FIGURE 2-20
Clear Disk Cache in Navigator

Deleting the files in cache can speed up your browsing. What if, however, you do not want to delete these files? There is also another way you can increase browsing speed. If you have a large hard drive with plenty of extra space, you may prefer to increase the amount of cache disk space. This will also increase your browsing speed. See Figure 2-21.

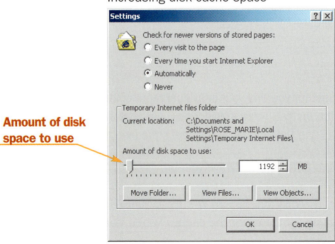

FIGURE 2-21
Increasing disk cache space

Copy and Save Text, Web Pages, and Images

As you view pages on the Web, you will find things you would like to save so that you can refer to them later. Both Internet Explorer and Navigator provide options to save a complete Web page or any part of a Web page. This includes text, images, or hyperlinks.

To copy and save text:

- Click Edit on the menu bar, and then click Select All or use your mouse to select a specific part of the page.
- Click Edit on the menu bar, and then click Copy.
- Paste the text into a Word document or other program.

To copy and save a hyperlink from a Web page:

- Select and then right-click the link to display the shortcut menu.
- For Internet Explorer, select Copy Shortcut to copy the link into the computer's memory. See Figure 2-22. For Navigator, select Copy Link Location to copy the link's address into the computer's memory.
- Paste the link into another document.

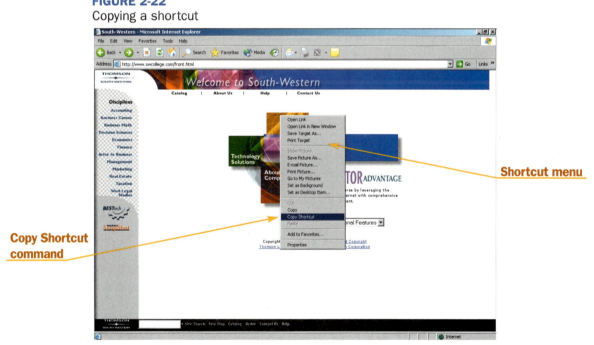

FIGURE 2-22
Copying a shortcut

To save an entire Web page:

- Click File on the menu bar, and then click Save As.
- Select the folder into which you want to save the image.
- In the File name box, type a name for the page.

- In Internet Explorer, in the Save as type box, select Web Page, complete. This option saves all of the files needed to display this page in its original format. This includes images and any other Web page elements.

To save an image:

- Right-click the image to display a shortcut menu.
- In Internet Explorer, select Save Picture As to display the Save Picture dialog box. In Navigator, select Save Image.
- Select the folder into which you want to save the image.
- Type the name for the image.
- Click the Save button.

If you need a printed copy of a Web page, click the Print button in Internet Explorer. In Navigator, click File on the menu bar, and then click Print.

Download and Install a Program

As you browse the Internet, you eventually will find a program you want to download. To *download* means to transfer from the Web server to your computer. The program could be a plug-in or enhancement for your browser, a utility program to help you better manage your computer system, a shareware game, and so on. Many companies that sell software allow you to pay for a new program online and then download the program directly from their site. Before completing this Step-by-Step and downloading a program, obtain permission from your instructor.

Technology Careers

PREPARING FOR THE JOB INTERVIEW

You have made it to the first step in the process of getting that new career opportunity—that first interview. So how do you prepare? You can never be sure what questions your potential employer might ask. You can, however, prepare for some of the more obvious questions. These might include:
- Are you generally on time?
- How do you work under pressure?
- What are your plans five years from now?
- Do you plan to go to college?
- Tell me about some of the things you are learning in school.

Most people are nervous when being interviewed. There is no way that you are going to totally eliminate being nervous, but prepare with a positive attitude. There are a number of useful job-related sites on the Web—try searching for "job interview tips." Imagine what the interview might be like and rehearse in your mind. Or, better yet, find a classmate to play the role of the potential interviewer.

Lesson 2 The Internet and the World Wide Web   45

STEP-BY-STEP 2.8

To download a program:

1. Create a separate folder on your hard drive for your downloaded programs.

2. Go to the Web site where the program is located.

3. Follow the Web site's download instructions. This will vary from site to site, but most sites have some type of Download Now button. Click that button. The File Download dialog box appears.

4. Select the folder on your computer where you want to store the downloaded program. See Figure 2-23.

FIGURE 2-23
Save As dialog box

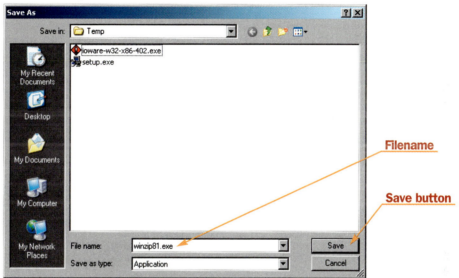

5. Click **Save** to start the downloading process.

6. A downloading box displays; estimated download time and transfer rate are displayed.

7. Now you wait while the download takes place. When the download is completed, click **OK**.

8. Next, you need to install the program. Using Windows Explorer, locate the file you downloaded and double-click the filename. Follow the installation instructions as provided by the program.

9. Close your browser and turn off your computer if instructed to do so.

SUMMARY

In this lesson, you learned:

- No one person or organization can claim credit for creating the Internet.
- Origins of the Internet can be traced to the United States Department of Defense.
- The original name for the Internet was ARPANET.
- Mosaic was the Internet's first graphical interface.
- To connect to the Internet from school, you probably have a direct connection via a local area network and a network interface card.
- For the home user, the most common type of Internet connection is with a modem and telephone line.
- To connect to the Internet, you need an Internet connection, telecommunications software, and a browser.
- Other types of Internet connections include DSL, cable modem, T1 and T3 lines.
- Interoperability means that all brands, models, and makes of computers can communicate with each other.
- A protocol is a standard format for transferring data between two devices.
- TCP/IP is the agreed upon international standard for transmitting data.
- The domain name identifies a site on the Internet.
- The Internet is made up of many services.
- The Web is an application that makes use of the Internet.
- Web pages can be linked through hyperlinks.
- Microsoft Internet Explorer and Netscape Navigator are the two most popular Web browsers.
- The HTTP protocol defines how Web messages are formatted and transmitted.
- A Web site address is referred to the as a URL or Universal Resource Locator.
- Every Web page on the Internet has its own unique address.
- HTML is another protocol that controls how Web pages are formatted and displayed.
- A Web page is coded with HTML markup tags.

VOCABULARY Review

Define the following terms:

Address bar	Hypertext markup	Online service
AutoSearch	language (HTML)	provider (OSP)
Bookmark	Hypertext transfer proto-	Protocol
Browser	col (HTTP)	Transmission control
Content Advisor	Internet Keywords	protocol and Internet
Disk cache	Internet service	protocol (TCP/IP)
Domain name	provider (ISP)	Uniform Resource
Favorites	Interoperability	Locator (URL)
Home page	Location bar	Web page
Host computer	NetWatch	World Wide Web
Host node		

REVIEW Questions

MULTIPLE CHOICE

Select the best response for the following statements.

1. A URL is the same as the _____.
   A. Web site address
   B. Location bar
   C. Address bar
   D. toolbar

2. The process that enables all makes and models of computers to communicate with each other is called _____.
   A. services
   B. T1
   C. interoperability
   D. internetwork

3. The first graphical browser was named _____.
   A. Internet Explorer
   B. Navigator
   C. Microsoft
   D. Mosaic

4. A software program used to retrieve documents from the WWW is called a _____.
   A. Packet
   B. Home page
   C. Browser
   D. Web server

5. To display a record of sites you have previously visited, use the _____ feature.
   A. Bookmark
   B. Favorites
   C. URL
   D. History

TRUE/FALSE

Circle T if the statement is true or F if the statement is false.

T   F   1. A T1 line is a high-speed connection to the Internet.

T   F   2. You must use a modem to communicate over a regular telephone line.

T   F   3. The home page is the first page that is displayed when you launch your browser.

T   F   4. You can use AutoSearch or Internet Keywords to locate Web pages on the Internet.

T   F   5. You can view saved pages offline.

FILL IN THE BLANK

Complete the following sentences by writing the correct word or words in the blanks provided.

1. The original name for the Internet was _____.

2. _____ software enables your computer to connect to another computer.

3. A(n) _____ modem uses coaxial cable.

4. The language used to create documents on the WWW is called _____.

5. _____ and _____ are the two most popular Web browsers.

PROJECTS

CROSS-CURRICULAR—MATHEMATICS

The Math Is Power Web site, located at *http://www.mathispower.org/Intro1.html*, is sponsored by the National Science Association and emphasizes the importance of high-quality math education for all students. Visit the Arcade Room or Take a Challenge. Complete at least two exercises at this site, and then sit back and congratulate yourself on a job well done.

CROSS-CURRICULAR—SCIENCE/MATH/LANGUAGE ARTS

The World Weather Watch is an interactive cross-curricular Internet project. To participate in the project, you collect weather data once a week for a specified time period. Your class can register to participate in the project or you can just post your data and use it for comparison discussions. The Web site is located at *http://youth.net/weather/welcome.html*.

CROSS-CURRICULAR—SOCIAL STUDIES/LANGUAGE ARTS

Visit Friends of the Desert located at *http://www.eduplace.com/ss/act/unity.html*. This activity provides instructions on how you and your fellow classmates can hold a conference. Through the conference, you learn how cooperation might solve a problem that affects Africa. A list of what you need and procedures on what to do are listed at this Web site. Your instructor will provide leadership for this project.

CROSS-CURRICULAR—LANGUAGE ARTS/MATH

At the Education Place, located at *http://www.eduplace.com/math/brain/index.html*, a new Brain Teaser is posted each Wednesday evening. You will also find an archive of previous Brain Teasers. Check out this site and have a class contest. Organize into teams and see which team can solve the most teasers.

WEB PROJECT

The job interview process was discussed briefly in the Technology Careers feature. The interview is the first step to obtaining that special job. Using the Internet and other resources, you are to research and report on job interview techniques.

TEAMWORK PROJECT

Ms. Perez is impressed with your knowledge of the Internet. She has asked you to coordinate a project with two other Vista Multimedia employees. There is no Internet connection at Vista Multimedia. Ms. Perez wants to convince the company president that an Internet connection could be a vital enhancement for the store. Your goal is to create a persuasive presentation for Ms. Perez that she can present to the company president.

LESSON 3

HOW A COMPUTER PROCESSES DATA

OBJECTIVES

Upon completion of this lesson, you should be able to:

- Identify computer system components.
- Explain how the CPU works.
- Differentiate between RAM and ROM.
- Describe how data is represented.

Estimated Time: 1.5 hours

VOCABULARY

American Standard Code for Information Interchange (ASCII)

Arithmetic/logic unit (ALU)

Bit

Byte

Cache memory

Central processing unit (CPU)

Control unit

Controller

Execution cycle (E-cycle)

Extended Binary Coded Decimal Interchange Code (EBCDIC)

Instruction cycle (I-cycle)

Main memory

Memory

Modem

Motherboard

Random access memory (RAM)

Read-only memory (ROM)

Universal Serial Bus (USB)

With today's technology a little knowledge about what's inside a computer can make you a more effective user and help you select the right computer for the job you need it to do. In this lesson you will learn how the CPU processes data and turns it into information. And you will learn about some of the basic components contained on the computer's motherboard.

Computer System Components

We use computers for all kinds of tasks—to predict weather, to fly airplanes, to control traffic lights, to play games, to access the Internet, to send e-mail, and so on. You might wonder how a machine can do so many things.

To understand what a computer really does takes a degree in computer engineering. But most of us don't need that level of understanding. Instead, we need an overview for a basic understanding.

Just about all computers, regardless of size, take raw data and change it into information you can use. The process involves input, process, output, and storage (IPOS). For example,

- You input data with some type of input device.
- The computer processes it to turn it into information.
- You output the information to some type of output device.
- You store it for later retrieval.

Input, output, and processing devices grouped together represent a computer system. In this lesson, we look at the components that the computer uses to process data. These components are contained within the system case. See Figure 3-1.

> **Hot Tip**
>
> Research companies and universities are designing wearable computer systems.

FIGURE 3-1
Computer system components

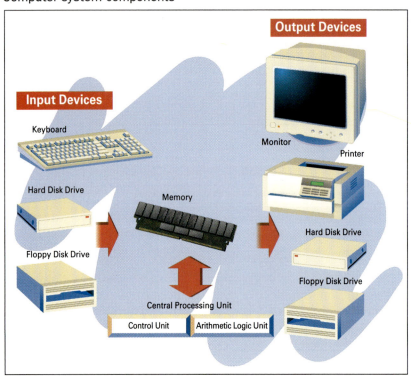

System Components

The PC system case is the metal and plastic case that houses the main system components of the computer. Central to all of this is the *motherboard* or system board that mounts into the case. The motherboard is a circuit board that contains many integral components. A circuit board is simply a thin plate or board that contains electronic components. See Figure 3-2. Some of the most important of these components are as follows:

- The central processing unit
- Memory
- Basic controllers
- Expansion ports and expansion slots

FIGURE 3-2
Simplified motherboard

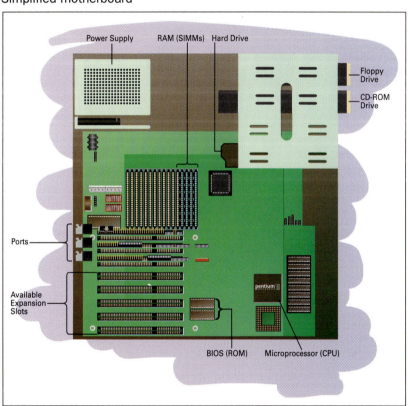

The Central Processing Unit

The *central processing unit* (CPU), also called the microprocessor, the processor, or central processor, is the brains of the computer. The CPU is housed on a tiny silicon chip. See Figure 3-3. This chip contains millions of switches and pathways that help your computer make important decisions. The switches control the flow of the electricity as it travels across the miles of pathways. The CPU knows which switches to turn on and which to turn off because it receives its instructions from computer programs. Programs are a set of special instructions written by programmers that control the activities of the computer. Programs are also known as software.

FIGURE 3-3
The brains of the computer

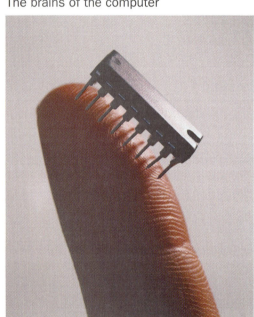

The CPU has two primary sections: the arithmetic/logic unit and the control unit.

The Arithmetic/Logic Unit

The *arithmetic/logic unit* (ALU) performs arithmetic computations and logical operations. The arithmetic operations include addition, subtraction, multiplication, and division. The logical operations involve comparisons. This is simply asking the computer to determine if two numbers are equal or if one number is greater than or less than another number. These may seem like simple operations. However, by combining these operations, the ALU can execute complex tasks. For example, your video game uses arithmetic operations and comparisons to determine what displays on your screen.

The Control Unit

The *control unit* is the boss, so to speak, and coordinates all of the CPU's activities. Using programming instructions, it controls the flow of information through the processor by controlling what happens inside the processor.

We communicate with the computer through programming languages. You may have heard of programming languages called BASIC, COBOL, C++, or Visual Basic. These are just a few of the many languages we can use to give the computer instructions. For example, we may have a programming statement such as Let X = 2 + 8. With this statement, we are using a programming language to ask the computer to add 2 + 8. However, when we input this instruction, something else has to happen. The computer does not understand our language. It only understands machine language, or binary, which is ones and zeros. This is where the control unit takes over.

The control unit reads and interprets the program instruction and changes the instruction into machine language. Recall that earlier we discussed the CPU and pathways and switches. It is through these pathways and the turning on and off of switches that the CPU represents the ones and zeros. When electricity is present, it represents a one. The absence of electricity represents a zero. After changing the instructions into machine language, the control unit then sends out the necessary messages to execute the instructions.

> **Internet**
>
> Jones Telecommunications and Multimedia Encyclopedia Web site has a wealth of information on computer history and development. You can find this Web site at *www.digitalcentury.com/ encyclo/update/comp_hd.html*.

Memory

Memory is also found on the motherboard. Sometimes understanding memory can be confusing because it can mean different things to different people. The easiest way to understand memory is to think of it as "short term" or "long term." When you want to store a file or information permanently, you use secondary storage devices such as the computer's hard disk drive or a floppy disk. You might think of this as long term.

Random Access Memory

You can think about the memory on the motherboard as short term. This type of memory is called *random access memory,* or *RAM*. You may have heard someone ask, "How much memory is in your computer?" Most likely they are asking how much RAM is in your computer. Data, information, and program instructions are stored temporarily on a RAM chip or a set of RAM chips. See Figure 3-4.

FIGURE 3-4
RAM chip: memory

When the computer is turned off or if there is a loss of power, whatever is stored in the RAM memory chips disappears. Therefore, it is considered volatile. The computer can read from and write to this type of memory. RAM is also referred to as *main memory* and primary memory.

> **Hot Tip**
>
> Can't afford that new computer, but need more speed? Try adding more RAM or purchase one of the optimizer software programs.

To better understand how RAM works and how the computer processes data, think about how you would use a word-processing program to create an address list of your family and friends. First, you start your word-processing program. The computer then loads your word-processing program instructions into RAM. You would input the names, addresses, and telephone numbers (your data). Your data is also stored in RAM. Next you would give your word-processing program a command to process your data by arranging it in a special format. This command and your processed data, or information, is also now stored in RAM. You would then click the Print button. Instructions to print are transmitted to RAM and your document is sent to your printer. Then, you click the Save button. Instructions to provide you with an opportunity to name and save your file are loaded into RAM. Once you save your file, you exit your word-processing program and turn off the computer. All instructions, data, and information are erased from RAM.

This step-by-step process is known as the **instruction cycle** or I-cycle and the **execution cycle** or E-cycle. When the CPU receives an instruction to perform a specified task, the instruction cycle is the amount of time it takes to retrieve the instruction and complete the command. The execution cycle refers to the amount of time it takes the CPU to execute the instruction and store the results in RAM. See Figure 3-5.

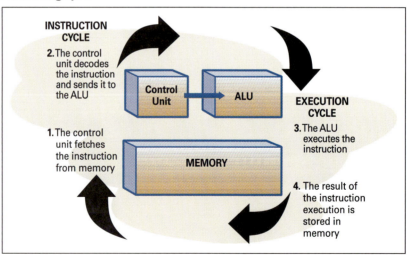

FIGURE 3-5
Processing cycle

Together, the instruction cycle and one or more execution cycles create a machine cycle. Machine cycles are measured in microseconds (millionths of a second), nanoseconds (billionths of a second), and even pico seconds (trillionths of a second) in some of the larger computers. The faster the machine cycle, the faster your computer processes data. The speed of the processor has a lot to do with the speed of the machine cycle. However, the amount of RAM in your computer can also help increase how fast the computer processes data. The more RAM you have, the faster the computer processes data. See Figure 3-6.

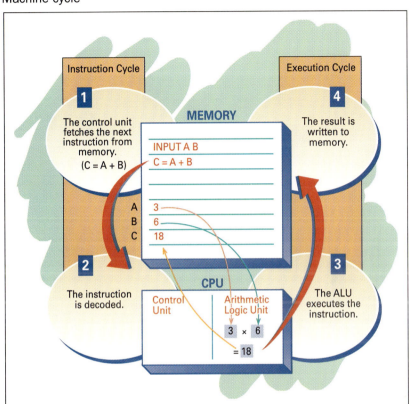

FIGURE 3-6
Machine cycle

Read-Only Memory

Another type of memory you will find on the motherboard is *ROM*, or *read-only memory*. ROM chips are found throughout a computer system. The computer manufacturer uses this type of chip to store specific instructions that are needed for the computer operations. This type of memory is nonvolatile. These instructions remain on the chip regardless if the power is turned on or off. The most common of these is the BIOS ROM. The computer uses instructions contained on this chip to boot or start the system when you turn on your computer. A computer can read from a ROM chip, but cannot write or store data on the chip.

> **Did You Know?**
> Another type of memory is called *cache memory*. This very high-speed RAM is used to increase the speed of the processing cycle.

Basic Controllers

The motherboard also contains several controllers. A *controller* is a device that controls the transfer of data from the computer to a peripheral device and vice versa. Examples of common peripheral devices are keyboards, mouse, monitors, and printers. Controllers are generally stored on a single chip. When you purchase a computer, all the necessary controllers for the standard devices are contained on the motherboard. See Figure 3-7.

FIGURE 3-7
A close-up of a motherboard

Serial and Parallel Ports and Expansion Slots

We use serial and parallel ports to connect our peripheral devices to the computer. Serial devices transmit data one *bit* at a time. Parallel devices transfer several bits at a time. A bit is a zero or one. Most computers have at least one parallel port and one serial port. You will most likely find a printer connected to your parallel ports and perhaps a modem connected to your serial port. A *modem* is a device that allows one computer to talk to another.

The *Universal Serial Bus (USB)* is a new standard that supports data transfer rates of up to 12 million bits per second. You can use a single USB port to connect up to 127 peripheral devices. USB is expected to replace serial and parallel ports.

Expansion slots are openings on the motherboard where a circuit board or expansion board can be inserted. Let's suppose that you want to add pictures to your list of names and addresses. You need a scanner to scan the pictures and you need some way to connect the scanner to the computer. You could accomplish this by adding an expansion board and then connecting the scanner to the board.

Perhaps you would like to add more memory. Motherboards contain special expansion slots for additional memory. Expansion boards are also called expansion cards, add-ins, and add-ons. See Figure 3-8.

FIGURE 3-8
Expansion card

Data Representation

Earlier in this lesson, you read about binary and that a bit is either a zero or a one. You may wonder, though, just exactly how the computer determines what combination of zeros and ones represent the letter A or the number 1. It's really very simple. This is accomplished through standardized coding systems. The most popular system is called *ASCII* (pronounced as-kie) and stands for *American Standard Code for Information Interchange*. There are other standard codes, but ASCII is the most widely used. It is used by nearly every type and brand of microcomputer and by many large computers as well.

Eight bits or combinations of ones and zeros represent a letter such as A. Eight bits are called a *byte* or character. Each capital letter, lowercase letter, number, punctuation mark, and various symbols has its own unique combination of ones and zeros.

Another type of standard code is called *Extended Binary Coded Decimal Interchange Code*, or *EBCDIC* (pronounced EB-si-dik). This code is mostly used in very large computers.

> **Internet**
> Find out more about the ASCII standard by visiting the Webopedia Web site located at *webopedia.internet.com/TERM/A/ASCII.html*. Key the URL exactly as shown here.

SUMMARY

In this lesson, you learned:

- Just about all computers perform the same general options: input, process, output, and storage.
- Input, output, and processing devices grouped together represent a computer system.
- The motherboard is the center of all processing.
- The motherboard contains the CPU, memory, and basic controllers for the system.
- The motherboard also contains ports and expansion slots.
- The central processing unit is the brains of the computer.
- The computer is given instructions through computer programs.
- The CPU has two main sections—the arithmetic logic unit and the control unit.
- All calculations and comparisons take place in the ALU.
- The control unit coordinates the CPU activities.
- The motherboard contains different types of memory.
- Random access memory is volatile and is used to store instructions, data, and information temporarily.
- The machine cycle is made up of the instruction cycle and the execution cycle.
- Read-only memory is nonvolatile and is used to store permanent instructions needed for computer operations.
- A controller is used to control the transfer of data between the computer and peripheral devices.
- Peripheral devices are connected to the computer through serial and parallel ports.
- The Universal Serial Bus is a new standard expected to replace serial and parallel ports.
- Expansion boards are used to connect specialized peripheral devices or to add more memory to the computer.
- The ASCII code is a standard code used to represent the alphabet, numbers, symbols, and punctuation marks.

Lesson 3 How a Computer Processes Data

VOCABULARY Review

Define the following terms:

American Standard Code for Information Interchange (ASCII)
Arithmetic/logic unit (ALU)
Bit
Byte
Cache memory
Central processing unit (CPU)
Control unit
Controller
Execution cycle (E-cycle)
Extended Binary Coded Decimal Interchange Code (EBCDIC)
Instruction cycle (I-cycle)
Main memory
Memory
Modem
Motherboard
Random access memory (RAM)
Read-only memory (ROM)
Universal Serial Bus (USB)

REVIEW Questions

MULTIPLE CHOICE

Select the best response for the following statements.

1. Eight _____ make one character.
   A. characters
   B. bits
   C. bytes
   D. codes

2. The _____ contains the CPU, memory, and basic controllers.
   A. memory
   B. motherboard
   C. processor
   D. expansion slot

3. The _____ is considered the brains of the computer.
   A. program
   B. ALU
   C. CPU
   D. control unit

4. Random access memory is _____.
   A. permanent
   B. volatile
   C. nonvolatile
   D. the same as ROM

5. A printer would be considered a(n) _____.
   A. controller
   B. peripheral device
   C. input device
   D. USB

TRUE/FALSE

Circle the T if the statement is true or F if the statement is false.

T   F   1. You would most likely use a serial port to connect a modem to your computer.

T   F   2. The ASCII code is the most widely used standardized coding system.

T   F   3. A bit has eight bytes.

T   F   4. The two primary sections of the CPU are the ALU and the control unit.

T   F   5. The computer only understands machine language.

FILL IN THE BLANK

Complete the following sentences by writing the correct word or words in the blanks provided.

1. You can think of RAM as _____-term memory.

2. The instruction cycle and the execution cycle create a(n) _____ cycle.

3. The _____ the machine cycle, the faster your computer.

4. A(n) _____ is a board that contains electronic components.

5. You would add memory to a computer by inserting it into a(n) _____ slot.

CROSS-CURRICULAR *Projects*

MATH/LANGUAGE ARTS/SCIENCE

Collect three or four computer ads from your local Sunday paper. Using either a spreadsheet program or paper and pencil, complete a comparison table. Include the following elements in your table: processor speed, amount of memory, number of expansion slots, and price. Based on your comparisons, write a short paragraph explaining which computer you would purchase and why.

SCIENCE/LANGUAGE ARTS

If possible, find a computer system with the case removed. Examine the motherboard and the components connected to the motherboard. Locate and count the number of available expansion slots. Locate the RAM chips. See if you can find the CPU. Can you see the chip itself? Create a drawing of the system and label as many of the components as you can.

SOCIAL STUDIES/LANGUAGE ARTS

Using the Internet or other resources, see what you can find about the history of computers. See if you can find the answers to the following questions: (1) What is the name of the first commercially available electronic digital computer? (2) In what year was the IBM PC first introduced? (3) What software sent Bill Gates on his way to becoming the richest man in the world? (4) In what year did Apple introduce the Macintosh computer? Use your word processing program to answer each of these questions and/or to provide some additional historical facts.

CRITICAL *Thinking*

ACTIVITY 3-1

Many people compare the computer to our brain. We input data into the computer, process the data, and then output it in the form of information. Consider how we function as a human—that we input through our five senses, process what we input by thinking about it, and then talk or perform some action as output. If we as humans can function like a computer, then what's so great about this technology and why do we need it? Do you think there will ever be a computer that can rival the human brain?

WEB PROJECT

Launch your Web browser and key the following URL: *www.AskJeeves.com*.

When the Web site is displayed, ask Jeeves "Who invented the microprocessor?" and click **ASK**. Jeeves will provide several answers for you. Choose the one most appropriate and click **ASK**. This takes you to the Web site where you can find the answer to your question. Use your presentation systems program to create a presentation on what you found at this Web site. Include the name of and an overview of the person who developed the first transistor. Add two or three more slides to your presentation with information you find at this Web site. Share your presentation with your friends or coworkers.

LESSON 4

KEYBOARDING

OBJECTIVES

Upon completion of this lesson, you should be able to:

- Define keyboarding.
- Identify the parts of the standard keyboard.
- Identify the home row keys.
- Identify the parts of a word-processing screen.
- Identify correct keyboarding techniques.
- Key (type) text without watching the keys.
- Save, print, retrieve, spell check, and format documents.
- Identify keyboarding software programs.
- Describe the purpose of speech recognition software.

Estimated Time: 1.5 hours

VOCABULARY

Ergonomic keyboard
Formatting
Hard return
Home row keys
Keyboarding
Menu bar
Modifier keys
QWERTY
Ruler
Status bar
Text area
Timed writings
Title bar
Toolbar
Touch typing
Word wrap

A major part of your work at Vista Multimedia involves inputting data into the computer. You enter data when customers rent videos and CDs as well as when you create letters and other documents for the store. Because of the amount of typing required, it is important that you develop good keyboarding skills. Some people think it is not necessary to have good keyboarding skills to use a computer. Good keyboarding skills are an asset to those who take the time to develop them. Other inputs, however, such as voice, handwriting, and mouse are also important skills.

Many who have not learned the appropriate method for keyboarding use the "hunt and peck" method. This involves using at least two fingers; sometimes more, to "peck" the needed keys after "hunting" the keyboard to find them. This method is slow and frustrating for most individuals.

It is not necessary to be a speed typist, but having adequate keyboarding skills will enable you to use the computer much more effectively. This will make you more productive. It will take you less time to key your term papers, calculate your grades, compose your e-mail messages, or complete other computer tasks.

Unit 1 Computer Basics

The skill of typing, or *keyboarding*, as it is called today, is the ability to enter text by using the correct fingers without looking at the keys. This is also called *touch typing*. Developing keyboarding skills requires much practice. It is a skill that will empower you to operate a computer much more efficiently! It is essential for using application programs such as word processing, database, spreadsheet, desktop publishing, presentation, data communications, and other miscellaneous programs.

Mastering this skill will enable you to use your time on the computer concentrating on your work instead of "hunting" for keys!

> **Hot Tip**
> Christopher Sholes is given credit for having invented the first typewriter.

The Keyboard Layout

There are several styles of keyboards, but the **QWERTY** is more popular. Pronounced KWER-tee, the name refers to the arrangement of keys on a standard English computer keyboard. See Figure 4-1. Your keyboard may look different. All keyboards, however, have the same basic parts.

> **Did You Know?**
> The Dvorak keyboard replaced the QWERTY keyboard. It was much faster and required less work by the typist. The Chiclet keyboard was a very small keyboard that was first used on the PC Jr.

FIGURE 4-1
The QWERTY keyboard

- Alphanumeric keys are the parts of the keyboard that look like a typewriter. They are arranged the same way on most keyboards.
- *Modifier keys:* These keys are used in conjunction with other keys.
    - Ctrl for control
    - Alt for alternate
    - Shift

> **Did You Know?**
> The arrangement of the keys on the first typewriter was alphabetical. This arrangement of keys made typing very slow and was soon changed.

- The numeric keypad is usually located on the right side of the keyboard. It looks like a calculator. The keys look like the ones on a calculator; however, if you look closely, you will see some additional symbols on the keys. These are used for specialized tasks in conjunction with various software programs.

- The function keys are usually located in a row at the top of the keyboard. You use these to give the computer commands. The software application being used determines the purpose of each of these function keys.

- The directional keys control the movement of the insertion point on the screen. The insertion point is sometimes referred to as the cursor.

- The special-purpose keys perform specialized functions.
    - Esc: The function of this key depends on the software application. It is usually used to "back up" one level in a multilevel environment, that is, back up one step in a multistep process.
    - Print Screen: Pressing this key sends a copy of what appears on your screen directly to the printer.
    - Scroll Lock: Despite the term, this key does not allow you to scroll documents necessarily. The way this key functions depends on the software being used.
    - Pause/Break: In some software programs, this key can be used to stop a command in progress.

> **Internet**
>
> Visit *www.officemuseum.com/typewriters.htm* to read about early writing machines and typewriters in the early office.

Some keyboards are designed to relieve stress that can result from repeated or longtime use. These are called *ergonomic keyboards*. See Figure 4-2.

FIGURE 4-2
An ergonomic keyboard

Unit 1 Computer Basics

The Display Computer Screen

Once you start your word processing program, a screen similar to Figure 4-3 will display. Refer to Figure 4-3 to learn about the following features.

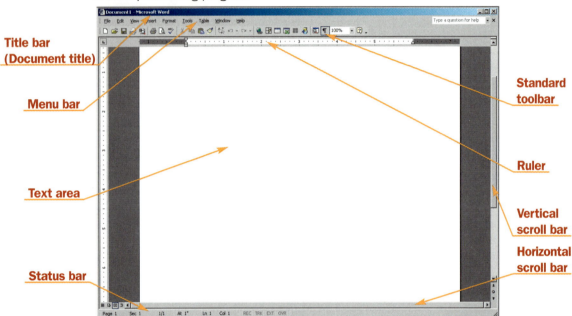

FIGURE 4-3
A word processing program

Technology Careers

MANAGER OF INFORMATION SYSTEMS

The manager of information systems directs the operation of the computer system in an organization. He or she also provides the employees with any computer-related services they may need to perform their jobs.

An element of the manager's job is to keep abreast of new technology and evaluate it for possible use in the organization. Security of information is also a major responsibility.

The person in this position must have excellent communication skills because he or she has to work with both the users in the organization and senior administrators. Organizational skills are very important.

A bachelor's degree in computer science or engineering is preferred. A master's degree in computer science would allow you the opportunity to advance quickly in the field of information systems. It is also helpful to have experience as a programmer, systems analyst, or project manager.

The salary range for this job is between $60,000 and $80,000. Salary varies depending on location of position, size of organization, and experience level.

- Document title: You will give each of your documents a name. The name will appear in this area. This area is sometimes called the *title bar*.
- *Menu bar*: A menu displays a list of commands.
- Standard *toolbar*: Displays commonly used commands accessed through buttons.
- Formatting toolbar: Use the buttons on this to change the appearance of your document.
- *Ruler*: Use the ruler to change paragraph indentations and margin settings and add tab settings.
- Display window or *text area*: The area that contains the information you key. As you key in this area, the insertion point continues to move to the right.
- The insertion point: The point where the next characters keyed from the keyboard will appear on the display screen. The insertion point is usually represented by a blinking vertical line.
- Vertical scroll bar: This bar is used to scroll vertically through your document.
- Horizontal scroll bar: This bar is used to scroll horizontally through your document.
- *Status bar*: This bar displays information about your document, including current page number, total pages in document, location of insertion point, and the status of some of the specialized keys.

Your screen may look a little different. Different software programs have slightly different screens. However, basically they are the same. As you key data and the insertion point moves to the right, the text will drop down to the next line. This is called *word wrap*. The text will wrap around at the right margin and continue on the next line. You do not need to press Enter to get to the next line. However, you do need to press Enter if you are keying paragraphs and want to start a new paragraph.

Correct Keyboarding Techniques

Several basic techniques are required to learn to touch keyboard effectively. These include using the correct posture, holding the hands and wrists properly, striking the keys correctly, and using the home row keys properly.

Position

The correct keyboarding position refers to your posture. See Figure 4-4.

FIGURE 4-4
Correct posture is important

- Sit up straight and lean forward slightly from the waist. Your body should be about a hand's length from the front of the keyboard and centered with the keyboard.
- Keep your feet flat on the floor.
- Let your elbows hang naturally at your sides.
- Rest your fingers lightly on the keyboard.
- Focus your eyes on the book or whatever you are keying from unless you are composing at the keyboard; in that case, keep your eyes on the computer screen.

Keystroking

Using the correct fingers to key is very important. Your hands should be placed in a curved position over the home row. The *home row keys* include a, s, d, f, j, k, l, and ;. These keys are called the home row because they are in the position from which all keystrokes are made. After the keystroke is made, the finger returns to the home row. See Figure 4-5.

FIGURE 4-5
Correct finger position

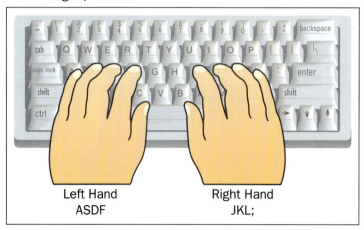

Left Hand
ASDF

Right Hand
JKL;

Figure 4-6 provides a closer look at which fingers are used for which keys.

- Rest your fingertips lightly on the keys.
- Keep your fingers slightly curved and upright. Make sure that the palm of your hand does not touch the keyboard or your desk.
- Strike the key with a quick, snappy stroke and return the finger to the home row.

FIGURE 4-6
Finger position for all keys

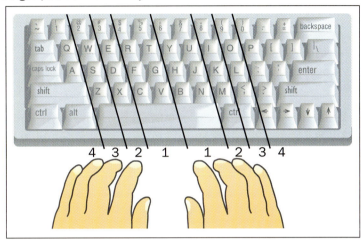

There are two additional keys you will learn to use. These are the Enter key and the spacebar. Look at Figure 4-7 to see how to use these keys.

FIGURE 4-7
Finger position for Enter key and spacebar

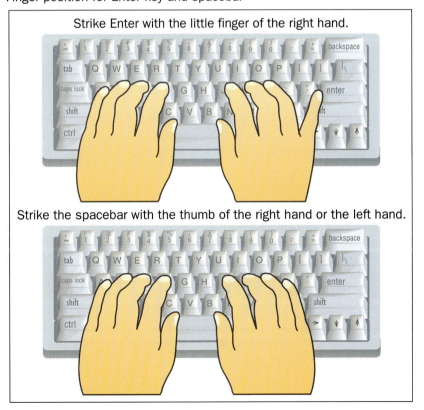

- The Enter key is used to move down to the next line. Use the "semicolon" key finger to strike the Enter key.

- The spacebar is used to insert horizontal spaces between words, punctuation marks, and so forth. Press this key with the right thumb.

Your Workstation

Your workstation, which includes your desk, chair, computer, printer, supplies, and reference materials, should always be organized. Place materials you will key on the right side of the computer and supplies on the left side. Keep any items you are not using off your desk.

Developing Beginning Keyboarding Skills

Developing keyboarding skill requires a lot of practice. The most important factor in mastering keyboarding skill is good technique. Speed and accuracy are built around good technique. At this point, however, you do not need to concern yourself with speed. Concentrate on being accurate, and the speed will come later.

The first part of learning to keyboard is learning to key the alphabetic keys. Your instructor may place a large diagram poster on the board that shows the correct finger position for reaching to other keys from the home row.

Ethics in Technology

PLAGIARISM

"Plagiarism is stealing a ride on someone else's train of thought."—*Author unknown*

This definition of plagiarism is very accurate. The basis of plagiarism involves using information as if it were your own.

Why is plagiarism illegal? Even though you may consider it as just borrowing words, pictures, or music from someone, you are still taking something that belongs to someone else. It is his or her possession just like a person's car, house, and so on. Paraphrasing someone else's thoughts is also a form of plagiarism unless you give the originator credit for the work.

With widespread use of the Internet, incidents of plagiarism have risen at an astonishing rate. It does not take as much time to find information electronically as it does to go through volumes of books to find the same information. A research paper easily can be created using the cut-and-paste function in your word processing program. We could say that it is just easier to find and copy resources on the Internet.

Easy it may be, but it is also illegal! It is a form of theft. You are taking the thoughts, words, and ideas of another person and using them as if they were your own.

How can you avoid plagiarism? You must give credit whenever you use another person's thoughts, ideas, or opinions or you must ask permission to use their work in your document.

Learning to key all of the alphabetic keys will take several weeks to learn. You will complete many, many drills to acquire the desired skills. Some of the drills will be repetitious, however, they are necessary in developing your keyboarding skill.

STEP-BY-STEP 4.1

Learning the alphanumeric keys:

1. Start your software program.

2. Organize your workstation.

3. Check your posture to be sure you are following the guidelines mentioned earlier in this lesson.

4. Place your fingers on the home row keys. Curve your fingers so the tips of your fingers are resting on the home row keys. Your fingers are named for the home keys on which they rest: A finger, S finger, D finger, and so on.

5. Press the spacebar to space between words. It is operated with the right or left thumb. Practice using the spacebar. Tap the spacebar once; tap it twice, tap it once, tap it twice, tap it once, tap it twice.

6. Press **Enter** when you are ready to move to the next line. This is called a **hard return**. To press the Enter key, extend the "Semi" finger to the Enter key, and press lightly. Practice using the Enter key. Press the spacebar once, twice, once, twice, once, twice. Reach and press **Enter**. (Remember to return the Semi finger to the ; key.)

7. Practice the "f" key. You will use the following line:

   fff fff ff ff f f ff ff f f

   Key **fff** (press the spacebar once), key **fff** (press spacebar once), key **ff** (press spacebar once), key **ff** (press spacebar once), key **f** (press spacebar once), key **f** (press spacebar once), key **ff** (press spacebar once), key **ff** (press spacebar once), key **f** (press spacebar once), key **f** (press **Enter** once).

8. Key the same line again. Press **Enter** twice.

9. Practice the home row keys.

   j jj f ff k kk d dd l ll s ss ; ;; a aa jkl; fdsa   (Press **Enter**)
   j jj f ff k kk d dd l ll s ss ; ;; a aa jkl; fdsa   (Press **Enter** twice)

10. Keep your practice file open for the next Step-by-Step.

The remainder of the alphabetic keys are learned using the same method. After learning the alphabetic keys, you begin drills focusing on accuracy and later, speed. Drills used to develop speed and accuracy are called *timed writings*. After learning the alphabetic keys, you will learn to key the numeric keys and the symbols on the keyboard. You will use the same procedure to learn these keys.

Saving Your Practice Work

After completing your practice, your instructor may want you to save your work on a diskette. Before you save your work, review the following steps on how to take care of your diskettes.

- Store your diskettes away from extreme temperatures.
- Insert and eject diskettes carefully from the disk drive.
- Never remove or insert a disk while the drive is running. Check for the light on the drive. When the light is lit, the drive is running.
- Make backup copies of your diskettes.

STEP-BY-STEP 4.2

1. Click **File** on the menu bar and then click **Save As**.
2. The Save As window is displayed. Your instructor will tell you where to save your work. Select the appropriate drive on which to save your work. If you are saving your work on your own diskette, it will be saved on the disk in Drive A.
3. In the File name box, key the name of the lesson or the name your instructor tells you to use. For this practice, use **practice** as the filename.
4. Click the **Save** button.
5. Close your file and keep your word-processing program open for the next Step-by-Step.

Printing a File

Your instructor may ask you to print your practice session. If so, complete the following steps:

- Click File on the menu bar and then click Print.
- Once the Print dialog box opens, click the OK button.
- You are returned to your screen while the document is printing.
- If you are going to work on a new document, click File on the menu bar, and then click Close on the drop-down menu.

Exiting the Program

When you finish, you need to exit the software program. Click File on the menu bar and then click Exit. The desktop displays.

Retrieving a File

Once a file has been saved, you can open that file to add additional information, to delete information, or just to read it. To open a file:

- Click File on the menu bar and then click Open.
- The Open dialog box is displayed.
- Once the Open dialog box opens, be sure the drive where your file is located is displayed.
- Click on the name of the file you want to open.
- Click the Open button. A copy of the file displays on your screen.

Additional Concepts

Checking the Spelling in Your Document

If you make a spelling error as you are keying your document, the misspelled word may be displayed with a wavy red line under it or with some other type of identification. You can manually correct the error or you can use the built-in spell checker.

If you want to correct the word yourself, use one of the following methods:

- Use the **Backspace** key to delete text to the left of the insertion point. For example, if the insertion point is in front of the "p" in *computer* and you press Backspace, the "m" will be erased.
- Use the **Delete** key to delete text to the right of the Insertion point. For example, if the insertion point is behind the "m" in *computer* and you press Delete, the "p" will be erased.

The spell checker in your software will check your document for any misspelled words or words that are not in the software's spelling dictionary. Many word-processing programs also include a grammar checker either with the spell checker or separately. To access the spell checker in most word-processing programs, click Tools on the menu bar and then click Spelling (it may be called Spelling and Grammar). See Figure 4-8. Another option is to click the spell checker button on the toolbar.

- The Speller dialog box is displayed. A word that the software does not recognize displays. You have several options from which to choose.

- If the word is misspelled, click the correct word from the list provided, and then click Change. If the word is not misspelled, click Ignore.

FIGURE 4-8
Spelling and grammar checking

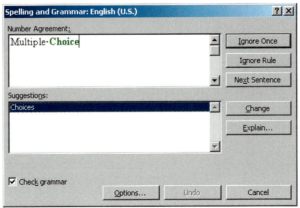

The spell check does not check for word usage such as *their* and *there*, or *site*, *cite*, and *sight*. Therefore, it is still necesssary to proofread your documents carefully.

> **Did You Know?**
> You can use keyboard shortcuts to access commands instead of the mouse.

Formatting Your Documents

Once you have learned to keyboard, you will begin to key various types of documents such as letters and reports. These documents will need to be formatted for margins, spacing, and so on. You may even want to change the style of the text, the size of the letters, or bold, underline, or italicize the text. All of these enhancements, and more, can be applied to your document. This is called *formatting* your document.

You can enter commands to format your document before you key the document or you can format your text after it has been entered. The commands for formatting documents are accessed through different methods in different software programs. The way that you format once the command has been selected, however, is pretty much the same. Example: You have keyed a report and now want to go back and format the title to be bold.

1. Select the title by clicking on the first letter of the title, holding down the left mouse button, and dragging to the end of the title.
2. Once the title is highlighted (selected), click the Bold button on the formatting toolbar.

Special Characters and Spacing

Traditional typewriters used different characters than those found on computer keyboards. Some characters that were available on typewriter keys are not available on computer keys. The cents (¢) symbol is such a key. To print this symbol, you would use the Symbol option on the Insert menu. The hyphen (-) key on the typewriter is not used the same as the hyphen key on the computer. Other special keys include:

- **em dash:** This character was represented by two hyphens in typewritten copy. It introduces a sentence break, a sudden break in thought, or a parenthetical statement. It is a stronger break than a comma, but not as strong as a period. It is also used to indicate an open range. It is approximately the width of a capital letter M (—). Select the Special Characters tab, then click the Em Dash symbol. Example: I was going to — when are the grades due?

- **en dash**: This character is used to separate ranges or durations, or in compound words. Spaces are not used before or after an en dash. It is approximately the width of a capital letter N (–). Example: 1997–2007.

- **smart quotes**: Typewriters insert straight marks for quotation marks. Computer software, however, can insert curly quotation marks. These characters show more easily whether the quoted section is the beginning or ending. Example: "Word processing" instead of "word processing".

- Many typeset characters that were not available on traditional typewriters are available with computer programs; for example, the copyright symbol (©) or a stacked fraction (½). They are accessed through the Insert, Symbol menu on the Menu Bar.

- Characters typed on a traditional typewriter occupy the same amount of space regardless of the size of the character. This is referred to as *monospaced* type. Computer typefaces are proportional, meaning that each letter occupies a slightly different width; for example, an M is wider than an I.

- Because monospaced type did not leave enough space after ending punctuation, typists were instructed to insert two spaces after end-of-sentence punctuation such as periods and question marks. When you are using computer software with its proportional type, only one space is necessary.

Keyboarding Software

There are many different keyboarding software programs available for learning to keyboard. These programs provide instruction, drills, and testing for developing keyboarding skills. Some of the more popular of these keyboarding software programs include *Keyboarding Made Easy*, *Kid Keys*, *Mavis Beacon Teaches Typing*, *Typing Tutor*, *MicroType Multi-media*, *Mario Teaches Typing*, and *All the Right Type Three*.

Some of these programs are designed for persons with special needs, such as those having poor vision or who can use only one hand. Some even have voice instructions. No matter what the program, it is important to use appropriate techniques as discussed previously in this lesson.

Speech Recognition Software

Computer programmers have developed a way for computer users to "talk" to their computers to input data rather than manually keying it in. This is called speech recognition software. You speak through a microphone that is connected to your computer, and the information displays on your screen.

You will need to train your computer to recognize your voice. This may take some time but the result of this new skill will be that you can get your work done faster. Many students say that this voice input is fun and worth the 10 to 12 hours it takes to train the computer to recognize the user's voice. Studies have shown that voice input can easily exceed 100 words a minute and with practice 130 words a minute. The average keyboarder can do 40 to 50 words a minute. So you can see the benefit of using your voice—you'll be more productive!

Using Your New Keyboarding Skill

Now that you have learned to keyboard efficiently, you are ready to produce a correctly formatted letter, save the letter, and then print it. Use the letter in Figure 4-9 to complete the task in Step-by-Step 4-3.

FIGURE 4-9
Letter

Current Date

Ms. Lakita McDaniel
1106 College Drive
Cincinnati, OH 45226

Dear Ms. McDaniel

Our class has been studying various plays in our Theater class during this semester. Reading plays can sometimes transform you into a totally different person in a totally different place.

As wonderful as it is to read plays, it is even more exciting to actually see one on stage. Well, we have gotten permission and financial assistance from our principal to see the play Ragtime on the second Friday of next month at 2 p.m. at the Wilder Performing Arts Center.

The cost of the tickets has been taken care of by our principal. However, we do need you to send us signed permission for your child to attend the play with our class. Your child will be bringing home a permission slip for you to sign. Please sign it promptly and return by the second Monday of next month.

We look forward to having your child on the field trip with us.

Sincerely

Mr. David Snead

Theater Teacher

cc

STEP-BY-STEP 4.3

1. Start your word-processing software, if it is not already started. Open a New document.

2. Press **Enter** two times.

3. Key the date and press **Enter** three times.

4. Key the inside address. Remember to press **Enter** at the end of each line. After you key the last line of the inside address, press **Enter** twice.

5. Key the salutation and press **Enter** two times.

6. Key the first paragraph. Remember that you do not press Enter until you complete the paragraph; then press it two times.

7. Key the second paragraph and press **Enter** two times.

8. Key the third paragraph and press **Enter** two times.

9. Key the closing and press **Enter** four times.

10. Key the writer's name and press **Enter** twice.

11. Key the writer's title and press **Enter** three times.

12. Key your initials in lowercase letters. Example: Carnell Cherry would key *cc*.

13. Spell check your document.

14. Save the letter with the filename **Field Trip**.

15. Print one copy of the letter.

16. Close the letter.

17. Exit the word-processing program.

SUMMARY

In this lesson, you learned:

- Keyboarding is the ability to enter text by using the correct fingers and without watching your keys.
- The standard keyboard is divided into six major sections:
    - Alphanumeric keys
    - Modifier keys
    - Numeric keypad
    - Function keys
    - Directional keys
    - Special-purpose keys
- All keying should begin from the home row. The home row consists of the following keys: A S D F J K L and ;.
- Parts of the computer screen are:
    - Title bar (document title)
    - Menu bar
    - Standard toolbar

- Formatting toolbar
- Ruler
- Text area
- Vertical scroll bar
- Horizontal scroll bar
- Status bar

■ Using correct techniques is very important in developing keyboarding skill.
  - Posture
  - Keystroking
  - Workstation

■ You should save your work often.

■ You can retrieve files that have been saved.

■ The spell checker checks the document for words it doesn't recognize. It gives you several options when incorrectly spelled words are displayed.

■ You may enhance the appearance of your document by using any of the many formatting features available in the software.

■ Keyboarding software is available for learning to keyboard.

■ Speech recognition software allows you to "talk" to your computer to enter data.

VOCABULARY Review

Define the following terms:

Ergonomic keyboard	Modifier keys	Timed writings
Formatting	QWERTY	Title bar
Hard return	Ruler	Toolbar
Home row keys	Status bar	Touch typing
Keyboarding	Text area	Word wrap
Menu bar		

REVIEW Questions

MULTIPLE CHOICE

Select the best response for the following statements.

1. Standard keyboards have the _____ layout.
   A. QWARTY
   B. QWERTY

C. QWAZXY
D. QWYTRE

2. _____ keys perform specialized functions.
   A. Shift keys
   B. Special-purpose keys
   C. Backspace keys
   D. Cursor keys

3. The _____ displays information about a document including current page number, total pages in document, location of cursor, and so on.
   A. Formatting toolbar
   B. Status bar
   C. Vertical scroll bar
   D. Horizontal scroll bar

4. The home row keys include _____.
   A. a, b, c, d, k, l, ;,
   B. q, w, e, r, t, y
   C. a, s, d, f, j, k, l, ;
   D. y, r, t, q, k l, j

5. Using just two fingers to strike keys is called the _____ method of keyboarding.
   A. peck and hunt
   B. hunt and peck
   C. touch
   D. QWERTY

TRUE/FALSE

Circle T if the statement is true or F if the statement is false.

T F 1. Keyboarding is also referred to as touch typing.

T F 2. Ergonomic keyboards relieve stress that can be incurred from repeated and/or longtime use of a keyboard.

T F 3. Christopher Sholes is given credit for inventing the first typewriter.

T F 4. Slouching down in the chair while keyboarding affects your keyboarding skill in a positive way.

T F 5. Voice recognition software will identify everyone's voice who uses your computer.

FILL IN THE BLANK

Complete the following sentences by writing the correct word or words in the blanks provided.

1. You do not watch the keys or your fingers when using the _____ method of keyboarding.

2. The _____ keys are usually located in a row at the top of the keyboard.

3. The correct keyboarding position refers to your _____.

4. The most important factor in mastering keyboarding is good _____.

5. If you concentrate in the beginning on being accurate, the _____ will come later.

PROJECTS

CROSS-CURRICULAR—MATH

Most word-processing programs have mathematical features built in. Use the software manual or the Help feature in your software to find out what formulas are available. Prepare a typewritten report and share with your classmates describing what these formulas are, how to access them, and how to use them.

CROSS-CURRICULAR—SCIENCE

Use the Internet and any other resources to locate information on El Niño. You are looking for information that will explain what it is and how it affects our weather. Write a one- to two-page report of your findings using your word-processing software. Look up El Niño using a search engine.

CROSS-CURRICULAR—SOCIAL STUDIES

Use the Internet and any other resources to locate information on how a bill becomes a law. Use a word-processing program to write a report listing the steps involved in the lawmaking process. Use *www.AskJeeves.com* to find information for this project.

CROSS-CURRICULAR—LANGUAGE ARTS

Use the site listed in "The Internet" sidebar to gather information to prepare a one-page summary of five early typewriters. Include the name of each typewriter, who invented it, and a brief description of the typewriter.

 ### WEB PROJECT

Many careers require keyboarding skills. These include Administrative Assistant, Receptionist, or Secretary, just to name a few. Use *www.AskJeeves.com* and other Internet sites to locate information regarding these and other careers that require keyboarding skill. Prepare a word-processed report on two of these careers. Include the duties performed, the level of skill required, and expected salary.

 ### TEAMWORK PROJECT

Ms. Perez, your supervisor at Vista Multimedia, has read about speech recognition software. She has asked you and another employee to research this topic. She would like to know the capabilities of speech recognition software, its advantages and disadvantages, and the names and prices of three speech recognition software programs. Search the Internet for this information and create a report for Ms. Perez.

LESSON 5

Input, Output, Storage, and Networks

OBJECTIVES

Upon completion of this lesson, you should be able to:

- Identify and describe the most common input devices.
- Identify and describe the most common output devices.
- Identify and describe how input and output devices are connected to the computer.
- Identify and describe storage devices.
- List and describe the types of networks.
- List and describe communications media.
- Describe the different network topologies.
- Describe network architecture and protocols.

Estimated Time: 3 hours

VOCABULARY

Bus topology
Clients
Client/server network
Ethernet
Hard disk drives
Input devices
Local area network (LAN)
Magnetic tape drives
Modem
Monitors
Network
Optical storage devices
Output devices
Parallel ports
Peer-to-peer network
Printers
Ring topology
Scanners
Serial ports
Server
Star topology
TCP/IP
Token ring
Topology
Transmission media
Voice recognition
Wide area network (WAN)

We all can agree it is the computer that does all of the work of processing data! However, it needs help. Data must be entered into the computer. Once the data has been entered and processed, it has to be "presented" to the user. Special devices are used for these tasks. Such devices are called input and output devices.

When customers come into the video store to rent videos, they leave with the rented videos and a receipt. In order for the receipt to be printed, you enter the customer's information into the computer and the printer produces a receipt. You use the keyboard or a scanner to enter the information or to input the data. The printer produces a copy of the transaction, or the output of the information.

Input devices enable you to input data and commands into the computer and *output devices* enable the computer to give you the results of the processed data. Some devices perform both input and output functions. The modem is an example. It is an input device when the sender inputs an e-mail message to be sent to a receiver. The modem is an output device when it sends the message.

As companies grow and purchase more computers, they often find it advantageous to connect those computers through a network. This allows users to share software applications and to share hardware devices such as printers, scanners, and so forth.

Input Devices

The type of input device used is determined by the task to be completed. An input device can be as simple as the keyboard or as sophisticated as those used for specialized applications such as voice or retinal recognition.

Keyboard

The keyboard is the most common input device for entering numeric and alphabetic data. Therefore, if you are going to use the computer efficiently, it is very important that you learn to keyboard. When you enter information into the computer at the video store, it is important to be able to enter the information in a reasonable amount of time. As you learned in Lesson 4, the keyboard comes in many different sizes and shapes.

Many companies specialize in developing ergonomic keyboards that minimize the stress caused by keying data for long periods of time. Use a search engine such as *www.AskJeeves.com* or *www.Dogpile.com* to locate several of these companies and see the types of products they produce.

Mouse

The *mouse* is a pointing device that rolls around on a flat surface and controls the pointer on the screen. The *pointer* is an on-screen arrow-shaped object used to select text and access menus. As you move the mouse, the "arrow" on the screen also moves.

The mouse fits conveniently in the palm of your hand. It has a ball located on the bottom that rolls around on a flat surface as the mouse is moved. Most of these devices have two buttons; some have three buttons. You use the left button for most mouse operations. Once you place the on-screen pointer where you want it, press a button on the mouse. This will cause some type of action to take place in the computer; the type of action depends on the program being used.

Everything that you do with the mouse uses these techniques:

- *Pointing:* placing the on-screen pointer at a designated location
- *Clicking:* pressing and releasing the mouse button
- *Dragging:* pressing down the mouse button and moving the mouse while continuing to hold down the button
- *Double-clicking:* pressing and releasing the mouse button twice in rapid succession

■ *Right-clicking:* pressing the right mouse button. See Figure 5-1.

FIGURE 5-1
The mouse is used as a pointing device to select an option

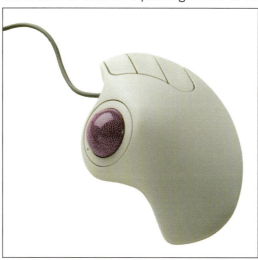

Joystick

The *joystick* is also a pointing device. It consists of a plastic or metal rod mounted on a base. It can be moved in any direction. Some joysticks have switches or buttons that can input data in an on/off response. Joysticks are most often used for games. See Figure 5-2.

FIGURE 5-2
Joystick

Trackball

The *trackball* is a pointing device that works like a mouse turned upside down; the ball is on top of the device. You use your thumb and fingers to operate the ball, thus controlling the arrow on the screen. See Figure 5-3. Trackballs are often found on the keyboards of laptop and notebook computers.

FIGURE 5-3
Trackball

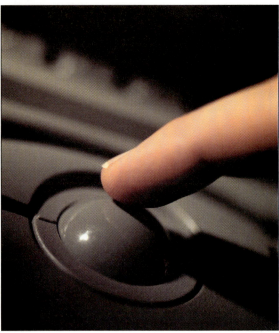

Technology Careers

PC SUPPORT SPECIALIST

The PC support specialist provides support for application software and related hardware via telephone and/or site visits to all workstation users.

As a PC support specialist you need to be knowledgeable about current software and have good oral communication and organizational skills. You will be required to interact with all departments within the company and users with various skill levels ranging from novice to expert. You must be willing to learn other areas of Management Information Systems (MIS) such as networking, printer maintenance, and e-mail.

A bachelor's degree is preferred for most of these jobs; however, impressive experience is also accepted. Experience performing actual hands-on hardware and software upgrades is important.

Graphics Tablet

A *graphics tablet* is a flat drawing surface on which the user can draw figures or write something freehand. The tablet is connected to the computer. Once the drawing has been inputted to the computer, it can be manipulated like a regular graphic.

Touch Display Screen

The *touch display screen* is a special screen with pictures or shapes. You use your fingers to "point" to the desired object to make a selection. These screens can be found in many public establishments such as banks, libraries, delivery services, and fast-food restaurants. These are very user-friendly input devices. See Figure 5-4.

FIGURE 5-4
Touch screens are often used in retail stores where keyboards are impractical

Voice Recognition Devices

Voice recognition devices are used to "speak" commands into the computer and to enter text. These devices are usually microphones. The computer must have some type of voice recognition software installed

> **Did You Know?**
>
> Microsoft has a text-only version of Internet Explorer, and Netscape has a version of its Navigator browser that incorporates voice recognition capabilities in an effort to assist visually impaired persons.

before a voice recognition device can be used. Directory assistance is also a type of voice recognition technology. Voice recognition technology has also enabled disabled persons to command wheelchairs and other objects that will make them more mobile. See Figure 5-5.

FIGURE 5-5
Persons with disabilities can use voice recognition devices to command wheelchairs

Scanners

Scanners are devices that can change images into codes for input to the computer. There are various sizes and types of scanners:

- *Image scanners* convert images into electronic form that can be stored in a computer's memory. The image can then be manipulated.
- *Bar code scanners* read bar lines that are printed on products (for example, in a grocery store or department store). See Figure 5-6.
- *Magnetic scanners* read encoded information on the back of credit cards. The magnetic strip on the back of the cards contains the encoded user's account number.

FIGURE 5-6
Optical character reading equipment is frequently used in grocery stores to read the price on an item

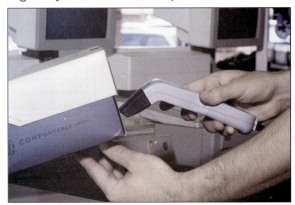

Video Input

Video input allows images generated with camcorders and VCRs to be transferred to the computer. Once input into the computer, the images can be viewed on the screen and edited.

Digital Cameras

The pictures taken with a digital camera are stored in the camera's memory and can be transferred to the computer's memory. These pictures can be viewed quickly and any imperfections can be edited. See Figure 5-7.

FIGURE 5-7
A digital camera stores photographs that can later be transferred to a computer system and viewed on a monitor

Output Devices

Output devices display information. Examples of output are printed text, spoken words, music, pictures, or graphics. The most common output devices are monitors and printers.

> **Did You Know?**
> You don't need a digital camera to have digital pictures. Your photo lab can deliver your photos to you via the Internet or on a disk in digital format.

Monitors

Monitors are called video display screens because images are displayed on the screen. They can be either monochromatic or color. A monochrome monitor screen has a one-color display. It could be white, green, or amber. Color monitors display thousands of colors. Most monitors today are color.

Factors that influence the quality of a monitor are screen size, resolution, and dot pitch. *Screen size* is the diagonal measurement in inches from one corner of the screen to the other. Common measurements for monitors are 15, 17, 19, and 21 inches. With large monitors you can make the objects on the screen appear larger, or you can fit more information on the screen. The larger screens are more expensive. Most computers are sold with 15- or 17-inch monitors.

Resolution is the number of pixels or dots that a monitor can display. Most 15-inch monitors have pixel grid settings of 640 × 480, 800 × 600, and 1024 × 768. *Dot pitch* measures the distance between pixels. See Figure 5-8.

FIGURE 5-8
Monitors come in various sizes, while notebook computers use flat-panel displays that are built into the lid

Printers

Printers are used to produce a paper or hard copy of the processing results. There are several types of printers with tremendous differences in speed, print quality, price, and special features.

When selecting a printer, consider the following features:

- *Speed:* Printer speed is measured in ppm, pages per minute. The number of pages a printer can print per minute varies for text and for graphics. Graphics print more slowly than regular text.

- *Print quality:* Print quality is measured in dots per inch, dpi. This refers to the resolution.

- *Price:* The price includes the original cost of the printer as well as what it costs to maintain the printer. A good-quality printer can be purchased very inexpensively; a high-output system can cost thousands of dollars. The ink cartridges and toners need to be replaced periodically.

The three most popular types of printers are laser, ink jet, and dot matrix. Printers are classified as either impact or nonimpact. *Impact printers* use a mechanism that actually strikes the paper to form images. Dot matrix printers are impact printers. *Nonimpact printers* form characters without striking the paper. Laser printers and ink jet printers are examples of nonimpact printers.

> **Hot Tip**
> Downloading graphic and text files from the Internet is another form of computer input. Once you download a file from the Internet, you can save it on your computer's hard drive or to a floppy disk if there is enough space to hold it.

Laser Printers

Laser printers produce images using the same technology as copier machines. The image is made with a powder substance called toner. A laser printer produces high-quality output. The cost of a laser printer has come down substantially. Color laser printers are much more expensive, costing thousands of dollars. See Figure 5-9.

FIGURE 5-9
How a laser printer works

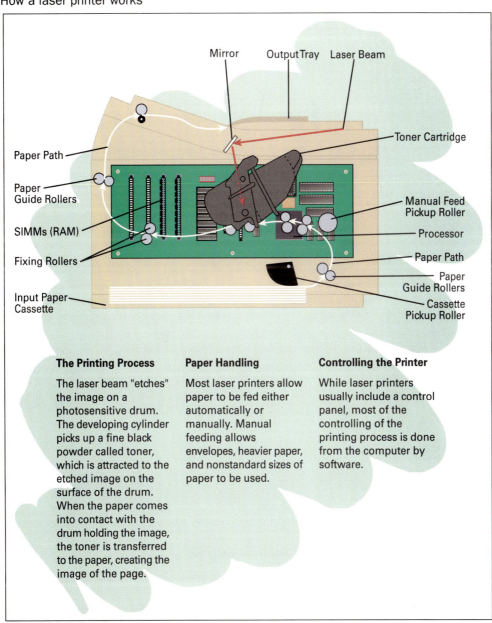

The Printing Process

The laser beam "etches" the image on a photosensitive drum. The developing cylinder picks up a fine black powder called toner, which is attracted to the etched image on the surface of the drum. When the paper comes into contact with the drum holding the image, the toner is transferred to the paper, creating the image of the page.

Paper Handling

Most laser printers allow paper to be fed either automatically or manually. Manual feeding allows envelopes, heavier paper, and nonstandard sizes of paper to be used.

Controlling the Printer

While laser printers usually include a control panel, most of the controlling of the printing process is done from the computer by software.

Ink Jet Printers

Ink jet printers allow less expensive color printing. The color is sprayed onto the paper. The same process used in laser printers is used in ink jet printers; it just works more slowly. Unlike earlier versions of the ink jet printer, the new versions can use regular photocopy paper. Ink jet printers are also combined with other technologies to create complete "three-in-one" office machines. These machines combine printer, copier, and fax capabilities into one. See Figure 5-10.

FIGURE 5-10
How an ink jet printer works

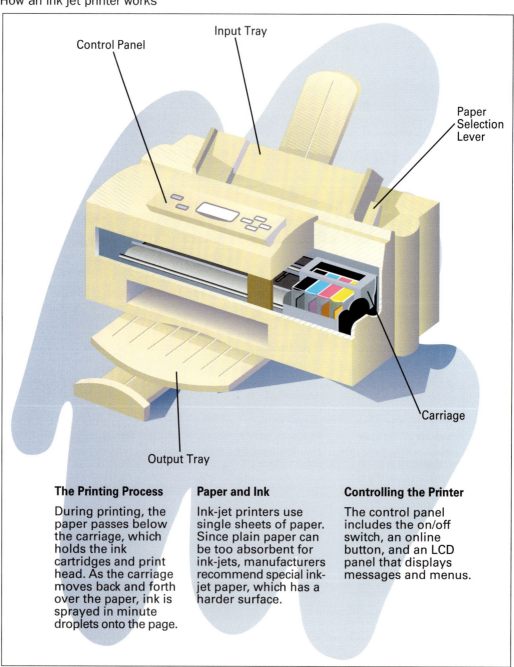

The Printing Process

During printing, the paper passes below the carriage, which holds the ink cartridges and print head. As the carriage moves back and forth over the paper, ink is sprayed in minute droplets onto the page.

Paper and Ink

Ink-jet printers use single sheets of paper. Since plain paper can be too absorbent for ink-jets, manufacturers recommend special ink-jet paper, which has a harder surface.

Controlling the Printer

The control panel includes the on/off switch, an online button, and an LCD panel that displays messages and menus.

Dot Matrix Printers

Impact printers have been around for a long time. They print by transferring ink to the paper by striking a ribbon with pins. The higher the number of pins (dpi), the better the resolution or output. The mechanism that actually does the printing is called a *printhead*. The speed of the dot matrix printer is measured in characters per second (cps). With the reduction in cost of laser and ink jet printers, dot matrix printers are used less often today.

Connecting Input/Output Devices to the Computer

Input and output (I/O) devices must be physically connected to the computer. There are two ways to connect these devices to a computer. You can plug the device into an existing socket or port located on the back of the computer, or you can install a circuit board with the port you need already included.

Serial and Parallel Ports

Computers can have several types of ports, including the following:

- *Parallel ports* transmit data eight bits at a time.
- *Serial ports* transmit one bit at a time. It is like a narrow one-lane road. A mouse, keyboard, and modem are connected in serial ports.

Special Ports

- SCSI (pronounced "scuzzy") stands for small computer system interface. One SCSI port can provide connection for one or more peripheral devices; they allow many devices to use the same port.
- MIDI (pronounced "middy") ports are used to connect computers to electronic instruments and recording devices.
- PC cards are used to add memory and to connect peripheral devices to notebook computers. They act as the interface between the motherboard and the peripheral device. The use of expansion cards in notebook computers is impractical because of the size of the notebook computer. These slots allow for the attachment of printers, modems, hard disks, and CD-ROM drives.
- USB ports can replace other types of ports such as serial and parallel ports, and they can accommodate up to 127 devices.

Storage Devices

As data is entered into the computer and processed, it is stored in RAM. If you want to keep a permanent copy of the data, you must store it on some type of storage medium such as the following:

- Floppy diskettes
- Hard disks

- CDs
- Magnetic tape cartridges
- WORM disks (Write once, read many)
- Zip and Jaz diskettes
- Super floppies

Storage devices are categorized by the method they use to store data. Magnetic storage devices use oxide-coated plastic storage media called Mylar. As the disk rotates in the computer, an electromagnetic read/write head stores or retrieves data in circles called *tracks*. The number of tracks on a disk varies with the type of diskette. The tracks are numbered from the outside to the inside. As data is stored on the disk it is stored on a numbered track. Each track is labeled and the location is kept in a special log on the disk called a *file allocation table* (FAT).

The most common types of magnetic storage medium are floppy diskettes, hard drives, and magnetic tape.

Floppy Diskettes

Floppy diskettes, usually just called diskettes, are flat circles of iron oxide-coated plastic enclosed in a hard plastic case. Most floppy diskettes are 3½-inches, although you may see other sizes. They have a capacity to hold 1.44 MB or more of data. To protect unwanted data from being added to or removed from a diskette, write protection is provided. To write-protect a diskette, open the write protect window on the diskette. See Figure 5-11.

FIGURE 5-11
The parts of a diskette

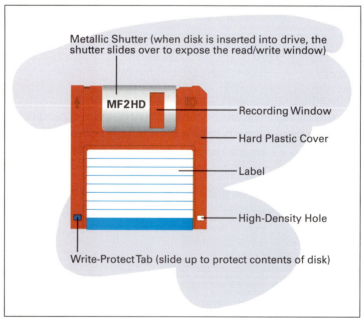

Hard Disk Drives

Hard disk drives are used to store data inside of the computer. They provide two advantages: speed and capacity. Accessing data is faster and the amount of data that can be stored is much larger than what can be stored on a floppy diskette. The size of the hard drive is measured in megabytes or gigabytes. See Figure 5-12.

FIGURE 5-12
How a hard drive works

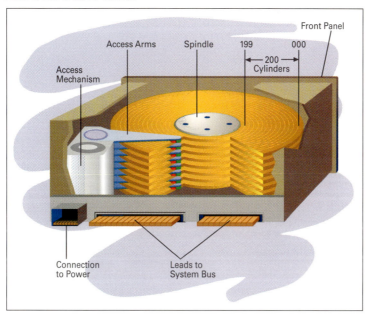

 Ethics in Technology

COMPUTER VIRUSES

The word "viruses" can put fear into anyone who uses the Internet or exchanges diskettes. How can such a small word cause such fear? It is because a virus can cause tremendous damage to your computer files!

A virus is simply a computer program that is intentionally written to attach itself to other programs or disk boot sectors and duplicates itself whenever those programs are executed or the infected disks are accessed. A virus can wipe out all of the files that are on your computer.

Viruses can sit on your computer for weeks or months and not cause any damage until a predetermined date or time code is activated. Not all viruses cause damage. Some are just pranks; maybe your desktop will display some silly message. Viruses are created by persons who are impressed with the power they possess because of their expertise in the area of computers and sometimes they create them just for fun.

To protect your computer from virus damage, install an antivirus software program on your computer and keep it running at all times so that it can continuously scan for viruses.

Zip Drives and Jaz Drives

Zip drives and Jaz drives house disks that are capable of holding tremendous amounts of storage. Even though they are only the size of a 3½-inch diskette, they can hold as much as 1 GB of data. Zip drives are slower than Jaz drives; they can hold as much as 70 floppy diskettes and are less expensive than the Jaz drive. The Jaz drive is much faster and can store up to 1 GB of data. See Figure 5-13.

FIGURE 5-13
Types of removable storage

Magnetic Tape Drives

Magnetic tape drives are used for making backup copies of large volumes of data. This is a very slow process and therefore is not used for regularly saving data. The tape can be used to replace data that may have been lost from the hard drive.

Optical Storage Devices

Optical storage devices use laser technology to read and write data on silver platters.

CD-ROM

The *CD-ROM* (Compact Disk Read-Only Memory) can store up to 680 MB. This is the equivalent of about 450 floppy diskettes! You can only read data from the CD; you cannot store data on a CD unless you are using the new writable CDs.

WORM Disks

WORM disks (Write Once, Read Many) are optical disk storage devices that use laser beams and optical technology. They are usually used for permanently storing large volumes of data. The data is stored by making imprints into the surface of the disk that cannot be removed.

CD-R

CD-R (Recordable) drives make it possible for you to create your own CD-ROM disks that can actually be read by any CD-ROM drive. Once information has been written to this type of disk, it cannot be changed.

PhotoCD

The *PhotoCD* is used to store digitized photographic images on a CD. The photos stored on these disks can be uploaded into the computer and used in other documents.

DVD Media

Full-length movies can be stored on the *DVD* (Digital Versatile Disk). It is the size of a regular CD and can be played in a regular CD player. However, the DVD movie player can connect to your TV and play movies like a VCR.

Caring for Removable Storage Media

Removable storage media require special care if the data stored is to remain undamaged. Here are some safeguards that should be taken:

- Keep away from magnetic fields such as those contained in televisions and computer monitors.
- Avoid extreme temperatures.
- Never open the data shutter or attempt to disassemble a removable disk cartridge. Never touch the surface of the media itself.
- Remove media from drives and store them properly when not in use.
- Write-protect important data to prevent accidental erasure.
- When handling CD-ROMs and other optical discs, hold them at the edges.
- Never try to remove the media from a drive when the drive indicator light is on.
- Keep disks in a sturdy case when transporting.

Introducing Networks

When most people think of networks, they envision something fairly complicated. At the lowest level, networks are not that complex. In fact, a **network** is simply a group of two or more computers linked together. As the size of a network increases and more and more devices are added, the installation and management does become more technical. Even so, the concept of networking and the terminology remains basically the same regardless of size.

In this lesson we discuss **local area networks (LANs)** and **wide area networks (WANs)**. The primary difference between the two is that a LAN is generally confined to a limited geographical area, whereas a WAN covers a large geographical area. Most WANs are made up of several connected LANs.

Most organizations today rely on computers and the data stored on the computers. Many times they find they need to transmit that data from one location to another. The transmission of data from one location to another is known as *data communications*. To transmit that data requires the following components, as shown in Figure 5-14:

- A sending device, which is generally a computer
- A communications device, such as a *modem*, that converts the computer signal into signals supported by the communications channel
- A communications channel or path, such as telephone lines or cable, over which the signals are sent
- A receiving device that accepts the incoming signal, which is generally a computer
- Communications software

FIGURE 5-14
Communications components

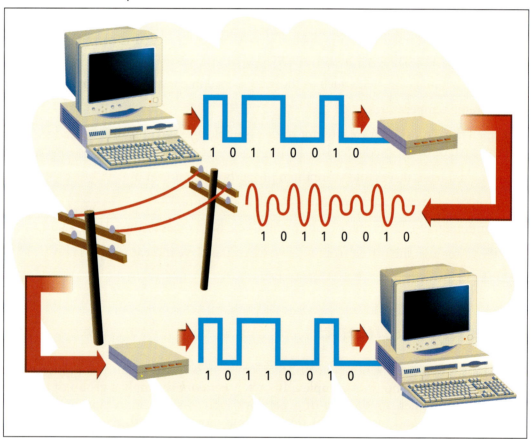

Network Benefits

To consider the topic of network benefits, you might first think about the biggest network of all, the Internet. Think about some of the changes that have occurred in our society because of the Internet. Perhaps the most profound of all of these changes is electronic mail. A network provides almost instant communication and e-mail messages are delivered almost immediately. Other benefits include the following:

- *Information sharing:* Authorized users can use other computers on the network to access and share information and data. This could include special group projects, databases, and so forth.

- *Hardware sharing:* It is not necessary to purchase a printer or a scanner or other frequently used peripherals for each computer. Instead, one device connected to a network can serve the needs of many users.

- *Software sharing:* Instead of purchasing and installing a software program on every single computer, it can be installed on the server. All of the users can then access the program from one central location. This also saves companies money because they purchase a site license for the number of users. This is much less expensive than purchasing individual software packages.

- *Collaborative environment:* Enables users to work together on group projects by combining the power and capabilities of diverse equipment.

Communications Media

To transfer data from one computer to another requires some type of link through which the data can be transmitted. This link is known as the *communications channel*. The worldwide telephone network is an important part of this channel. The telephone system is actually a collection of the world's telephone networks, including cellular, local, long-distance, and communications satellite networks. Although it was originally designed to handle voice communications, it's now used to transmit data, including fax transmissions, computer-to-computer communications such as e-mail, and live video from the Web.

At one end of the communications channel, you have a sending device, such as a computer or fax machine. A communications device, such as a modem, connected to the sending device converts the signal from the sender to a form that transmits over a standard dial-up telephone line or a dedicated line. A dial-up line provides a "temporary" connection, meaning each time a call is placed, the telephone company selects the line to transmit it over. A dedicated line, on the other hand, provides a permanent or constant connection between the sending and receiving communications devices. The transmission is moved or "switched" from one wire or frequency to another. A switch is a device located at the telephone company's central office that establishes a link between a sender and receiver of data communications. At the receiving end, another modem converts the signal back into a format that the receiving device can understand.

To send the data through the channel requires some type of *transmission media,* which may be either physical or wireless.

Physical Media

Several types of physical media are used to transmit data. These include the following:

- *Twisted-pair cable:* This is the least expensive type of cable and is the same type used for many telephone systems. It consists of two independently insulated copper wires twisted around one another. One of the wires carries the signal and the other wire is grounded to absorb signal interference. See Figure 5-15.

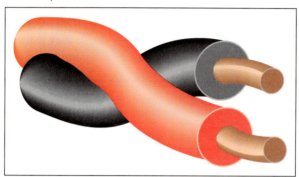

FIGURE 5-15
Twisted pair cable

- *Coaxial cable:* Coaxial cabling is the primary type of cabling used by the cable television industry and it is also widely used for computer networks. Because the cable is heavily shielded, it is much less prone to interference than twisted-pair cable. However, it is more expensive than twisted-pair. See Figure 5-16.

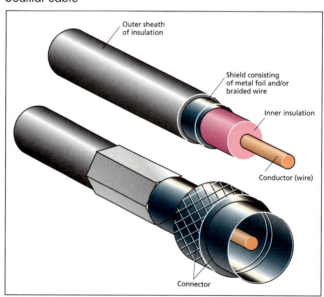

FIGURE 5-16
Coaxial cable

- *Fiber-optic cable:* Fiber-optic cable is made from thin, flexible glass tubing. Fiber optics has several advantages over traditional metal communications line. The bandwidth is much greater, so it can carry more data; it is much lighter than metal wires; and is much less susceptible to interference. The main disadvantage of fiber optics is that it is fragile and expensive. See Figure 5-17.

FIGURE 5-17
Fiber-optic cable

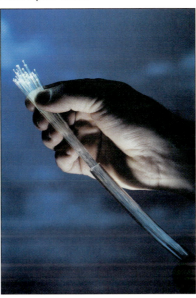

Wireless Media

Just like physical media, several wireless options are also available:

- *Radio signals:* Transmissions using radio signals require line of sight; that is, the signal travels in a straight line from one source to the other. For radio transmission, you need a transmitter to send the signal and a receiver to accept the signal.

- *Microwaves:* A microwave signal is sent through space in the form of electromagnetic waves. Just like radio signals, they must also be sent in straight lines from one microwave station to another. To avoid interference, most microwave stations are built on mountaintops or placed on the top of large buildings. See Figure 5-18.

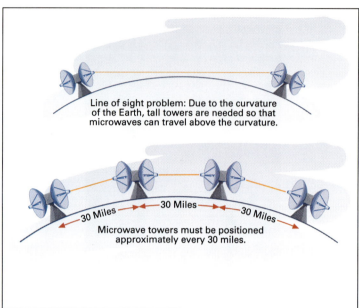

FIGURE 5-18
Microwave tower

- *Satellites:* Communication satellites are placed in orbit 22,300 feet above the surface of the earth. This allows the satellite to maintain a constant position above one point on the earth's surface by rotating at the same speed as the earth. The satellite contains equipment that receives the transmission, amplifies it, and sends it back to earth. See Figure 5-19.

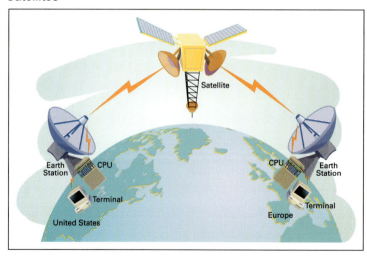

FIGURE 5-19
Satellites

The type of communications media an organization may select to use within a network is determined by several different factors: the type of network, the size of the network, and the cost.

Communications Hardware

Communications hardware devices facilitate the transmitting and receiving of data. When we think about communications hardware, the first thing that generally comes to mind is the desktop computer and modem. However, many other devices send and receive data. Some examples are large computers such as supercomputers, mainframe computers, and minicomputers; handheld and laptop computers; and even fax machines and digital cameras. Two of the more commonly used transmitting devices for personal use are as follows:

- *Modem:* The word MODEM is an acronym for *modulate-demodulate,* which means to convert analog signals to digital and vice versa. This device enables a computer to transmit data over telephone lines. Computer information is stored digitally, whereas information sent over telephone lines is transmitted in the form of analog waves. Both the sending and receiving users must have a modem. See Figure 5-20.

FIGURE 5-20
Computer with modem attached

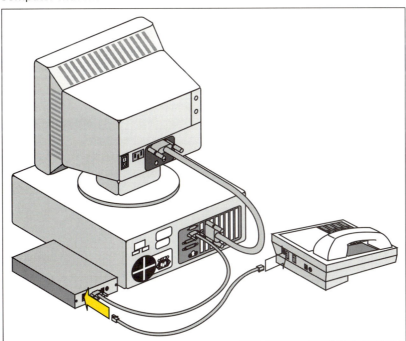

- *Cable modem:* A cable modem uses coaxial cable to send and receive data. This is the same type of cable used for cable TV. The bandwidth, which determines the amount of data that can be sent at one time, is much greater with a cable modem. A cable modem can be connected directly to your computer or connected to a set-top box used with your television. With a set-top box, you can access and surf the Web from your TV.

Network Transmission Hardware

Modems work well for personal computers and a small one- or two-person office. However, when it comes to transmitting data across LANs and WANs, the devices are considerably different. Some of the more widely used of these devices are as follows:

- *Network interface cards (NICs):* This is an add-on card for either a desktop PC or a laptop computer. Each computer on a network must have a NIC. This card enables and controls the sending and receiving of data between the PCs in a LAN.

- *Hub:* You may have heard the word *hub* applied to airports. Travelers make connections through various hubs to go from one location to another. A hub works similarly in data transmission. At a hub or junction data arrives from one or more directions and is forwarded out in one or more other directions. Hubs contain ports for connecting computers and other devices. The number of ports on the hub determines the number of computers that can be connected to a hub. See Figure 5-21.

FIGURE 5-21
Computers connected to a hub

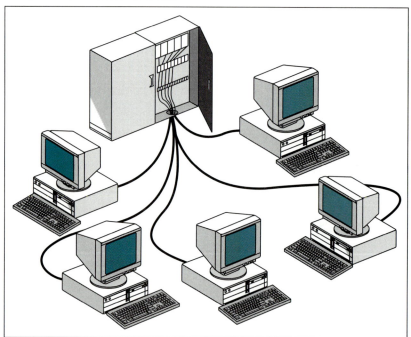

- *Bridge:* A bridge is a special computer that connects one LAN to another LAN. Both networks must use the same protocol, or set of rules. Think about the bridge as a device that determines if your message is going to the LAN within your building or to the building across the street.

- *Gateway:* A gateway is a combination of software and hardware that links two different types of networks that use different protocols. For instance, gateways between electronic mail systems permit users on different systems to exchange messages.

- *Router:* A router is like a traffic policeman—this intelligent device directs network traffic. When you send data through a network, it is divided into small packets. All packets don't travel the same route; instead one may go one in one direction and another in a different direction. When the packets reach their final destination, they are reassembled into the original message. A router connects multiple networks and determines the fastest available path to send these packets of data on their way to their correct destination. And, just like our traffic policeman, in the event of a partial network failure, the router can redirect the traffic over alternate paths.

Types of Networks

Many types of networks exist, but the most common types are *local area networks (LANs)* and *wide area networks (WANs)*. As explained earlier, a LAN is generally confined to a limited geographical area and a WAN covers a wide geographical area.

Local Area Networks

Most LANs connect personal computers, workstations, and other devices such as printers, scanners, or other devices. There are two popular types of LANs—client/server and peer-to-peer. The basic difference is how the data and information are stored.

- *Client/server network:* This is a type of architecture in which one or more computers on the network acts as a *server*. The server manages network resources. Depending on the size of the network, there may be several different servers. For instance, there may be a print server to manage the printing and a database server to manage a large database. In most instances, the server(s) is a high-speed computer with lots of storage space. The network operating system software and network versions of software applications are stored on the server. All of the other computers on the network are called *clients*. They share the server resources. See Figure 5-22.

FIGURE 5-22
Client/server network

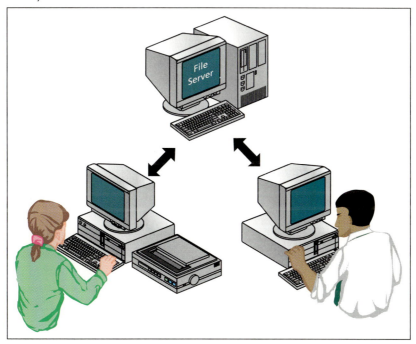

- *Peer-to-peer network:* In this type of architecture, all of the computers on a network are equals. There is no computer designated as the server. People on the network each determine what files on their computer they will share with others on the network. This type of network is much easier to set up and manage. Many small offices use peer-to-peer networks. See Figure 5-23.

FIGURE 5-23
Peer-to-peer network

Wide Area Networks

A WAN covers a large geographical network. This area may be as large as a state or a country or even the world, since the largest WAN is the Internet. Most WANs consist of two or more LANs and are connected by routers. Communications channels can include telephone systems, satellites, microwaves, or any combination of these.

Two variations on a WAN are intranets and extranets. An *intranet* is designed for the exclusive use of people within an organization. Many businesses have implemented intranets within their own organizations on which they make available files such as handbooks and employee manuals, newsletters, and employment forms.

An *extranet* is similar to an intranet, but it allows specified users outside of the organization to access internal information systems. Like the Internet, intranets and extranets use and support Web technologies, such as hyperlinks and Web pages coded in hypertext markup language (HTML).

Network Topologies

Networks can be designed using a variety of configurations. These configurations are referred to as topologies. A *topology* is simply the geometric arrangement of how the network is set up and connected. There are three basic topologies.

- *Bus topology:* Within this type of topology, all devices are connected to and share a master cable. This master cable is called the bus or backbone. There is no single host computer. Data can be transmitted in both directions, from one device to another. This type of network is relatively easy to install and inexpensive. See Figure 5-24.

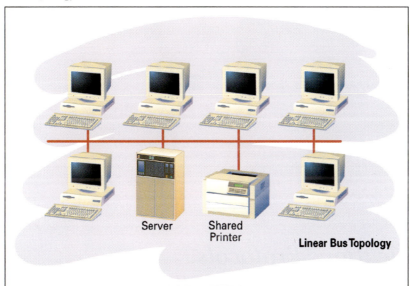

FIGURE 5-24
Bus topology

- *Ring topology:* A ring topology is somewhat similar to a bus. However, the devices are connected in a circle instead of a line. Each computer within the circle is connected to adjoining devices on either side. Data travels from device to device around the ring. This type of topology is more difficult to install and manage and is more expensive. However, it does provide for faster transmission speeds and can span large distances. See Figure 5-25.

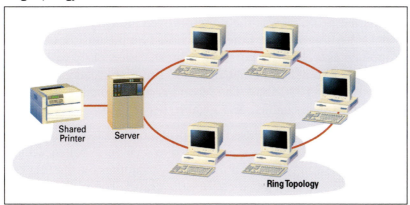

FIGURE 5-25
Ring topology

- *Star topology:* Within a star topology, all devices are connected to a central hub or computer. All data that transfer from one computer to another must pass through the hub. Star networks are relatively easy to install and manage, but bottlenecks can occur because all data must pass through the hub. This type of network requires more cabling than the other types. See Figure 5-26.

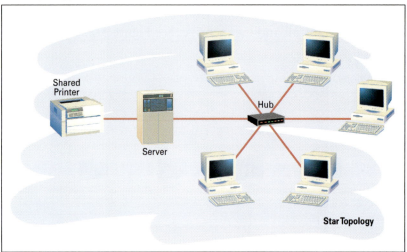

FIGURE 5-26
Star topology

These topologies can also be mixed or combined to produce hybrid topologies.

Communications Protocols

A protocol is simply an agreed on set of rules and procedures for transmitting data between two or more devices. Some of the features determined by the protocol are as follows:

- How the sending device indicates it has finished sending the message
- How the receiving device indicates it has received the message
- The type of error checking to be used

Many protocols have been developed over the years. However, within networking and LANs, the two most widely used protocols are Ethernet and token ring. On the Internet, the major protocol is TCP/IP.

- *Ethernet:* The Ethernet protocol was the first approved industry standard protocol. It is one of the most popular LAN protocols. Ethernet is based on the bus topology, but can work with the star topology as well. It supports data transfer rates of up to 10 megabits per second (Mbps). There are two new Ethernet versions. The first is called Fast Ethernet and supports data transfer rates of 100 Mbps. The second is called Gigabit Ethernet and supports data transfer rates of 1,000 megabits, or 1 gigabit, per second.

- *Token ring:* The second most widely used LAN protocol is called *token ring*. Within this type of network, all of the computers are arranged in a circle. A token, which is a special signal, travels around the ring. To send a message, a computer on the ring catches the token, attaches a message to it, and then lets it continue to travel around the network.

- **TCP/IP:** TCP/IP is the acronym for Transmission Control Protocol/Internet Protocol. This protocol is used by both LANs and WANs and has been adopted as a standard to connect hosts on the Internet. Even network operating systems, such as Microsoft NT or Novell Netware, support TCP/IP.

Network Operating Systems Software

All computers require an operating system. The operating system, among other functions, manages the computer's resources. Some of the operating systems with which you may be familiar are Windows, Mac OS, and UNIX.

Two types of operating systems are necessary in computer networking. The first is the desktop operating system, such as Windows or Mac OS. The second is the network operating system. Some desktop operating systems, such as Windows, UNIX, and the Mac OS, have built-in networking functions. These functions work adequately within a very limited environment. To really utilize a network, however, full function network operating systems (NOS) software is required.

Network operating systems run on the server and provide features such as administration, file, print, communications, security, database, management, and other services to personal computer clients.

SUMMARY

In this lesson, you learned:

- Input devices enable you to input data and commands into the computer.
- The most common input devices are the keyboard and mouse.
- The mouse is a pointing device used to input data.
- Other types of input devices include joysticks, trackballs, graphics tablets, touch display screens, voice recognition devices, scanners, and electronic pens.
- Printers are used to produce a paper or hard copy of the processed result.
- Criteria for selecting a printer include speed, print quality, and cost.
- Input and output devices must be physically connected to the computer.
- There are two ways to connect I/O devices to a computer: Plug the device into a port in the back of the computer or install a circuit board with the needed port included.
- There are several types of ports: USB, SCSI, MIDI, parallel, and serial.
- To maintain a permanent copy of data, you must store it on some type of storage medium. These may include floppy diskettes, hard drives, CDs, magnetic tape cartridges, and WORM disks.
- A network is a group of two or more computers linked together.
- A local area network is generally confined to a limited geographical area.
- A wide area network is made up of several connected local area networks.

- Data communication is the transmission of data from one location to another.
- The Internet is the biggest network of all.
- You can use a network for information sharing, hardware sharing, software sharing, and as a collaborative environment.
- The link through which data is transmitted is the communications channel.
- Transmission media can be either physical or wireless.
- Physical media includes twisted-pair cable, coaxial cable, and fiber-optic cable.
- Wireless media includes radio signals, microwaves, and satellites.
- Most networks consist of a network server and computer clients.
- A modem is a type of communications device.
- Network interface cards enable the sending and receiving of data between the PCs in a LAN.
- A hub is a device that controls the incoming and forwarding of data.
- A bridge connects one LAN to another.
- A gateway links two different types of networks.
- A router directs the Internet or LAN traffic.
- The two popular types of LANs are the client/server network and peer-to-peer network.
- Network topologies include bus, ring, and star.
- A protocol is an agreed on set of rules and procedures for transmitting data between two or more devices.
- The Ethernet protocol is one of the most popular LAN protocols.
- Token ring is the second most widely used LAN protocol.
- TCP/IP is a protocol used by both LANs and WANs to connect to the Internet.
- All computers require an operating system.
- Networks require network operating systems.

VOCABULARY Review

Define the following terms:

Bus topology	Monitors	Serial ports
Clients	Network	Server
Client/server network	Optical storage devices	Star topology
Ethernet	Output devices	TCP/IP
Hard disk drives	Parallel ports	Token ring
Input devices	Peer-to-peer network	Topology
Local area network (LAN)	Printers	Transmission media
Magnetic tape drives	Ring topology	Voice recognition
Modem	Scanners	Wide area network (WAN)

REVIEW Questions

MULTIPLE CHOICE

Select the best response for the following statements.

1. Laser, ink jet, and dot matrix are types of _____.
   A. Monitors
   B. Printers
   C. Storage devices
   D. Input devices

2. Monitors and printers are types of _____.
   A. Input devices
   B. Output devices
   C. Storage devices
   D. Ports

3. All of the following are types of ports, *except* _____.
   A. MSO
   B. USB
   C. SCSI
   D. MIDI

4. Floppy diskettes are also called _____.
   A. Diskettes
   B. Hard drives
   C. CDs
   D. Magnetic disks

Unit 1 Computer Basics

5. A _____ is confined to a limited geographical area.
   A. Wide area network
   B. Local area network
   C. Tiny area network
   D. Metropolitan area network

6. The least expensive type of physical communications media is _____.
   A. Twisted-pair cable
   B. Fiber-optics cable
   C. Coaxial cable
   D. Radio signals

7. A _____ changes analog signals to digital signals and digital signals to analog.
   A. Satellite
   B. NIC
   C. Bridge
   D. Modem

8. A _____ is a combination of software and hardware that links two different types of networks.
   A. Hub
   B. Bridge
   C. Gateway
   D. Router

9. A geometric arrangement of a network is called a _____.
   A. Bridge
   B. WAN
   C. LAN
   D. Topology

TRUE/FALSE

Circle T if the statement is true or F if the statement is false.

T F 1. Input and output devices perform the same function.

T F 2. The mouse is a pointing device that rolls around on a flat surface and controls the pointer.

T F 3. Factors that influence the quality of a monitor are screen size, resolution, and dot pitch.

T F 4. ppm refers to the number of pages that a printer prints per minute.

T F 5. Within a bus topology, all devices are connected to a master cable.

T F 6. A protocol is a type of topology.

T F 7. Token ring is the most widely used LAN protocol.

T F 8. Satellites orbit the earth.

T F 9. Software sharing is one of the benefits of networking.

FILL IN THE BLANK

Complete the following sentences by writing the correct word or words in the blanks provided.

1. A/An _____ is used to enter data into the computer.
2. _____ and _____ are the most popular output devices.
3. Input and output devices are connected to computers through _____.
4. The two types of ports are _____ and _____.
5. Hard disks and floppy diskettes are types of _____ mediums.
6. The least expensive type of cable is _____.
7. _____ signals must be sent in straight lines.
8. Fiber-optic cable is made from _____.
9. An add-on card that allows a computer to connect to a network is called a _____.
10. The _____ protocol was the first approved industry standard protocol.

CROSS-CURRICULAR *Projects*

MATH

Contact computer vendors, read computer magazines, research the Internet, and use any other resources to collect data concerning the prices of at least five storage devices. Find sales information for the same product from three vendors. Determine the average cost of each device. Prepare a chart like the one here to show your findings.

STORAGE DEVICE	CAPABILITIES	VENDOR	COST	VENDOR	COST	VENDOR	COST	AVG. COST

SCIENCE

There are many styles of keyboards for computers. Many of the designs were developed to address various health issues related to keyboard use. Use appropriate research sources to locate information on various keyboard designs and report on the theory on which they are designed. You may also visit retail stores that sell computers to obtain information and sales documents. Prepare a written report of the information you locate.

SCIENCE/LANGUAGE ARTS

Your teacher has assigned you a science project. You are to work with several of your classmates. However, it is difficult for everyone to get together at the same time. Write a paper, giving a short overview of the science project you have been assigned and an explanation of how using a computer network would help your group accomplish its goal.

SOCIAL STUDIES

Prepare a written report in table format of early storage media. Your table should have the columns shown here. Include at least five types of early storage media.

TYPE	MEDIA	CAPACITY	ADVANTAGES	DISADVANTAGES

LANGUAGE ARTS

Prepare a report describing several applications in which a user would need to use the Jaz or Zip drive to store data. Describe the application and explain why it would be necessary to use the Zip or Jaz drive. Also explore the alternatives to using these drives. You may find useful information at *www.iomega.com*.

LANGUAGE ARTS

The goal for this project is to describe an existing network. Interview someone at your school, a family member, or a neighbor who works with a network. Find out what kind of network he or she uses and for what purposes. Prepare a presentation and share it with your class.

WEB PROJECT

Two of the most popular networking operating systems are Microsoft NT and Novell Netware. Search the Web for information on both of these network operating systems. Prepare a report and chart comparing the features of these two NOSs.

CRITICAL *Thinking*

ACTIVITY 5-1

Your supervisor, Ms. Perez, is interested in setting up a teleconference with several of the stores throughout the state. However, she would like to get more information on this capability. She has asked you and the assistant manager to research this technology for her and let her know the steps needed to set up such a conference. Research the Internet and any other materials to prepare a step-by-step guide for setting up a teleconference. Include an introduction that gives basic information about teleconferencing.

ACTIVITY 5-2

Ms. Perez is very pleased with the research you have completed on networking. She would now like for you and two or three of your teammates to put together a proposal for a network for Vista Multimedia. Ms. Perez has asked that you determine the type of network, what devices should be on the network, what network operating system to use, and what communications media to use. She has requested a brief description of why you selected each item.

LESSON 6

Operating Systems and Software

OBJECTIVES

Upon completion of this lesson, you should be able to:

- Distinguish between software and hardware.
- Describe the difference between applications software and systems software.
- Describe the three categories of system programs.
- Describe operating systems for microcomputers.
- Describe network operating systems.

Estimated Time: 1.5 hours

VOCABULARY

Applications software
Graphical user interfaces (GUIs)
Hardware
MS-DOS
Multitasking
Network operating system
Operating systems
Software
Systems software
Unix
User interface

Over the last 50 years or so, computer technology has changed the world. Not so long ago, workers would not have used computers. Customers would not have ID cards that could be scanned. Accounting was done using ledgers.

When most of us think about computers, we think of hardware and how the hardware has changed—that computers have become smaller and faster. If we look at the history of computers, however, we find that the early computers were used for little more than high-speed calculators. This alone would not have had such a major influence on our culture and economy. The reason that computers have had such an impact is through the vision and desire of software developers. These software creators came up with hundreds of ideas and ways in which to use computers. They created programs that affect us in every aspect of our lives.

Hardware vs. Software

You have probably heard the words software and hardware many times. Sometimes it is difficult to distinguish between these two terms. *Hardware* refers to anything you can touch. This includes objects such as the keyboard, mouse, monitor, printer, chips, disks, disk drives, and CD recorders. You cannot touch software because it has no substance. *Software* is instructions issued to the computer so that specific tasks may be performed. Another word for software is program.

For example, a computer programmer may write a program that lets the user download music from the Internet. Or suppose the Vista Multimedia bookkeeper has a problem with his computer. You might hear him say, "The problem lies in the software." This means there is a problem with the program or data, and not with the computer or hardware itself. He may also say, "It's a software problem." A good analogy here is a book. The book, including the pages and the ink, is the hardware. The words and ideas on the pages are the software. One has little value without the other. The same is true of computer software and hardware.

Types of Software

There are two basic types of computer software: ***applications software*** and ***systems software.*** Applications software helps you perform a specific task. Systems software refers to the operating system and all utility programs that manage computer resources at a low level. Figuratively speaking, applications software sits on top of systems software. Without the operating system and system utilities, the computer cannot run any applications program.

Applications Software

Applications software is widely referred to as productivity software. Applications software is comprised of programs designed for an end user. Some of the more commonly used application programs are word processors, database systems, presentation systems, spreadsheet programs, and desktop publishing programs. Some other applications categories are as follows:

- Education, home, and personal software—reference, entertainment, personal finance, calendars, e-mail, browsers

- Multimedia software—authoring, animation, music, video and sound capturing and editing, virtual reality, Web site development

- Workgroup computing software—calendars and scheduling, e-mail, browsers, electronic conferencing, project management

Systems Software

Systems software is a group of programs that coordinate and control the resources and operations of a computer system. Systems software enables the many components of the computer system to communicate. There are three categories of systems software: operating systems, utilities, and language translators.

Operating Systems

Operating systems provide an interface between the user or application program and the computer hardware. See Figure 6-1. There are many brands and versions of operating systems software. Each of these is designed to work with one or more particular processors. For example, an operating system like Windows is designed to work with a processor made by Intel. Many IBM PC-compatible computers contain this brand of processor. Most Macintosh computers contain a processor manufactured by Motorola. The Windows operating system does not work with this Motorola processor.

> **Did You Know?**
> Some operating systems software programs are DOS, Windows 2000, Windows NT, Macintosh OS, and Unix. Some software applications include word processing, spreadsheets, database, and desktop publishing. These software applications are frequently sold as suites, such as Microsoft Office.

FIGURE 6-1
Operating systems: an interface between users and computers

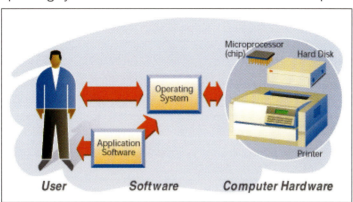

Utilities

Utility programs help you perform housekeeping chores. You use these programs to complete specialized tasks related to managing the computer's resources, file management, and so forth. Some utility programs are part of the operating system, and others are self-contained programs. See Figure 6-2. Some examples of utility program functions are as follows:

- You format a disk—a disk formatting utility provides the instructions to the computer on how to do this.

- You copy a file from the hard drive to a floppy disk—the file management utility provides the instructions to the computer.

- To do a backup of the hard drive, you use the backup utility.

FIGURE 6-2
File conversion utility

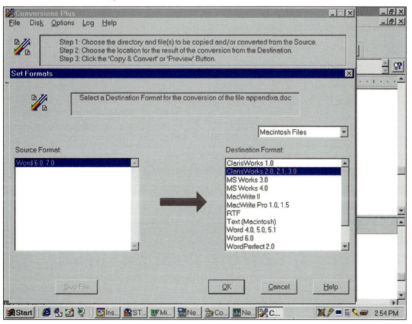

See Table 6-1 for a list and purpose of the most commonly used utilities.

TABLE 6-1
Utlility programs

TYPE OF UTILITY	PURPOSE
Disk formatting	Prepares a disk to have files stored on it
File management	Allows the user to perform tasks such as copying, moving, and deleting files
File recovery	Attempts to recover a file that has been erased
Disk defragmentation	Attempts to place the segments of each file on the hard disk as close to one another as possible
Uninstall	Removes an application that is no longer needed
Diagnostic	Provides detailed information about the computer system and attempts to locate problems
File conversion	Converts a file from one format to another
Disk compression	Frees up storage space on a disk by compressing the existing files
Backup	Makes a duplicate copy of the contents of a secondary storage device
Antivirus	Protects the computer system from viruses

Language Translators

Language translators convert English-like software programs into machine language that the computer can understand. Vista Multimedia hires a programmer to write a software program to inventory all of the items in the store. The programmer writes the program statements using a programming language called Visual Basic. A program statement directs the computer to perform a specified action.

The computer, however, cannot read the Visual Basic programming statements because they are written in a language that we understand. This is where the language translator takes over. The translator changes each of the Visual Basic programming statements into machine language. A single statement in a high-level language can represent several machine-language instructions. Now the statements can be executed and Vista Multimedia's inventory can be processed.

> **Hot Tip**
>
> If you have a computer, you should have an emergency boot disk. Sooner or later, your computer may not boot from the hard drive. You can use your emergency boot disk to get your computer started. Each operating system has its own unique way of creating a boot disk. Check your operating system help files for information on how to create this disk. Then be sure to store it in an easy-to-find and safe place.

Microcomputer Operating Systems Interfaces

All computers, big and small, have operating systems. For most of us, however, the computer we most often use is a microcomputer. So our focus in this lesson is on microcomputer operating systems.

The *user interface* is the part of the operating system with which we are most familiar. This is the part of the operating system we interact with when using our computer. The two most common types of user interfaces are command-line interfaces and graphical interfaces.

Command-line Interfaces

All early computers used command-line interfaces. With this type of interface, you must type the exact command you wish to execute. One of the most widely used command-line interfaces for microcomputers is *MS-DOS*. Using DOS, you want to look at a list of files on your computer's hard drive. You key the DOS command dir and press Enter. See Figure 6-3. This type of interface is not considered very user friendly. You must memorize the commands and key them without any spelling errors. Otherwise, they do not work.

FIGURE 6-3
Command-line interface

Graphical User Interfaces

As microcomputer technology developed, so did the operating system interface. The next step in this progression was menus. The user could choose commands from a list.

The big breakthrough in ease of use came with the development of *graphical user interfaces (GUIs)*. When the user turns on the computer and starts the operating system, a symbolic desktop is displayed. On this desktop are various objects, or icons. These graphical symbols represent files, disks, programs, and other objects. GUIs permit the user to manipulate these on-screen icons. Most people use a pointing device such as a mouse to click on the icons and execute the commands. See Figure 6-4.

FIGURE 6-4
Graphical user interface

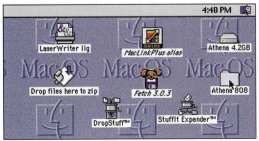

Microcomputer Operating Systems

There are several popular operating systems for microcomputers. If you are using a Macintosh or a Macintosh clone, you will most likely be using a version of the Mac OS.

If your computer is what is commonly referred to as a PC or an IBM PC compatible, you most likely are using one of these three operating systems:

- DOS
- A combination of DOS and Windows
- A standalone version of Windows

Mac OS

The Mac OS is used with Apple's Power Macintosh computers and Power Macintosh clones. The Macintosh was introduced in 1984. One of the main features of this new computer was a GUI. The GUI was called the Finder and contained icons or symbols that represented documents, software, disks, and so forth. To activate the icon, the user clicked on it with a mouse. See Figure 6-5. This operating system was also the first OS to provide on-screen help or instructions. In 2002, Macintosh released OS v.X.

> **Internet**
>
> The history of Apple Computer and Steve Jobs and Steve Wozniak is a fascinating story. For an overview of this story and some interesting facts about the Macintosh operating system, check out the Web site at www.hypermall.com/History/ah01.html.

> **Did You Know?**
>
> Macintosh popularized the first graphical user interface; however, Apple did not invent the interface. Xerox Corporation developed the idea for a graphical user interface.

FIGURE 6-5
Macintosh operating system

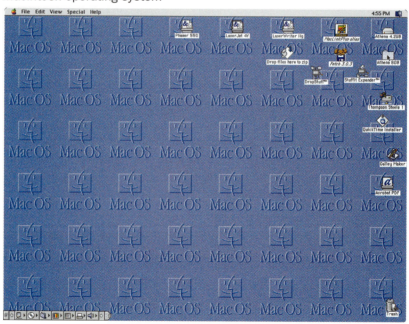

DOS

IBM introduced its first IBM PC in 1981. With the introduction of this new microcomputer came a new operating system (OS). This system was called DOS (Disk Operating System). IBM referred to this operating system as PC DOS. They licensed this software from a small start-up company called Microsoft. But as agreements go, Microsoft retained the rights to market its own version of the OS. Microsoft called their version MS-DOS. This OS was the catalyst that launched Microsoft into the multibillion dollar company it is today.

DOS is a character-based operating system. The user interacts with the system by typing in commands. DOS is a single-user or single-tasking operating system because the user can run only one program at a time.

Windows

In response to the competition from the Macintosh, Microsoft introduced its own GUI in 1987. This OS was called Windows.

- The first versions of Windows contain a graphical shell and were called operating environments because they work in combination with DOS.
- The different applications installed on a computer appear as icons.
- The user activates the icons by clicking on them with a mouse.
- These early versions of Windows are consecutively numbered beginning with Windows 3.0, Windows 3.1, and so forth.

Technology Careers

SOFTWARE DEVELOPER

A software developer maintains and helps develop new application and operating systems programs. When you see a job listing for software developer, it could include many requirements.

A company may be looking for someone to develop software using a particular programming language such as Visual Basic, C, or C++. Or a company may be looking for someone to develop add-ons to operating systems programs. This could include enhancements to utility programs, updates to language translators, or new additions to the operating system itself. Many companies seek employees with skills in operating systems programs such as Unix and Windows NT.

If you go online and look for software developer jobs, you will find that many of them refer to Oracle, a large information technology software company. Oracle products support database technology, data design and modeling, Web applications, and much more.

There is a great variation in salaries and educational requirements. Salaries can range from $25,000 to $100,000 plus. Educational requirements range from some college to a bachelor's or master's degree or maybe even a Ph.D. Generally, but not always, the more education you have, the higher your starting salary. Most companies require some experience, but a few have entry-level positions.

Windows 95 was Microsoft's first true multitasking operating system. *Multitasking* allows a single user to work on two or more applications that reside in memory at the same time. Some advantages of Windows 95 include the following:

- An improved graphical interface
- Programs run faster than with earlier Windows versions
- Includes support for networking, which allows a group of two more computers to be linked
- Uses Plug and Play technology, the goal of which is to just plug in a new device and immediately be able to use it, without complicated setup maneuvers

Windows 98 is easier to use than Windows 95 and has additional features. Some of these new features include the following:

- Internet integration
- Windows Explorer has a Web browser look option
- Faster system startup and shutdown
- Support for the Universal Serial Bus that is used to easily add and remove devices on the computer

Windows 2000 is an update to the Windows 98 and Windows NT operating systems. See Figure 6-6. Some new features include the following:

- Tools for Web site creation
- Wizards that guide the user through various operations
- Monitoring programs

> **Internet**
>
> Want to learn more about Windows CE, Microsoft's operating system for small handheld devices? Access the Web site *www.whatis.com*; in the Quick Search text box, key **Windows CE** and click **Go**. You can also find additional information at *www.microsoft.com/windowsce/*.

FIGURE 6-6
Windows 2000 operating system

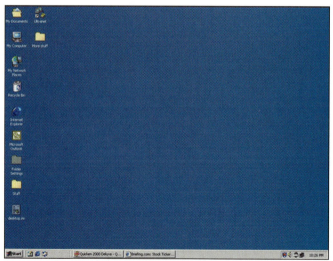

One of the most recent update is Windows XP, which provides increased stability and improved device recognition. Even though the Windows versions have changed, some features remain consistent, such as the Start menu, taskbar, and desktop.

Windows CE is a scaled-down Windows operating system. It is used on small handheld computers and wireless communication devices.

Still another operating system is *Unix*. Unix is frequently used by scientists and programmers. This operating system, developed by AT&T, is considered a portable operating system. This means it can run on just about any hardware platform. There are several variants of the language, such as Linux and IBM's AIX. See Figure 6-7.

FIGURE 6-7
Unix operating system

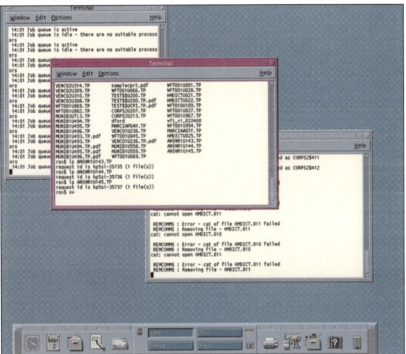

STEP-BY-STEP 6.1

When you start your computer, operating system commands are loaded into memory. Each operating system boots or starts the computer in its own individual way. Understanding the boot process is the key to diagnosing many computer startup problems.

The Step-by-Step given in this example is based on the Windows OS system. Keep in mind, however, that the boot process is similar for all operating systems.

1. When you turn on the computer, the first thing that happens is POST, an acronym for Power-on Self Test. This is a series of diagnostic tests to check RAM and to verify that the keyboard and disk drives you may have are physically connected to the computer.

2. The BIOS (Basic Input Output System) searches for the boot record—first on drive A and then on drive C. The BIOS is built-in software that is normally placed on a ROM chip. It contains all of the code that controls the most common devices connected to your computer. This includes the monitor, keyboard, disk drives, and other components. This chip comes with your computer when you purchase it.

STEP-BY-STEP 6.1 Continued

3. The boot record is loaded into RAM. The boot record contains several files. These files contain programming configuration instructions for hardware devices and software applications that you may have installed on your computer.

4. Next, the software drivers are loaded. Drivers are what enable you to use your printer, modem, scanner, or other devices. Generally, when you add a new device to your system, you install drivers for that device.

5. Next to be loaded is the GUI or graphical user interface. In this instance, the GUI is Windows. When loading the GUI, the operating system reads the commands for your desktop configuration. It also loads whatever programs you have previously specified into the Windows Startup folder.

6. If everything goes as it should, the GUI displays and the computer is ready to use.

Network Operating Systems

Network operating systems allow a group of two or more microcomputers to be connected. There are several brands of network operating systems. Three of the most popular are as follows:

- Microsoft Windows NT
- Novell's Netware
- IBM's Warp Server

Sharing Files on Different Operating Systems

In many business and educational settings, it is necessary to share files across operating system platforms. A business may have workers using both Macintosh and Windows computers, depending on the task: often artists and designers use Macintosh computers, while accountants and writers may have PCs. In the classroom all of the computers may be the same type, but students may have different kinds of computers at home for doing homework. These situations require the ability to read disks and share files created on different operating systems. It may even be necessary to run programs on one system that were written only for another system. There are both hardware and software solutions available for these problems.

One type of hardware solution is an expansion card that is added to the motherboard of the computer. These cards provide the ability for the computer to run a program that was designed for a different operating system. For example, a card can be added to a Macintosh that will allow it to run Microsoft programs. There are also software programs available to provide this ability; for example, SoftWindows® is a program that displays Windows on a PowerMac.

Macintosh computers have software installed that allows them to read disks that were formatted on PCs. Additional software finds a compatible program to run a PC file once the user double-clicks on the file's icon.

Another solution to the file-sharing issue is to save files in a format that is readable on different operating systems. One example for word-processing documents is the basic text format (.txt). This format is usually readable by most word-processing programs on different systems. However, documents saved as .txt do not retain complicated formatting. Another text format, called Rich Text Format (.rtf), does retain most formatting commands, such as paragraph breaks, fonts, and styles such as bold and italic. To save a file in Rich Text Format, you use the Save As command in your word-processing program and specifically select Rich Text Format as the file type.

Ethics in Technology

WHAT IS COMPUTER ETHICS?

Webster's Online Dictionary[1] offers the following definition of ethics:
(1) the discipline dealing with what is good and bad and with moral duty and obligation
(2) a: a set of moral principles or values, b: a theory or system of moral values <the present-day materialistic ethic>, c: plural but singular or plural in construction: the principles of conduct governing an individual or a group <professional ethics>, d: a guiding philosophy.

Ethical judgments are no different in the area of computing than they are in any other. The use of computers can raise many issues of privacy, copyright, theft, and power, to name just a few. In 1990 the Institute of Electrical and Electronics Engineers created the following code of ethics. Many businesses and organizations have adopted this code as their code. Remember that this is just a code—not a law. People choose to follow it voluntarily.

CODE OF ETHICS

We, the members of the IEEE, in recognition of the importance of our technologies affecting the quality of life throughout the world, and in accepting a personal obligation to our profession, its members, and the communities we serve, do hereby commit ourselves to the highest ethical and professional conduct and agree:

1. to accept responsibility in making engineering decisions consistent with the safety, health, and welfare of the public, and to disclose promptly factors that might endanger the public or the environment;
2. to avoid real or perceived conflicts of interest whenever possible, and to disclose them to affected parties when they do exist;
3. to be honest and realistic in stating claims or estimates based on available data;
4. to reject bribery in all its forms;
5. to improve the understanding of technology, its appropriate application, and potential consequences;
6. to maintain and improve our technical competence and to undertake technological tasks for others only if qualified by training or experience, or after full disclosure of pertinent limitations;
7. to seek, accept, and offer honest criticism of technical work, to acknowledge and correct errors, and to credit properly the contributions of others;
8. to treat fairly all persons regardless of such factors as race, religion, gender, disability, age, or national origin;
9. to avoid injuring others, their property, reputation, or employment by false or malicious action;
10. to assist colleagues and co-workers in their professional development and to support them in following this code of ethics.

[1] Webster's Online Dictionary: courses.ncsu.edu:8020/classes-a/computer_ethics/basics/principles/

SUMMARY

In this lesson, you learned:

- Hardware refers to anything you can touch.
- Software is instructions that tell the computer what to do.
- Software is also called a program.
- The two basic types of computer software are applications software and systems software.
- Applications software is also known as productivity software.
- Systems software coordinates and controls the resources and operations of a computer system.
- Three major categories of systems software are operating systems, utilities, and language translators.
- Operating systems provide an interface between the user and application program and the computer hardware.
- Utility programs help users complete specialized tasks such as file management.
- Language translators convert English-like software programs into machine language.
- A programmer uses a programming language to write program statements.
- All computers have operating systems.
- The user interface is the part of the operating system with which we are most familiar.
- The two most common user interfaces are command-line interfaces and graphical user interfaces.
- The Mac operating system is used with Apple's Power Macintosh computers and Power Macintosh clones.
- Icons are symbols that represent documents, software programs, disks, and so forth.
- DOS was introduced with the IBM PC in 1981 and is a character-based operating system.
- Microsoft introduced the first version of Windows in 1987; this was an operating environment.
- Windows 95 was Microsoft's first true multitasking operating system.
- Windows CE is a scaled-down Windows operating system used for small handheld computers.
- Unix is a portable operating system.
- Network operating systems allow a group of two or more microcomputers to be connected.
- There are several methods for sharing files on different operating systems.

VOCABULARY Review

Define the following terms:

Applications software	MS-DOS	Software
Graphical user interfaces (GUIs)	Multitasking	Systems software
	Network operating system	Unix
Hardware	Operating systems	User interface

REVIEW Questions

MULTIPLE CHOICE

Select the best response for the following statements.

1. Another word for software is _____.
   A. hardware
   B. program
   C. programming statement
   D. interface

2. The two basic types of computer software are _____ and _____.
   A. program, applications
   B. productivity, applications
   C. applications, systems
   D. systems, networking systems

3. A group of programs that coordinate and control the resources of a computer system is called _____.
   A. systems software
   B. applications software
   C. language translator
   D. utility program

4. The _____ is the part of the operating system with which we are most familiar.
   A. formatting utility
   B. programming statement
   C. language translator
   D. user interface

5. DOS was first introduced with the _____.
   A. Apple Macintosh
   B. IBM PC
   C. Unix operating system
   D. Windows

TRUE/FALSE

Circle T if the statement is true or F if the statement is false.

T F 1. The first version of Windows was a true operating environment.

T F 2. DOS is a multitasking operating system.

T F 3. Apple Computer Company developed the GUI.

T F 4. Computer hardware is anything you can touch.

T F 5. There are five categories of systems software.

FILL IN THE BLANK

Complete the following sentences by writing the correct word or words in the blanks provided.

1. The second step in the progression of the operating system interface was _____.

2. Word processing is an example of _____ software.

3. Novell NetWare is an example of _____ system.

4. One of the main features of Apple's Power Macintosh was the _____ interface.

5. DOS is a(n) _____-user operating system.

CROSS-CURRICULAR *Projects*

MATH/LANGUAGE ARTS

To use a floppy disk, you must first format it. Use the Internet or other written resources and write step-by-step instructions on how to format a floppy disk. If you have a computer available, give your instructions to one of your friends or coworkers. Ask them to use your instructions and format a floppy disk. Were they able to follow the instructions easily? At the end of the formatting process, a summary displays telling you the number of available bytes on the disk. Include the name in your report. If there are any bad bytes in bad sections, include that information as well.

SCIENCE

Operating systems have come a long way over the last few years. They are much easier to use and support many more features. If you were going to design an operating system for computers for the year 2010, what features would you include? How would your operating system be different from those that are currently available? Use your word-processing program to write a report or give an oral report to the class.

SOCIAL STUDIES

The more recent versions of operating systems include accessibility options for people with visual or hearing disabilities. Research the operating system on your computer and complete a report on the accessibility options.

LANGUAGE ARTS

You have been hired to create an icon to represent a new software program that has just been developed. This is an interactive encyclopedia. It also contains games to help reinforce the topics presented in the encyclopedia. Think about the icons on your computer's desktop or that you see in the figures throughout this chapter. Using graph paper or a computer drawing program, create an icon for this new interactive encyclopedia.

WEB PROJECT

Office 2000 is a popular applications suite of programs. For an online tutorial of some of the ways you can use Office 2000, go to *www.actden.com/o2k/HTML/index_h.htm*.

When you complete the tutorial, use your word-processing program to write an overview of what you learned. Your report should be at least one page.

TEAMWORK PROJECT

You and two team members have been given the responsibility for purchasing new computers for Vista Multimedia. One team member wants to purchase an Apple Macintosh with the Mac OS v.X with the latest software suite, another wants to purchase a PC with the latest version of the Windows OS, and the third wants to purchase a PC with the Unix operating system. The manager has requested that your team do some research and present her with a report so that she can make the best choice. Your report should include the positives and negatives for each of these operating systems.

COMPUTER BASICS

UNIT 1 REVIEW

REVIEW Questions

FILL IN THE BLANK

Complete the following sentences by writing the correct word or words in the blanks provided.

1. A(n) _____ includes hardware, software, data, and people.
2. _____ _____ is the technology that enables computers to communicate with each other and other devices.
3. A(n) _____ is a standard format for transferring data between two devices.
4. A(n) _____ is the software program you use to retrieve documents from the WWW and display them in readable format.
5. The _____ is the brain of the computer.
6. _____ _____ is used to increase the speed of the processing cycle.
7. _____ is the ability to enter text by using the correct fingers without looking at the keys.
8. The most popular type of keyboard is the _____ keyboard.
9. A(n) _____ is a computer program that is intentionally written to attach itself to other programs or a disk boot sector and duplicates itself whenever those programs are executed or the infected disks are accessed.
10. DOS is a(n) _____-user operating system.

MULTIPLE CHOICE

Select the best response for the following statements.

1. _____ worked with IBM to develop the operating system for the IBM PC in 1981.
   A. Bill Gates
   B. Steve Jobs
   C. Steve Wozniak
   D. Christopher Sholes

2. A _____ computer is used mostly for addresses and calendars.
   A. notebook
   B. palm
   C. mainframe
   D. desktop

3. A _____ is a group of two or more computer systems linked together via communication devices.
   A. network
   B. server
   C. client
   D. node

4. _____ is the ability to enter text by using the correct fingers without looking at the keys.
   A. Scrolling
   B. Touch typing
   C. Formatting
   D. Keystroking

5. Drills used to develop typing speed are called _____.
   A. practice
   B. timed writings
   C. keyboarding
   D. touch typing

6. A _____ connects computers and devices within a limited geographical area.
   A. cable
   B. Digital Subscriber Line
   C. local area network
   D. wide area network

7. The _____ is a circuit board that contains many integral components of the computer.
   A. motherboard
   B. CPU
   C. control unit
   D. modem

8. Eight bits are called a _____.
   A. bite
   B. byte
   C. RAM
   D. USB

9. Voice recognition devices are examples of _____ devices.
   A. input
   B. output
   C. storage
   D. network

10. A group of programs that coordinate and control the resources of a computer system is called _____.
    A. systems software
    B. applications software
    C. a language translator
    D. a utility program

TRUE/FALSE

Circle T if the statement is true or F if the statement is false.

T F 1. One of the major areas of change in the evolution of computers will be connectivity.

T F 2. There are five categories of computers.

T F 3. The "hunt and peck" method of typing is the most efficient method.

T F 4. Ergonomic keyboards are designed to relieve stress that can result from repeated and/or longtime use of a keyboard.

T F 5. A search engine is a software program.

T F 6. Use of the Internet is showing a decline.

T F 7. The WWW and the Internet are the same.

T F 8. An online service provider (OSP) is less expensive than a local Internet service provider (ISP).

T F 9. All computers require an operating system.

T F 10. A protocol is an agreed on set of rules and procedures for transmitting data between two or more devices.

CROSS-CURRICULAR *Projects*

MATH

Use store catalogs, the Internet, and other resources to research the cost and capabilities of palm computers and laptop computers. Include at least five types of each. Present your findings in a report.

SCIENCE

The Internet can be used to find all kinds of information. Use it to find out what the weather will be in your town for the next seven days. Present this information in a report in columnar format. You are to include the day/date, the forecast, and the high and low temperature for each day. You can find this information at *www.weather.com*. You may also use any other Web sites.

SOCIAL STUDIES

Use the Internet and other resources to locate information on the history of the Internet. Include information about persons who were instrumental in its development as well as specific information on how it was used originally and its explosion into our lives today. Prepare a two-page report to share with your classmates.

LANGUAGE ARTS

The computer has changed the way many tasks are completed in various fields such as health care, banking, education, and so forth. Conduct research on at least three fields where computers have changed the way tasks are completed. Present your findings in a report.

 ## WEB PROJECT

Internet etiquette is a very important topic for anyone who uses the Internet for e-mail, newsgroups, and other Internet features. Conduct an Internet search to locate information regarding Internet etiquette. Prepare a report to share this information with your classmates. Here are some URLs to get you started:

www.iwillfollow.com/email.htm

www.dtcc.edu/cs/rfc1855.html

www.albion.com/netiquette/

www.fau.edu/netiquette/netiquette.html

 ## TEAMWORK PROJECT

Your supervisor at the video store has begun to develop discomfort in her wrists from using the standard keyboard on her computer. She has asked you and your coworker to research information regarding various types of keyboards that would eliminate stress on the wrists. Prepare a chart on ergonomic keyboards. Include a brief discussion on ergonomic keyboards. Include as many different keyboards as you are able to locate. Include information regarding the name, characteristics, cost, and benefits of each keyboard. If possible, include a graphic of the keyboards in your chart.

SIMULATION

Ground Works is a landscaping business that is a full-service lawn and landscaping company. It offers residential and commercial services that include professional landscape design and installation, quality lawn and landscape maintenance, fertilization and pest control programs, and shrub and tree care.

The company is owned and operated by Robert Randolph. His entire family works in the business in some capacity. All of the company's records and correspondence have been done by hand. Mr. Randolph has decided that using a computer would vastly enhance the operation of his business and also give his company a more professional image.

He has decided to purchase a computer system for the business. Before actually going out to purchase the computer, he would like to find out as much information as possible about computers. He would also like to know more about the Internet and how he can use it in his business. Even though he will not be the one who will use the computer the most, at least not in the beginning, he would also like to learn to use the keyboard correctly.

JOB 1-1

Mr. Randolph has asked you to do some research to assist him in making a decision as to what type of computer to purchase for the business. He has heard about desktop, notebook, and palm computers, but is unsure about which would be best for the business. He has asked you to investigate the advantages and disadvantages of each and recommend which he should purchase. Use the Internet and any other resources to locate this information. Prepare a report that includes characteristics of each as well as the cost and size. Select the computer that you recommend and justify your choice.

JOB 1-2

Mr. Randolph took a keyboarding class in high school many years ago. His speed and accuracy have gotten very rusty. He knows that if he is going to really use the computer, he needs to be able to key properly. He also knows that it will take quite a bit of time for him to develop accuracy and speed.

He heard you talking about being able to "talk" to the computer instead of having to actually key data and information. He knows that you have done some research on speech recognition software. He would like for you to select one speech recognition program and prepare a proposal that would indicate the reasons for selecting this particular program for him to purchase. He would like the proposal to include the features of the program, the technical requirements, and the cost.

JOB 1-3

Mr. Randolph is interested in offering a few new services to his customers. He has asked you to search for other lawn care companies on the Internet to get an idea of other types of services he could offer. Prepare a chart of companies that you select. Include the name of the company, the URL for the company, and the services that you think would be good to add to the ones that Ground Works is currently offering.

PORTFOLIO *Checklist*

Include the following activities from this unit in your portfolio.

_____ Lesson One Mathematics Cross-Curricular Report

_____ Lesson Two Teamwork Project Report

_____ Lesson Three Social Studies Cross-Curricular Report

_____ Lesson Five Science Cross-Curricular Report

SOFTWARE

Unit 2

Lesson 7 — 1.5 hrs.
Word Processing

Lesson 8 — 1.5 hrs.
Spreadsheets

Lesson 9 — 1.5 hrs.
Databases

Lesson 10 — 1.5 hrs.
Presentation Graphics and Multimedia

Lesson 11 — 1.5 hrs.
Integration

🕐 **Estimated Time for Unit: 7.5 hours**

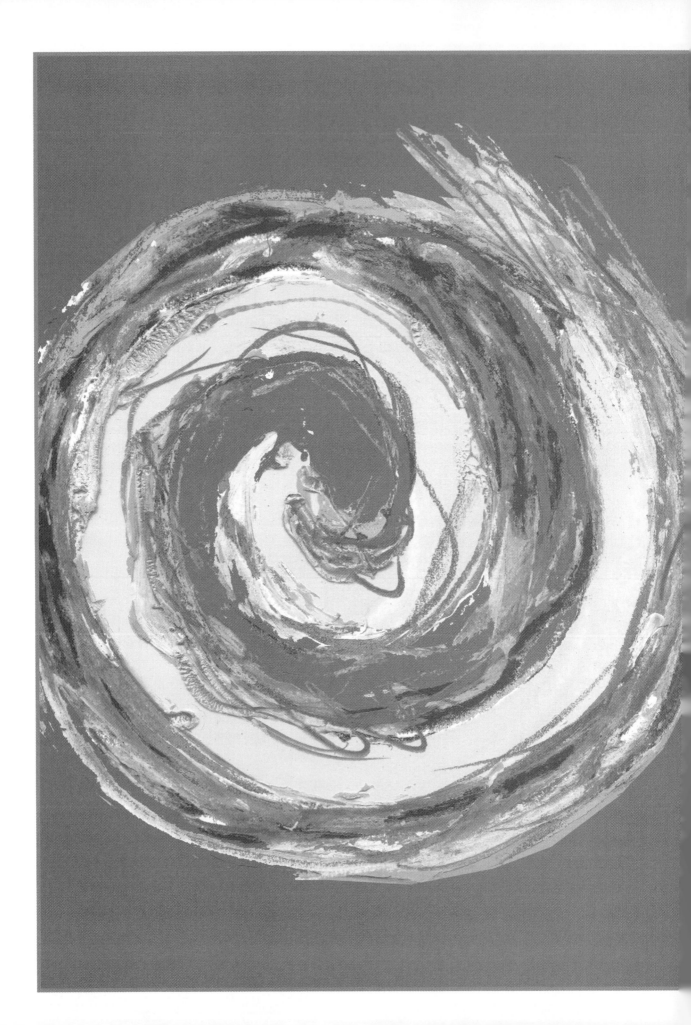

LESSON 7

WORD PROCESSING

OBJECTIVES

Upon completion of this lesson, you should be able to:

- Identify the components of the word-processor window.
- Select commands using menus and toolbars.
- Create and edit a document.
- Correct spelling in a document.
- Apply character, paragraph, and document formatting, including setting custom tabs.
- Insert and modify pictures and drawn objects.
- Create, edit, and format a table.
- Save, open, and print a document.

Estimated Time: 1.5 hours

VOCABULARY

Cell
Drawn objects
Editing
File menu
Font style
Footer
Format Painter
Formatting
Header
Insertion point
Justification
Line spacing
Margins
Points
Sans serif
Selecting
Serif
Sizing handles
Spell Checker
Styles
Symbols
Table
Tab stop
Word-processing software
Word wrap

Ms. Perez, your supervisor at Vista Multimedia, has asked you to type a letter to one of the customers who won the drawing for two free video rentals. She would like the letter to look very professional. She has given you the draft of the letter. See Figure 7-1.

You are taking a word-processing class at school and are very excited about being able to use your new skills. Word-processing software makes preparing professional-looking documents a very easy task. Let's see what you can do!

FIGURE 7-1
Letter

January 15, 200_

Mrs. Elizabeth Stevenson
1204 Drumcastle Court
Chesapeake, Virginia 23323

Dear Mrs. Stevenson

Congratulations! You are the winner of this month's drawing. Your name was drawn from more than 1,000 entries.

As the winner, you will receive two free movie rentals of your choice. Just think, you get to see two exciting, entertaining movies absolutely free!

You may come into the store anytime within thirty days of the date of this letter to make your selection. Bring this letter with you. This is our way of saying thanks for your patronage. Enjoy your movies.

Sincerely

Ms. Marie Perez
Store Manager
xx

What Is Word-Processing Software?

It would be almost impossible to spend a day in a business office, a hospital, a home, or even your school without seeing a word-processing program in use. The tests and worksheets that your teachers give you are most likely created with a word-processing program; so are the letters that are sent home to your parents. Most people have had some experience with word-processing. For many individuals, word processing is the most-used computer application program.

Word-processing software is one of the more common applications for computers today. It provides the capability to handle text and graphics, which makes it easy to create and modify all kinds of documents—from simple one-page documents to multipage reports, to flyers, brochures, newsletters, and books! You also can create Web pages with word-processing software.

Most word-processing programs share the same basic features, although the way you access these commands may differ. Some of these common commands include Open, Close, Save, Save As, Print, Cut, Copy, Paste, and Speller or Spell Check. Word-processing programs also contain a menu structure, graphic toolbars with icons representing most common commands, and scroll bars or some other mechanism for allowing you to move around in documents.

Two of the more popular word-processing programs are Microsoft Word and Corel WordPerfect. Microsoft Works also includes a popular word-processing component. Microsoft Word 2002 is used in this textbook, but any software or version you use will have similar screens and commands.

> **Did You Know?**
> Sometimes word processing is referred to as computerized typing.

The Word-Processing Screen

Start your word-processing program by clicking the Start button in the lower left corner of the Windows taskbar. Click Programs or All Programs and then the name of your word processor from the menu that displays. Once you open the word-processing program, the main editing window is displayed on your screen as a blank document. The following list describes the tools available in most word-processing programs. See Figure 7-2.

FIGURE 7-2
Blank document screen

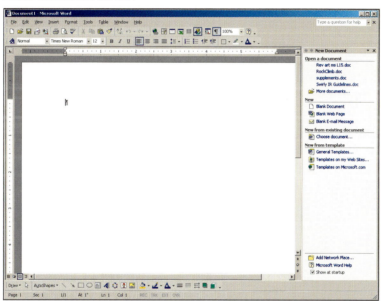

- *Title bar* displays the name of the software program. It also displays the name of the document on which you are working after you have saved and named the document.
- *Menu bar* contains commands needed to operate the word-processing software.
- *Standard and Formatting toolbars* contain icons from which the more frequently used commands may be chosen quickly. For example, if you wanted to print your document, you could click the picture of the printer on the toolbar and your document would be sent to the printer to be printed.
- *Insertion point* shows your location in the document.
- *Ruler* shows you the positioning of text, tabs, margins, and any other elements on the page.
- *Document window* is where you actually type and see your document.
- *View buttons* allow you to switch between different view modes such as Normal view, Print Layout view, Web Layout view, and Outline view.

- *Scroll bars* allow you to scroll through a document that is too large to fit in the document area.
- *Status bar* across the bottom of the window contains information related to your position in the document, the page count, and the status of keyboard keys.
- *Task pane* is a windowpane that displays recently used documents as well as frequently used features. Click one of the listed options to select it. To close the task pane, click the Close button.
- *Taskbar* shows the Start button, the Quick Launch toolbar, and all open programs.

Menu Options

Most word-processing programs are menu driven and have similar menus. This characteristic makes the programs easy to use. Once you click a menu item on the menu bar, a drop-down menu displays. See Figure 7-3.

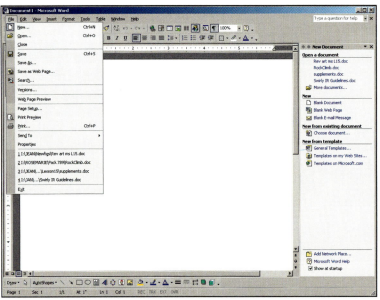

FIGURE 7-3
Drop-down menu

The *File menu* is usually the first selection on the menu bar and offers options common to most word processing programs. Click File and a drop-down menu displays. The following list describes some of the more common File menu commands:

- New—to begin a new document.
- Open—to open a file that has been saved.
- Close—to close or remove a file from the screen.
- Save—to save a file permanently on either the hard drive or a disk.
- Save As—to save the same document using a different name or in a different location.
- Print—to print your document.
- Page Setup—to set margins, select orientation, determine paper size, and so on.
- Print Preview—to see a full-page view of your document before printing.

- Exit—to close the word-processing program. This command prompts you to save any unsaved work before you quit the program.

Entering Text

When you start the word-processing program, a blank screen displays with a blinking line in the upper left corner. This line is called the *insertion point.* It indicates the location where text will be placed when you begin keying. As you enter text, the insertion point moves across the screen, indicating where the next character will be placed. See Figure 7-4.

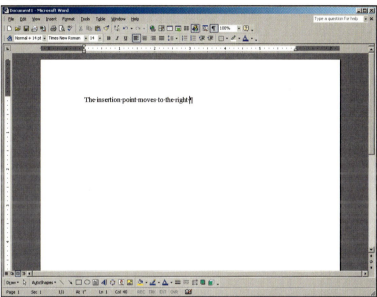

FIGURE 7-4
Typing a line of text

When you type a short line such as a date or the salutation in a letter, you will need to press the Enter key to move to the next line. If you continue to type, as your text reaches the right edge of the screen, the insertion point automatically moves down to the next line; you do not have to press Enter to move down to the next line. This feature is called *word wrap.* The text automatically wraps around the right margin and continues onto the next line. The only time you need to press Enter is at the end of a paragraph.

STEP-BY-STEP 7.1

1. Open Word if you have not already done so.

2. If you prefer, close the task pane by clicking the "X" in the upper-right corner of the task pane.

3. Key the following text. Do not press **Enter**. Watch the text wrap around the right margin and move down to the next line. Do not worry about correcting errors; you will learn to do that later in this lesson.

STEP-BY-STEP 7.1 Continued

Word-processing software is one of the most common applications for computers today. It provides the capability to handle text, which makes it easy to create (and modify) all kinds of documents.

> **Did You Know?**
>
> When word-processing software is capable of showing the document on the screen the same way it will look when printed, it is said to have WYSIWYG capability. WYSIWYG stands for "What You See Is What You Get."

4. Keep your file open for the next Step-by-Step.

Saving a File

To create a permanent copy of a document, you save it to the hard drive on your computer or to a disk, or to a folder on a network server. To save a file:

1. Click Save As on the File menu. The Save As dialog box is displayed. See Figure 7-5.

2. Click the down arrow on the right side of the Save in box until you see the drive and folder in which you will save your work.

3. Click in the File name box and key the name that you are assigning to the document.

4. Click Save.

FIGURE 7-5
Save As dialog box

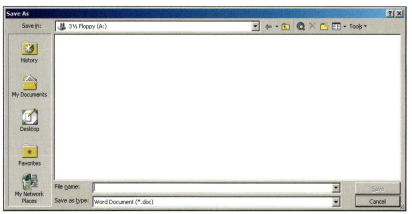

Opening an Existing File

To open a saved document, retrieve it to the screen. To open a file:

1. Click Open on the File menu. The Open dialog box is displayed. See Figure 7-6.

2. Click the down arrow on the right side of the Look in box until you see the drive on which the saved document is located.

3. Click the name of the file you want to open.

4. Click Open.

FIGURE 7-6
Open dialog box

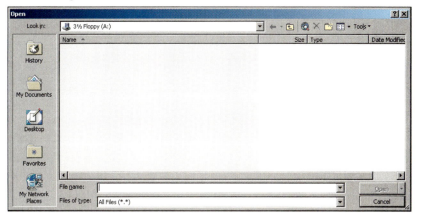

Printing a File

To get a hard copy of a document, print the document. You can print an entire document, a single page, or selected pages. To print a document:

1. Select Print on the File menu. The Print dialog box opens. See Figure 7-7.
2. To print the entire document, click OK.
3. To print the current page on which the insertion point is located, select Current page, then click OK.

FIGURE 7-7
Print dialog box

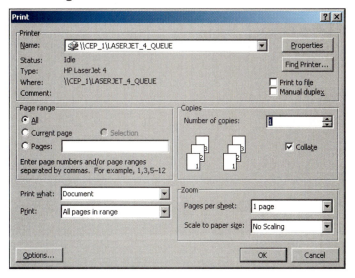

STEP-BY-STEP 7.2

1. You are ready to key the letter to Mrs. Stevenson that was shown in Figure 7-1. This letter will be typed on company stationery so you will need to begin typing approximately 2.5 inches from the top margin of the paper. You are to key the errors that appear in the letter.

STEP-BY-STEP 7.2 Continued

2. Open a New document. Press **Enter** eight times. This will place the insertion point approximately 2.5 inches from the top margin. You can check this location in the status bar.

3. Key the date, **January 15, 200_**. (Don't key the period.)

4. Press **Enter** four times.

5. Key the following lines, pressing **Enter** once after each line except the third line. Press **Enter** two times after the third line.
   Mrs. Elizabeth Stevenson
   1204 Drumcastle Court
   Chesapeake, VA 23323

6. Key the salutation, **Dear Mrs. Stevenson**. Press **Enter** two times to leave one blank space between the salutation and the body of the letter.

7. You are now ready to key the body of the letter. As you key the paragraphs, do not press Enter until you have completed the paragraph; then press **Enter** two times. You will notice that the text in the sentence will automatically wrap to the next line.
   Congratulations! You are the winner of this month's drawing. Your name was drawn from more than 1,000 entries.

8. Press **Enter** two times.

Technology Careers

WORD-PROCESSING OPERATOR

The word-processing operator performs a variety of routine word-processing tasks to produce various printed materials such as manuscripts, correspondence, labels, reports, lists, statistical information, tables, and other printed materials from rough draft and/or machine dictation.

Duties and responsibilities are usually routine. They are accomplished by following established work methods and procedures. Maintaining electronic filing systems including cataloging, coding, and filing documents and instructions for future use also is part of the word-processing operator's job description.

A high school diploma or an associate's degree is usually required for this position along with one year of word-processing experience. Keyboarding skill of 50 words per minute also is usually required. The salary for this position ranges between $20,000 and $25,000, depending on the applicant's experience and the size and location of the company.

STEP-BY-STEP 7.2 Continued

9. Key the following two paragraphs, pressing **Enter** twice after the first paragraph.

   As the winner, you will receive two free movie rentals of your choice. Just think, you get to see two exciting, entertaining movies absolutely free.

   You may come into the store anytime within thirty days of the date of this letter to make your selection. Bring this letter in with you. This is our way of saying thanks for your patronage. Enjoy your movies.

10. Press **Enter** two times.

11. Key **Sincerely**. Press **Enter** four times.

12. Type **Ms. Perez**. Press **Enter** one time.

13. Key **Store Manager**. Press **Enter** two times.

14. Key your initials in lowercase letters.

15. Click **Save**. In the File name box, key **Drawing Letter** followed by your initials. Click **OK**.

16. Keep the file open for the next Step-by-Step.

Editing Text

Probably the greatest advantage of word-processing software is the capability to change text without retyping the entire page or document. Changing an existing document is called *editing* the document. The insertion point can be moved to any position in a document in order to make corrections or to insert text. It is moved with either the directional keyboard control keys (the cursor keys) or the mouse.

Several simple methods exist for quickly correcting text:

- The *Backspace key:* The Backspace key deletes text to the left of the insertion point. Each time you press Backspace, a character of text or blank space is deleted. For example: If your insertion point is behind the "r" in Computer| and you press Backspace, the "r" will be deleted.

- The *Delete key:* The Delete key deletes text to the right of the insertion point. Each time you press Delete, a character or space in front of the insertion point is deleted. For example, if the insertion point is in front of the "p" in Com|puter and you press Delete, the "p" will be deleted.

- The *Insert key:* Most word processing software is in the Insert Mode by default. This means that wherever you place the insertion point, the text that you key enters at that point and the text to the right of the insertion point moves to the right. Pressing the Insert key causes the new text to overwrite the existing text. In other words, the old text disappears and the new text takes its place.

- *AutoCorrect:* Many of the latest word processing programs have a feature called AutoCorrect. Preselected errors automatically correct themselves. These are commonly misspelled words. For example, if you accidentally type "teh" instead of "the," the software automatically makes the correction for you. You may customize this feature to include words that you often misspell.

STEP-BY-STEP 7.3

1. Use the **Delete** and **Backspace** keys to correct the errors in the letter.

2. Click the **Save** button on the **Formatting** toolbar after you make the corrections.

3. Select **Close** on the **File** menu to close the document.

4. Select **Exit** on the **File** menu to exit the word-processing program if you are finished working for the day.

Checking Spelling

Correcting spelling errors with the Backspace and Delete keys can be very time consuming, and you may still miss errors. The AutoCorrect feature will correct some errors, but you still may have other spelling errors. You use the *Spell Checker* to check a document for errors.

However, even though you use the Spell Checker, you still need to read the document carefully. The Spell Checker will not check for correct word usage. For example, if you key *cite* in a document when *sight* is the correct word, the Spell Checker will not detect it. To correct spelling errors:

1. Select Spelling and Grammar from the Tools menu. The Spelling and Grammar dialog box opens. See Figure 7-8.

2. The first spelling error displayed in the document displays, along with suggestions for replacement. If the correct word is in the list of suggestions, click it.

3. Several buttons are located on the right side of the dialog box. Click the Change button to accept the highlighted word in the Suggestions box.

FIGURE 7-8
Spelling and Grammar dialog box

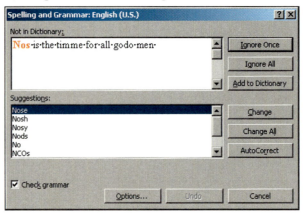

Selecting Text

When you are editing a document, you must indicate which text you want to change. You do this by *selecting* the text you want to edit. When you select a block of text, it is highlighted, which indicates that it has been selected. To select a block of text, you can use the mouse, the keyboard, or both. With the mouse, you click at the beginning of the text you want to change and drag it to the end of the text you want to change. You can double-click on a word to select it. To select an entire paragraph, you can triple-click. Once you have selected the text, you can select the command you want, such as bold or underline. See Figure 7-9.

FIGURE 7-9
Selected text

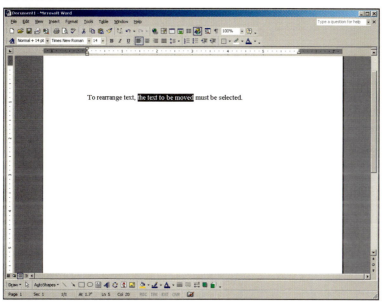

If you have selected a block of text and decide that you do not want to change it in any way, you can deselect the block of text. Click the mouse anywhere on the screen or press any arrow key.

A block of text also can be copied, cut, and pasted. To repeat pasting a block of text to another portion of the document or even into another document, you select the block of text and click the Copy tool on the Formatting toolbar. You will not see anything happen on the screen. A copy of the blocked text is placed in a special part of memory called the clipboard.

Using the Cut command works the same way, except the text is deleted from the document and placed in memory. Once you have decided where you want the block of text to be inserted, position the insertion point at that location and click the Paste button. The contents of the clipboard are copied into the document at the location of the insertion point.

Formatting Text

Another advantage of word processing software programs is the ability to control formatting. *Formatting* refers to the appearance and layout of text. You can format characters, paragraphs, or the entire document.

Character Formatting

You can change the way a character or letter looks like by changing the *font style*. Fonts have names such as Times New Roman, Arial, and Courier.

This is Times New Roman

This is Arial

```
This is Courier
```

Fonts are described as either *serif* or *sans serif* fonts. Serif fonts have little extra strokes at the ends of the letters. Sans serif fonts do not have these extra strokes. Many people use serif fonts for the body of text because serif fonts are easier to read in large blocks of text. Sans serif fonts are often used for headings.

Times New Roman is a serif font.   Arial is a sans serif font.

The size of fonts is measured in *points*. Seventy-two points equal one inch. Sizes vary from one font to the next; 10 point in one font may look bigger than 12 point of another font. The most common font size for most text is a 12-point font. Sizes over 18 points are good for headlines and banners.

This is 10-point Times New Roman Type

This is 12-point Times New Roman Type

This is 14-point Times New Roman Type

This is 18-point Times New Roman Type

This is 36-point Times New

You also can add attributes such as bold, underline, italics, and color to characters. These attributes can be added as you key the text or after you have finished keying.

You can **bold** your text.

You can <u>underline</u> your text.

You can <u>double underline</u> your text.

You can add color to your text.

You can add ***<u>more than one attribute</u>*** to your text.

You can key your text in *italics*.

You can outline your text.

All these formats and more are found in the Format menu. After accessing the Format menu, click Font. See Figure 7-10.

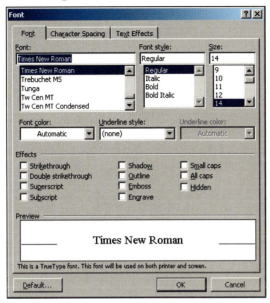

FIGURE 7-10
Font dialog box

To apply the same formatting to different text within a document, such as all headings having the same formatting, or the same word having the same formatting, you can save time by using the *Format Painter*. In addition to saving time, the document formatting will be consistent. The Format Painter button is located on the Formatting toolbar.

STEP-BY-STEP 7.4

1. Open your word-processing program. Start a new document.

2. Key the name of your school and press **Enter** two times.

3. Select the name of your school. Click **Bold**.

4. Place the insertion point beneath your school's name. Click the **Underline** button. Key the name of your principal.

5. Click the **Underline** button to remove the Underline command. Press **Enter** two times.

6. Click the **Italics** button. Key the name of the city and state in which you live. Click the **Italics** button to remove the **Italics** command.

7. Select the name of your school and change the font style to Technical, 18 point. (If you do not have Technical as a font option, choose some other font.)

8. Select the name of your principal. Apply the "sparkling" text effect.

9. Place the insertion point at the end of the text on the page and press **Enter** two times. Key the following paragraph.

STEP-BY-STEP 7.4 Continued

> Word-processing software is used to produce documents such as letters, reports, flyers, envelopes, etc. Word-processing software will also allow you to enter text into a document and later make changes to the text. This is called editing.

10. Double-click *editing*. This highlights the entire word with its Bold attribute.

11. Click the **Format Painter** button on the **Formatting** toolbar. The insertion point turns into a "paintbrush."

12. Place this paintbrush to the left of *Word processing* and drag it to the end of *processing*. Release the mouse button. *Word Processing* should now be bold. Apply Bold to the next occurrence of *Word processing* the same way.

13. Save this document as **Formatting Drill** and your initials. Print and close the document. Close the word-processing program if you are finished working for the day.

Many other formatting features are available that will enable you to enhance your document. These additional features can be found on the Format menu.

STEP-BY-STEP 7.5

1. Start your word-processing program.

2. Open the Drawing Letter document.

3. Select all of the text.

4. Change your font style to a serif font of your choice. Use a font size between 10 and 12.

5. Bold the word "Congratulations" in the first paragraph and add italics to "two free movie rentals" in the second paragraph.

6. Click **Save** to save the document with the changes.

7. Print the document.

8. Close the letter and exit the word-processing program if you are finished working for the day.

Ms. Perez will be very impressed with the professional-looking letter you just prepared using word-processing software!

Line and Paragraph Formatting

Most documents are organized into paragraphs. In word processing, a paragraph is defined by pressing Enter after the last word in the paragraph. You can control the line spacing inside the paragraph and the justification of the paragraph. You also can indent lines within the paragraph, add bullets and numbered lists, and place a border around a paragraph.

Line spacing within a paragraph can be set at single, double, triple, or some other setting. The setting controls the amount of space between lines of text in a document. If you do not change the line spacing, your document defaults to single spacing.

Example of single-spaced text.
Word processing software is one of the more commonly used computer applications today.

Example of double-spaced text.
Word processing software is one of the more commonly used computer applications today.

To change the line spacing in a document to double spacing:

1. Select the text for which you want to change the line spacing.
2. Click Format on the Standard toolbar.
3. Click Paragraph.
4. Click the Line spacing box arrow. Select Double.
5. Click OK.
6. Click to deselect text.

Did You Know?
You can use keyboard shortcuts for many commands. Press Ctrl+2 to change selected text to double spacing. Press Ctrl+A to select the entire document.

Justification (alignment) refers to the placement of text between the left and right margins. Text can be aligned at left or right, centered, or justified.

Left justified text appears at the left margin.

Right justified text appears at the right margin.

Centered text is centered between the margins.

Full justified text is aligned at both the right and left margins. For example, columns in newspapers are justified so that all complete lines end directly under each other.

To change justification in a document:

1. Select the text for which you want to change the justification.
2. Click the Alignment button you want to use on the Formatting toolbar. See Figure 7-11.
3. You also can use these keyboard shortcuts:

   CTRL+L for left alignment

   CTRL+E for center alignment

   CTRL+R for right alignment

   CTRL+J for justify

FIGURE 7-11
Alignment tools

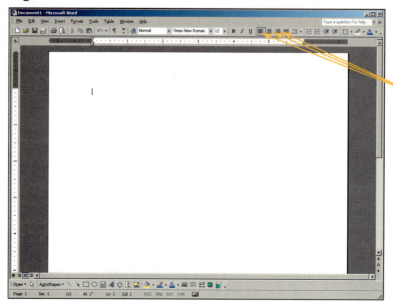

Indenting text moves text. The Tab key will move the first line of a paragraph one-half inch. You can indent a paragraph from the left margin, from the right margin, or from both margins. See Figure 7-12. To indent text within a document:

1. Place the insertion point at the beginning of each paragraph and press Tab. This indents the first line of each paragraph.

2. To indent a paragraph from both margins, click Format on the Standard toolbar and select Paragraph.

3. In the Indentation boxes, change the number to 0.5 for the left margin and 0.5 for the right margin. See Figure 7-13.

FIGURE 7-12
Indented text

STUDENT BUSINESS ORGANIZATIONS

Student organizations at the middle school, high school level and even the college level are a very important part of the instructional program. They provide opportunities for students in business and business/related fields to develop business competencies and to promote civic responsibilities. Students have the opportunity to "practice" what they learn in the classroom, they have the opportunity to compete in events that test their business knowledge and skills and they have the opportunity to learn and use leadership skills.

Future Business Leaders of America and Phi Beta Lambda are two of the most popular business organizations for students. They are basically the same organization with FBLA being at the secondary level and PBL Lambda being the college level organization. Both organizations are open to all business students.

> Future Business Leaders of America, a non-profit organization, was developed in 1937 by Dr. Hamden L. Forkner of Columbia University. The first chapter was charted in Johnson City, Tennessee, on February 3, 1942. Today, there are more than 250,000 active members in more than 13,000 chartered chapters. The first chapter of Phi Beta Lambda was chartered at the University of Northern Iowa in 1969.

The purpose of these organizations is to develop competent business leadership while strengthening the confidence of students in themselves and in their work. Volunteerism is a very important facet of life today. Both of these organizations take service to the community very seriously. In addition to having March of Dimes as their primary service organization, they participate actively in developing various projects that contribute to the community.

FIGURE 7-13
Paragraph dialog box (Indents and Spacing tab)

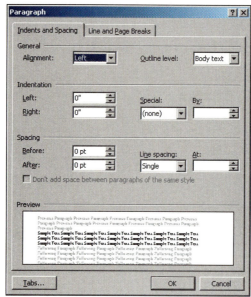

You can use bullets and numbering to emphasize a list of items. You can add a bullet in front of each item in the list. The bullet can be a circle, arrow, square, or some other symbol. You also can identify each item with a number or letter if you want the list in consecutive order. See Figure 7-14. To identify an item in a list with a bullet or number:

1. Select Bullets and Numbering on the Format menu.

2. Select the Bulleted tab if you want to use bullets. Click the style of bullets you want to use and then click OK.

3. Select the Numbered tab if you want to use numbers. Click the style of numbering you want (for example, Arabic or Roman numerals or letters) and then click OK.

4. You also may use the Bullets and Numbering tools on the Formatting toolbar.

FIGURE 7-14
Bullets and Numbering dialog box

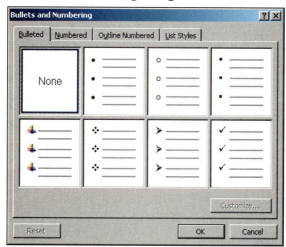

STEP-BY-STEP 7.6

1. Select **Open** on the **File** menu and open the **Student Organizations** document.
2. Save the document with the new filename **Student Organizations – Your Initials**.
3. Complete the following instructions to edit the document to look like Figure 7-12.
4. Press **Tab** to indent the first line of each paragraph.
5. Justify lines and paragraphs as shown.
6. Single-space the third paragraph.
7. Indent the single-spaced paragraph 0.5" from each margin as shown.
8. Select the first list. Click the **Bullets** button to apply bullets to this list.
9. Select the next list. Click the **Numbering** button to apply numbers to the list.
10. Save the file again and print.
11. Close the file and exit the word-processing program if you are finished for the day.

Document Formatting

You can format your document so that all pages have the same formatting.

Margins are the white space around the edge of the page where the text ends. The margins "frame" the document. The margins can be adjusted to be wider or smaller. Each margin, top, bottom, left, and right, can be changed individually. New documents have 1" top and bottom margins and 1.25" left and right margins by default.

Headers and footers are special areas at the top of the page and at the bottom of the page, respectively. The information that is keyed in the header or footer will print on every page.

Other document formatting features include page numbering, styles, borders and shading, graphics, symbols, page and section breaks, vertical centering, tabs, tables, and automatic formats.

To set margins:

1. Position the insertion point at the top of the document.
2. Click Page Setup from the File menu.
3. Click the appropriate box and change the margins to the size you want. See Figure 7-15.

FIGURE 7-15
Page Setup dialog box

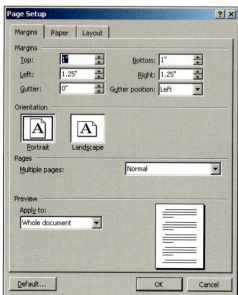

To divide a document into pages at points other than where the software automatically divides text into pages, you can insert a page or section break:

1. Position the insertion point at the point where the page is to be divided.
2. Click Break on the Insert menu. See Figure 7-16.
3. Click Next page. The Section Break will be indicated by a double-dotted line.

FIGURE 7-16
Break dialog box

You may need to center a short page vertically (up and down) between the top and bottom margins. For example, a title page is usually centered vertically. To center text vertically:

1. Position the insertion point at the top of the document. This can also be done by pressing Ctrl+Home.
2. Select Page Setup on the File menu. Click the Layout tab. See Figure 7-17.
3. In the vertical alignment box for the Page section, select Center.
4. In the Apply to box, you will see Whole Document. This means that every page in the document will be centered vertically.

5. If you want only the first page centered, position the insertion point at the beginning of the second page, open the Page Setup dialog box, select Top for the Page Alignment box, and From this Point Forward in the Apply to box.

6. Click OK.

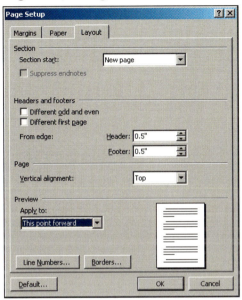

FIGURE 7-17
Page Setup dialog box

STEP-BY-STEP 7.7

1. Open the **Types of Computer Software** document.

2. Save this file with the new file name **Types of Computer Software – Your Initials**.

3. Select **Page Setup** from the **File** menu. Click the **Margins** tab.

4. Click inside the Top margin box and key **1.5** to change the top margin to 1.5 inches. Do the same for the left margin. Change the right margin to 1 inch. Click **OK**.

5. Position the insertion point at the end of the last line of text on the first page and press **Enter** three times.

6. To insert a section/page break for the first page and to center the text on the first page, select **Break** from the **Insert** menu, then **Next page**. Click **OK**.

7. Position the insertion point at the top of the first page. To center the information on the first page vertically, select **Page Setup** from the **File** menu. Click the **Layout** tab.

8. Select **Center** in the Vertical Alignment section. Click **OK**.

9. Save and close the document.

The Header and Footer feature allows you to have the same information on every page, either at the top or bottom of the page. The information keyed at the top of the page is called a *header*, and the information keyed at the bottom of the page is called a *footer*. You can key any information in the header or footer such as page numbers, your name, the name of the document, and so forth. The Header and Footer toolbar includes tools for inserting the date, page number, the time, and other options. See Figure 7-18.

FIGURE 7-18
Head and Footer toolbar in a document

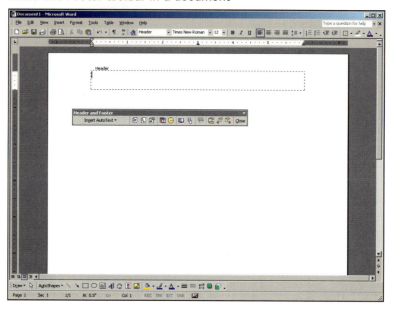

To insert a header:

1. Place the insertion point at the beginning of the document.
2. Select Header and Footer from the View menu. See Figure 7-18. The Header and Footer pane and toolbar will be displayed.
3. You will key the header information in the Header pane. Pressing the Tab key moves the insertion point to the center and right margin of the pane, or select one of the buttons on the toolbar.
4. After keying your information, click Close to remove the toolbar from your screen.

Page numbering can be inserted within a header or footer, or it can be inserted through the Page Number option. To insert page numbers in your document:

1. Place the insertion point at the beginning of the document.
2. Click the Insert menu and then click Page Numbers. See Figure 7-19.
3. Select the position and alignment for your page numbers by clicking the down arrows in the Position and Alignment boxes.
4. Click OK.

FIGURE 7-19
Page Numbers dialog box

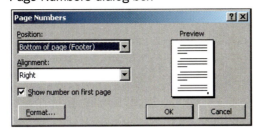

Other Formatting Features

Using Styles

Styles are predesigned formatting options that have been saved. Each option is given a name. Using styles will save you time in formatting your document as well as ensure consistency of formatting throughout the document. To apply styles:

1. Select the text on which to apply a style.
2. Select Styles and Formatting from the Format menu. The Styles and Formatting pane is displayed. Scroll down the pane until you see the style you want. Click it. The selected text will have the attributes of the style you selected. See Figure 7-20.

FIGURE 7-20
Styles and Formatting task pane

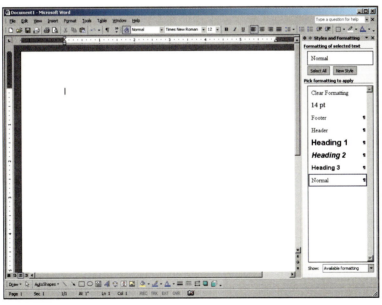

Borders and Shading

Borders and shading added to a paragraph can add emphasis to the information in the paragraph. The border can be a single line, a double line, or a dotted line; it can surround the entire paragraph or selected sides. You can even add color to borders. Shading also can be in color or it can be various shades of gray. When adding shading, however, be careful that it is light enough so that the text is easily readable.

To apply a border around text and add shading:

1. Select the paragraph you want to enclose in a border.
2. Select Borders and Shading from the Format menu. See Figure 7-21.
3. In the Borders and Shading dialog box, select the Box setting under the Borders tab.
4. In the Style box, select the style of border. You also may select the thickness of the border using the Width box. Change the color of the border by selecting your desired color in the Color box.
5. To add a gray shading or a color, click the Shading tab and select the desired color in the Fill box.
6. Click OK.

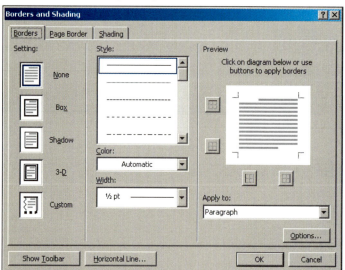

FIGURE 7-21
Borders and Shading dialog box

STEP-BY-STEP 7.8

1. Open the **Types of Computer Software – Your Initials** document.

2. Select **Header and Footer** from the **View** menu. When the Header pane appears, key your name and press **Tab** two times. Click the **Insert Date** button on the **Header and Footer** toolbar.

3. Click **Close**.

4. Select the first side heading (Word Processing) in the document.

STEP-BY-STEP 7.8 Continued

5. Select **Styles and Formatting** on the **Format** menu. Add the **Heading 1** style to the side heading in the document. Repeat this for each side heading.

6. Select the last paragraph in the document. Place a red double border around it by selecting **Borders and Shading** on the **Format** toolbar.

7. Click **Box** in the **Setting** section.

8. Select the style of border in the **Style** box, the color Red in the Color box, and a 1½ point thickness in the Width box.

9. Click the **Shading** tab and add 15% gray shading by clicking the fifth box in the **Fill** box.

10. Click **OK**.

11. Click **Save** to save the document again. Close the document.

Setting Custom Tab Stops

A *tab stop* is a location on the horizontal ruler that tells the insertion point to stop when Tab is pressed. Tab stops are used to indent text and align columns in a document.

When you press Tab, the insertion point moves one-half inch to the right. Word has one-half inch tabs preset, as do most other word-processing programs. You also can set custom tab stops. These can be left, right, center, bar, or decimal tabs. You can add leaders to each type of tab. *Leaders* are characters that fill in blank spaces between columns. Leaders can be periods, dashes, or underlines. See Figure 7-22. Table 7-1 summarizes the different types of tab stops.

FIGURE 7-22
Table with different types of tabs

Team	Date Received	Calendars Sold	Amount Paid
\multicolumn{4}{c}{FBLA CALENDAR SALE}			

FBLA CALENDAR SALE
Financial Report

Team	Date Received	Calendars Sold	Amount Paid
Red	March 8	37	$185.00
White	March 10	58	290.00
Blue	March 10	19	95.00
Green	March 9	59	295.00
Gold	March 8	35	175.00
TOTALS		198	$1,040.00

TABLE 7-1
Tab names and functions

TAB NAME	FUNCTION
Left Tab	The left tab is the default tab. It aligns text at the left.
Right Tab	Aligns text at the right. This tab is used for aligning numbers. It is also useful for aligning lines of text in a written program.
Center Tab	Centers text. It is useful for keying titles or headings over columns.
Decimal Tab	Aligns text on the decimal point. This tab is especially useful when keying numbers containing decimals.
Bar Tab	Draws a vertical line at the tab stop.

To set custom tabs:

1. Position the insertion point at the point where the tabs are to begin.
2. Select Tabs on the Format menu. The Tabs dialog box is displayed. See Figure 7-23.
3. Clear all old tabs by clicking Clear All.
4. Key the tab stop position and type of tab you want. Click Set. Set additional tabs using the same steps.
5. Once all tabs are set, click OK.

Hot Tip

You can also set tabs directly on the horizontal ruler using the tab buttons to the extreme left of the horizontal ruler. Access the Help menu to learn to set tabs using this feature.

 Ethics in Technology

DIGITAL SIGNATURES

It is possible to send an e-mail message disguised as coming from someone else. Sometimes that can be a security problem. A security device that guards against this type of computer crime and protects e-mail messages is called a digital signature.

A digital signature consists of several lines of code that appear at the end of the e-mail message. It guarantees that the message was originated by the person who signed the message, that it has not been forged, and that the message has not been altered in any way in transmission or by anyone else in an attempt to change the message.

FIGURE 7-23
Tabs dialog box

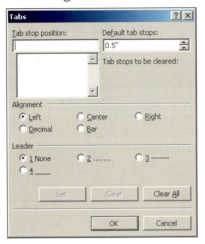

STEP-BY-STEP 7.9

1. Select **New** from the **File** menu to display a blank document. You will key the table in Figure 7-24.

2. Key the title **SPRING CLASS ENROLLMENTS**. Make it bold and center it. Click **Bold** to turn off the bold formatting.

3. Press **Enter** three times. Click the **Align left** button.

4. Select **Tabs** from the **Format** menu.

5. Click **Clear All Tabs**.

6. Set a Center tab at 2.25 inches by keying **2.25** in the **Tab stop position** box, clicking the **Center** radio button, and clicking **Set**. Follow the same steps to set a right tab at 4.0 and a right tab at 5.75.

7. Click **OK**.

8. Key the information in Figure 7-24. Double space the text.

9. Save the document as **Table Practice – Your Initials**.

10. Print and close the document. Close the program if you are finished working for the day.

FIGURE 7-24
Table for Step-by-Step 7.9

SPRING CLASS ENROLLMENTS			
Division	Course	Sections	Enrollment
Business	Accounting	10	235
Business	Economics	4	79
Business	Computer Concepts	19	295
Biology	General Biology	12	262
Biology	Human Anatomy	7	163
TOTALS		52	1,034

Graphics

You can enhance your document by adding photos, symbols, drawings, or clip art. Many software programs come with a gallery of graphics that can be used in your documents. Once you have selected a graphic and inserted it into your document, you can move and size it; you can also control the alignment of text around the graphic.

Hot Tip

You can download free clip art from the Web.

To insert clip art:

1. Select Picture from the Insert menu, then Clip Art. The Insert Clip Art task pane opens. See Figure 7-25.

FIGURE 7-25
Insert Clip Art task pane

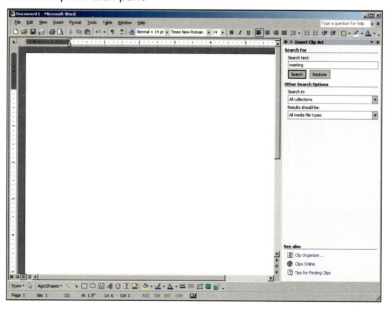

2. In the Search text box, key the name of clip art you want to insert in your document. Example: If you need a picture of an apple, key the word "apple."

3. Click Search.

4. Word will search for apple clip art and display the images in the task pane. Scroll through the images until you find the one you want.

5. Double-click the picture, and it is inserted at the insertion point in your document.

6. You can change the size of your picture by sizing it. To do this, click any place on the picture. A box with eight small squares will surround the picture. These squares are called *sizing handles*. Click and drag on these handles to increase or decrease the size of the picture. See Figure 7-26.

> **Extra for Experts**
>
> If you create a text box and then insert the clip art into the text box, it will be easier to move the graphic around in your document.

7. When you double-click on the picture, the Format Picture dialog box also appears. You can use this toolbar to make additional changes to your picture.

FIGURE 7-26
Graphic with sizing handles

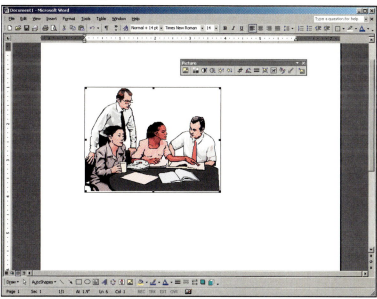

Symbols are small pictures and special characters such as mathematical symbols and foreign language symbols that can be used in documents. To insert a symbol:

1. Select Symbol from the Insert menu. See Figure 7-27.

2. There are different groupings or sets of symbols. Scroll down the Font box, and select the group that you want.

3. Select the symbol you want by clicking it.

4. Click Insert, then click Close. Your symbol is inserted at the insertion point location in your document.

FIGURE 7-27
Symbol dialog box

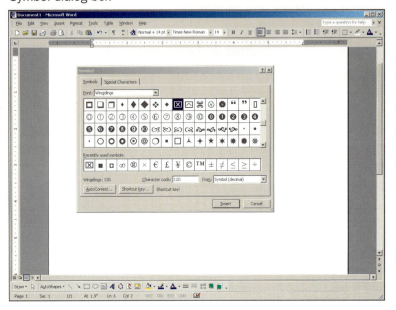

Drawn objects are graphic images that are created using tools available in Word. You use the Drawing toolbar to access these tools. These tools include lines, ovals, circles, and rectangles, among others. To insert a drawn object into your document:

1. Select Toolbars from the View menu, then Drawing on the submenu. The Drawing toolbar displays at the bottom of your screen. See Figure 7-28.

2. Click the tool you want to use. The pointer changes to a crosshair. Position the crosshair where you want the object to appear.

3. Click and hold the left mouse button and drag to draw the object to the size you want.

4. Release the mouse button.

FIGURE 7-28
Drawing toolbar

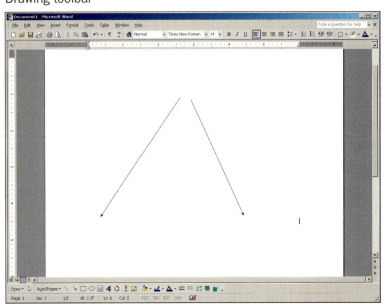

STEP-BY-STEP 7.10

1. Select **New** from the **File** menu to display a blank document.

2. Key "FBLA MEETING" centered in all capital letters in a 36-point bold font. Remember to remove this formatting before pressing **Enter**.

3. Press **Enter** five times. Center the insertion point so that the graphic will be centered horizontally on the page.

4. Select **Picture** from the **Insert** menu, and then select **Clip Art** to insert a graphic.

5. When the Insert Clip Art pane opens, key **meeting** in the Search text box and click **Search**.

6. Scroll through the displayed images and click to select one. It displays in your document. Click the image so that you can size it appropriately for your flyer.

7. Press **Enter** five times.

8. Key the remainder of the information for the flyer in an appropriate font and point size:
   Tuesday, April 23, 200_
   Room B210
   2:30 p.m.
   Important business will be discussed.

9. Center the information vertically on the page.

10. Save the document as **FBLA Flyer** and your last name.

11. Print the document.

12. Close the document and exit from the word-processing program, if you are finished working for the day.

Extra for Experts

Research how to add text in a drawn oval.

Creating a Simple Table

A *table* is an arrangement of information in columns and rows. This arrangement makes it easier to read and understand presented information. Information is keyed in a cell. A *cell* is the point at which a row and a column meet or intersect. See Figure 7-29.

FIGURE 7-29
Sample table

FUTURE BUSINESS LEADERS OF AMERICA
H. L. Boone High School Chapter
Officer Roster

NAME	OFFICE	CLASSIFICATION	YEARS IN FBLA	HOMEROOM
Bernadette Banks	President	Senior	3	Mrs. Jones
Susan Downs	Vice President	Junior	2	Mr. Powell
Robert Chevez	Secretary	Sophomore	1	Mrs. Winston
Michelle Ito	Financial Secretary	Junior	3	Mr. Fadee
Brian Boitano	Treasurer	Junior	2	Mr. Lamb
Miriam Watson	Chaplain	Freshman	1	Ms. Taborn
Markita Cherry	Sergeant-at-Arms	Senior	2	Mrs. Lawson

To create a table:

1. Select Insert on the Table menu, then select Table on the submenu. The Insert Table dialog box opens. See Figure 7-30.

2. Specify the number of rows and columns that are to appear in your table, then click OK. The empty table appears in the document.

3. Position the insertion point in the cell where you want information to display and begin keying. To move to the next cell, press Tab or the appropriate arrow key. Press Enter only if you want to include a second line of text in the cell.

FIGURE 7-30
Insert Table dialog box

Formatting and Modifying a Table

Once a table has been created, it can be changed. Columns and rows can be added or deleted. Cells can be merged or split. Column widths can be increased or decreased, and row heights can be increased or decreased. The table can be formatted manually or using the AutoFormat features.

To format and modify a table:

1. **Insert rows and columns.** Position the insertion point inside the first cell (or at the point where you want the insertion to occur). Insert rows and columns by selecting Insert on the Table menu. Select the command you want from the submenu.

2. **Delete rows and columns.** Select rows or columns you want to delete. Select Delete on the Table menu. Select Rows or Columns from the submenu.

3. **Merge cells.** Select the group of cells you want to merge. Select Merge Cells on the Table menu.

4. **Split cells.** Select the group of cells you want to split. Select Split Cells on the Table menu.

5. **Increase column width and row height.** Position the insertion point on the vertical line and drag left or right to change column width. Position the insertion point on the horizontal line and drag up or down to change row height.

6. **Split table.** Position the Insertion point in the row that you want to be the first row of the second table. Select Split Table on the Table menu. The table will split.

7. **Borders and shading.** Select the area for which you want to add a border. It can be around the entire table, a row, a column, or cell. Select Borders and Shading on the Format menu. Click your selections.

8. **AutoFormatting.** Select Table AutoFormat on the Table menu. After the Table AutoFormat dialog box opens, scroll the Style box to preview various available styles. Click Apply to select the one you want to use.

9. **Manual Formatting.** You can add additional formats by adding color to your text, aligning the text within the cells, and so on.

STEP-BY-STEP 7.11

1. Open the word-processing program. You will create the table shown in Figure 7-31.

2. Key the title (your name) and subtitles of the table. Center them and make them bold.

3. Select **Insert**, **Table** from the **Table** menu.

4. In the Insert Table dialog box, indicate the number of columns and rows. Click **OK**.

5. Select the first row. On the **Format** menu, click **Borders and Shading**. Select shading of 12.5% gray. Click the fourth box on the first row for 12.5%.

6. Select the first row. Click the **Center** button to center the column title.

7. Key the data into each cell. Adjust the column width as necessary.

8. Save your document as **Class Schedule – Your Initials** and print.

9. Close the document and the word-processing program.

FIGURE 7-31
Table for Step-by-Step 7.11

YOUR NAME
Class Schedule
200_ – 200_

BELL	TIME	COURSE	INSTRUCTOR	ROOM
Bell 1	7:55 a.m. – 8:45 a.m.	English	Brown	208
Bell 2	8:55 a.m. – 9:45 a.m.	Math	Mandez	204
Bell 3	9:55 a.m. – 10:45 a.m.	P.E.	Coley	Gym
Bell 4	10:55 a.m. – 11:45 a.m.	Lunch		Cafeteria
Bell 5	11:55 a.m. – 12:45 p.m.	Computer Concepts	Vinoo	106
Bell 6	12:55 p.m. – 1:45 p.m.	History	Duke	200
Bell 7	1:55 p.m. – 2:45 p.m.	Theater	Vito	Theater

SUMMARY

In this lesson, you learned:

- Word processing software is used to create documents such as letters, reports, memos, brochures, and even Web pages.
- Commands for using the features of a word-processing program are selected from menus and toolbars. Keyboard shortcuts make using commands quicker.
- Formatting features may be added to characters, paragraphs, or the entire document.
- Word-processing software allows for easy formatting and modification (editing) of documents by selecting blocks of text and applying changes such as cutting, copying, and pasting or adding attributes such as bold, underline, or italics or changing font style or justification.
- The Spell Checker checks the documents for possible misspelled words.
- Documents should be saved often. When saving a document, you must give it a name and indicate where it is to be saved.
- Hard copies of documents are generated through printers.

VOCABULARY Review

Define the following terms:

Cell	Insertion point	Sizing handles
Drawn objects	Justification	Spell Checker
Editing	Line spacing	Styles
File menu	Margins	Symbols
Font style	Points	Table
Footer	Sans serif	Tab stops
Format Painter	Selecting	Word-processing software
Formatting	Serif	Word wrap
Header		

REVIEW Questions

MULTIPLE CHOICE

Select the best response for the following statements.

1. The _____ is used to access commands.
   - A. menu bar
   - B. title bar
   - C. scroll bar
   - D. status bar

2. The _____ toolbar contains tools you can use to draw and manipulate objects.
   A. Formatting
   B. Drawing
   C. Standard
   D. Tables and Borders

3. Times New Roman, Arial, and Courier are types of _____.
   A. templates
   B. commands
   C. font styles
   D. formatting

4. To place the name of a document at the top of every page in the document, create a(n) _____.
   A. margin
   B. justification
   C. header
   D. footer

5. When clicked on, a graphic will be enclosed with a box with eight small squares. These squares are called _____.
   A. sizing handles
   B. borders
   C. symbols
   D. Clip art

TRUE/FALSE

Circle T if the statement is true or F if the statement is false.

T F 1. Word-processing software is used for calculation applications.

T F 2. Editing documents means making changes to existing text.

T F 3. A table consists of rows and columns.

T F 4. You can create your own graphic images.

T F 5. Styles are used to ensure consistency of formatting in documents.

FILL IN THE BLANKS

Complete the following sentences by writing the correct word or words in the blanks provided.

1. All documents should be _____ if you want to keep a permanent copy.

2. The tool for inserting the date in a footer is found on the _____ toolbar.

3. A list of options from which to choose commands is a(n) _____.

4. Left, right, center, bar, and decimal are types of _____ in Word.

5. _____ are predesigned sets of formatting options that add consistency to documents.

PROJECTS

CROSS-CURRICULAR—MATH

Word processing programs have the capability to perform various mathematical operations using mathematical symbols. Check your software's manual or use the Help feature to identify which symbols are available and how to access them. Prepare a table consisting of the symbol, the meaning of the symbol, and how to access it. Title your report "Mathematical Symbols in Word-Processing Software."

CROSS-CURRICULAR—SCIENCE

Use your word-processing program to write a two-page report on acid rain. Search the Internet to gather information for your report. In your report, include an introduction paragraph describing acid rain. Include side headings for causes, effect on the environment and humans, and solutions. The last paragraph should be a summary of the report. Double-space the report.

CROSS-CURRICULAR—SOCIAL STUDIES

Many people think that their individual vote decides who wins a presidential election. This is not true. The Electoral College determines the winner. Using the Internet and other resource options, find information about the Electoral College. Explain its origin, its function, and how it operates. Use word processing software to write a report on your findings. You may decide on the setup of your findings. Use various formatting commands to enhance the appearance of your report.

CROSS-CURRICULAR—LANGUAGE ARTS

Most word-processing programs have features that are especially useful to writers, such as Styles and Formatting and Comments. Use the software's manual, the Internet, brochures, and any other resources to identify other features that are useful to writers. Prepare a report that includes the name and description of each feature. The title of your report will be "Writers' Aids in Word-Processing Software." Insert this information into a table. Format the table.

WEB PROJECT

Security problems regarding computers were briefly discussed in the Ethics in Technology feature. Computer crimes have increased rapidly. These crimes involve illegal use of or the unauthorized entry into a computer system or computer data to tamper, interfere, damage, or manipulate the system or data. You are to use the Internet and other resources to research and prepare a report on various security devices to guard against computer crime. Include graphics in your report if possible.

TEAMWORK PROJECT

Ms. Perez, your supervisor at Vista Multimedia, would like to see how the store could take advantage of templates that are available in the video store's word-processing program. She would like to see actual samples with the store's information included.

Because there are quite a few templates available in the software, you have asked the other part-time employee to assist you. After viewing the available templates, decide on three that would be appropriate for the store. Add the store's name to each of the templates.

LESSON 8

SPREADSHEETS

OBJECTIVES

Upon completion of this lesson, you should be able to:

- Understand the purpose and function of a spreadsheet.
- Identify the major parts of a spreadsheet window.
- Enter labels, values, formulas, and functions into a spreadsheet.
- Change column width and row height.
- Insert and delete rows and columns.
- Format data in a spreadsheet.
- Create graphs.
- Save and print a spreadsheet.

Estimated Time: 1.5 hours

VOCABULARY

Absolute cell reference
Active cell
AutoFormat
Cell
Cell range
Formula
Formula bar
Function
Label
Name box
Relative cell reference
Sorting
Spreadsheet
Task pane
Value
What-if analysis
Workbook
Worksheet

Many small businesses like Vista Multimedia use spreadsheet software for various activities that require calculation, such as their payroll. Preparing the payroll using a spreadsheet is an easy task to perform. Once the hours worked and wage and deduction information have been entered, it's just a matter of minutes before the entire staff's pay can be determined.

Ms. Perez completes the payroll for Vista Multimedia. However, she has never learned how to chart the information. She also has never tried to use the "what-if" function. She's been thinking about giving a small bonus to those employees who work more hours than their usual 20 per week. The store has been very busy and she wants to show her appreciation for those who have helped out by working extra hours. The what-if analysis will allow her to determine if she can afford the bonuses.

In addition to preparing the payroll with the regular information, she has decided to try to create a chart displaying the payroll information visually and to determine the amount of bonus each employee would receive.

What Is the Purpose of Spreadsheets?

A *spreadsheet* is simply a row and column arrangement of data. Spreadsheet software allows you to calculate, manipulate, and analyze numbers. Spreadsheets are used to prepare budgets, financial statements, and as an inventory management tool. They are also used to make forecasts and to assist in making decisions. Spreadsheet software performs calculations faster and more accurately than doing the calculations manually.

Once data has been entered into a spreadsheet, calculations can be performed with it easily. The data can be formatted in various ways. It can even be presented in a chart. But the best feature of all is that when information is changed the spreadsheet will recalculate automatically! We will use Microsoft Excel spreadsheet program in this lesson.

> **Did You Know?**
> Spreadsheets can be used to create budgets, maintain inventories, prepare payrolls, and calculate students' grades.

The Anatomy of a Spreadsheet

A spreadsheet form looks much like a page from a financial journal. It is a grid with columns and rows. This grid is often called a **worksheet**. The terms *worksheet* and *spreadsheet* are used interchangeably. The columns are identified by letters in the alphabet, and the rows are identified by numbers. The point at which a column and a row intersect or meet is called a *cell*. This cell has a name that is represented by the column letter and the row number. For example, the first cell in a worksheet is cell A1. It is located in column A and on row 1. The *active cell* is the cell in which you are currently working. It will have a thick border around it. See the active cell C4 in Figure 8-1.

FIGURE 8-1
Active spreadsheet cell

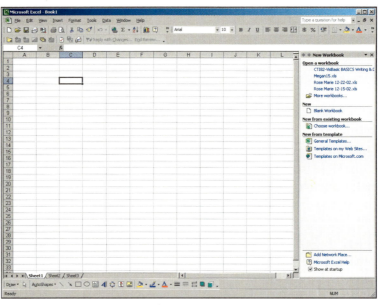

You would think only 26 columns would be available in a spreadsheet because there are only 26 letters in the English alphabet. Spreadsheet developers decided to use two letters for the additional columns, much like we use two digits to indicate numbers above 9. The 27th cell is AA, then AB, and AC, and so on, until IV, which is the last column. It is column 256. Rows are numbered 1 to 65,536. There are 16,777,216 cells in an Excel spreadsheet! See Figure 8-2.

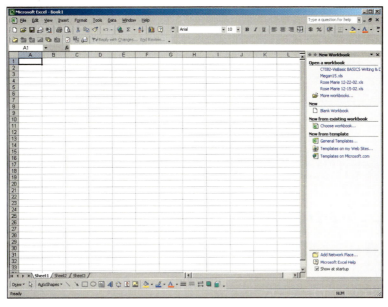

FIGURE 8-2
The spreadsheet window

- The *title bar* contains the name of the software program and the name of the document that you are working on if you have saved it.
- The *menu bar* located at the top of the screen contains menu items such as File, Edit, View, Insert, and so on.
- The *Standard toolbar* has icons for commands that are used frequently.
- The *Formatting toolbar* has icons that are used frequently for formatting the appearance of the spreadsheet.
- The *Name box* identifies the active cells.
- The *Formula bar* displays the content of the active cell.
- *Column letters* identify the vertical columns, whereas *row numbers* identify the horizontal rows.
- The *scroll bar* allows you to display all areas of the spreadsheet.
- The *task pane* is a separate window to the right of the spreadsheet. It opens automatically when you start a program and displays commonly used commands. If you do not want it to remain open, simply click the Close button.

Moving Around in a Spreadsheet

Before you can enter data into a cell or edit a cell, you need to select that cell to make it active. You can do this by using either the mouse or the keyboard.

You can quickly select a cell with the mouse by pointing to the cell and clicking the left mouse button. If you want to select a cell that is not currently on the screen, you can use the vertical and horizontal scroll bars to display the area of the spreadsheet that contains the cell(s) you want to select. Several keys on the keyboard will allow you to select a cell. See Table 8-1.

TABLE 8-1
Keystrokes and their actions

KEYSTROKE	ACTION
Arrow Keys	Moves up, down, left, or right one cell
Page Up	Moves the active cell up one full screen
Page Down	Moves the active cell down one full screen
Home	Moves the active cell to Column A of the current row
Ctrl+Home	Moves the active cell to cell A1
F5 (Function Key)	Opens the Go To dialog box, in which you enter the cell address of the cell you want to make the active cell

Entering Data into a Spreadsheet

The data entered into a spreadsheet will be one of three types. It will be a label, a value, or a formula. A *label* is alphabetical text and aligns at the left side of the cell. A *value* is a number and aligns at the right side of the cell. A *formula* is a statement that performs a calculation. A *function* is a built-in formula that is a shortcut for common calculations such as addition and average. Each type of data in the spreadsheet program has a particular use and is handled in a unique way. Once data has been keyed into a cell, it can be changed or corrected by using Delete or Backspace. It can also be corrected by rekeying the data.

Now that we have gone over the basics of a spreadsheet, let's enter information for the part-time payroll. See Figure 8-3.

FIGURE 8-3
Part-time payroll spreadsheet

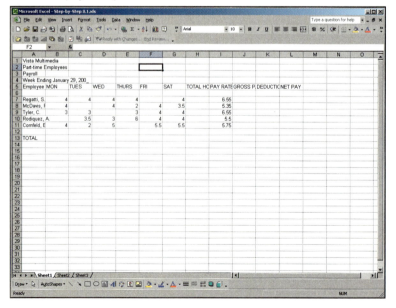

STEP-BY-STEP 8.1

Use the information in Figure 8-3 to enter the labels and values into the spreadsheet.

1. Start your spreadsheet program.

2. Key **Vista Multimedia** in cell A1. Press **Enter**. (Don't be concerned if some of the words extend into nearby cells.)

3. Key **Part-time Employees** in cell A2. Press **Enter**.

4. Key **Payroll** in cell A3. Press **Enter**.

5. Key **Week Ending January 29, 200_** in cell A4. Press **Enter**.

6. Key **Employee** in cell A5. Press the right arrow key.

7. Key **MON** in cell B5. Press the right arrow key.

8. Continue until all information in rows 5 through 13 has been keyed. Don't be concerned if some of the words extend outside of the cells or are cut off. You will learn to adjust column width later. Remember to correct any errors using Backspace or Delete or by rekeying the information.

9. Save this spreadsheet as **Part-time Payroll – Your Initials**.

10. Leave the file open for use in the next Step-by-Step.

Entering Formulas and Functions

A *formula* is an equation that performs a calculation in a spreadsheet. Whenever you enter a formula, you must inform the program that you are entering a formula and not a label. You do this by keying the equals sign (=). To key a formula, you combine numbers, cell references, arithmetic operators, and/or functions. The arithmetic operators indicate the desired arithmetic operations. These include addition (+), subtraction (-), multiplication (*), and division (/).

To save keying time, a function can be used instead of a formula. A *function* is a prewritten formula that performs various types of calculations automatically. Some of the functions are very simple, like SUM for addition; others are more complex like PMT. Table 8-2 shows a list of commonly used functions.

TABLE 8-2
Common functions

FUNCTION NAME	DESCRIPTION
AVERAGE	Gives the average of specified arguments.
COUNT	Counts the number of cells in a range.
IF	Specifies a logical test to perform; then performs one action if test result is true and another if it is not true.
MAX	Gives the maximum value of a range of cells.
MIN	Gives the minimum value of a range of cells.
ROUND	Rounds a number to a specified number of digits.
SUM	Totals a range of cells.

To use the SUM function to add a range of cells, you key =*SUM(B9:G9)*. The range of cells you want to add, sometimes referred to as an *argument*, is keyed inside parentheses with the first cell of the range, a colon (:), and the last cell of the range. A **cell range** is a group of cells that are closely situated.

The AutoSum button makes it easy to total long columns of data. It is identified on the Formatting toolbar as the Greek letter Sigma (Σ). To use AutoSum, click in the cell where the answer is to appear and click the AutoSum button. Excel will display an outline around the group of cells in the column above the highlighted cell or row of cells adjacent the highlighted cell. If the highlighted cells are not the ones you want, click the first of the group you want and drag to the last cell in the range you want to add. Press Enter or click AutoSum again.

You should be very careful when entering formulas. Keying the incorrect cell reference, using a semicolon instead of a colon to identify a range, or even misspelling a function could cause your result to be incorrect. If you enter a formula incorrectly, you can make the correction in the Formula bar. Just click the cell in which the formula appears, then place the insertion point at the point of the needed correction in the Formula bar and make the correction.

Hot Tip

A very useful feature of spreadsheet software is the macro, a recorded series of keystrokes that can be replayed as needed. For example, all of the keystrokes necessary to print a section of a spreadsheet to a certain printer can be recorded as a macro.

STEP-BY-STEP 8.2

1. Calculate Total Hours worked by S. Regatti in cell H7.

2. Key **=B7+C7+D7+E7+F7+G7**. Press **Enter**.

3. Calculate Total Hours worked by R. McDavis in cell H8.

4. Key **=B8+C8+D8+E8+F8+G8**. Press **Enter**.

5. Calculate the total number of hours worked by C. Tyler in cell H9.

6. Use the **SUM** function to determine total hours worked for A. Rodiquez in cell H10. Key **=SUM(B10:G10)**. Press **Enter**.

7. Use the **SUM** function to determine the total hours worked for B. Cornfeld.

8. Place the cell pointer in cell **B13**. Use the SUM function to determine the total hours worked on Monday.

9. Save the file. Keep it open for use in the next Step-by-Step.

Copying Data

The same formula is used to calculate the number of hours worked the remainder of the week. Instead of keying the same formula five more times, you can copy the formula to the other cells. There are several ways to copy data. You can copy and paste, use the drag-and-drop method, or you can fill cells.

To Use Copy and Paste:

1. Click in the cell to be copied.
2. Select Copy from the Edit menu on the menu bar.
3. Move the cell pointer to the cell into which you want to paste the formula. You may also select a range of cells in which to paste the formula.
4. Select Paste from the Edit menu to paste the formula into the selected cell or cells.

To Use Fill Cells:

1. Click to select the cell to be copied.
2. The cell will be outlined with a thick black border with a detached black square at the lower right corner of the cell.
3. Click and drag the corner square, highlighting the cells into which you want data copied.
4. Release the mouse button.

When you copy cells that contain formulas, the program automatically adjusts the formula to the location into which it is copied. This is called a *relative cell reference*. If the value of either of the cells in the formula must remain the same when copied into another cell, you must make a change to the formula so that it will contain an *absolute cell reference*. This means the content of the formula will not change when copied or moved to another cell. To create an absolute cell reference, key a $ before the column letter and row number in the cell reference. For example, *A4* is an absolute cell reference for cell A4.

STEP-BY-STEP 8.3

1. Click **B13** and look in the Formula bar. You will see the formula =SUM(B7:B11).

2. Make sure cell **B13** is selected. Select **Copy** from the **Edit** menu.

3. Click in cell **C13** and drag over to cell **H13**.

4. Select **Paste** from the **Edit** menu. Columns B through H should now be totaled.

5. Click cell **J7**. Enter **=H7*I7** to determine Gross Pay for S. Regatti. Copy the formula to determine Gross Pay for the other employees.

6. Click cell **K7**. Enter **=J7*.27** to determine the amount of deductions taken from S. Regatti's pay. Copy the formula to determine Deductions for the other employees.

7. Click cell **L7**. Enter **=J7-K7** to determine net pay for S. Regatti. Copy the formula to determine Net Pay for the other employees.

Technology Careers

DIRECTOR, INFORMATION TECHNOLOGY

The director of information technology is an administrator who is responsible for planning, promoting, and supporting information technologies within an organization. These technologies include computing, networking, and telecommunications. By planning, organizing, directing, and supervising all information technology activities, the director ensures that all users are able to apply technologies in performing their daily tasks.

The director of information technology should be knowledgeable about principles, practices, and techniques for operating microcomputers as well as large-scale, high-volume data processing operations; personnel management; and budget development and administration.

A bachelor's degree in business administration, computer science, or a closely related field is usually required. However, a master's degree is often preferred. Many firms require significant experience, including experience at a managerial level. The salary for this position ranges between $45,000 and $55,000 a year, depending on experience and the size and location of the company.

STEP-BY-STEP 8.3 Continued

8. Total the Gross Pay, Deductions, and Net Pay columns using AutoSum.

9. Save the file. Your spreadsheet should look like Figure 8-4. Keep the file open for the next Step-by-Step.

FIGURE 8-4
Partially completed spreadsheet

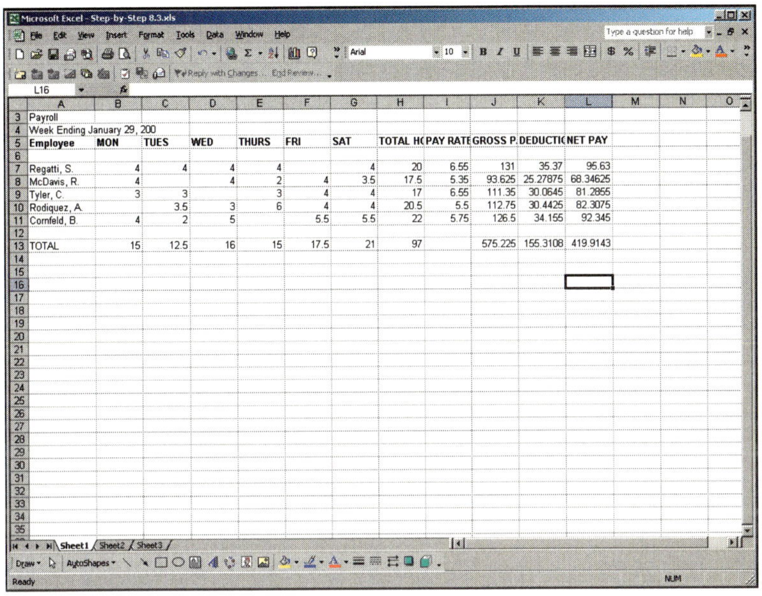

Printing the Spreadsheet

Once you have completed your spreadsheet, you can preview it to see what it will look like before you print it. Click the Preview tool on the Formatting toolbar.

Formatting and Printing the Spreadsheet

You can change special format settings by selecting Page Setup on the File menu. Once the dialog window opens, click the Sheet tab. Select the settings you desire and then click OK.

- To print the column headings on each page of a multipage spreadsheet, click Row and Column Headings. Then click the "Rows to repeat at top" box area. The spreadsheet will appear on screen so that you can select the row you want repeated on all pages.

- To print the worksheet sideways (called *landscape orientation*), select Page Setup on the File menu. Select the Page tab and click the Landscape radio button.

- To print only a portion of the spreadsheet, you can define the part you want to print by selecting the range. Click Selection in the Print Dialog box. See Figure 8-5.

- To divide the spreadsheet into pages at a certain point, you can force a page break at the row above the selected row by placing the cell pointer on any cell on the row above which the spreadsheet will split. Select Page Break on the Insert menu. To remove a page break, select a cell below the page break and select Remove Page Break on the Insert Menu.

To print the spreadsheet, click the Print tool on the Formatting toolbar. Make your selections, such as the number of copies you want to print, then click OK.

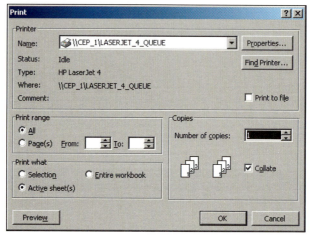

FIGURE 8-5
Print dialog box

You can print the spreadsheet with the borders or gridlines showing around the cells.

1. Select Options on the Tools menu.
2. Click the View tab if it is not already selected.
3. Click Gridlines and a check mark will appear in the box. Click OK. This is the default setting.
4. To remove the gridlines, click the Gridlines box so that the check mark disappears.

You can force the data to fit on a specified size of paper or number of pages. The "Fit to" command is used for this application.

1. Select Page Setup on the File menu. See Figure 8-6.
2. Click the Page tab and the Fit to radio button.
3. Click the spin buttons to indicate the number of pages wide and tall.

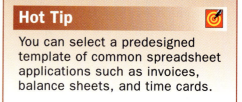

Hot Tip

You can select a predesigned template of common spreadsheet applications such as invoices, balance sheets, and time cards.

FIGURE 8-6
Page Setup dialog box

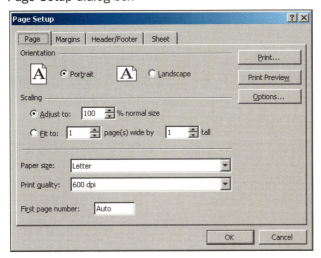

Formatting a Spreadsheet

The appearance of the spreadsheet is just as important as the accuracy of the text that it contains. Formatting can be used to emphasize specific entries. It can also help to make the information easier to understand. Compare Figures 8-7a, 8-7b and 8-7c.

FIGURE 8-7a
Unformatted spreadsheet

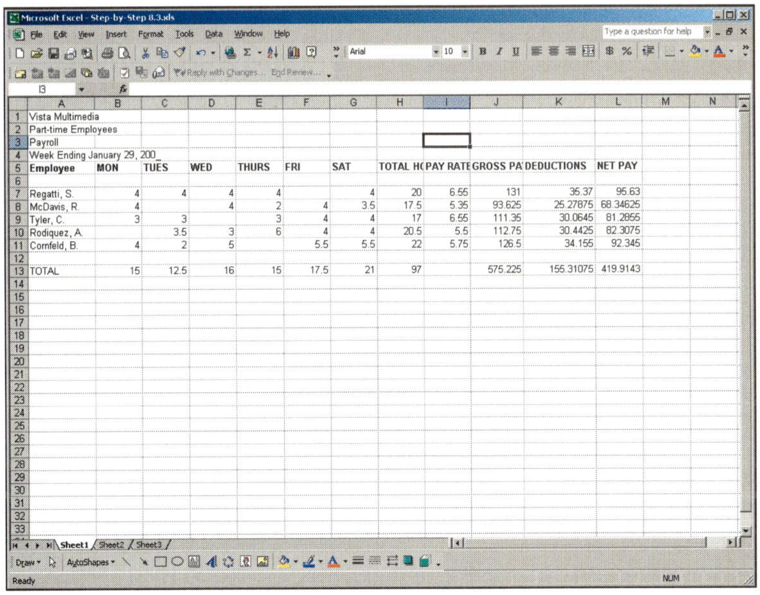

FIGURE 8-7b
Formatted spreadsheet

FIGURE 8-7c
AutoFormatted spreadsheet

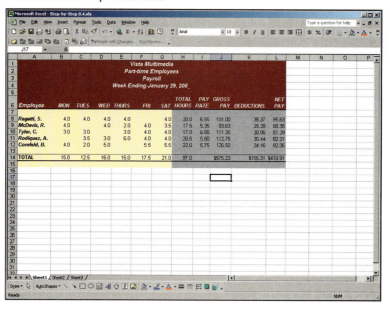

Changing Column Width and Row Height

Sometimes when you enter text in a cell it is too long for the width of the cell. If this occurs, you may see a series of ##### in the cell, or the text may spill over into the next cell, or some of the characters may be cut off.

To change the column width and row height:

1. Position the insertion point on the vertical line between the column letters. The insertion point becomes a double-headed bold black arrow.

2. Click and drag to the right to widen the column. Drag to the left to decrease the column width.

3. To adjust row height, place the pointer below the row number (at the left) until the pointer becomes a double-headed arrow.

4. Click and drag upward to increase the height and downward to decrease the height of the row.

Formatting Data

The appearance of the data in a spreadsheet can have an impact on how well the information is understood.

- The labels in cells can be aligned using the alignment tools (left, right, center, justify) on the Formatting toolbar. Select the cells you want to align and click the appropriate tool.

- Text in cells can be rotated or wrapped by selecting Cells on the Format menu. Then select Alignment and the formatting feature you want to use.

- The font size, font style, and font color can be changed by selecting the appropriate tool on the Formatting toolbar.

- The Format Painter can be used to format data in a spreadsheet. Using the Format Painter will ensure consistency of the formatting. To use this feature, select the text that has the formatting you want to copy. Click the Format Painter tool on the Formatting toolbar. The insertion point turns into a brush. Click in front of the text to be formatted and drag the brush to the end of the text.

- Styles, which are pre-established cell formats, can be applied to data. This command is found on the Format menu.

- The title of the spreadsheet can be centered over the columns in the spreadsheet. To do this, click the first cell of the title and drag over to the last column in the spreadsheet. Select Cells on the Format menu. Then click the Alignment tab and select Center Across Section in the Horizontal box. Or, you can use the Center Across Section Tool. See Figure 8-8.

FIGURE 8-8
Center Across Section tool

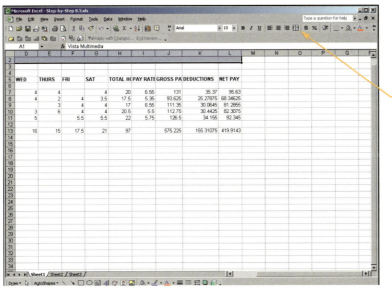

Formatting Numbers

Numbers can be formatted with decimals, commas, or dollar signs.

1. Select the cells you want to format.
2. Select Cells on the Format menu.
3. Select the Number tab and select the style you want in the Category area. Click OK.

Borders and Shading

You can add a border and shading to a range of cells in your spreadsheet.

1. Select the range of cells you want to enclose in a border or shade.
2. Select Cells on the Format menu.
3. To add a border, select the Border tab. In the Presets area, select Outline. In the Border area, click on the Top, Bottom, Left, and Right squares. You will see the border selected. Select the style of border you want by selecting it in the Style box and the color in the Color box and then click OK. See Figure 8-9.
4. To add shading to the range of cells, select Patterns tab in the Format Cells dialog box.

FIGURE 8-9
Format Cells dialog box with Border tab selected

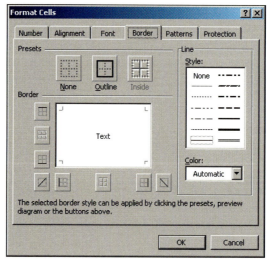

AutoFormat

There are many other features that you can use to format your worksheet manually, but this can be very time consuming. Using AutoFormat to format the body of the worksheet will save time as well as give your worksheet a professional look. *AutoFormats* are customized preset styles. See Figure 8-10.

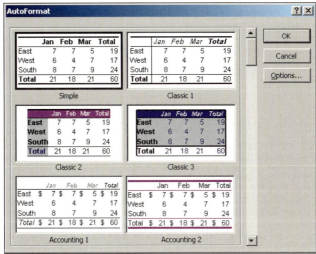

FIGURE 8-10
AutoFormat dialog box

Inserting and Deleting Cells, Rows, and Columns

Sometimes you may need to insert additional information into your worksheet. To insert a cell, row, or column:

1. Select Cells on the Insert menu. You must select whether you want cells to shift to the left or down in order to insert your desired cell(s).

2. Select Rows on the Insert menu. One row will be added above the row on which the cell pointer is located.

3. Select Columns on the Insert menu. A column will be added to the left of the column in which the cell pointer is located.

4. Delete cells, rows, and columns by selecting Delete from the Edit menu.

> **Did You Know?**
> You can also insert cells in a spreadsheet by selecting a range of cells and clicking Insert and Cells. You will be asked where to insert the new cells.

S TEP-BY-STEP 8.4

1. Center the title lines over the spreadsheet by clicking in cell **A1** and dragging over to cell **L1**. Select **Cells** from the **Format** menu. Then click the **Alignment** tab on the **Format Cells** menu. Click the down spin arrow in the **Horizontal Text alignment** box and click **Center Across Selection**. Click **OK**. Repeat for each title line.

2. To insert a blank row between the last title line and the body of the spreadsheet data, click on row 5. Click **Insert, Rows**.

STEP-BY-STEP 8.4 Continued

3. Select cells **A6** through **L6**. Click the **Center** and **Bold** tools.

4. To widen column A, place the pointer on the vertical line between **column A** and **column B**. Drag pointer to the right until column A is wide enough to hold all names.

5. Select cells **H6** through **L6**. Select **Cells** from the **Format** menu. Click **Alignment, Wrap text, OK**. Widen column K.

6. To format the hours for one decimal place and the money for two decimal places, select cells **B8** through **H14**. Select **Cells** and **Number** on the **Format** menu. Select **Number** in the **Category** box. Click **1** in the **Decimal places** box, then click **OK**. Select **I8** through **L14**. Follow these steps again, but click **2** in the **Decimal places** box.

7. Select cells **J14** through **L14**. Follow the steps above to place **$** in front of these amounts by choosing **Currency**.

8. Select cells **B14** through **L14** to enclose in a shaded border. Click **Format**, **Cells**, and **Border**. Click the **Top**, **Bottom**, **Left**, and **Right** boxes. Select the double lines in the **Style** box. Click the **Patterns** tab. Select a color for your shading color. Click **OK**.

9. Select cell **A12**. Click **Insert**, **Cells**, and **Shift Cells Down** to move **TOTAL** to the same row as the total amounts.

10. Save and print the file. Keep it open for the next Step-by-Step.

Sorting Spreadsheet Data

Sorting is organizing or rearranging data in either ascending or descending order. When you sort data in *ascending* order, the alphabetic information will be arranged in ABC order and numeric information will sort from the lowest to the highest number. When you sort data in *descending* order, alphabetic information will be sorted from Z to A and numbers from highest to lowest. To sort data:

1. Select the text to be sorted.
2. Choose Sort from the Data menu.
3. When the Sort dialog box opens, the column you selected is identified. Click either the Ascending or Descending radio button.
4. If the Sort Warning dialog box appears, click Continue with current selection.
5. Click Sort.

Extra for Experts

Use AutoFormat to format the spreadsheet with a professional look. The format you choose should depend upon the type of spreadsheet you need and the audience for your spreadsheet.

Hot Tip

You can sort on more than one criterion by selecting Sort on the Data menu. For example, a list of students can be sorted-first by class, then by last name, then by first name.

Extra Challenge

Open the *Television Habits.xls* spreadsheet data file and sort it first by Show Type, then by Show Name.

Workbooks

A *workbook* is a group or collection of worksheets. You work on an individual worksheet by selecting a Sheet tab in the lower left area of the screen. Each worksheet can be assigned a name by double-clicking *Sheet#* on the tab and keying the name of the worksheet. You can insert a new worksheet by selecting Worksheets on the Insert menu. See Figure 8-11. To work on a different worksheet within a workbook, simply click on the desired sheet tab. If a worksheet in a workbook is no longer needed, right-click on the name of the worksheet (sheet tab) and click Delete. To change the name of a worksheet, right-click on the name of the worksheet (sheet tab) and click Rename.

You can also link worksheets in a workbook by creating a reference between cells on different worksheets. In other words, you can transfer data from one worksheet to another.

FIGURE 8-11
Sheet Tabs in a workbook

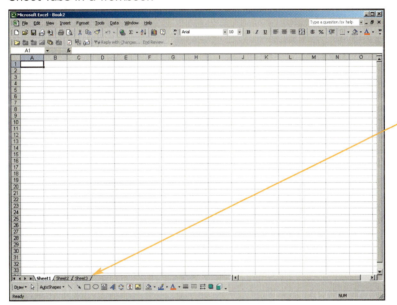

Hiding Data

If you don't want a portion of your worksheet available for others to see, or if certain information does not need to be displayed, you can hide this data. To hide a column:

1. Select the column you want to hide by clicking the column letter.
2. Right-click and select **Hide**. That column will disappear.
3. To unhide the column, position your insertion point between the columns adjacent to the hidden column, then right-click and select **Unhide**.

Headers and Footers

To repeat information at the top of every page of your spreadsheet, you can insert a header by selecting Headers and Footers on the View menu. You can place information at the bottom of every page of your spreadsheet by inserting a footer. You can choose a standard or custom header or footer. See Figure 8-12.

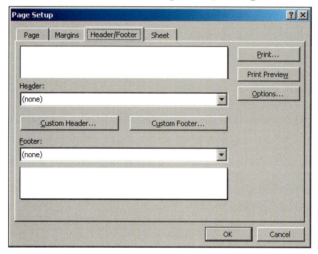

FIGURE 8-12
Header and Footer tab of Page Setup dialog box

 Ethics in Technology

PHYSICAL SECURITY

With all the concern about major computer crime, the subject of internal security may be overlooked. It is usually fairly easy for an unauthorized person to access systems by simply going to a valid user's desk.

Machines and consoles should be kept in a secure place. Only a limited number of persons should have access. A list of persons with access should be kept up to date. Some organizations actually have security guards to monitor computer rooms and control entry.

Remember that limited access means less opportunity for computer equipment and/or data to be stolen. That is why no alternative methods for getting into a computer room should be available. This includes hidden spare keys in an unsecured place.

Some organizations have taken computer security an extra step by securing equipment physically to desks and tables. This may seem like overkill, but you should protect your investment and your data by whatever means necessary.

Adding Objects in a Spreadsheet

Pictures and drawn objects can be added to a spreadsheet to enhance its appearance. If you want to add additional text, you can put it in a text box and position the text box anywhere on the spreadsheet. You can place arrow shapes on the spreadsheet to point out specific information.

> **Hot Tip**
>
> When resizing pictures, use only the corner handles. If you click and drag any of the middle handles, the picture will stretch out of proportion.

To insert a picture:

1. Select Picture from the Insert menu.
2. Select Clip Art. The Sort dialog box will appear. Click **OK** to close.
3. Click the Later button in the Add Clips to Organizer dialog box, if necessary.
4. Key the type or category of picture that you want in the Search text box in the Insert Clip Art task pane.
5. Click Search.
6. Scroll through the pictures that are shown using the vertical scroll bar at the right of the task bar.
7. Once you have located the picture you want, click it and the picture will appear in your document. See Figure 8-13.

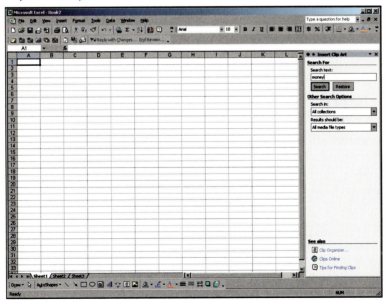

FIGURE 8-13
Clip Art task pane

8. If the picture is too large, click on the sizing handles and drag until the picture is the desired size. Move the picture to another location by clicking on it. When the pointer turns into a four-headed arrow, drag the picture to the desired position.

To insert a drawn object in your spreadsheet:

1. Click the object you want to use from the Drawing toolbar.
2. The insertion point will change to a crosshair. Place it in your document where you want it.
3. Click and drag the object until it has the shape and size you want.

STEP-BY-STEP 8.5

1. Select **Page Setup** on the **File** menu. Click the **Page** tab if it is not already selected. Click the **Landscape** radio button if it is not already selected. Click **OK**.

2. Select the names in column A. Click **Data** and **Sort**. Click **OK**. If a warning window appears, click **Continue with the current selection**. Click **Sort**. Click **OK**.

3. Hide column I, which shows the employees' pay rates. Click the **I** column to highlight it. Click the right mouse button. Select **Hide**.

4. Create a footer to show your name as the preparer of this payroll. Select **Header and Footer** on the **View** menu. Once the **Page Setup** dialog box opens, select **Custom Footer**. Click the left panel and key "Prepared by *Your Name*." Tab to the right panel and click the **Insert Date** tool. Click **OK**. Click **OK** again.

5. Insert a picture related to money in the upper left portion of the spreadsheet. Select **Picture** on the **Insert** menu. Select **Clip Art**. The Clip Art pane will display at the right of the screen. Key "**money**" in the **Search** text box. Click **Search**. Scroll through the pictures shown until you see one you want, and select it. If necessary, click on the sizing handles and adjust the size of the clip art. Drag it to the top left portion of the spreadsheet.

6. Save and print your file, then close it.

Creating Charts

Graphing the contents of a spreadsheet provides a visual arrangement of the data that makes it easier to understand. There are various types of chart formats available, including pie chart, column chart, bar chart, and line chart. Once a chart has been created, its type and elements can be modified.

To create a pie chart of the payroll spreadsheet:

1. Select the range of cells to be included in the chart.
2. Select Chart from the Insert menu.
3. Select Pie as the type of chart to be created.
4. You will see what your chart will look like. A screen showing the Data Range/Series will appear. Click Next.
5. A box with information identifying the data will appear at the left of the chart. This is called the legend. Click Next again.

> **Extra for Experts**
>
> Use the Part-time Payroll spreadsheet to prepare a pie chart to show the Net Earnings for employees. Print the chart. Select a different chart type showing the same data and move the legend to the right of the chart. Print the chart.

6. Enter the title of the chart in the Chart title box.
7. Click Next.
8. Click Finish.
9. The chart will appear on the screen. You can click on its border and move it to any location in the spreadsheet.

Using a Spreadsheet

Once spreadsheets have been created, the information can be analyzed to help make decisions, make changes, forecast future performance, or whatever is needed. One commonly used feature is the *what-if analysis*. It is the process of using a spreadsheet to test different scenarios or to apply a certain condition if a predefined condition exists. The IF function is used to perform this task.

> **Extra for Experts**
> Determine the bonus for each employee. Display the data in column M. Prepare a pie chart graphing the bonuses earned.

Ms. Perez has decided to give employees who work more than 20 hours per week a bonus of 2% of their gross pay. Those who do not work more than 20 hours will not get the bonus. The IF function to determine the bonus would be keyed as "IF(H7>20),(J7*2%),0." This means, "If the number in cell H7 (the hours per week) is greater than 20, then multiply the number in cell J7 (the gross pay) by 2%; otherwise, do nothing."

SUMMARY

In this lesson, you learned:

- The purpose of spreadsheet software is to enter, calculate, manipulate, and analyze numbers.
- An important part of a spreadsheet window consists of the toolbars.
- Columns are identified by letters. There are 256 columns in a spreadsheet.
- Rows are identified by numbers. There are 65,536 rows in a spreadsheet.
- The point at which a column and a row intersect is a cell.
- A cell that has been selected (highlighted or outlined with a black border) is referred to as an active cell.
- A range of cells is a group of closely situated cells.
- Cells containing alphabetic information are referred to as labels, and cells containing numeric information that can be calculated are referred to as values.
- A formula is a statement that performs a calculation. All formulas begin with the equal sign.
- A function is a built-in formula that is a shortcut for common calculations such as addition and average.
- Formulas may be copied to other cells by using several methods such as the copy-and-paste method.

- New rows and columns may be added to an existing spreadsheet; likewise, unwanted rows and columns can be deleted.
- Formatting can be added to a spreadsheet to improve its appearance.
- Selected data in a spreadsheet can be hidden so it will not be displayed or printed.
- A relative cell reference refers to cells that change when they are copied into other locations.
- An absolute cell reference refers to cells that do not change regardless of where they are copied.
- A spreadsheet should be saved often so that commands and formats entered are not lost.
- The contents of a spreadsheet can be displayed in chart format.
- Spreadsheet programs have many features available to make spreadsheets more efficient and attractive.

VOCABULARY Review

Define the following terms:

Absolute cell reference	Formula bar	Spreadsheet
Active cell	Function	Task pane
AutoFormat	Label	Value
Cell	Name box	What-if analysis
Cell range	Relative cell reference	Workbook
Formula	Sorting	Worksheet

REVIEW Questions

MULTIPLE CHOICE

Select the best response for the following statements.

1. The point at which a column and a row intersect is called a(n) _____.
   A. cell
   B. pointer
   C. value
   D. label

2. There are _____ columns in a spreadsheet.
   A. 65,536
   B. 26
   C. 256
   D. 2,182

3. The formula is keyed in the _____.
   A. Standard toolbar
   B. Formula bar
   C. Menu bar
   D. Formatting toolbar

4. Pie, bar, stacked, and line are examples of types of _____.
   A. spreadsheets
   B. cells
   C. formulas
   D. charts

5. Labels, values, formulas, and functions are types of _____ that can be entered into a spreadsheet.
   A. fonts
   B. data
   C. formats
   D. headings

TRUE / FALSE

Circle T if the statement is true or F if the statement is false.

T F 1. A spreadsheet program can be used to type letters.

T F 2. A spreadsheet is also referred to as a worksheet.

T F 3. The point at which a column and row intersect is a cell.

T F 4. Spreadsheets can also be printed in chart format.

T F 5. You can move around in a spreadsheet by using keys on the keyboard.

FILL IN THE BLANK

Complete the following sentences by writing the correct word or words in the blanks provided.

1. A cell address consists of a(n) _____ letter and a(n) _____ number.

2. Four types of data entered into a spreadsheet are _____, _____, _____, and _____.

3. To identify a cell as absolute, key a(n) _____ before the letter and number in the cell address.

4. The point at which a column and row meets is called a(n) _____.

5. All formulas should begin with a(n) _____.

PROJECTS

CROSS-CURRICULAR—MATH

During the past five years the cost of cars has increased quite drastically. Research the cost of at least five cars that were on the market five years ago and are still on the market today. Find the cost of those cars five years ago and their cost today. Record the information in a spreadsheet. Calculate the amount of increase in price for each car. Also create a chart showing the percentage of increase for each car. If you do your research on the Internet, the URL for most cars is *www.*, the name of the car, and *.com*. For example, the URL for Lexus is *www.lexus.com*.

CROSS-CURRICULAR—SCIENCE

Create a spreadsheet to record and compare the nutritional value of the same foods at three fast-food restaurants. Include the number of calories, amount of sodium, and the number of fat grams. Include a clip art object in the spreadsheet. Format the spreadsheet using AutoFormat.

CROSS-CURRICULAR—SOCIAL STUDIES

Use the Internet and other resources to find information concerning the most recent population figures in the five largest cities in your state. Record the information in a spreadsheet. Determine total population for the cities for each year. Prepare a chart for each year to show the population changes visually.

CROSS-CURRICULAR—LANGUAGE ARTS

The students in your class have had a reading contest during this past year. Create a spreadsheet to enter the information concerning the number of books read by each member in the class who participated. You may make up this information. Create formulas to determine the total number of books read by boys, the total number of books read by girls, and the total number of books read. Also determine the percentage of books read by the boys and the percentage read by the girls.

STUDENT	1ST SEMESTER	2ND SEMESTER	TOTAL	% READ
Girls				
Name				
Name				
Name				
Total				
Boys				
Name				
Name				
Name				
Total				
Grand Total				

 **WEB PROJECT**

Your math teacher has assigned you to compare the salaries of the current five top-paid athletes in baseball, basketball, and football. Include a column to indicate if the player is a college graduate; if so, include the name of the school from which he graduated. Also determine the average salary of these players. Search the Internet for the information to complete your task.

 TEAMWORK PROJECT

Many spreadsheet programs have templates available that make using them even more efficient. Access the Internet and use your search engine to find information about spreadsheet template files that can be used for spreadsheet applications. Identify the template file(s) found, and describe how it/they can be used with a spreadsheet program. Use search terms such as *spreadsheet*, *template*, *files*, and so on, to help narrow your search.

Your supervisor has asked you and one other employee to identify spreadsheet templates that would increase the efficiency of the video store. You are to identify the templates and give a description of each.

LESSON 9

DATABASES

OBJECTIVES
When you complete this lesson, you will be able to:
- Define the purpose of a database.
- Identify uses of databases.
- Identify and define the components of a database.
- Plan, design, and create a database.
- Create a table and enter records.
- Modify a table structure.
- Perform queries.
- Sort tables.
- Modify data in a table.
- Create and use forms and reports.

Estimated Time: 1.5 hours

VOCABULARY
Ascending sort
Database
Datasheet view
Descending sort
Design view
Field
Form
Primary key
Query
Record
Report
Table

You were recently elected secretary of your school's Future Business Leaders of America chapter and have decided to create a database to maintain many of the records for the chapter. Previously, secretaries recorded this information manually in a notebook, which was not a very efficient way to have the information available for use. Recording information regarding the membership in a database would be very helpful to the chapter. Information could be retrieved in many different ways. A printout of just officers could be done; a printout of various committee members would be a snap. Even a list of members who have not paid dues could be generated quickly!

What Is Database Software?

A *database* is a collection of related data. Database software is used to enter, store, maintain, and retrieve data as useful information. Individuals at home can also use a DBMS (database management system) to maintain address lists of friends and business contacts, a property inventory, or membership lists for organizations to which they belong. Businesses use database software to maintain customer files, inventory files, and personnel files. The files in a database can also be used to merge with other documents such as letters and sets of labels (such as address labels).

Creating a Database

Before you actually begin to design and develop your database, you must do some planning. You need to answer questions such as what information to include and how the information will be used. Once you have made these decisions, you are ready to create your database.

> **Did You Know?**
> Some popular examples of databases include libraries, the telephone directory, encyclopedias, and even the almanac!

Database Structure

Let's look at the structure of a database for organizing your FBLA membership:

- A *field* is an individual piece or item of information. Examples of fields would be the member's name, address, telephone number, classification, office held, and dues paid.
- A *record* is a collection of fields. Each member would have a record consisting of all the fields that had been identified.
- A *table* is a group of records.

Figure 9-1 shows how fields and records are displayed in a table.

FIGURE 9-1
Fields and records

Before entering data into a database program, its structure must be created. This means that you will identify what information you want in your database, in other words, what field names you will use. Once this structure has been completed and saved, you can begin to enter the information about each member.

Now you are ready to create a database and table to organize and arrange the data to make it useful to you.

Lesson 9 Databases 207

To Create a Database

1. Launch your database program. You will see a Startup screen similar to Figure 9-2.

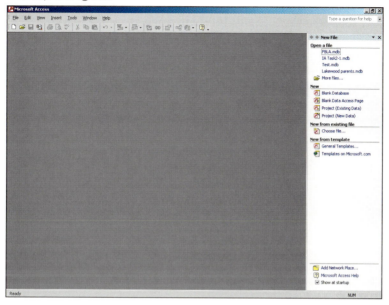

FIGURE 9-2
Startup dialog box

2. Click Blank Database in the New File task pane at the right of the screen. The File New Database dialog box will display. See Figure 9-3.

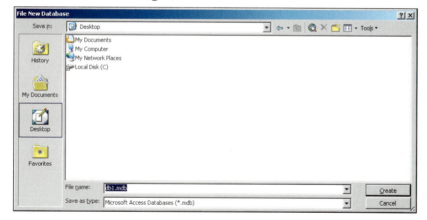

FIGURE 9-3
File New Database dialog box

3. Identify the location where your database will be stored and the name of your database in the File name box. Click Create.

4. You will see the name of the database in the title bar.

To Create a Table

Once the database has been created, the table will be created. You will identify the fields that you will use, their type, and a description. You will also include any additional information regarding a field such as its size or format.

1. While the Database dialog box is displayed, double-click Create table in Design view. See Figure 9-4. The Table Structure dialog box will open.

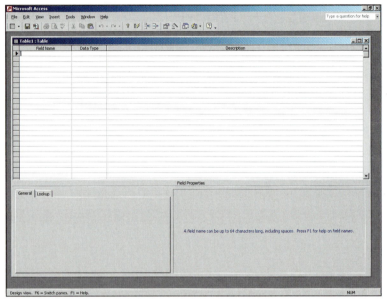

FIGURE 9-4
Table Structure dialog box

2. In the Field Name box, key the name of your first field. Field names may have up to 64 characters and spaces. However, it is best to make field names short and descriptive. Examples would be Last Name, First Name, Address, Birth Date, etc.

3. In the Data Type box, click the spin button to see a list of the different types of data. Click on the type that you need. It is important to select the accurate type of data. This will determine how the program is able to use the data. For example, a telephone number would not be a Number type, because it would not be used in mathematical computations. Sometimes you may need to format numbers to represent money. This would be a Currency type. See Table 9-1 for descriptions of the various data types available.

TABLE 9-1
Data type descriptions

DATA TYPE DESCRIPTIONS	
Data Type	**Description**
Text	The default data type. Consists of words and numbers that are not used for calculations. Entries can be up to 255 characters in length. Name, zip code, state, and phone number would be examples of Text type.
Memo	Memo type is used for alphanumeric data that is longer in length than Text data. It is usually used for longer information such as a note about a record. A Memo field can hold 65,535 characters.

TABLE 9-1 Continued
Data type descriptions

DATA TYPE DESCRIPTIONS	
Data Type	Description
Number	Number type is for digits only. This data can be used for calculations.
Date/Time	Date/Time type holds dates and times.
Currency	Currency data has decimal places and the dollar sign.
AutoNumber	The unique sequential number assigned by Access for each record entered.
Yes/No	Yes/No data consists of only Yes or No, True or False, and On or Off entries.
OLE Object	Used for more advanced features such as storing or linking objects in a table.
Hyperlink	Stores a hyperlink to a URL, other document, or other object.
Lookup Wizard	Creates a field that can be used to choose a value from another table or query.

4. List a brief description of the field in the Description box. This will not display in the table but will display in the status bar whenever you select the field.

5. Once you enter the name of a field and tab over to the Data box, the Field Properties box at the bottom of the screen will appear. See Figure 9-5. It is here you will change the field size and other formatting.

FIGURE 9-5
Table Structure Field Properties

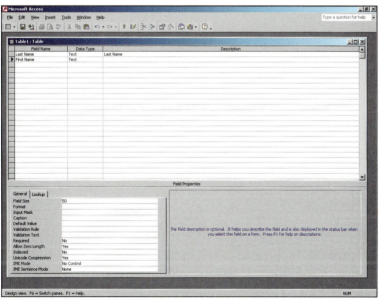

6. After you enter the field information, you will save the structure or design. Select Save on the File menu and the Save As dialog box will open. Key the name of the table in the Table Name box. Click OK.

7. You will be prompted to enter a primary key. A *primary key* uniquely identifies a field for each record. The information in this field will be different for each record. For example,

only one person would have an account number or social security number. The description that you would give to the field that you select as the primary key is *primary key*.

8. Click Yes, and then click the field that will be identified as the primary key. You may need to scroll to locate the field. Click the "key" icon on the Formatting toolbar. A "key" will appear to the left of the field name.

9. Select Close on the File menu. You will be returned to the Database dialog box and will see the name of your table listed.

> **Hot Tip**
> The primary key must always be identified.

STEP-BY-STEP 9.1

1. Launch your database software program. Click **Blank Database** in the **New File** task pane at the right of the screen.

2. Identify the location where your files will be stored and enter **FBLA** as the name of your database. Cick **Create**.

3. Now that the database has been created, create the Membership table. Double-click **Create table in Design view**.

4. Enter **LastName** in the **Field Name** box. Tab over to the **Data Type** box. You do not need to change the type because LastName is a Text type. Tab over to the **Description** box. Key **Member's last name**. (Some fields really don't require a description.)

5. The Properties area at the bottom of the screen appears. Change the **Field Size** to **15** by clicking in the space provided and keying **15**.

6. The first field has now been entered. To enter the next field, click on the second row in the table (just below the first field). Enter the following information for all fields:

Field Name	Type	Description	Field Size
FirstName	Text	Member's first name	15
Address	Text	Member's address	15
City	Text		15
State	Text		2
Zip	Text		5
Telephone	Text		8
StudentNo	Text		5
Office	Text	Office Held	15
Committee	Text	Committee Assignment	15
Dues Paid	Currency	Amount of dues paid	
Homeroom	Text	Homeroom Teacher	15

7. Once you have entered all fields, select **Save** on the **File** menu. Enter **Membership** as the Table Name.

8. Designate the StudentNo field as the primary key. Close the table.

STEP-BY-STEP 9.1 Continued

9. Figure 9-6 shows the table you just created.

10. Keep the database open for the next Step-by-Step.

FIGURE 9-6
FBLA membership table structure

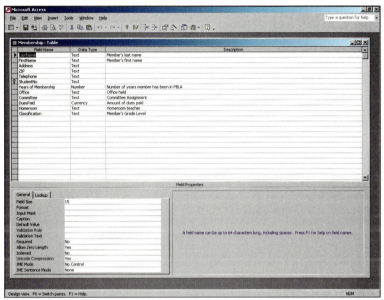

Modifying the Table Structure

Sometimes you may find that you need to make some changes to the table's structure. The field size may be too small or you may have misspelled a field name. You may want to add or delete fields. You can easily add fields at the bottom of your list of fields.

To Modify the Table Structure

1. Open the table. Switch to Design view (if you are not already there). Select the field that needs to be changed. If you want to correct spelling, delete incorrect text and replace with correct text. If you want to change the Data Type, click the spin arrow until the list appears, then click the type you want.

2. To insert a field between two fields, right-click the field that will appear below the new field. Select Insert Rows from the menu. This will place a blank row in your table just above the field you clicked on.

3. Some structure changes can be made from Datasheet view, such as widening the width of a field. Place the insertion point on the vertical line between the Field Name and Data Type columns, press and hold the left mouse button, and drag to the right to enlarge. Fields can also be deleted by clicking on the field name and then right-clicking and selecting Delete Columns.

Entering Data into a Table

The table structure was created in Design view. Datasheet view will be used to enter the data for each record. Views are formats used to display and work with the various objects such as queries, forms, and tables. There are four basic views:

- *Design view* — Used to create a table, form, query, and report
- *Datasheet view* — Displays a row-and-column view of the data in tables, forms, and queries
- *Form view* — Displays the records in a form
- *Preview* — Displays a form, report, table, or query as it will appear when printed

You can switch between Datasheet view and Design view by clicking the View tool on the Formatting toolbar.

Once you have created the table structure, you are ready to enter records. To enter data into a table:

1. Open the table by double-clicking the name of the table. You should be in Datasheet view. If you are not, click the View tool. See Figure 9-7.

2. Once the table opens, you will see the field names at the top of the table or grid.

3. Click in the box just beneath the first field name to key the first record. Key the first field information. Tab to the next field and key that information. Continue until all fields have been entered.

4. Key the data for the second record in the same manner. Continue until all records are entered.

> **Extra for Experts**
>
> Information in records can be cut or copied by highlighting the record in Datasheet view and clicking **Cut** or **Copy** on the **Edit** menu. Select Delete Record on the **Edit** menu to delete the record from the table.

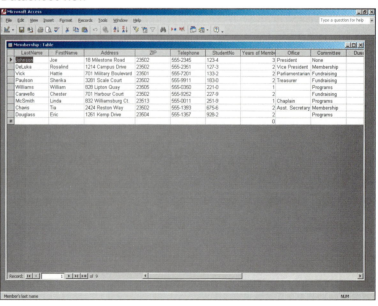

FIGURE 9-7
Datasheet view

Printing a Table

The entire table can be printed from Datasheet view. To print the table in landscape, select Page Setup on the File menu. Click the Page tab and the Landscape radio button. Select Print from the File menu. Once the Print dialog box opens you can select what you want to print. You have a choice of printing only selected records. See Figure 9-8.

FIGURE 9-8
Print dialog box

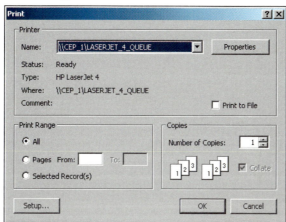

Sorting a Table

The information in a table can be sorted either in ascending or descending order. An *ascending sort* arranges records from A to Z or smallest to largest. A *descending sort* arranges records from Z to A or largest to smallest. Click the field name that you want sorted (in Datasheet view); the column will be highlighted. Click the Ascending Sort or Descending Sort tool on the Formatting toolbar. You may sort on any field.

> **Hot Tip**
> Data recorded in a table can be used to create mailing labels and mail merge documents.

STEP-BY-STEP 9.2

1. Open the table structure in Design view.

2. Add the following field at the bottom of the list:

Field Name	Type	Description	Field Size
Classification	Number	Member's grade level	10

3. Change the size of the Address field to be 25 instead of 15.

STEP-BY-STEP 9.2 Continued

4. Change to Datasheet view, and add the following records:

Joe Johnson	Rosalind DeLuka	Hattie Vick
18 Milestone Road	1214 Campus Drive	701 Military Boulevard
Norfolk, VA 23502	Norfolk, VA 23513	Norfolk, VA 23502
555-2345	555-2345	555-7201
12348	25190	12732
President	Vice President	Parliamentarian
None	Membership	Fundraising
$15	$15	$15
Smith	Martinez	Johnson
Senior	Junior	Sophomore
Sherika Paulson	Linda McSmith	Eric Douglass
3281 Scale Court	832 Williamsburg Ct.	1261 Kemp Drive
Norfolk, VA 23504	Norfolk, VA 23502	Norfolk, VA 23501
555-9911	555-0011	555-1357
92829	18301	13329
Treasurer	Chaplain	None
Fundraising	Programs	Programs
$15	$15	$0
Smith	Johnson	Wright
Sophomore	Freshman	Junior

5. Save these records by selecting **Save** on the **File** menu.

6. Print the datasheet in landscape.

7. Sort the table by **LastName** field. Print.

8. Keep the database open for the next Step-by-Step.

> ### Extra Challenge
> Create a database and table for a CD collection. Include fields such as Title, Artist, Type of Music, Date Purchased, and Cost. Print the table.

Querying a Database

A *query* is a question you ask about the data stored in a database. Querying a database means to search a database for specific records that meet a given criteria. For example, you may ask for a list of all members who live in the 23502 zip code. You may want to know the sophomores who live in that zip code.

You will need to use a comparison operator to match the range of information in your fields. For example, if you want to know which members live in the 23502 zip code, the comparison operator for Zip Code (the field to be searched) would be "*equal to.*" A data item can be equal to another, not equal to another, greater than another, greater than or equal to another, less than another, or less than or equal to another. You may also combine some of the operators. Some database programs may use additional operators. See Table 9-2.

TABLE 9-2
Comparison operators

COMPARISON OPERATORS	
Operator	**Meaning**
=	Equal to
>	Greater than
>=	Greater than or equal to
<	Less than
<=	Less than or equal to
< >	Not equal to
Between and **And**	Includes a range

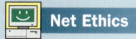
Net Ethics

JUNK E-MAIL

How many times have you received e-mail messages from unknown persons or organizations? Such messages are referred to as junk e-mail. It is much like junk mail you receive through the postal service: solicitations to purchase something. The difference between the two, however, is that many times the electronic junk mail contains obscene materials.

Junk e-mailers use two methods: spamming and spoofing. In spamming, the sender sends hundreds of thousands of e-mail messages at the same time to persons across a wide geographic location. They are able to use unique ways to get e-mail addresses. Some purchase authentic mailing lists; some purchase hacked (illegally obtained) mailing lists. They hope the more their so-called ads are seen, the greater the possibility of sales.

Spoofing enables junk e-mailers to hide their identity from the recipient. This makes it difficult to stop the excessive messages because the recipient does not know who is sending the messages.

You may ask how all these people get your e-mail address. Your e-mail is not private. It does not have the security of first-class mail. Whenever you enter personal information on the Internet, you make it possible for others to locate information about you.

There are ways for you to protect yourself when sending e-mail messages. The most effective method is encryption software. It scrambles letters according to a mathematical formula, and the person receiving the message uses the same formula to unscramble the letters and read your message.

To Create a Query in Design View

1. Open the database. Click Queries in the Objects menu of the Database dialog box. Select Create Query in Design view. See Figure 9-9.

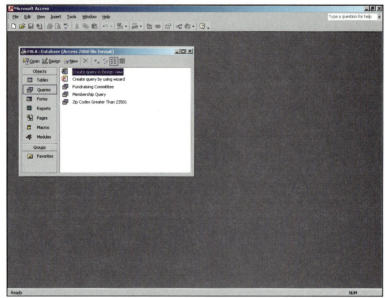

FIGURE 9-9
Create Query dialog box

2. The Show Table dialog box will display. See Figure 9-10. Click the name of the table you want to use. Click Add. Click Close.

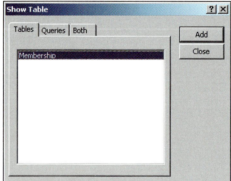

FIGURE 9-10
Show Table dialog box

3. The Select Query dialog box is in two sections. The top shows a Field Box that shows the fields in the table. The bottom shows a grid where you will enter the information needed to perform a query. See Figure 9-11.

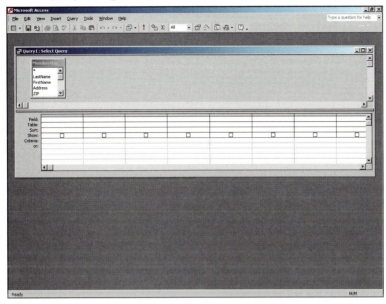

FIGURE 9-11
Select Query dialog box

4. You will need to enter the field name that you want the query to be based on in the Field box in the lower section of the grid. You may also add additional field names. You may do so by double-clicking the field name in the Field box and it will display in the lower grid. You may also click the spin arrow in the Field box in the lower grid. You will see a list of all the fields in the table. Click the field that you want.

5. In the Criteria row of the field you want to query, key the information you are looking for if it is exact. For example, key the zip code you want if you are looking for a specific zip code. If your search requires an operator, key it in the criteria row along with the information you are searching. Example: Key >23501 if you want zip code numbers that are higher than 23501. See Figure 9-12.

FIGURE 9-12
Filled-in Select Query dialog box

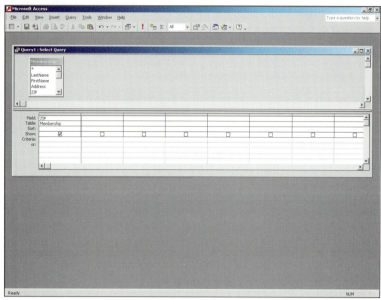

6. Once you have entered all query information, click the Run tool on the Formatting toolbar. You will see all the records that fit the query you entered. See Figure 9-13.

FIGURE 9-13
Query results

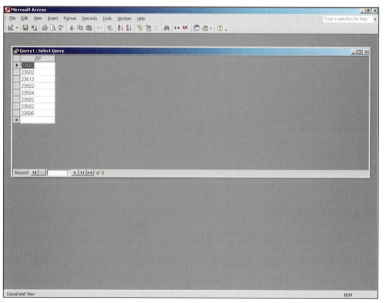

7. You may print the list of records.
8. If you want to keep this query, you must save it. Select Save on the File menu. Assign a name for the query (for example, **Zip Codes Greater Than 23501**) when prompted to do so. See Figure 9-14.

FIGURE 9-14
Save Query dialog box

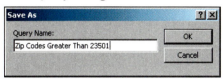

STEP-BY-STEP 9.3

1. Open the FBLA database, if it is not already open. You will create a query to print a list of all members in Johnson's homeroom.

2. Click **Queries** in the **Objects** box. Double-click **Create query in Design view**.

3. Click **Add**. Click **Close**.

4. Double-click the **Homeroom** field.

5. Key **Johnson** on the **Criteria** row.

6. Add the **LastName** and **FirstName** fields to the grid.

7. Click the **Run** tool.

8. Print the datasheet. Save it as **Homeroom**.

9. Keep the FBLA database open for the next Step-by-Step.

Creating and Using Forms

A *form* is an object you use to input, maintain, view, and print records in a database one record at a time. Although these activities can be performed using other functions of the software, forms allow you to customize the appearance of the form. The form can even be formatted attractively to include a logo. A form can be created in Design view, or more quickly, using the Form Wizard.

To Create a Form Using the Form Wizard:

1. Open the desired database file.
2. Click the Forms button in the Objects box.
3. Double-click Create form by using wizard. The Form Wizard dialog box will display. See Figure 9-15.

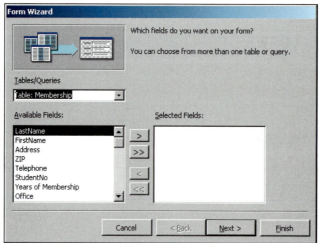

FIGURE 9-15
Form Wizard dialog box

4. The name of the current table should show in the Tables/Queries box. If it does not, click the spin arrow to see a list of tables. Click the one that you want to use.
5. In the Available Fields box you will see the list of fields in the table. You are to select the fields that you want in your form. Click the field you want,

> **Hot Tip**
>
> In some database software programs, the same form used to define the database fields can be used as a form to enter or edit data.

then click the > box. The field name should appear in the Selected Fields box. If you want to include all of the fields, click the >> button. See Figure 9-16.

FIGURE 9-16
Select fields

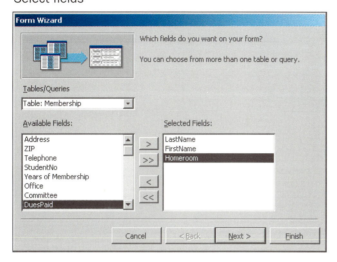

6. Click the Next button. Select the type of layout you want for your form. See Figure 9-17.

FIGURE 9-17
Form Wizard Layout dialog box

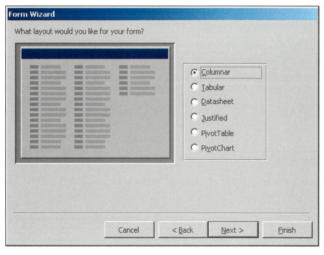

7. Click the Next button. Select the style of form you want. See Figure 9-18.

FIGURE 9-18
Form Wizard Style dialog box

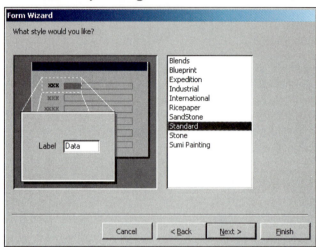

8. Click the Next button. Give your form a name. See Figure 9-19.

FIGURE 9-19
Form Wizard Query Title dialog box

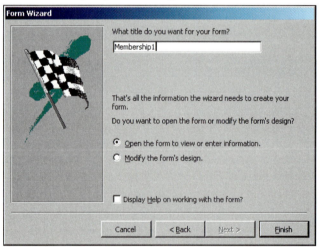

9. Click Finish. A completed form will appear on your screen.

Creating and Using a Report

An important feature of database management software is the ability to generate sophisticated *reports* that contain the contents of the database. These reports can be used to summarize data, pulling out only what is needed. You can decide what formatting you want to use, such as headings, spacing, and graphics. Once the report has been generated, you can decide which records you want included in the report, you can sort the report, and you can even insert a picture in the report.

To Create a Report

1. Open the desired database.
2. Click Reports in the Objects box.
3. Double-click Create report by using wizard. The Report Wizard dialog box will display. See Figure 9-20.

FIGURE 9-20
Report Wizard

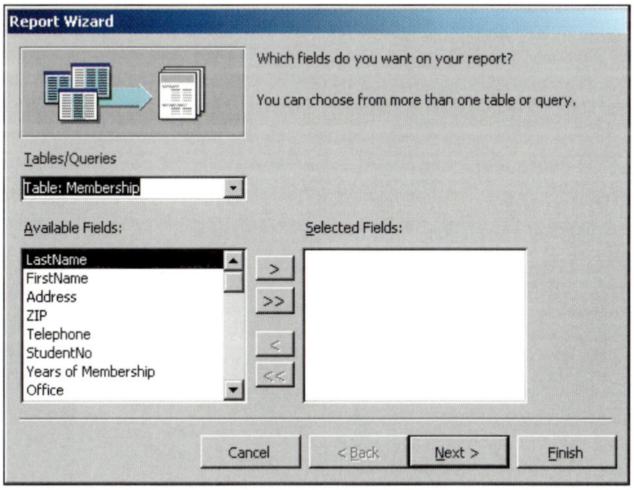

4. The name of the current table should show in the Tables/Queries box. If it does not, click the spin arrow until you see the name of the table you want. Click it.

5. In the Available Fields box you will see a list of the fields in the table. You are to select the fields that you want included in your report by clicking the field names and the > button. You may also double-click the field name to move it to the Selected Fields box. See Figure 9-21.

FIGURE 9-21
Report Wizard Selected Fields box

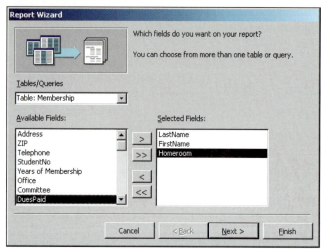

6. Click the Next button. If you want a special grouping by an identified field, select the field. See Figure 9-22.

FIGURE 9-22
Report Wizard Grouping dialog box

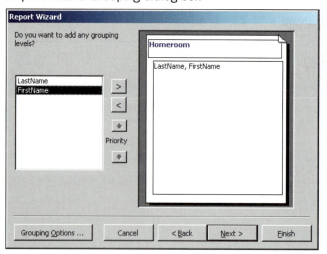

7. Click the Next button. Indicate which field you want to use to sort the report. See Figure 9-23.

FIGURE 9-23
Report Wizard Sorting dialog box

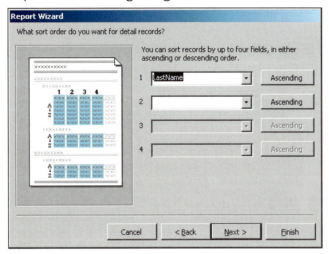

8. Click the Next button. Indicate the layout and style of the report by clicking the appropriate choices. See Figure 9-24.

FIGURE 9-24
Report Wizard Layout dialog box

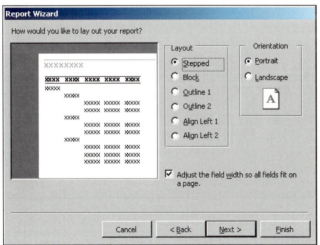

9. Click the Next button. Select the style of format you want for the report. See Figure 9-25.

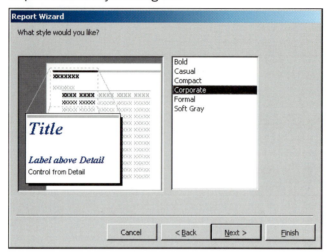

FIGURE 9-25
Report Wizard Style dialog box

10. Click the Next button. Give the report a name by keying the name in the appropriate box. See Figure 9-26.

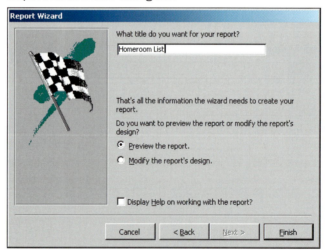

FIGURE 9-26
Report Wizard Title dialog box

11. Click Finish.
12. Save the report.

STEP-BY-STEP 9.4

1. Open the **Membership** table in the FBLA database.
2. Create a form using the Form Wizard.

STEP-BY-STEP 9.4 Continued

3. The name of the current table should appear in the **Tables/Queries** box. If not, click the spin arrow to see a list of tables from which you may choose.

4. Include all of the fields in the form by clicking **>>**. Click **Next**.

5. Select the **Columnar** layout for your form. (This is the default layout so you do not have to actually select it.) Click **Next**.

6. Select the **Standard** style for your form. (This is also the default style so you do not have to actually select it.) Click **Next**.

7. Name the form **Membership**.

8. Click **Finish**.

9. Select **Close** on the **File** menu. Leave your database software open for the next Step-by-Step.

STEP-BY-STEP 9.5

1. Open the **Membership** table in the FBLA database.

2. Create a report using the Report Wizard.

3. The name of the current table should appear in the **Tables/Queries** box. If not, click the spin arrow to see a list of tables from which you may choose.

4. Include the following fields in the report: **FirstName**, **LastName**, **Classification**, **Committee**, and **Dues Paid** by clicking **>** after selecting each field. Click **Next**.

5. Group the report by Classification by selecting the **Classification** field and clicking **>**. Click **Next**.

6. Sort the report by the **LastName** field by selecting this field in the box to the left of the **Ascending** box. Click **Next**.

7. Choose the default layout and orientation. Click **Next**.

8. Select a style of your choice by clicking your choice. Click **Next**.

9. Name this report **Classification**. Click **Finish**.

10. Print the report.

11. Select **Close** on the **File** menu.

12. Close your database software if you are finished working for the day.

SUMMARY

In this lesson, you learned:

- Databases allow for organizing, storing, maintaining, retrieving, and sorting data.
- The components of a database are fields, records, and tables.
- The database structure is designed and created first.
- The fields to be used in a table are identified in the structure. Any special attributes including field data type and size are also included in the structure.
- Once the table structure has been created, records may be added to the table.
- The structure may be modified to include any necessary changes.
- Data in a table may be sorted in ascending or descending order.
- Specific records may be selected based on a given criteria. This process is called performing a query.
- Forms are used to display the data of one record. Forms may be formatted in customized formats.
- A report is a formatted display (printed or on screen) of the contents of a table in a database.

VOCABULARY Review

Define the following terms:

Ascending sort	Design view	Query
Database	Field	Record
Datasheet view	Form	Report
Descending sort	Primary key	Table

REVIEW Questions

MULTIPLE CHOICE

Select the best response for the following statements.

1. To perform a query to select a *greater than* criteria, use the following comparison operator: _____.
   A. <
   B. =
   C. >
   D. >=

2. The size of a field is determined by the _____.
   A. Number of spaces required for the data that will fill the field
   B. Number of fields in the table
   C. Data type of the field
   D. Description of the field

3. The _____ uniquely identifies a field.
   A. Foreign key
   B. Primary key
   C. Memo field
   D. Esc key

4. _____ are not prepared with a database management program.
   A. Membership rosters
   B. Customer accounts
   C. Monthly budgets
   D. Resumes

5. A _____ is a group of records.
   A. Field
   B. Table
   C. Database
   D. File

TRUE/FALSE

Circle T if the statement is true or F if the statement is false.

T F 1. The foreign key uniquely identifies a record in a table.

T F 2. Updating a database is the process of adding, changing, and deleting records in a table to keep them current and accurate.

T F 3. Designing the table structure includes naming the fields, identifying the data type, choosing the size, and writing the description.

T F 4. It is better if field names are long and descriptive.

T F 5. Data in a table may be sorted in ascending or descending order.

FILL IN THE BLANK

Complete the following statements by writing the correct word or words in the blanks provided.

1. A(n) _____ is an organized collection of data.

2. A(n) _____ is a group of fields.

3. Perform a(n) _____ when you want to display specific records and fields.

4. The _____ feature of a database program allows you to generate printouts formatted with headings and other user-defined features.

5. Text, numeric, date, and memo are examples of _____.

CROSS-CURRICULAR *Projects*

MATH

Use the Internet and other resources to locate statistical information on six NFL teams. Create a database named NFL and a table named Stats. The table will consist of statistical information for the teams. Use the following fields: Team Name, Games Played, Games Won, Games Lost, Sudden Death, Yards Ran, Yards Rushed, and Season Points. Once you have entered the information into the table, print the entire table in Datasheet View. After the first printing, add information for two additional teams. Prepare a report and print the report with selected fields. You can find information at *www.espn.go.com* and also *www.askjeeves.com*.

SCIENCE

There have been quite a few hurricanes in certain parts of the country in recent years. Some of these hurricanes have been very costly in lives and dollars. Use the Internet to locate information on hurricanes during the past 10 years. Use your favorite search engine and the keyword *hurricanes*.

Create a database file containing the following information: name, year, state, classification, dollar damages, and lost lives. After entering the information in the database, print the entire file sorted by hurricane name, and again by the year of the hurricane. Answer the following questions using data from your database: (1) Which state had the most hurricanes during the 10-year period? (2) Which hurricane caused the most financial damage?

SOCIAL STUDIES

Use the Internet and other resources to find information on at least 15 African American inventors. Use your search engine with the keyword *inventors*. You can also visit *www.askjeeves.com* for the information.

Create a database to store the information you find. You will need the inventor's first name and last name, gender, nationality, invention, year of invention, and brief description of invention if necessary. Once you have entered the data, print a copy of the entire file. Use the query feature to organize and print your data in various ways. For example, print a query of all inventions made by women; print a query of all inventions that were made during a certain year.

LANGUAGE ARTS

Your instructor will give you a list of writers. Use the Internet and any other resources to find additional information on the writers such as birth date, place of birth, sex, type of writing, most recent book, publication date, and theme of book. Create a database containing these authors' information. Print the entire file sorted by authors' last names. Prepare additional printouts by performing queries requesting various scenarios such as a printout of female authors. Create a report listing the authors' names and most recent books and their publication dates.

WEB PROJECT

You have decided it is time to begin investigating various colleges and universities to determine which you will attend when you graduate. You have decided what you want to study and now need to find the best school for that field of study. However, there are other features that must be considered. These may include tuition, distance from home, required SAT score, student population, etc. Create a database to record college features and include as many fields as you feel necessary. You are to research at least six possible schools. Produce a report and several printouts showing different sorts, such as all colleges with tuition under a certain amount or schools in a given state. Also generate a file of labels for the colleges' addresses.

 TEAMWORK PROJECT

Your store manager at Vista Multimedia, Ms. Perez, has asked you and the other part-time employees to work together to design a report format for displaying videos whose shelf lives have expired and are for sale at a reduced rate. The report should have an appropriate title and headings over columns (fields). You are to sort the videos in groupings by type of movie such as Comedy, Science Fiction, etc. You do not need to print the report from the database. She just wants to see what the format would look like. Use your word-processing software to prepare the report.

LESSON 10

Presentation Graphics and Multimedia

OBJECTIVES

Upon completion of this lesson, you should be able to:

- Describe presentation graphics software.
- Explain the advantage of using visuals.
- Create a presentation.
- Work in different views.
- Insert new slides.
- Delete slides.
- Select appropriate slide layouts.
- Add design.
- Add charts and WordArt.
- Add transitions and animations, and customize backgrounds.
- Print a presentation and handouts.
- Describe effective presentation rules.
- Identify some presentation tips and hints.
- Add animated GIFS to a presentation.
- Add a music background to a presentation.
- Describe advantages and disadvantages of adding multimedia effects to a presentation.

Estimated Time: 1.5 hours

VOCABULARY

Animated GIF
Animation
Charts
Design templates
Electronic presentation
Multimedia
Plug-ins
Presentation graphics program
Transitions

Have you given a report in front of a class recently? Or have you listened to a report by a classmate or a lecture by your teacher? If so, you may have noticed that no matter how interesting the subject matter or how dynamic the speaker, it's still hard to keep everyone's attention. One attention-holding technique is to include visuals, such as those in a presentation graphics program. This is not the complete answer to the problem, but presentation graphics software will help. If you have a flair for graphics, there's almost no limit to what you can do.

Using Visuals in a Presentation

Ms. Perez, Vista Multimedia store manager, is giving a presentation tomorrow on a new in-store feature. She has purchased special equipment for creating a Digital Versatile Disk (DVD). The general public can rent the equipment and create DVDs. The president and other officers of Vista Multimedia are eager to learn about the project.

Ms. Perez is anxious about the presentation and asks you for advice. You suggest that she use a *presentation graphics program.* You explain to her that she can use this software to create a slide sequence of ideas and pictures that support her presentation. Equipment requirements for the presentation include a portable projector and computer—all of which she has available. See Figure 10-1.

FIGURE 10-1
A presentation using a projector and presentation graphics

Overview

Presentation graphics programs are used in business and education. Using this software, a computer, and a projector for an on-screen or *electronic presentation* allows the speaker to present a variety of special effects and features. Presentation graphics programs are excellent for creating on-screen shows, but that's not the only output option. Other options include the following:

- *Self-running presentation:* For example, you are participating in a science fair. You can set up a self-running presentation illustrating your project. When the presentation is completed, it automatically restarts.

- *Online meetings:* You can use a program like Microsoft's NetMeeting and share a presentation in real time (occurring immediately) with classmates at a neighboring school or in a neighboring country.

- *Presentation broadcasting:* You can use the Web to broadcast your presentation to classmates all over the world.
- *Web presentation:* Once you create your presentation, you can save it as a Web or HTML document, and upload it onto your school's Web site.
- *Overhead transparencies:* If you don't have access to a computer and projector for your presentation, you can create and print either black and white or color transparencies using plastic transparency acetate sheets in your printer.
- *35mm slides:* Some schools may not have computers and projectors in every classroom, but most schools have slide projectors. You can save each screen as a separate slide, then have them converted to 35mm slides.
- *Audience handouts:* Printed handouts support your presentation. Smaller versions of your slides can be printed two, three, six, or nine to a page.

Several software companies produce presentation graphics programs. Some of the more popular of these include the following:

- Microsoft PowerPoint—both Macintosh and Windows versions
- Corel Presentations
- Lotus Freelance

Creating a Presentation

Ms. Perez is impressed with your presentation graphics knowledge. In fact, she is so impressed that she has asked you to help her create the presentation for the big meeting next week. Most presentation programs contain the same features. In this lesson, the illustrations are from Microsoft's PowerPoint 2002 presentation program.

Did You Know?

We are witnessing many innovative uses of presentation graphics software. Accountants, engineers, teachers, and other professionals all use this software. However, one of the most dramatic and unique uses of presentation graphics software is by attorneys in courtrooms.

Internet

Looking for tips, tools, techniques, and technology for creating and delivering more effective presentations? You can visit www.presentations.com for this information and more. You can even sign up for a free subscription to *Presentations* magazine.

To create a presentation:

1. Launch your presentation program. You will see the startup screen with the task pane. The task pane displays three options for creating new presentations and one option for using existing presentations. See Figure 10-2.

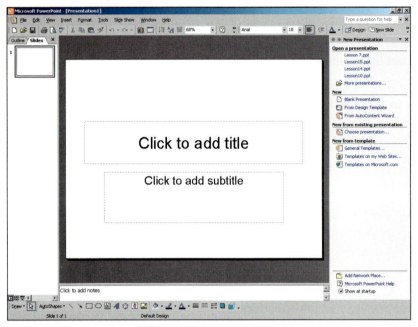

FIGURE 10-2
PowerPoint startup screen

2. You may select any of the three options to begin your presentation. However, you will use the Blank Presentation option in this lesson. Once you click Blank Presentation, you will see the Slide Layout task pane. See Figure 10-3.

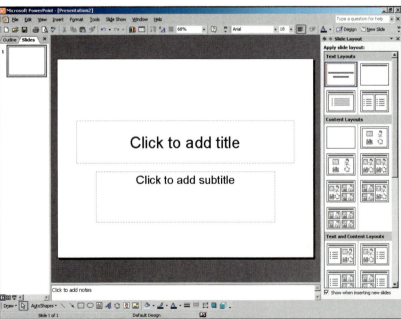

FIGURE 10-3
Slide Layout task pane

3. The software provides predesigned layouts for each slide. If you place your insertion point over each layout in the task pane, the slide layout will be revealed. The layout of a slide is determined by the type of information that will appear on the slide. The first slide in every presentation is the title slide. This is the layout of the current slide on the screen.

4. Click inside the first box on the slide and key the title of the slide presentation.

5. Click inside the second box on the slide and key the subtitle of the slide presentation or the name of the presenter or any other information that should appear on the title slide.

6. Next, you apply a design template. A *design template* contains color schemes with custom formatting and styled fonts, all designed to create a special look. Click Design on the Formatting toolbar to see a menu of the various designs available. Scroll the list to find one you would like to use. Click it to add this design to your slide. The same design can be used throughout the slide presentation, or you may change the design on selected slides.

7. Insert a new slide by clicking the New Slide tool on the Formatting toolbar. The design you chose for the Title slide will already be applied to the new slide. See Figure 10-4.

FIGURE 10-4
Design templates

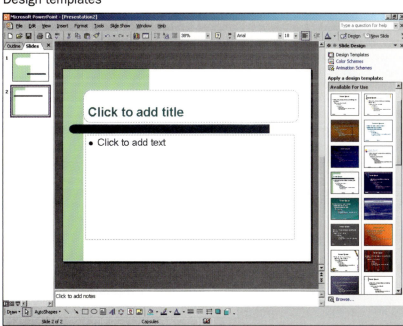

8. You can add animation to each of the bulleted items on a slide. When you add animation to a slide, you add a sound or visual effect. This is one of the elements that create a lively presentation for your audience. To add animation to a slide, click Animation Schemes in the task pane. If you want this animation applied to all slides, click the Apply to All Slides button. When the presentation is played, each bulleted item will appear individually in the selected animation scheme. See Figure 10-5.

Hot Tip

The color scheme can be changed on the designs. Font color as well as size can also be changed on slides.

FIGURE 10-5
Animation Schemes

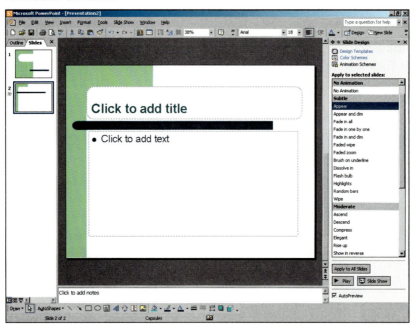

9. Transitions also add interest to presentations. *Transitions* are special effects that display when you move from slide to slide. If Slide Transition is not displayed at the top of the task pane, press the down arrow until you see Slide Transition, and then select it. You may choose the type of transition and change its speed. The same transition may be added to all slides, or a different transition can be added to each slide. See Figure 10-6.

FIGURE 10-6
Slide Transition task pane

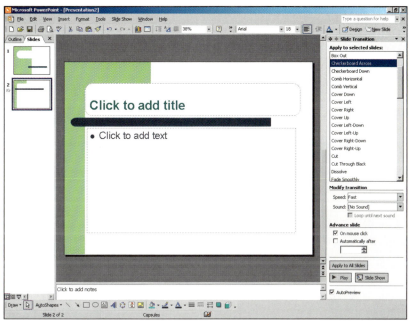

STEP-BY-STEP 10.1

1. Launch your presentation graphics program.

2. Click **Blank Presentation**.

3. The first slide is in the Title slide layout. Click inside the top text box and key **Vista Multimedia**. Click inside the bottom text box and key **DVD Creation Project**.

4. Select a design template of your choice.

5. Apply animation of your choice. Apply to all slides.

6. Apply the transition of your choice. Apply to all slides.

7. Add a new slide. Select **Title, Text, ClipArt** slide layout. Key **Status of DVD Creation Project** in the top text box. Key **On Time** as the first bullet item and press **Enter**. Key **Profitable** as the second bullet item and press **Enter**. Key **Popular** as the third bullet item.

8. Add a new slide. Select **Title and Text** slide layout. Key **Technology** as the title of this new slide. Key the following bullets: **Technical Problems, Copyright Issues, Software Problems, Hardware Problems,** and **Equipment Availability**.

> **Internet**
>
> Need a quick guide to preparing presentations? Check out www.mhhe.com/socscience/ comm/lucas/student/birdsell/ birdsell12.htm. You can find lots of tips and hints that will help make you a better presenter.

STEP-BY-STEP 10.1 Continued

9. Save the file with the name **DVD Creation Project**.

10. Close the file. Keep your presentation software program open for the next Step-by-Step.

Working in Different Views

Presentation software graphic programs come with different views to help you while you are creating a presentation. The two main views are Normal view and Slide Sorter view. You can easily switch between views by clicking the appropriate buttons. See Figure 10-7.

FIGURE 10-7
View buttons

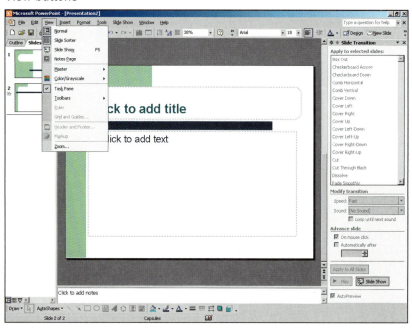

- **Normal view** contains four panes—the outline pane, slide pane, task pane, and notes pane. These panes let you work on all parts of your presentation from one screen. Adjust the size of the different panes by dragging the pane borders. Normal view was shown in Figure 10-3.

- **Notes Page view** displays your slides at the top of the page with speaker notes for each slide in the notes pane at the bottom of the page. To add speaker notes, click Speaker Notes on the Formatting toolbar. The Speaker Notes pane will display on the screen below the slide. Click in the pane and key notes or information related to the slide. You can print this view and use the notes as you give your presentation.

- **Outline view (pane)** shows an outline of the presentation's text. Use this view to organize and develop the content of your presentation.

- **Slide Sorter view** displays thumbnails or miniature images of all slides in your presentation. This view may be used to add transitions and animations and to add, delete, and move slides.

- **Slide view** displays a full-screen image of each slide. See Figure 10-8.

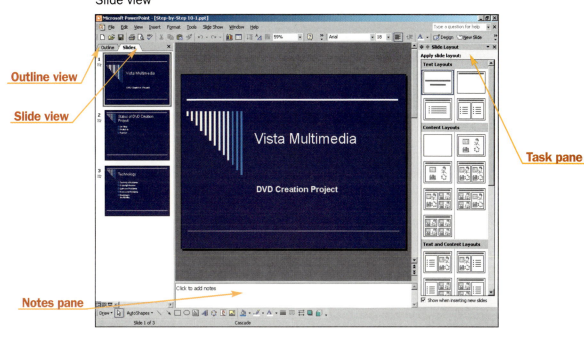

FIGURE 10-8
Slide view

- **Slide Show view** plays your presentation as you will present it to your audience.

Add Clip Art to Your Presentation

Adding clip art to your presentation will enhance its visual appeal and make your presentation look professional. PowerPoint has "moving clip art" that will make your presentations come alive. You can use moving clip art by selecting Movies and Sound on the Insert menu. In addition to clip art, other objects such as sound clips, videos, and photographs can be added to your presentation.

1. Chose a layout that has an open area for clip art and other objects. (However, you can insert clip art on any slide, no matter what its layout.)

2. If you select a slide with a clip art layout, you will see a box where the clip art will be added. Within that box is an icon of a man. Double click this icon and the clip art gallery will open. Key the name of the type of clip art you want and click Search.

3. Once a group of images appears, double-click the image you want to use and it will display on the slide. See Figure 10-9. You can move the image to various positions on the slide.

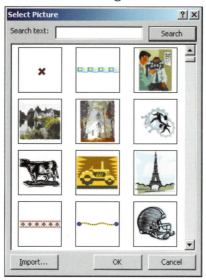

FIGURE 10-9
Select Picture dialog box

Adding a Chart to Your Presentation

Another popular feature of presentation software is charts. **Charts** help us to visualize statistical information and help to simplify complex data. Ms. Perez can use a chart in her presentation to show the projected growth for her DVD project over the next three years. Follow these steps to add a chart to a presentation:

1. Insert a new slide with the Title, Text and Chart layout. See Figure 10-10.

FIGURE 10-10
Title, Text, and Chart slide

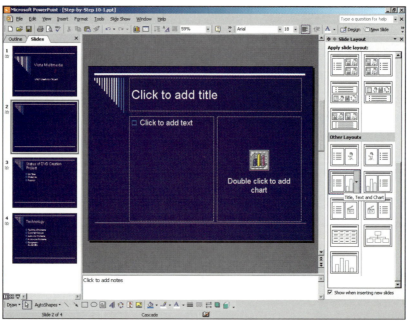

2. Click in the Click to add title box and key the title of the slide.
3. Click in the Click to add text box and key the text.
4. Double-click the chart icon on the slide to display the datasheet. See Figure 10-11.

FIGURE 10-11
Datasheet

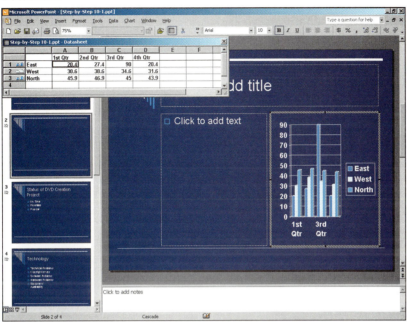

5. Select and delete all of the data in the datasheet. See Figure 10-12.

FIGURE 10-12
Datasheet with data deleted

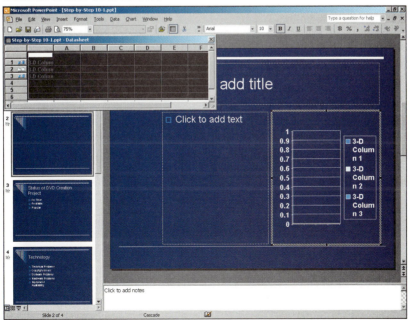

6. Click in the various cells to key the information for the chart.
7. Click the Chart Type tool on the Formatting toolbar. Select the desired type of chart.

Adding WordArt to a Presentation

After viewing the slide show, both you and Ms. Perez agree that Slide No. 3 could use a little more pizzazz. You suggest that perhaps some special text effects may be just what the slide needs. You can do this using a special feature called WordArt or TextArt. It will take support to accomplish the bullet points Ms. Perez listed on this slide. In this example, *support* is the word you will add to the slide.

> **Did You Know?**
> Most people read from left to right. Put the most important information in the upper-left corner and least important information in the lower-right corner.

 Ethics in Technology

COPYRIGHT ISSUES

The Internet and electronic media have made a major impact on copyright issues throughout the world. With one click of a mouse, anyone with an Internet connection can distribute copyrighted property to millions of Internet users. Many people feel that if it's on the Internet that it is fair game.

When people hear the word *copyright,* they tend to think of traditional media such as books, magazines, and so forth. Copyright applies to much more—it can include artwork, musical recordings, computer programs, videotapes, movies, maps, graphs, databases, and many other original creations. Copyright law would seem to be a simple one to enforce. However, the copyright law also grants a right of "fair use" to the public. This is where the confusion comes in—no one can agree on what's fair.

To evaluate the issue of "fair use," the law includes four aspects: (1) the purpose of the use, including a nonprofit educational purpose; (2) the nature of the copyrighted work; (3) the amount of the copying; and (4) the effect of the copying on the potential value of the original work.

One major issue of digital copyright is the future of music on the Internet. MP3, which is the technical abbreviation for a method of compressing audio files into digital format, allows users to download songs from the Internet to play back via their own computers or on Walkman-like players. Protection schemes are being developed in an effort to prevent copyright theft. An example of a protection scheme is that the music would expire after a certain date. However, many people point to the unsuccessful implementation of protection schemes for software some years back. These schemes did not work and it is doubtful if they will work for music.

1. From the Drawing toolbar located at the bottom of the screen, click Insert WordArt. See Figure 10-13.

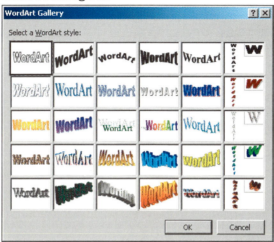

FIGURE 10-13
WordArt dialog box

2. Select the WordArt style of your choice and then click OK to display the Edit WordArt Text dialog box.

 Technology Careers

PRESENTATION EXPERT

Presentations are an organization's most direct communication effort. Many times, a presentation can make or break a sale or prevent a company from landing that big contract. As more and more employees are using computers and presentation graphics programs, companies are beginning to realize the importance of this media.

A growing trend in large companies is to hire a presentation expert to oversee the creation and delivery of presentations within the organization. Depending on the size of the company and the number of presentations required, this person might work alone or work as part of a media department. The media department generally functions as a service bureau for the rest of the company. The presentation manager may also be responsible for design. They must keep updated and be aware of technological advances in the areas of multimedia. This position will most likely require additional education such as workshops, conferences, and classes.

Many large companies may have a set of master slides and templates. All employees are expected to use these standards. The presentation manager may be responsible for creating these masters and templates and may even be responsible for teaching physical presentation delivery skills or coaching frequent speakers.

Since there are no certifications or degrees for presentation managers, many people employed in this field have graphics design and/or Web design backgrounds. They may or may not have a four-year degree. It is not unusual to find someone with a community college two-year degree in design or someone with design certifications employed in this type of job.

Salaries are varied and can range from as little as $20,000 to as much as $80,000 or more.

3. In the Edit WordArt Text dialog box, type the text you want to format, select any other options you want, and then click OK. See Figure 10-14. The WordArt is pasted into your slide. See Figure 10-15. WordArt is an *object*, which means you can click it to select it, move it, and resize it. You can also add or change effects to the text by using the tools on the WordArt and Drawing toolbars.

FIGURE 10-14
Edit WordArt Text dialog box

FIGURE 10-15
Slide with WordArt inserted

4. On the Standard toolbar, click Save.

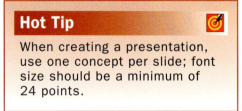

Hot Tip

When creating a presentation, use one concept per slide; font size should be a minimum of 24 points.

Playing Your Presentation

Once you have created the slides, you can run your presentation at any time.

1. Click the Slide Show View button. Your slides will be displayed with the transitions and animations that you applied. Click the left mouse button to advance slides.
2. To view the previous slide, click the right mouse button. Click Previous.
3. To end the slide show before it reaches the final slide, press Esc.

Printing Your Presentation

Most presentation programs provide many print options. For example, you can print your entire presentation—the slides, outline, notes, and audience handouts—in color, grayscale, or black and white. You can also print specific slides, handouts, notes pages, or outline pages. In this example, you print a handout for your audience.

1. On the File menu, click Print to display the Print dialog box.
2. In the lower-left corner, click the Print what: drop-down arrow and select Handouts. To the right under Handouts, notice that the number defaulted to 6 per page. You can easily change this to 2, 3, 4, or 9. See Figure 10-16.
3. Click OK to print your handout.

FIGURE 10-16
Print dialog box

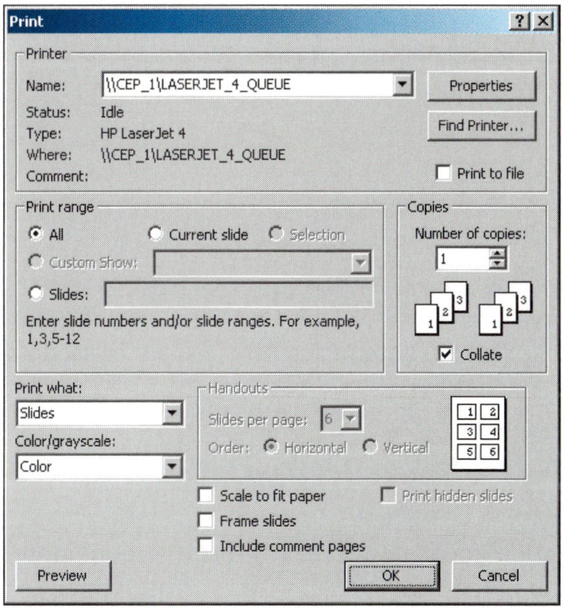

STEP-BY-STEP 10.2

1. Open the **DVD Creation Project** presentation, if it is not already open.

2. Display the second slide. Insert a CD graphic in the object box. (*Tip:* Key **CD** as your search word.)

3. Adjust the size of the graphic if it is too small by clicking on one of the corner sizing handles and dragging. You can also move the graphic to place it in the perfect spot.

4. Display the third slide. Insert a WordArt object. You may select your favorite style. Key **Support** as the text. Position the object on the screen where you would like it.

5. Insert a new slide with Title, Text, Chart layout. Key **Projected Growth** as the title.

6. Key the following bullets:
   - Three-Year growth
     - Year 1 – 12%
     - Year 2 – 18%
     - Year 3 – 22%

7. Double-click the chart icon and the datasheet will appear. Select and delete the data in the datasheet.

8. Click the first cell in column A and key **Year 1**. Key **Year 2** under column B and **Year 3** under column C.

9. In the cell under Year 1, key **12**; under Year 2, key **18**; and under Year 3, key **22**.

10. Click the **Chart Type** icon on the Formatting toolbar and select the **Column** chart. Close the datasheet.

11. Save the presentation.

12. Run the slide show.

13. Print the presentation as handouts with two slides per page.

14. Close the presentation. Shut down your computer if you are finished working for the day.

Preparing an Effective Presentation

You can use presentation tools to make any presentation more effective and interesting. However, beware! Presentation programs contain so many features and so many options, it is difficult to keep from getting carried away. The first-time user tends to add distracting sounds, animations, and excessive clip art to each slide. Some general presentation rules to consider are as follows:

- Keep it simple—this includes words and images.
- Use words or phrases—no sentences and no fine detail.

- Don't clutter the slide—leave a lot of white (blank) space.
- Be consistent—use the same design template, the same font, and so forth, on all of your slides.
- Project an image—use visuals to clarify or emphasize a point, to add variety, and to change focus.
- Organize the information—it should be easy to follow such as in an outline format.
- Create high contrast between the background and the text.
- Use color wisely.

A popular rule used by many designers is the rule of three. You divide your screen into thirds, both horizontally and vertically, and place your images one third of the way in. For example, the Figure 10-17 shows a screen divided into thirds, horizontally and vertically. Place the images at the points where the lines intersect. (See Figure 10-17.)

FIGURE 10-17
Rule of three table

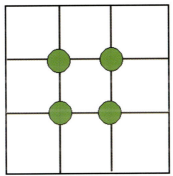

Delivering a Presentation

The TV show *60 Minutes* did a survey on people's worst fears and found that the number one fear is public speaking. Most of us, however, will at one time or another find ourselves in a position where we must talk to a group or give an oral presentation. Professional organizations like Toastmasters and companies such as Dale Carnegie train people in presentation skills. Even with training, most people will not become professional speakers overnight. But there are some special techniques you can use. If you practice and use some of the following suggestions, you may find that you actually enjoy public speaking.

- Plan—know the purpose of your presentation, plan your content, and know your audience.
- Prepare—have an attention-getting opener, be positive, and develop a memorable closing.
- Outline your main points—outlining helps you stay focused, but don't be afraid to skip some points or move ahead if that's what your audience wants.
- Talking—don't talk too slow or too fast; watch your audience and take your cue from them.
- Present—make eye contact, be natural and sincere; involve your audience.
- Questions—be sure to leave time at the end of your presentation to answer questions.

Using Multimedia

In the presentations you have created so far in this lesson, you have already seen a small example of a multimedia presentation. The presence of both text and graphics in a single slide show qualifies that presentation as a multimedia presentation because the combination of words and pictures in a presentation unites two different media in one package. Today however, the term multimedia has come to mean much more than the simple combination of text and pictures. While there are multiple definitions of exactly what comprises multimedia, in general *multimedia* has come to mean the use of text, graphics, audio, and video in some combination to create an effective means of communication and interaction. Multimedia technology can be a very effective tool in both non-Web-based applications, such as PowerPoint, or in Web-based projects.

Web-based Multimedia

Although you will not be creating any Web-based projects in this lesson, an overview of how multimedia is being used on the Internet will be helpful in understanding the overall concept of multimedia. The use of multimedia has caused a major stir on the Internet in the last few years. In the early years of the Internet and the World Wide Web (WWW), Web pages usually consisted of mainly text, and occasionally some graphics were added to a Web page to provide some visual appeal to the page. But, as anyone surfing the Web today can tell you, Web pages now make liberal use of multimedia effects to attract your attention. The Web has become a designer's paradise, with almost no limit to the effects a Web page can incorporate, including:

- **Simple animation**—Animated GIFs are easy to create and add motion to an otherwise simple Web page. An *animated GIF* is a series of GIF images that are each displayed for some period of time, and then the next image in the sequence is displayed. Depending on the time slice allocated to each image, the animation can appear to be very slow or very fast. Java applets and JavaScript code can also be added to Web pages to create basic animations and provide user interactivity.

- **Audio files**—Many Web sites now incorporate sound clips as background music when the page is loaded. Other Web sites include hyperlinks that can be accessed to play or download audio files that the creator of the site has created or obtained from some other source. MP3 is a very popular audio format today because MP3 files are compressed files, so they load or download very quickly, yet they retain high audio quality because of their digital format. Newer Web browsers include or can obtain plug-ins that can launch and play audio clips automatically. (*Plug-ins* are small software programs designed to work with a Web browser to perform a specific function that the browser cannot do by itself, such as play audio or video files.)

- **Video files**—Some Web sites now include movies that begin to play as soon as the page that contains the video clip is loaded. The page may launch an external video viewer or have one built in to the site that can be used to show the movie. Other sites have movies available for the user to view by selecting a hyperlink to load or download the clip. As with audio clips, Web browsers can include plug-ins to load the correct viewer based on the format of the movie, such as MPEG, WAV, MOV, or other formats.

- **Animated movies**—With modern software such as Macromedia's Flash and Director products, among others, you can create your own movies and animations that can play automatically as the page is loaded, or can be activated by the user through the use of interactive controls added to the Web page. Some of these products allow you to create very sophisticated effects and can really attract a user's attention to a Web page.

Presentation-based Multimedia

Most of the same multimedia effects used in Web-based projects can also be incorporated in a presentation software slide show. Audio and video clips can be added to presentations to make them more interesting and to attract and focus the viewer's attention at crucial moments in the slide show. For example, a business presentation may require a "question and answer" or a discussion period for each slide. Not all members of the audience will have the same interest in each slide, and their attention may wander during the course of a discussion. Adding a simple audio clip or even just an audio tone that sounds as new slide is displayed adds a multimedia effect to the presentation that alerts everyone in the audience to the fact that a new slide has just been shown.

Self-running presentations are sometimes found in small kiosks or display stands in shopping centers, advertising the stores that are found in the shopping center and the type of merchandise or product each merchant offers. A silent slide show running by itself would not attract much attention. Most shoppers would just walk by the display without ever noticing it. But, adding a catchy or popular song that plays in the background as each slide is displayed might cause a passerby to stop and watch the presentation for a few minutes.

A multimedia slide show can also include controls and navigation buttons that allow the user to interact with the presentation and control how it is presented. A department store could have a small display stand inside the main entrance with a user-controlled presentation. It might have a slide that lists the main departments of the store, with a link to a slide containing more information about that department. When the shopper selects the link using the specified controls, a new slide would display listing the merchandise that can be found there and directions to that part of the store. Each department slide could also include a small movie to show the merchandise the shopper will find in that department. After a set period of time, or at the user's control, the slide show would return to the main page, ready for the next shopper.

Multimedia Design Considerations

While multimedia can be used to add interest to a presentation or a Web site, there are consequences associated with the use of multimedia effects. Incorporating a lot of graphic images and audio and video/movie files into a Web site or a slide show increases the overall size of the site or slide show. The larger the size of a Web site or slide show, the longer it takes to load and the more disk space it takes to store it. Size is much more of a critical factor for a Web site than it is for a slide show, however. If a Web page that contains large audio or video files takes too long to load into a user's browser, the user may cancel and jump to some other Web site. When planning a multimedia Web site or slide show, keep the following design factors in mind.

Graphic Image Formats

There are many types of graphic images that can be used when creating a multimedia slide show. You can insert bitmapped images, such as TIF or BMP or EPS images, into a slide. You can insert vector images such as those created in Adobe Illustrator, Macromedia Freehand, or Corel Draw into your slides. You can also use compressed images, such as JPEG or GIF. Each image type has its own advantages and disadvantages.

Bitmapped images offer extremely high quality, but the price you pay for that quality is typically a very large file size. A vectored image also offers a high-quality image, but usually at a much smaller size. A vectored image with a lot of detail can be quite large, but generally will not be as large as a corresponding bitmapped file. Bitmapped and vectored images are typically used in printed material, which usually requires high-resolution images in the range of 300 to 600 dpi (dots per inch), or more. Compressed images such as JPEG and GIF offer a reasonable tradeoff between quality and size. JPEG and GIF images work very well in a video environment, such as a slide show or Web site, where screen resolution is typically only 72 dpi.

For example, study the images in Figure 10-18. This figure shows three different versions of a smiley face image, created in three different formats. The bitmapped file created at 300 dpi requires over 2.7M of storage space, and would require a considerable amount of time to download if being accessed over the Internet. The vector file was also created at 300 dpi, and being a fairly simple image without intricate detail, it only requires 103K of storage space. Converting that image to a JPEG format reduced the size to only 27K, but the image quality has not suffered greatly. The JPEG image works very well for "screen" viewing, but would not look as good printed as the bitmapped or vector image would. The JPEG version would load very quickly in a Web page and could be quickly transported over the Internet to a user's computer. When used in slide shows, JPEG images can greatly reduce the overall disk storage capacity and RAM memory required for the presentation yet still present a reasonably high level of quality when viewed on a monitor or projection screen.

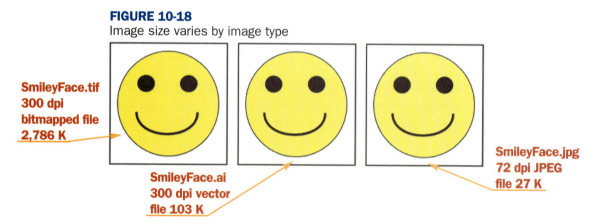

FIGURE 10-18
Image size varies by image type

Image format and size does not affect a slide show presentation nearly as much as it would a Web site. In most cases, only JPEG and GIF images are used on the Web. You can create hyperlinks to bitmapped and vector images so they can be downloaded, but most Web browsers cannot read and display those types of images. When creating or using images for a Web site, it is important to keep the overall size of the images as small as possible so they will download quickly and display easily.

Audio and Video Files

As with graphic images, the use of audio and video files can greatly increase the size of a Web page or a slide show, and in the case of a Web page can dramatically affect the download time required for the page. Music and video clips are usually fairly large files, no matter what format they are. They both can be used to add interest to either type of project, but take care not to overuse them. They should be used to enhance the message you are trying to convey, not just to impress the viewer with high-tech trickery.

When using an audio clip or music file for a presentation, you must consider the environment in which the presentation will be used. For example, the business presentation discussed earlier that includes a discussion period for each slide would not be a good place to include background music that plays for the duration of the slide show. It would be distracting and irritating for the people viewing the presentation. However, the shopping center kiosk presentation is an ideal place for a musical background. In a Web-based multimedia project, using the right music in the background can greatly enhance the overall "feel" of the Web site, but may also become annoying if someone is viewing or reading the page for a lengthy period of time. Many multimedia Web designers include a control somewhere on the page that enables the viewer to turn off the music if it becomes annoying or distracting.

The same basic guidelines for audio clips also apply to video clips. They can add interest to your project, but don't overuse them. In addition to the already discussed considerations, there are other factors to consider with video clips. Web browsers cannot automatically play most video clips, and you must somehow embed a viewer that can play the clip, or provide users with a link where they can obtain the viewer required to play the video. Movie clips can also be a problem with a slide show, as PowerPoint must know how to play the clip. It is possible to use the Windows Media Player to play most formats of video clips, but you cannot always be certain the computer used to play the presentation will have that software installed. PowerPoint can handle simple video clips, as provided in the PowerPoint Clip Organizer, but be cautious when attempting to imbed an MPEG, or MOV, or other type of movie into a PowerPoint slide.

> **Did You Know?**
>
> The use of multimedia effects in a Web-based project or a slide show has copyright implications, as discussed earlier in this lesson. Graphic images, audio clips, and video clips are all subject to copyright law. Unless you are creating them yourself, you may need permission to use them in your projects. This is particularly true of music clips downloaded from the Internet. Before downloading and using any type of graphic/audio/video, examine the page or site where you find each element and determine the reuse policy of the site or creator of the element.

Creating a Multimedia Presentation

Ms. Perez has asked you to create a self-running presentation that will be installed on the display booth in the shopping center where Vista Multimedia is located. The presentation should contain animation effects for the slide text, and will include some animated GIFs as well. The animated GIFs all contain a series of images of CD covers, DVDs, VHS movies, and video game titles to represent items that can be found at Vista Multimedia. The final animated GIF will be used to illustrate the Internet Café that is located at Vista Multimedia.

The presentation should include a song or audio clip that plays in the background while the presentation runs. The slide bullet points should indicate what type of merchandise can be found at Vista Multimedia, and the final slide in the slide show should indicate the store's location within the mall. The presentation can run a maximum of 45 seconds from start to finish.

STEP-BY-STEP 10.3

1. Launch your presentation graphics program. (PowerPoint 2002 was used to create the steps involved in this Step-By-Step exercise.)

2. Click **Blank Presentation**.

3. The first slide is in the Title slide layout. Click inside the top text box and key **Vista Multimedia**. Click inside the bottom text box and key **Your One-Stop Multimedia Rental Center**.

4. Select a design template of your choice.

STEP-BY-STEP 10.3 Continued

5. Apply animation of your choice for the slide title and subtitles. Apply to all slides.

6. Apply the transition effect of your choice. Set the slide to advance automatically after **6** seconds to create the self-running effect. Apply to all slides.

7. Add a new slide. Select the **Title**, **Text** and **Content** slide layout. Key **We Have CDs Of Every Type** in the title text box. Key **Pop/Rock** as the first bullet item and press **Enter**. Key **Country** as the second bullet item and press **Enter**. Key **Jazz** as the third bullet item, **Classical** as the fourth bullet item, and **Oldies** as the fifth and final bullet item.

8. Set a transition for each bullet point so each one enters immediately after the previous element, and set the speed to **Fast**. Apply any entrance effect of your choice. Click the **Content** placeholder, click the **Insert** menu, select **Picture**, and then click **From File**. Locate the file titled **CD_Animation.gif** supplied with this lesson and insert it. Size it to nicely fit the right half of the slide. Apply a transition effect of your choice, but reorder this element so it appears at the same time the first bullet point enters the slide.

9. Repeat steps 7 and 8 for four new slides. The slides should have titles of your choice pertaining to DVDs, VHS movies, video games, and the store's Internet Café. Each slide should have three to four bullet points pertaining to the title subject, and each will have an animated GIF in the content pane. The animated GIF files to use for these slides are, respectively, **DVD_Animation.gif**, **VHS_Animation.gif**, **GAME_Animation.gif,** and **Internet**. You may want to load the GIF images and play the slide to see the images before defining your bullet points. Apply the same transition/animation effects and sequences to these slides as were applied to the CD slide in step 8.

10. Insert a new slide, using the **Title and Text Over Content** layout. Add a title referring to the fact that Vista Multimedia is in the mall and close to the display stand. Add a text line indicating the store is near the mall's food court. Insert the image **Mall_Layout.jpeg** in the Content area. Apply animation effects similar to the other slides.

11. Save the file with the name **Mall Kiosk Show**.

12. Adjust the timing of the show so it runs no more than 45 seconds. You can cut the title slide down to 3 or 4 seconds to start with. Other slides may need to be trimmed back to 5 seconds, but you want the final slide to display at least 6 seconds so shoppers can easily find the store.

13. You now need to add the audio background. Return to and select slide 1, the Title slide. Insert an audio clip of your choice into this slide, and set it to play in a never-ending loop so the music will play as long as the slide show plays. A clip called **Jamaican.mid** has been supplied with the other files for this project if you are unable to find a satisfactory clip elsewhere. Position the animation element for the sound clip immediately after the Title element, and set its Start option to **With Previous**. Set the Timing options for the sound clip to play continuously. Set the Effect options so it plays through all seven slides, and select the **Hide while not playing** check box.

STEP-BY-STEP 10.3 Continued

14. Play the slide show, If your audio clip does not play through the entire slide show, modify its timing settings until it does. Be certain the show does not exceed the maximum allowable time of 45 seconds. When all slides look good to you and the show plays, with sound, for about 45 seconds, save your presentation.

15. Close the file and close your presentation software program.

SUMMARY

In this lesson, you learned:

- With presentations graphic software you can create a presentation to illustrate a sequence of ideas.
- Use presentation graphics software for on-screen shows, self-running presentations, online meetings, presentation broadcasting, Web presentation, overhead transparencies, audience handouts, and 35mm slides.
- Some of the more popular presentation graphics programs are Microsoft PowerPoint, Corel Presentation, and Lotus Freelance.
- Presentation graphics programs come equipped with different views to help you while you are creating a presentation. These views include Normal, Outline, Slide Sorter, Slide, and Slide Show.
- Presentation graphics programs come with a collection of professionally designed templates.
- The addition of clip art and animation can make your presentation more entertaining.
- You use WordArt or TextArt to create special text effects.
- When creating a presentation, do not use a feature unless it adds to the presentation.
- Some general presentation rules to consider are these: Keep it simple, use words or phrases, don't clutter, be consistent, project an image, organize the information, use contrast between the text and background, and use text wisely.
- When creating page or screen layouts, many designers use the rule of three.
- Some techniques to help you give a better presentation include planning, preparing, outlining, talking at a moderate rate, natural presence, and leaving time for questions.
- The use of multimedia effects can add interest to a presentation or a Web-based project.
- The use of multimedia effects can dramatically increase the size of a presentation or a Web page.
- Choosing the right format for graphics and audio/video clips is critical when creating a multimedia project.

Unit 2 Software

VOCABULARY *Review*

Define the following terms:

Animated GIF	Design templates	Plug-ins
Animation	Electronic presentation	Presentation graphics program
Charts	Multimedia	Transitions

REVIEW *Questions*

MULTIPLE CHOICE

Select the best response for the following statements.

1. With a presentations graphics software program, you can _____.
   A. create slides
   B. create handouts
   C. create overhead transparencies
   D. all of the above

2. Online meetings are conducted in _____.
   A. real time
   B. late time
   C. after 12 noon
   D. before 12 noon

3. Using a presentation program in Normal view, the screen is divided into _____ pane(s).
   A. one
   B. two
   C. three
   D. four

4. _____ are special effects that display when you move from slide to slide.
   A. Animations
   B. Programs
   C. Formats
   D. Transitions

5. A tool for creating special text effects is called _____.
   A. animation
   B. WordArt
   C. shadowing
   D. AutoShapes

TRUE/FALSE

Circle T if the statement is true or F if the statement is false.

T F 1. One presentation attention-holding technique is the use of visuals.

T F 2. Each slide in your presentation should contain a lot of detail.

T F 3. You should rarely use visuals in your presentation.

T F 4. Outline view shows an outline of the presentation's text.

T F 5. The only output option for presentation graphics programs is on-screen shows.

T F 6. The use of multimedia in a presentation does not affect the file size.

FILL IN THE BLANK

Complete the following sentences by writing the correct word or words in the blanks provided.

1. When in _____ view, image thumbnails are displayed.

2. _____ are special visual or sound effects that you can add to text or to an object.

3. To present an on-screen presentation, you need the software, a computer, and a _____.

4. A _____ presentation is one that automatically restarts.

5. You can put your presentation on the Web if you save it as a Web or _____ document.

6. _____ images provide high quality but a very large file size.

CROSS-CURRICULAR Projects

MATH

One of the most popular features of presentation graphics programs is charts or graphs. Look for some real-life statistical information. Check newspapers, sports data, magazines, and so on. Using this statistical information and using a presentation graphics program, create a three- or four-slide presentation.

SCIENCE

Select a topic dealing with a science issue that is in the news, such as nuclear weapons or anthrax. Conduct research on your topic and prepare a five- to six-slide presentation for your class. Include animation, sound, graphics, and other objects that will make the presentation interesting to your classmates. Print handouts to be distributed to the class.

SOCIAL STUDIES

Use the Internet and other resources to research an event in history such as the Civil War, the first man on the moon, the life of a notable person, the writing of the Constitution, or any topic in history that is interesting to you. Prepare an outline of the topic to use to create a presentation that you will give to your classmates. Make your presentation informative and exciting by using graphics, sound, animation, transitions, as well as various slide layouts.

LANGUAGE ARTS

Your Future Business Leaders of America chapter has volunteered to work at the local adult education center. The students at the center are all high school dropouts who are working to pass the GED test so that they will be able to either continue their education or find desirable employment. The members of your group will provide tutoring in math, computer skills, English, or writing. You have been asked to work with a group that is learning to write papers. You want to make this subject interesting to the students so you decide to develop a computer presentation. Include at least five slides, using graphics, sound, animation, various slide layouts, etc., in your presentation. Print a set of speaker's notes that you will use as you discuss each step in writing a paper. Print audience handouts for the students to use.

WEB PROJECT

You have just returned from a year abroad as an exchange student. You have been asked to prepare a slide presentation of your experience. Prepare an eight- to ten-slide presentation that should include information regarding the country and its culture, the school you attended, the family with which you lived, and any other interesting information. Research a country on the Web for information to use in your presentation. Use various slide layouts, animations, and graphics.

TEAMWORK PROJECT

Ms. Perez wants to share information regarding time management with the employees at Vista Multimedia. She asked you and the part-time employees to search the Web to find information on time management. She would like you to create a multimedia presentation showing five or six tips that employees can use to make better use of their time. Be sure to make the presentation interesting so it will be appealing to all employees.

LESSON 11

Integration

OBJECTIVES

Upon completion of this lesson, you should be able to:

- Import and export data between Microsoft Office applications.
- Create a form letter.
- Create mailing labels.

Estimated Time: 1.5 hours

VOCABULARY

Data source
Form letter
Integrated software
Mail merge
Main document
Software suites

The president of your Future Business Leaders of America chapter would like to send letters to members' homes regarding the candy sale and would like each member to receive an original letter addressed to him or her. He would also like the candy sale spreadsheet included in the body of the letter, rather than being sent as a separate sheet. This may sound like it will take quite a while to complete, but it will not.

You prepared the candy sale spreadsheet earlier. You already have the members' addresses in a database file. You only need to write one letter and import data from the database file and the spreadsheet file. Even the labels for the envelopes will be a breeze to prepare! This is possible by using the integration features of your software.

Software Integration

Integrated software is software that combines applications such as word processing, spreadsheet, database, and presentations into one program. The applications within an integrated software program can share data because of common user interfaces. In other words, many of the commands and features are the same or very similar. Once you have learned to use one software application in an integrated package, you are familiar with the menus, toolbars, etc., in the other applications. However, these applications are not full versions of the individual software programs. They generally contain only the main, basic commands. Microsoft Works is the most popular integrated software on the market. AppleWorks is another popular integrated software package.

Software suites, also known as application suites or office suites, are bundled sets of applications that are designed to work together. These software suites provide integration features such as cut and paste, and they also have additional tools that make it easy to move data from one application to another. The applications in a software suite are generally the full versions of the software.

Microsoft Office, WordPerfect Office, Lotus SmartSuite, and StarOffice are all popular software suites. In this book, we have been using Microsoft Office for all of the examples and illustrations.

Creating a Form Letter

Let's get started with your assigned task. First, you will create a form letter. A *form letter* is a letter prepared using word-processing software and information imported from a database file. This allows for individual original letters. In other words, all members will receive the same letter, addressed specifically to them. Other documents besides letters may also be prepared in which information from a database file may be imported.

To complete your FBLA mailing, you will first create a *main document*, which contains the information that will be in every letter. Then you will create the *data source*, which contains the data that varies in the letter, such as each recipient's name and address. Once these two documents are created, a *mail merge* is performed to "join" the two documents. *Merge fields,* or *field names,* are placeholders that are included in the main document. The merge fields show where data is to be inserted from the data source into the main document. Once the main document and the data source documents are merged, the merge fields will be replaced with individual information in every letter. Microsoft Office has a Mail Merge Wizard that guides you through creating form letters.

Create a Form Letter

1. Launch your word-processing program to create the main document. You will be creating a letter about the FBLA Candy Sale for this activity. (You may also use a document that already exists.)
2. Select Letters and Mailings on the Tools menu on the Formatting toolbar. Select Mail Merge Wizard on the submenu. The Mail Merge task pane appears at the right of the screen. See Figure 11-1.

FIGURE 11-1
Mail Merge Wizard task pane

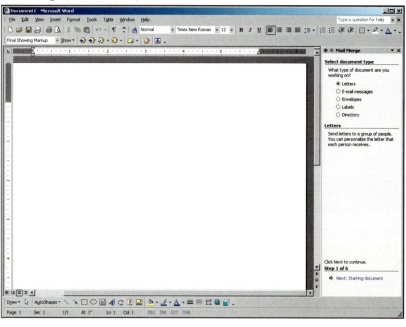

3. Letters should be selected in the Select document type section of the task pane. If it is not, select it.

4. Click Next: Starting document in the lower section of the task pane. A new task pane will appear. See Figure 11-2.

FIGURE 11-2
Mail Merge Wizard task pane

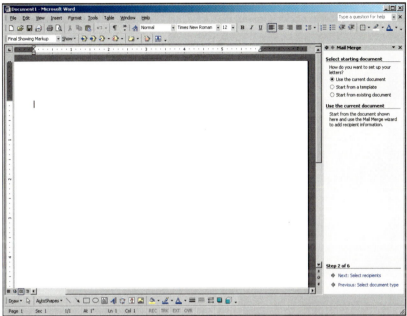

5. Select Use the current document. The Candy Sale letter will appear. See Figure 11-3.

FIGURE 11-3
Candy Sale letter

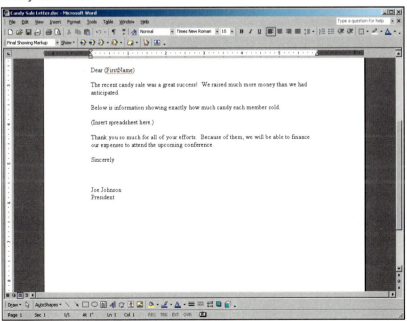

6. Click Next: Select recipients in the lower section of the task pane. A new task pane will appear. See Figure 11-4. Select Use an existing list.

FIGURE 11-4
Mail Merge Wizard task pane

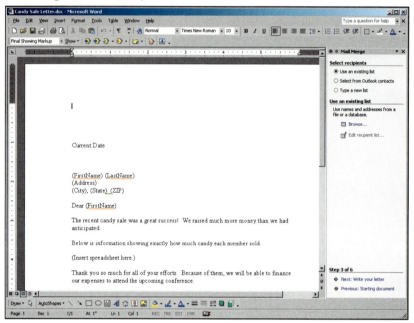

7. Click Browse to locate the data source file to be used. The Select Data Source dialog box will appear.
8. Click the down arrow in the Look in box until you locate the database file you want to use.
9. Click Next: Write your letter in the lower section of the task pane. Key the letter.

10. Click Address Block in the Write your letter section of the task pane. The Insert Address Block dialog box appears. See Figure 11-5. Scroll down the list to select the format you want to use for the address. The Preview Box at the bottom of the dialog box will show how the address will look. Select a format and click OK. The address merge field is inserted in the document. Press Enter twice.

FIGURE 11-5
Insert Address Block dialog box

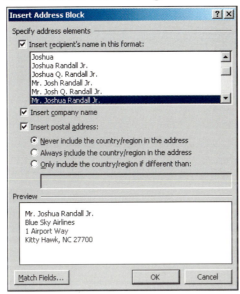

11. Key Dear and press the space bar once. Click More Items in the task pane. The Insert Merge Field dialog box appears. See Figure 11-6. Click the field you want inserted. Click Insert. Click Close. Follow the same procedure for other locations for merge fields. Press the Enter key twice after the salutation and key the remainder of the letter.

FIGURE 11-6
Insert Merge Field dialog box

12. When finished keying the letter, click Next: Preview your letters in the lower section of the task pane. You will see that the data from the database file is inserted into the merge fields. Scroll through the merged letters by clicking the Recipients button in the Preview Your Letters section of the task pane. There will be a letter for every person in your database. Save the file.

13. Click Next: Complete the merge in the lower section of the task pane. See Figure 11-7. You may print or edit all of the letters or selected letters from this pane.

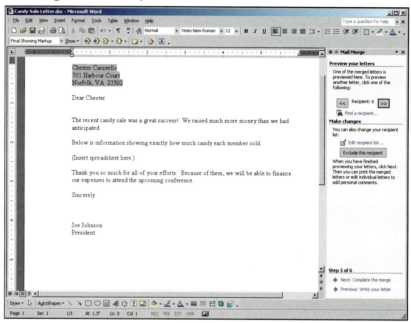

FIGURE 11-7
Mail Merge Wizard task pane

Now that we have gone over the steps for preparing a form letter, let's prepare the form letter for the candy sale. We will also import the Candy Sale spreadsheet into the letter.

STEP-BY-STEP 11.1

1. Launch Microsoft Access.

2. Open the Membership table in the FBLA database. Add the following two fields: **City** and **State**. (These fields were not included when the table was created.) Insert **Norfolk** as the city for each member and **Virginia** as the state for each member. Save the database file. Close Microsoft Access.

3. Launch Microsoft Word. Key the letter in Figure 11-3 as a form letter. Insert the merge fields as indicated in the letter.

4. Save the document as **Candy Sale Letter.doc**. Leave the document open.

5. Launch Microsoft Excel. Open the **FBLA Candy Sale.xls** file.

6. Select all of the spreadsheet except the title. Click the **Copy** tool on the Formatting toolbar.

7. Close Microsoft Excel. If you are asked if you wish to save the material that is on the Clipboard, click Yes.

8. The Candy Sale Letter document should be displayed on the screen. Place the insertion point at the position indicated in Figure 11-3 to insert the spreadsheet information.

9. Select **Paste Special** on the **Edit** menu. The cells that you copied from the FBLA Candy Sale spreadsheet will be inserted at the insertion point in the letter.

10. Press **Enter** so that there are two blank spaces below the table.

11. Print the letter. Save the document and exit Word.

Creating Mailing Labels

Now that the letter has been prepared, you are to prepare a set of mailing labels. This process is very similar to preparing the form letter. You will use a database file as your data source and a set of labels will be your main document. You will have an opportunity to select the database fields you want merged to the labels.

Create Mailing Labels

1. Launch Microsoft Word.

2. Select Letters and Mailings from the Tools menu on the Formatting toolbar. Select Mail Merge Wizard on the submenu. The Mail Merge task pane will appear at the right of the screen. See Figure 11-8.

FIGURE 11-8
Mail Merge Wizard task pane

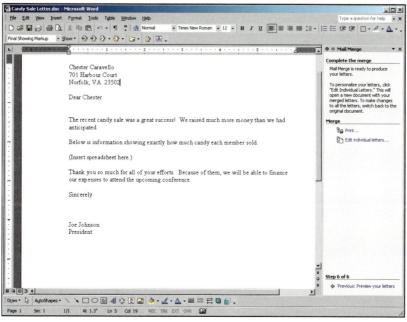

3. Select Labels in the Select document type section of the task pane. See Figure 11-9.

FIGURE 11-9
Labels Mail Merge task pane

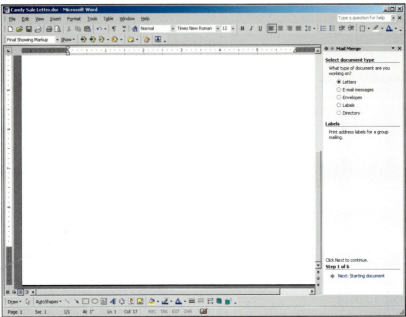

4. Click Next: Starting document in the lower section of the task pane. See Figure 11-10.

FIGURE 11-10
Labels Mail Merge task pane

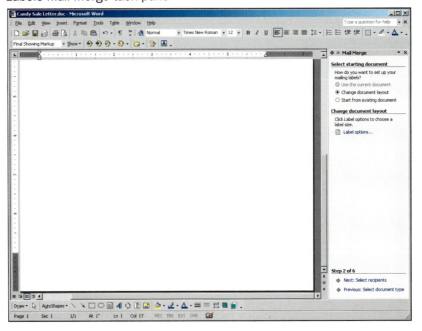

5. Click Label Options. The Label Options dialog box will open. See Figure 11-11. Select the Avery product number of the labels you will use. Click OK. A page of blank labels will appear.

FIGURE 11-11
Label Options dialog box

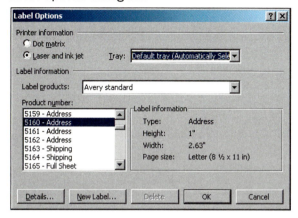

6. Click Next: Select recipients in the lower section of the task pane. A new pane will open. Use an existing list should be selected in the Select recipients section. See Figure 11-12.

FIGURE 11-12
Mail Merge Wizard task pane

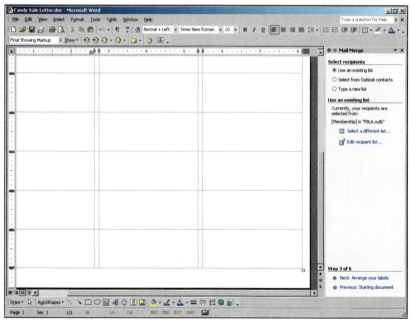

7. Click Browse. The Select Data Source dialog box appears. Scroll down until you locate the database file you want to use. See Figure 11-13.

FIGURE 11-13
Select Data Source dialog box

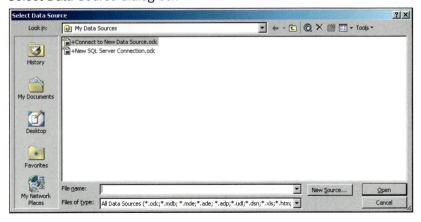

8. Click Next: Arrange your labels in the lower section of the task pane. Your insertion point should appear in the first label.

9. Click Address Block in the Arrange your labels section. The Insert Address Block dialog box appears. See Figure 11-14. Click OK. The Address Block merge field is inserted.

FIGURE 11-14
Insert Address Block dialog box

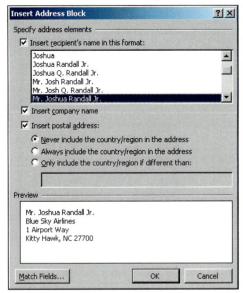

10. Scroll down to the bottom of the task pane and click Update all labels. The Address Block merge field will appear in all labels.

11. Click Next: Preview your labels in the lower section of the task pane. Scroll down to see all of the labels. See Figure 11-15.

FIGURE 11-15
Label preview

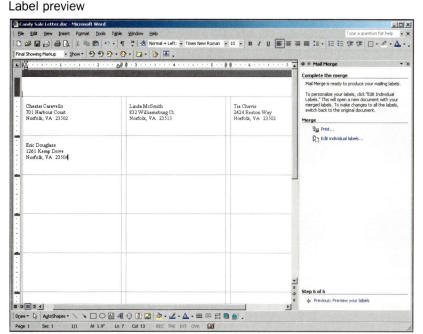

12. Click Next: Complete the merge in the lower section of the task pane. A new task pane appears. Click the print option to print the labels. You may choose to print all of the labels or specify which ones you want to print.

13. Save the label file.

STEP-BY-STEP 11.2

1. Launch Microsoft Word.

2. Prepare a set of mailing labels using the Membership Table in the FBLA database file. Use Avery 5160 address labels.

3. Save the label file as **Members Address Labels.doc**.

4. Print the labels and exit Word.

Importing Files

You can also link data from an Excel spreadsheet into an Access table. Remember, a spreadsheet is set up with rows and columns and so is a datasheet of an Access table. Each column represents a field and each row represents a record.

Link Data from an Excel Spreadsheet into an Access Table

1. Open the database file.
2. Select Get External Data on the File menu and select Import on the submenu. The Import dialog box appears. See Figure 11-16.

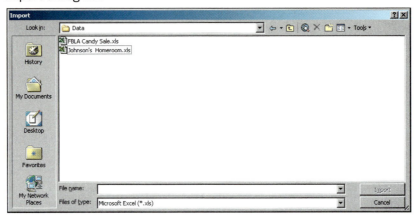

FIGURE 11-16
Import dialog box

3. Select Microsoft Excel in the Files of Type box at the bottom of the dialog box.
4. Locate the Excel file you want to use.
5. Click Import. The Import Spreadsheet Wizard dialog box will be displayed on the screen. See Figure 11-17.

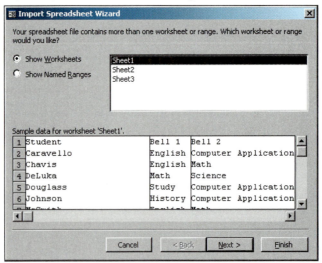

FIGURE 11-17
Import Spreadsheet Wizard dialog box

6. Click Next. The next dialog box will ask if the first row in the spreadsheet contains the column headings. This option should be checked. See Figure 11-18.

FIGURE 11-18
Import Spreadsheet Wizard dialog box

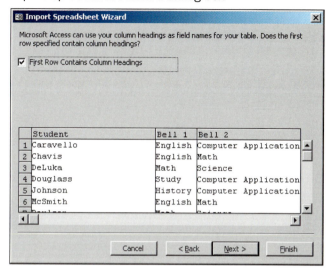

7. Click Next. A new dialog box will ask where you want to store your data. Select the In a New Table option. See Figure 11-19.

FIGURE 11-19
Import Spreadsheet Wizard dialog box

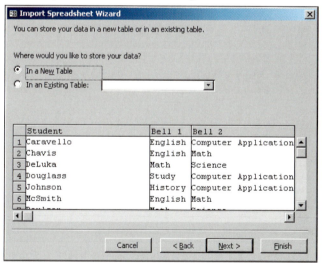

8. Click Next. You will identify the primary key in this dialog box or you can choose not to use a primary key. See Figure 11-20.

FIGURE 11-20
Import Spreadsheet Wizard dialog box

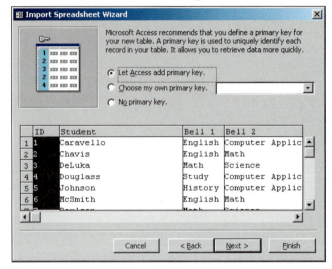

9. Click Next. Key the name of the new file in the Import to Table box. See Figure 11-21.

FIGURE 11-21
Import Spreadsheet Wizard dialog box

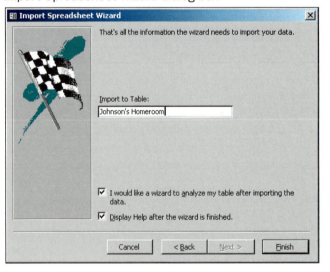

10. Click Finish.

11. Click OK to answer the message indicating that the wizard is complete.

12. The name of the new table will appear in the database window. You can now open the table.

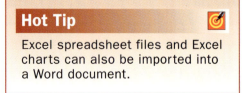

Hot Tip

Excel spreadsheet files and Excel charts can also be imported into a Word document.

Import a PowerPoint File into a Word File

1. Launch Microsoft PowerPoint.
2. Open a PowerPoint document.
3. Select Send to on the File menu on the Formatting toolbar. Select Microsoft Word on the submenu. The Send to Microsoft Word dialog box will appear. See Figure 11-22.

FIGURE 11-22
Send to Microsoft Word dialog box

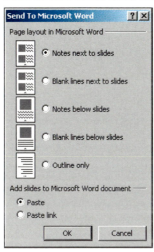

4. Select the layout you want. Click OK.
5. The selected layout will appear in a Word document. See Figure 11-23.

FIGURE 11-23
Word document with imported PowerPoint file

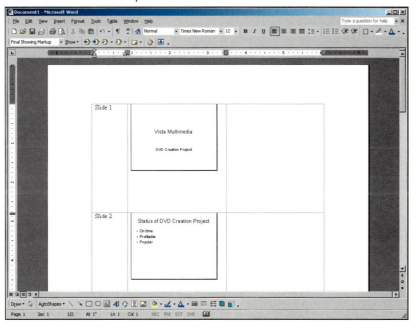

Import a Word File into a PowerPoint File

An outline created in Word can be used to create a PowerPoint presentation. Each heading level is adjusted to the bullet levels in slides.

1. Open PowerPoint and select Open on the File menu.
2. Once the Open dialog box displays, select All Outlines from the Files of type drop-down list box at the bottom of the screen.
3. Select the Word file you want to use; click Open.
4. PowerPoint imports the Word document into a presentation and formats it as slides.

> **Extra Challenge**
>
> Import the data in the Hickory Community College Alumni Association Word file located on your CD into a PowerPoint presentation. Add an appropriate design, animation, transitions, graphics, and so forth. Save the file as **Diversity** with your last name.

STEP-BY-STEP 11.3

1. Launch Microsoft Access.
2. Open the FBLA database file that you created earlier.
3. Link all of the data from the **Johnson's Homeroom.xls** file.
4. Save the new database table as **Johnson's Homeroom**.
5. Print the new table.
6. Exit Microsoft Access.
7. Launch Microsoft PowerPoint.

Technology Careers

VIDEO GAME PROGRAMMER

Video game programmers are engineers. They design the software that becomes the video games that are played by millions every day. They develop the characters, the actions, and all other features that make the games "come alive."

Game programmers are very intelligent and analytical people who enjoy solving problems. They can become obsessed with making their games faster and more exciting.

In the past, a college degree was not necessary to be a video game programmer. Many of the programmers learned what was needed on their own and practiced, practiced, and practiced. They usually like to work alone. Today, video games have become so complex and sophisticated that the programming format is very similar to other software applications. Hardware and operating systems are more powerful. A computer science degree as well as several years of programming experience would greatly increase one's prospects in the video game programming field. The salary for a beginning game programmer ranges between $23,000 and $25,000, depending on experience.

8. Open the **Vista Multimedia** PowerPoint file.

9. Link the information in this file to a new Word document. Select a layout of your choice.

10. Save the new Word document as **Vista Multimedia.doc**.

11. Print the new document.

12. Exit Microsoft Word and PowerPoint.

Extra Challenge

Prepare a database file consisting of the football players at your school. In addition to their names, include fields such as their grade level, their position, number of years on the team, and the name of their homeroom teacher. You will import this database into a letter written to the president of the Student Government Association indicating the list of football players arranged by grade level. The information the president needs includes the player's name, grade level, and number of years on the team.

SUMMARY

In this lesson, you learned:

- Integrated software is software that combines applications such as word processing, spreadsheet, database, and others into one program.
- Applications in an integrated software package are not full versions of the software.
- Software suites contain full versions of software applications that are designed to work together.
- Form letters created with mail merge are a popular use of integrated word-processing and database software.
- A main document and a data source are used to perform a mail merge to create form letters.
- Mailing labels can be created using word-processing and database software.
- Data created in a spreadsheet can be imported into a database table.
- Data created in a PowerPoint presentation can be imported into a Word document.

VOCABULARY *Review*

Define the following terms:		
Data source	Integrated software	Main document
Form letter	Mail merge	Software suites

REVIEW Questions

MULTIPLE CHOICE

Select the best response for the following statements.

1. _____ is software that combines full versions of applications such as word processing, spreadsheet, and database into a single package.
   A. A software suite
   B. Integrated software
   C. Dedicated software
   D. Private software

2. To create a _____, import data from a database file.
   A. main document
   B. data source
   C. form letter
   D. table

3. The _____ in a spreadsheet are the same as field names in a database file.
   A. column headings
   B. row letters
   C. cells
   D. formulas

4. Joining a data source and a main document will create a(n) _____.
   A. mail merge
   B. label
   C. software suite
   D. Address Block

5. _____ are entered in a main document to indicate what data will be inserted from the data source.
   A. Merge fields
   B. Address Blocks
   C. Labels
   D. Data sources

TRUE/FALSE

Circle T if the statement is true or F if the statement is false.

T   F   1. A PowerPoint file can be imported into a spreadsheet file.

T   F   2. A main document and a data source are needed to create a form letter.

T   F   3. The data source contains the information that stays the same in each document.

T   F   4. The mail merge option is used for form letters only.

T   F   5. Integrated software packages and software suites are identical.

FILL IN THE BLANK

Complete the following sentences by writing the correct word or words in the blanks provided.

1. The applications within an integrated package can be shared because of _____ features and commands.

2. _____ contain full versions of software.

3. Merge fields are also called _____ _____.

4. PowerPoint slides can be imported into a Word document by selecting the _____ option on the PowerPoint File menu on the Formatting toolbar.

5. The _____ task pane is used when creating mailing labels.

CROSS-CURRICULAR *Projects*

MATH

Use the Internet, local newspaper, and other resources to conduct some comparison shopping for a car you would like to buy. Get prices for the same car at three different car dealerships. Prepare a spreadsheet to display your data. Include information that would determine the monthly payments, the total amount of interest to be paid on the loan, as well as the total amount that the car will cost. Include a 20% down payment on the car. After completing the spreadsheet, write a letter to your parents to show them that you have conducted a thorough search for the perfect car. Import your spreadsheet into the letter.

SCIENCE

Plants are usually characterized as annuals, perennials, and biennials. Create a slide presentation about plants, describing each type. Include a plant of each type and include care instructions and any other information you decide would make your presentation interesting. Be sure to include a graphic in your presentation. Merge the presentation file into a Word document.

SOCIAL STUDIES

Prepare a six-slide show on an event in American history. The first slide will be the title slide and the last slide is to be the Bibliography slide. Link the slide show into a Word document.

LANGUAGE ARTS

Prepare a one-page family newsletter including information regarding your family members. Create a database file of at least 10 family members including their names, addresses, telephone numbers, and relationship to you. Create a set of mailing labels to mail newsletters. (If actual labels are not available, print the labels on a regular sheet of paper.)

WEB PROJECT

Your parents have told you that they are going to let you make all of the decisions to decorate your room. You are to do all of the research including getting all measurements, selecting colors, type of carpet, curtains and bedspread, as well as deciding on best prices and any other necessary details. You may use the Internet and any other resources to gather data. Once you have gathered all of your information, you are to prepare a PowerPoint presentation to give your parents a report of your decisions. Your presentation should include the name of each item, the cost, the description, where the item could be purchased, etc. You may add any additional information you think is necessary.

 TEAMWORK PROJECT

Ms. Perez has asked you and the other part-time employee to create a spreadsheet for a selected group of videos. The title of the spreadsheet will be:

Vista Multimedia

Selected Videos for Sale

Include the following column headings in the spreadsheet:

Title	Type	Date of Movie	No. of Copies	Price

(You may "create" the information for this spreadsheet. Use the names of at least ten videos.)

Once the spreadsheet has been created, import it into a letter to Ms. Perez informing her that this is the information that she requested.

UNIT 2 REVIEW

SOFTWARE

COMMAND SUMMARY

FEATURE	MENU COMMAND	LESSON
Align Text	Format, Paragraph, Alignment	7
Bold	Format, Font, Bold	7
Borders	Format, Borders and Shading	7
Bullets	Format, Bullets and Numbering	7
Clip art	Insert, Picture, Clip Art	7, 8, 10
Close	File, Close	7
New Document	File, New	7
Drawn Object	View, Toolbars, Drawing	7
Header and Footer	View, Header and Footer	7, 8
Italic	Format, Font, Italic	7
Line Spacing	Format, Paragraph	7
Margins	File, Page Setup, Margins	7
Numbering	Format, Bullets and Numbering	7
Open Document	File, Open	7
Page Break	Insert, Break	7
Print	File, Print	7, 9, 10
Save	File, Save	7
Section Break	Insert, Break	7
Shading	Format, Borders and Shading	7
Spell Check	Tools, Spelling and Grammar	7
Style	Format, Styles and Formatting	7
Symbols	Insert, Symbol	7
Table	Table, Insert, Table	7
Tabs	Format, Tabs	7
Underline	Format, Font	7
Align Data	Format, Cells, Alignment	8
Bold Data	Format, Cells, Font	8
Borders	Format, Cells, Border	8
Center Data Across Spreadsheet	Format, Cells, Alignment, Center Across Selection	8
Chart	Chart, Create	8

FEATURE	MENU COMMAND	LESSON
Slide Show	Slide Show, View Show	10
Slide	Slide Show, Slide	10
Views	View, Desired View	10
WordArt	Insert, Picture, WordArt	10

REVIEW Questions

FILL IN THE BLANKS

Complete the following sentences by writing the correct word or words in the blanks provided.

1. _____ contain icons from which the most frequently used commands may be quickly chosen.

2. _____ is the feature that allows text to automatically wrap around the right margin and continue onto the next line.

3. The _____ displays the content of a cell.

4. The _____ icon makes it easy to total long columns of data.

5. A _____ uniquely identifies a field for each record.

6. A _____ is a question you ask about the data stored in a database.

7. A _____ contains color schemes with custom formatting and styled fonts, all designed to create a special look.

8. The _____ view displays thumbnails or miniature images of all slides in a presentation.

9. _____ are a popular use of integrating word-processing and database software.

10. A _____ and a _____ are used to perform a mail merge to create form letters.

MULTIPLE CHOICE

Select the best response for the following statements.

1. _____ documents are printed sideways.
   A. Landscape
   B. Portrait
   C. Double spaced
   D. Normal view

2. _____ alignment arranges all lines to begin and end at the same point.
   A. Center
   B. Right
   C. Justified
   D. Left

3. A _____ is a shortcut for entering a command to calculate data in a spreadsheet.
   A. Formula
   B. Function
   C. Chart
   D. Wizard

4. A(n) _____ must precede all formulas.
   A. equal sign
   B. plus sign
   C. @ symbol
   D. command

5. The primary key field is identified by a(n) _____.
   A. asterisk
   B. key symbol
   C. plus symbol
   D. row selector

6. Create a _____ if you want to identify specific records in a table.
   A. report
   B. query
   C. form
   D. database

7. _____ view displays all slides in miniature images.
   A. Slide Sorter
   B. Notes Page
   C. Slide Show
   D. Outline

8. All of the following are ways that presentations can be printed except _____.
   A. Speaker notes
   B. Audience handouts
   C. Slides
   D. Books

9. All of the following are used to create form letters except a _____.
   A. main document
   B. data source
   C. label file
   D. word-processing software

10. _____ software is software that combines applications and allows for importing and exporting data between the applications.
    A. Specialized
    B. Integrated
    C. Networked
    D. Standalone

TRUE/FALSE

Circle T if the statement is true or F if the statement is false.

T F 1. Tabs are used to indent text to predefined positions.

T F 2. The Formatting toolbar contains shortcuts for menu items.

T F 3. A workbook may contain multiple worksheets.

T F 4. The AutoSum button is used to add long columns of numbers.

T F 5. A database is a collection of labels.

T F 6. Fields are the same as tables.

T F 7. The only layout of slides available in PowerPoint is the bullet layout.

T F 8. Clip art objects are the only types of objects that can be inserted on a slide.

T F 9. Integrated software packages contain full versions of various software programs.

T F 10. Mailing labels may be created by performing a mail merge.

CROSS-CURRICULAR *Projects*

MATH

Fourteen members and two advisers in your FBLA chapter will be attending the state conference in your state capital April 23–26. Prepare a spreadsheet to create a budget indicating the amount of money needed for the fourteen members and two advisers to fly (at the cheapest fare) to the conference (you will need to check with airlines to find the cheapest fare). The hotel rate is $98 per day plus 9.5% tax. Determine the cost of the stay in a hotel for three nights (two persons will share rooms). Each person must pay registration of $85 each. (You may make up the names of the members or use the name of members and advisers in your chapter.) Each member is being given $49.75 per day for food for four days. Your spreadsheet should include the total cost for each member, the total cost of each item for all members, and the total cost of the trip. *Note:* Two members have decided to drive instead of flying. The chapter will pay them 26 cents per mile to drive their cars. You will need to determine the distance from your city to your state's capital. Format the spreadsheet appropriately including adding a title. Create a chart showing the division of the various budgeted items. (*Hint:* Use *www.Mapquest.com* to find the distance to your state capital.)

SCIENCE

Use the Internet and other resources to locate information on at least 10 volcanoes in the United States. Create a database named Volcano and a table named United States containing the following fields: Name, Type, State, City, Date, and Elevation. You may include any other fields you wish to include. Print the table sorted by Volcano name. Perform and print several queries. Create and print a report with only the Name, State, City, and Elevation fields included.

SOCIAL STUDIES

Use the Internet to research information on the origin and history of the American flag. Create a PowerPoint presentation to present your findings. Include at least seven slides with clip art, sound, animation, and so forth, as well as several different slide layouts (a moving flag clip art would really enhance this presentation). Include a Reference slide that will contain the sources for the information used in your presentation. Print audience handouts.

LANGUAGE ARTS

Use the Internet and other resources to explore computer crimes and other computer violations. Prepare a two-page report on your findings. Include a description of several computer crimes as well as the penalty for committing these crimes and any other information regarding this subject that you think may be interesting to your classmates. Prepare copies for your classmates. Include a list of references you used for your report.

SIMULATION

Since Mr. Randolph purchased his new computer system and had Microsoft Office installed, he and his family have really begun to use its powerful capabilities. He has asked you to create a database of all of his customers, a spreadsheet to calculate the fees charged, a flyer announcing a special, and a presentation that will "showcase" his company.

PROJECTS

JOB 2-1

Use the following list of customers to create a database. Determine the fields from the list. Name the database *Ground Works*. Name the table *Customers*. Once you have created the table, print the entire table in alphabetical order. Create and print a label file with 30 labels on a sheet.

Customers

Jerome Biggs
1967 Jamesville Road
Norfolk, VA 23510
555-1234

Hilton Wallace
909 Harbor View Way
Norfolk, VA 23513
555-4567

Darrell Williams
104 Center Street
Norfolk, VA 23502
555-5678

Courtney Henley
5157 Central Mew
Norfolk, VA 23502
555-3456

Honnie Slade
371 Butt Station Road
Norfolk, VA 23503
555-9101

Molly Cage
13 Wavy Boulevard
Norfolk, VA 23510
555-2345

Willie Watts
839 College Drive
Norfolk, VA 23512
555-1213

Martha Harrington
789 Williams Court
Norfolk, VA 23512
555-6789

Carla Yates
7000 Pond Lane
Norfolk, VA 23510
555-1415

Allen Wales
876 Dunbarton Street
Norfolk, VA 23502
555-0099

Georgia D'Mario
293 Princeton Road
Norfolk, VA 23513
555-0987

Kathy Richards
777 Stoney Crescent
Norfolk, VA 23513
555-8888

John McDougal
3823 Washington Circle
Norfolk, VA 23502
555-6543

Clifton Mendez
345 Hampton Boulevard
Norfolk, VA 23502
555-1122

JOB 2-2

Ground Works is offering a 10% discount to all new customers in the month of June for lawn services. Prepare a flyer, using clip art, various fonts, color, lines, objects, and so forth. Print the flyer. Save the file as *Ground Works Flyer*.

JOB 2-3

Mr. Randolph has asked you to prepare a promotional computer presentation for Ground Works that he can use to show potential customers. He wants to include information regarding the history of his company, services he offers, prices, and so forth. The presentation should include approximately seven slides and include sound, animation, transitions, clip art, objects, and various layouts and designs. Moving clip art would really add impact to this presentation. Include all necessary information. Print speaker's notes for Mr. Randolph to use when delivering his presentation. Save this presentation as **Ground Works Presentation**.

JOB 2-4

Mr. Randolph has decided to use a spreadsheet to calculate his monthly earnings. He has started the spreadsheet. Open the **Monthly Earnings** file on your CD. Enter formulas to calculate the spreadsheet. Format the spreadsheet appropriately. Save the spreadsheet as *Monthly Earnings Your Last Name*. Create a chart to visually show the breakdown of services. You may select the type of chart of your choice.

PORTFOLIO *Checklist*

Include the following files from this unit in your portfolio:

_____ Ground Works database (Customers table)

_____ Ground Works Flyer.doc

_____ Ground Works Presentation.ppt

_____ Monthly Earnings.xls

_____ Candy Sale.doc

Advanced Computer Concepts

Unit 3

Lesson 12   1.5 hrs.
The Internet and Research

Lesson 13   1.5 hrs.
Evaluating Electronic Information

Lesson 14   1.5 hrs.
Desktop Publishing

Lesson 15   1.5 hrs.
Creating a Web Page

Lesson 16   2.5 hrs.
How Technology is Changing the Workplace and Society

Estimated Time for Unit: 8.5 hours

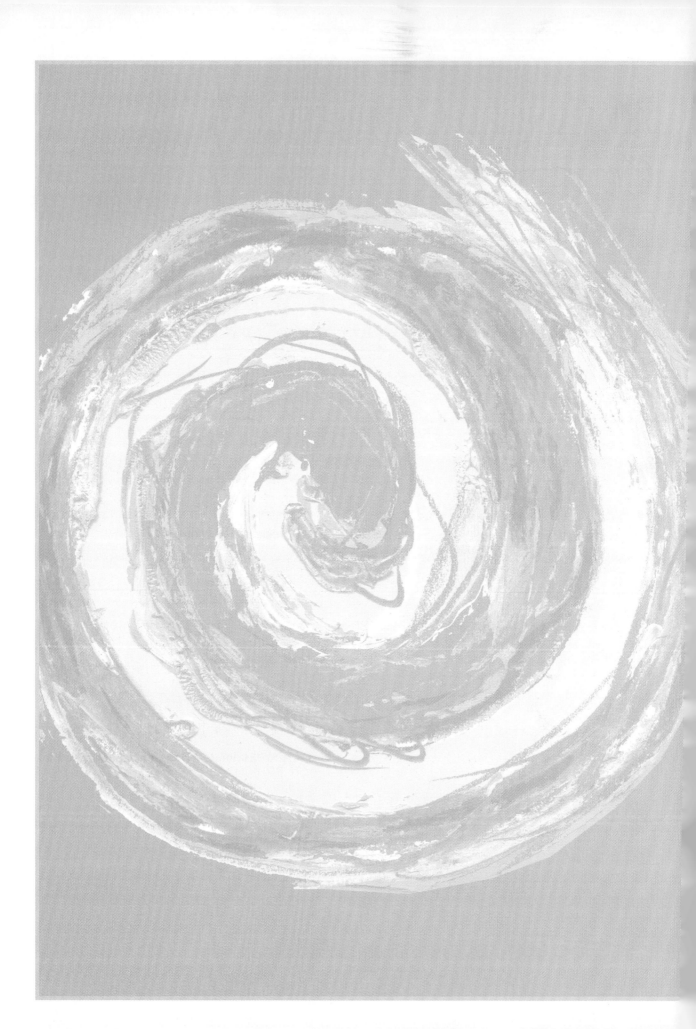

LESSON 12

THE INTERNET AND RESEARCH

OBJECTIVES

Upon completion of this lesson, you should be able to:

- List some reasons for searching the Internet.
- Describe different search approaches.
- Define a search engine.
- Explain how search engines work.
- Describe how search engines search.
- Identify some of the more popular search engines.
- List some of the specialty search engines.
- Describe the subject directory search approach.
- Describe some search tips and tricks.

Estimated Time: 1.5 hours

VOCABULARY

Algorithm
Boolean logic
Database
Hits
Keywords
Math symbols
Meta tags
Related search
Search engine
Spider
Subject directories
Uniform Resource Locator (URL)
Wildcard character

Ms. Perez needs some information for a report she is preparing for Vista Multimedia. After spending countless hours at the library searching through several reference books, she has not been able to locate some of the data she needs for her proposal. You suggest to her that the Internet could be the answer to her problem.

The Internet contains a wealth of information. In fact, you can find information on just about any topic you can imagine. The problem is that the Internet contains so much information it can be difficult to locate just what you need. You explain to Ms. Perez there are search tools and techniques that will help her locate information on just about any topic. If she masters some of these skills and understands how to use the tools, she most likely will be successful in finding what she needs.

The Key to a Successful Search

We live in the information age, and information continues to grow at an ever-spiraling rate. To conduct an effective online search on a particular topic can be a real challenge. You can be overwhelmed easily by the overabundance of raw data. With the right tools, however, the task becomes easier. One key to a successful Internet search is an understanding of the many search tools that are available. Some tools are more suitable for some purposes than others.

The two more popular tools that you can use for online searches are search engines and subject directories. You use a search engine to search for keywords. You use a directory to find specialized topics. The primary difference between these two search tools is that people assemble directories while search engines are automated. Search engines are discussed in the first part of this lesson, and an overview of directories is contained in the second part.

Why Search the Internet?

You might ask yourself, "Why would I want to search the Internet? What information does it contain that can help me?" Reasons why people search the Internet are varied and many. The following are just a few examples:

- You need to do research for the term paper due in your science class next week.
- Your grandfather is losing his hearing and has asked you to help him find some information on hearing aids.
- Your next-door neighbor is an attorney and needs some information for a court case.
- You plan to take a trip to Australia this summer and would like some information on some of the best places to stay.

As you can see from these illustrations, hundreds of reasons exist as to why you might want to conduct an Internet search. See Figure 12-1.

FIGURE 12-1
Searching the Internet

Search Engines

A *search engine* is a software program. The Internet contains hundreds of search engines. Each search engine may work a little differently, but most of them have some common search features. For example, all search engines support keyword searches. Although keyword searches may not be the most effective way to search, this is the search method used by most individuals.

Some search engines support an additional enhancement called concept searching. The search engine tries to determine what you mean and returns hits on Web sites that relate to the keywords. *Hits* are the number of returns or Web sites based on your keywords. If you search for "video games," the search engine also may return hits on sites that contain Nintendo and Playstation. One of the best-known search engines using concept-based searching is Excite. This search engine uses ICE (intelligent concept extraction) to learn about word relationships.

Another feature supported by some search engines is *stemming* or *truncation*. When you search for a word, the search engine also includes the "stem" of the word. For example, you enter the search word "play," and you also may receive results for plays, playing, and player.

> **Did You Know?**
>
> No single Web tool indexes or organizes the whole Web. When using an online search tool, you are searching and viewing data extracted from the Web. This data has been placed into the search engine's database. It is the database that is searched—not the Web itself. This is one of the reasons why you get different results when you use different search engines.

Keyword Searches

Keyword searches let you search for keywords within a Web document. A *keyword* is a descriptive word within the Web document. The Web page author can specify keywords using meta tags within the Web page header. *Meta tags* are special tags embedded within the Web page document; they do not display in the Web document. They do not affect how the page displays. Many search engines use these tags to create an index. For example, if your Web site is about Playstation 2, your meta tag may look something like this:

```
<meta name="keywords" content="Playstation 2, Tony Hawk, Myst, X-Men">
```

What if the Web page author does not specify meta tags? Then some search engines evaluate the document and index "significant" words. Depending on the search engine, significant words may be those words that are mentioned at the beginning of a document or words that are repeated several times throughout the document. Some search engines also index Alt text. This is the HTML text used to identify images and other objects on a Web page.

To search using keywords, the process is as follows:

- Launch your Web browser and display a search engine Web site.
- Complete and submit the online form displayed on the search engine page. This form contains your keywords. These keywords describe the information you are trying to locate.

> **Did You Know?**
>
> If you are using Web sources for your research paper, you need to give credit for the sources. You can find information on citing Internet sources at *www.lib.berkeley.edu/TeachingLib/Guides/Internet/Style.html*.

- The search engine matches as many keywords as possible by searching its own database. A *database* is a collection of organized information.

- The search engine returns a hyperlinked list of Web site addresses where the keywords are found. You click the hyperlinks to display and view the Web sites.

- If you are unable to find the information for which you are searching within these hyperlinked sites, you can revise your keywords and submit a new request.

> **Did You Know?**
> All search engines have banner ads, which is advertising using text or graphics. Several major search engines carry paid placement listings. Companies and organizations pay to guarantee the site a high ranking, usually in relation to desired words. The exact position of these listings can vary.

Your question may then be "How does a search engine find all of those links?" You can use the Internet to answer that question. In this instance, use the words "search engine" as the keywords. One popular search engine is AskJeeves. This search engine has a natural language software feature. You ask your question in plain English. AskJeeves compares your question to its database of questions and answers.

STEP-BY-STEP 12.1

1. Launch your browser and key **www.askjeeves.com**.

2. If you are asked to choose between USA and UK versions, select **USA**.

3. Key your question **How does a search engine work?** in the Search box and click the **Ask** button. See Figure 12-2.

FIGURE 12-2
Asking AskJeeves a question

Lesson 12 The Internet and Research **293**

STEP-BY-STEP 12.1 Continued

4. Within a few seconds, AskJeeves responds to your question based on its internal knowledge base of millions of questions and answers. See Figure 12-3. Scroll down to the You may find my search results helpful: section. Click on any of the links to display the page.

FIGURE 12-3
AskJeeves's response to the question

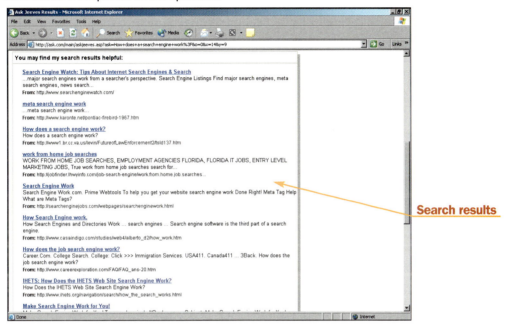

5. Click on one of the links and see if you can find the answer to your question. If the first link does not provide the information, click the browser's Back button and then try another link (Figure 12-4).

6. Leave your browser open for the next Step-by-Step.

FIGURE 12-4
Search Engine Watch Web site

So what is the answer to the question "How does a search engine find all of those Web sites?" To answer the question requires an overview of a search engine's three main parts:

- The search engine program or software itself is the main component. This program searches through the millions of records stored in its database.

> **Hot Tip**
> Have you been given a research assignment, but are having trouble coming up with a topic? Then check out *www.researchpaper.com* for a list of hot paper topics.

- The second part is a spider or crawler. The *spider* is a search engine robot that searches the Internet for the keywords. It feeds the pages it finds to the search engine. It is called a spider because it crawls the Web continually, examining Web sites and finding and looking for links. Every month or so, it may return to a previous Web site to look for changes.

- The third part of the search engine is the index or indexer. When the spider finds a page, it submits it to the index. Once a Web page is indexed, it becomes available to anyone using that search engine. Some search engines claim to index all words, even the articles, "a," "an," and "the." Other search engines index all words, except articles and stop words such as "www," "but," "or," "nor," "for," "so," or "yet." Some search engines index all words without reference to capitalization. Other engines differentiate uppercase from lowercase.

When you use a keyword search, the number of hits you receive can be in the thousands or even millions. Recall that hits are the number of returns on your keywords. Each hit is linked to a *Uniform Resource Locator (URL)*, which is the Web site address.

Suppose you are going to use the Internet to purchase some video games. In this example, you execute the search on video games using Google, one of the Internet's more popular keyword search engines.

STEP-BY-STEP 12.2

1. In the address bar, key the URL **www.google.com**.

2. In the Search box, key **video games for sale**. See Figure 12-5.

STEP-BY-STEP 12.2 Continued

FIGURE 12-5
Searching for "video games for sale"

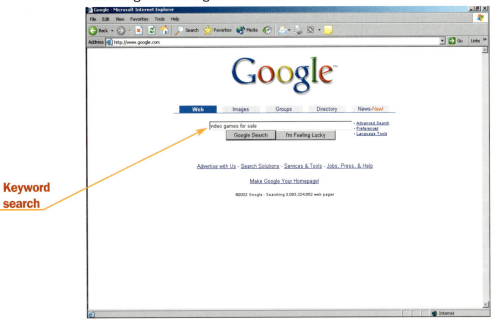

3. Click the **Google Search** button to display the results of your query. The hits are displayed—over 900,000. There is also a short paragraph describing each URL following the linked text. See Figure 12-6.

4. Leave your browser open for the next Step-by-Step.

FIGURE 12-6
Google "video games for sale" hits

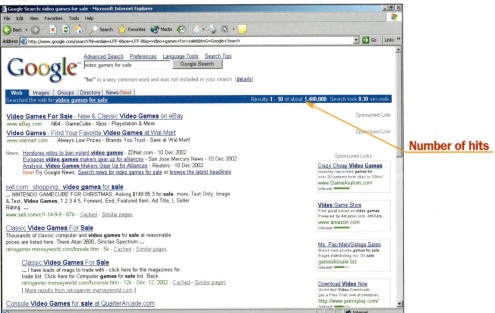

As you see from this example, the number of hits is a bit overwhelming. At this point, you have several options:

1. You can click on any of the links and review the information at a site.
2. You can redefine your keywords.
3. You can use another search engine.

Many times option three is your best choice. It is impossible for any one search engine to index every page on the Web. Each search engine also has its own personal algorithm it uses to index Web sites. An *algorithm* is a formula or set of steps for solving a particular problem. Using a different engine, therefore, may provide a totally different list of hits. Many popular search engine sites exist, and you may need to try several before you find the information you are seeking. See Table 12-1 for a list of some of the more popular search engines.

TABLE 12-1
Some popular general search engines

SEARCH ENGINE NAME	DESCRIPTION	CASE SENSITIVE
Northern Light at www.northernlight.com	more than 250 million pages, also articles from journals and business news sources	Ignores uppercase
Fast Search at www.alltheweb.com	Large and fast search engine; excellent ranking of Web sites	No
AltaVista at www.altavista.com	General database, supports advanced searches	Yes
Google at www.google.com	General database; excellent ranking of Web sites	No

Specialty Search Engines

So far in this lesson, we have discussed general search engines. There are, however, many specialized search engines on the Internet. These search engines sometimes are called *category-oriented search tools*. They generally focus on a particular topic. If you know you are looking for information in a particular format, your best bet is to search a site that specializes in indexing and retrieving that particular information. Some examples of uses for specialty search engines are as follows:

- You are looking up a former classmate or a long lost cousin; try the Switchboard Web site at *www.switchboard.com* or Yahoo's people search at *people.yahoo.com*.
- You want to download a shareware game called AdventureMaker; try the Shareware Web site at *shareware.cnet.com*.
- You want to do online jewelry shopping or item comparison—try Catalog City at *www.catalogcity.com* or Bottom Dollar at *www.bottomdollar.com*.
- Perhaps you are a sports fan and want to find out about the latest happenings in the wrestling world—try Sports Search at *www.sportsearch.com*.
- Are you thinking about your future and what career options you may have? If so, try CareerBuilder at *www.careerbuilder.com* to find a database of over 250,000 jobs.

These are just a few examples of the many hundreds of specialty Web sites. If you are looking for a particular information source, but you are not sure where to look, try the Beaucoup Web site at *www.beaucoup.com*. This site contains links to more than 3,000 specialty search engines. See Figure 12-7. For a super search, you can also enter keywords at this site and search several different search engines at one time.

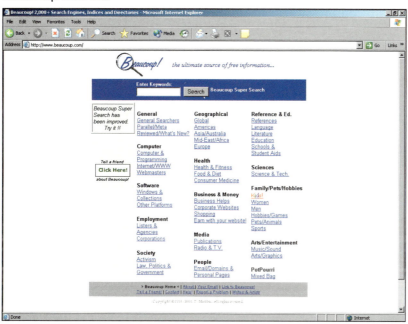

FIGURE 12-7
Beaucoup Web site

Another Web site similar to Beaucoup is the CNet site, located at *www.search.com*. This site has one of the Internet's best search engines, which includes databases, indexes, and directories in a single site. Table 12-2 lists some popular specialty search engines.

TABLE 12-2
Some popular specialty search engines

MAPS & TRAVEL INFORMATION	PEOPLE & COMPANIES	COMPANIES & CAREERS	WORLD DATA
Microsoft's *www.expedia.com*	People finder at *www.peoplesite.com*	Occupational Outlook Handbook at *www.bls.gov/oco*	World Health Organization at *www.who.int*
MapQuest at *www.mapquest.com*	Yellow Pages Search Power at *www.yellow.com*	America's Job Bank at *www.ajb.dni.us*	CIA World Factbook at *www.odci.gov/cia/publications/factbook*
Worldwide Online Reservations at *www.irsus.com/rooms.htm*	Toll-free numbers at *www.inter800.com*	Monster Job bank at *www.monster.com*	World Bank at *www.worldbank.org*
Great Outdoors at *www.gorp.com*	Canada Yellow Pages at *www.yellowpages.ca*	Career Resource Center at *www.careers.org*	World Data Center at *www.ngdc.noaa.gov/wdc/wdcmain.html*

Multimedia Search Engines

Are you interested in finding graphics, video clips, animation, and even MP3 music files? Then a multimedia search engine is probably the best way to go. For music and MP3, you might want to try the Lycos search engine at *music.lycos.com/downloads*, *mp3-music-search-engines.com*, or *www.audiofind.com*. MP3 is a file format that allows audio compression at near-CD quality. See Figure 12-8.

> **Hot Tip**
>
> Some search engines automatically include plurals; others do not. To be on the safe side, include the plural. For example, if you are searching for squirrels, use keywords such as "squirrel or squirrels."

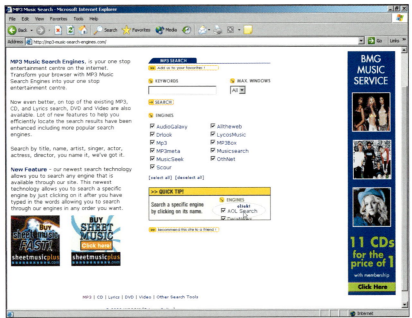

FIGURE 12-8
MP3 music search engine

Other specialty search engines include the following: Corbis at *www.corbis.com* boasts of "The world's largest collection of fine art and photography." AltaVista at *www.altavista.com* has a special tab for images, audio, and video. Or, try Ditto, the visual search engine, at *www.ditto.com*, to search for pictures, photographs, and artwork.

Meta-Search Engines

Have you searched and searched for the right information—going from search engine to search engine—and still not found what you need? If so, then you might want to try a meta-search engine. This type of search engine searches several major engines at one time. These search engines do not have their own databases. Instead, they act as a middle person. They send the query to major search engines and then return the results or hits. Meta-search engines generally work best with simple searches. Two popular meta-search engines are Dogpile at *www.dogpile.com* and MetaCrawler at *www.metacrawler.com*.

Subject Directory Searching

Recall that earlier in this lesson we discussed the primary difference between a search engine and a directory. Search engines use software programs to index sites and people assemble directories. Subject experts carefully check the Web sites to make sure they meet a particular set of standards before the site is included in the directory. Then they add the URL for the Web site to the database.

Most *subject directories* are organized by subject categories, with a collection of links to Internet resources. These resources are arranged by subject and then displayed in a series of menus. To access a particular topic, you start from the top and "drill down" through the different levels—going from the general to the specific. This is similar to a traditional card catalog or the telephone yellow pages.

Assume that your art teacher has asked you to prepare a report on jellyfish. You can use a search engine and keywords to try to locate information, or you can use a subject directory search tool. The Yahoo directory provides a list and links to approximately 14 subject directories. See Figure 12-9.

> **Internet**
>
> For education purposes, one of the best subject guides is the WWW Virtual Library. The VL is the oldest subject directory of the Web. This site is considered to have the highest-quality guides to particular sections of the Internet. You can find the Virtual Library at *www.vlib.org*.

FIGURE 12-9
Yahoo directory

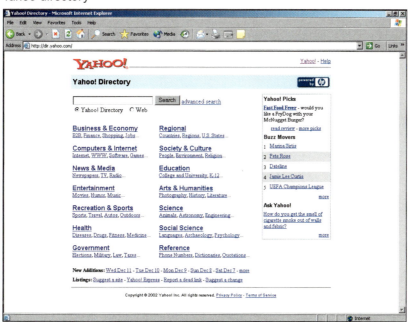

STEP-BY-STEP 12.3

1. Launch your Web browser, if necessary, and key the URL **dir.yahoo.com**. This takes you to the Yahoo directory site.

2. Click the **Science** category. See Figure 12-10. This drills down one level.

FIGURE 12-10
Yahoo directory—first level

3. Now displayed is a list of Science categories. Notice the number in parentheses to the right of each link. This is the number of links below that category. Remember that you are looking for jellyfish, so click **Oceanography@**. See Figure 12-11.

FIGURE 12-11
Yahoo directory—second level

STEP-BY-STEP 12.3 Continued

4. At the third level the category list is not quite as extensive and all categories relate to oceanography. Notice that Marine Biology is listed. Click **Marine Biology**. See Figure 12-12.

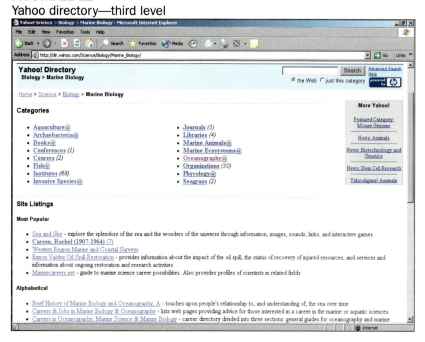

FIGURE 12-12
Yahoo directory—third level

5. You have moved down to the fourth level where all of the categories relate to marine biology. **Marine Animals** is one of the categories—click that category to move down to the fifth level.

6. At the fifth level, you find that Jellyfish is one of your category selections. Click **Jellyfish** to move to the sixth level.

STEP-BY-STEP 12.3 Continued

7. You have finally reached your goal. At this level are six or more links that will take you directly to Web sites devoted to jellyfish. See Figure 12-13. Just think how much you are going to impress your teacher.

FIGURE 12-13
Yahoo directory—sixth level

As you can see from Step-by-Step 12.3, drilling down through a subject directory is a more guided approach than entering keywords into a search engine. Additional benefits of directories are as follows:

- They are easy to use.
- You are not searching the entire Web.
- The Web sites have been handpicked and evaluated.
- Most links include some type of description.
- They produce better quality hits on searches for common items.

See Table 12-3 for a list of some other popular subject directories.

TABLE 12-3
Some popular subject directories

DIRECTORY NAME	DESCRIPTION	PHRASE SEARCHING
The Librarian's Index at *www.lii.org*	High quality; compiled by public librarians	No
Yahoo at *www.yahoo.com*	Biggest and most famous subject directory	Yes—use " "
Galaxy at *www.galaxy.com*	Good annotations; good quality	No

Tools and Techniques for Searching the Web

As the Internet continues to expand and more and more pages are added, effective searching requires new approaches and strategies. Remember that the more specific your search is, the more likely you will find what you want. Tell the search engine precisely the information for which you are searching. To find relevant information, you must use a variety of tools and techniques.

> **Internet**
>
> Meta-search engines send your search simultaneously to several individual search engines and their databases of Web pages. Find out about meta-search engines, how they work, and their limitations at *www.lib.berkeley.edu/ TeachingLib/Guides/Internet/ MetaSearch.html*.

Phrase Searching

If you want to search for words that must appear next to each other, then phrase searching is your best choice. Enter a phrase using double quotation marks, and phrase searching only matches those words that appear adjacent to each other and in the order in which you specify.

If you are searching for more than one phrase, you can separate multiple phrases or proper names with a comma. For example, if you are searching for baseball cards, enter the phrase "baseball cards" in double quotation marks. The results will contain Web sites with the words "baseball cards" adjacent to each other. Without the quotation marks, the search engine would find Web pages that contain the words baseball and cards anywhere within each page. To find Mickey Mantle baseball cards, you would enter "baseball cards", "Mickey Mantle". It is always a good idea to capitalize proper nouns because some search engines distinguish between upper- and lowercase letters. On the other hand, if you capitalize a common noun such as Bread, you will get fewer returns than if you keyed bread.

Search Engine Math

You can use *math symbols* to enter a formula to filter out unwanted listings. For example:

- Put a plus sign (+) before words that must display (also called an *inclusion operator*).
- Put a minus sign (-) before words that you do not want to display (also called an *exclusion operator*).
- Words without qualifiers need not display, but are still involved in sorting your search.

Suppose you are making cookies for the homeroom party and would like to try some new recipes. Your search words are *+cookie+recipes*. Only pages that contained both words would appear in your results. Now suppose you want recipes for chocolate cookies. Your search words are *+cookie+recipe+chocolate*. This would display pages with all three words.

To take this a step further, you do not like coconut. So you do not want any recipes that contain the word *coconut*. You will find that the minus (-) symbol is helpful for reducing the number of unrelated results. You would write your search phrase as *+cookie+recipe+chocolate-coconut*. This tells the search engine to find pages that contain *cookie, recipe,* and *chocolate* and then to remove any pages that contain the word *coconut*. To extend this idea and to get chocolate cookie recipes without coconut and honey, your search phrase would be *+cookie+recipe+chocolate-coconut-honey*. Simply begin subtracting terms you know are not of interest, and you will get better results. Almost all of the major search engines support search engine math. You also can use math symbols with most directories.

Boolean Searching

When you search for a topic on the Internet, you are not going from server to server and viewing documents on that server. Instead you are searching databases. A database is a collection of organized information. **Boolean logic** is another way that you can search databases. This works on a similar principle as search engine math, but has a little more power. Boolean logic consists of three logical operators:

- AND
- NOT
- OR

Returning to our cookie example, you are interested in a relationship between cookies and recipes. So you may search for "cookies AND recipes". The more terms you combine with AND, the fewer returns you will receive. Or, you want chocolate cookie recipes without coconut. You would search for "cookies AND recipes AND chocolate NOT coconut".

OR logic is more commonly used to search for similar terms or concepts. For example, you search for "cookies AND recipes OR chocolate" to retrieve results containing one term or the other or both. The more terms you combine in a search with OR logic, the more results you will receive from your search.

The power of the Boolean search comes the use of multiple parameters, which is not possible with the math symbols. For instance, you can create a search on "cookies AND recipes NOT (coconut OR honey OR spinach)".

Some search engines assist you with your logical search through the use of forms. For example, clicking on the HotBot search engine's Advanced Search tab brings up a form. Using this form, you can specify the language, words, and phrases to include and to omit, and even specify a time period. See Figure 12-14. Keep in mind that some search engines do not support Boolean logic. Check the search engine Help feature to determine if Boolean logic is supported.

FIGURE 12-14
HotBot's advanced search form

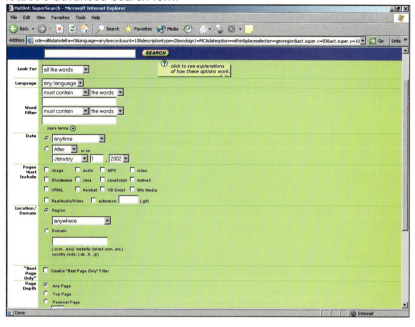

Wildcard Searching

The * symbol or asterisk is considered a *wildcard character*. If you do not know the spelling of a word or you want to search plurals or variations of a word, use the wildcard character. For example, you want to search for "baseball cards and Nolan Ryan," but you are not sure how to spell *Nolan*. You can construct you search using a wildcard—"baseball cards" and "N* Ryan". Some search engines only permit the * at the end of the word; with others you can put the * at the end or beginning. Some search engines do not support wildcard searches. Check the search engine Help feature to determine if wildcard searches are supported.

Title Searching

When a Web page author creates a Web page, the Web page generally contains an HTML title. The title is entered between title tags, such as

```
<Title>Learn the Net: An Internet Guide and Tutorial</Title>
```

When you go to a Web site, the title is what appears on the title bar at the top of the Web page. See Figure 12-15.

FIGURE 12-15
Title bar example

Many of the major search engines allow you to search within the HTML document for the title of a Web page. If you did a title search for *Internet Tutorial*, then most likely one of your results or hits would be the page shown in Figure 12-15. Not all search engines support title searches.

Other Search Features

Another feature provided by several search engines is a ***related search***. These are preprogrammed queries or questions suggested by the search engine. A related search can dramatically improve your odds of finding the information you are seeking. Several search engines offer this feature, although they may use different terminology. You may see terms such as "similar pages," "related pages," or "more pages like this." WebCrawler and Google use "Similar Pages." All of these terms basically mean the same thing. See Figure 12-16.

FIGURE 12-16
Google uses the term "Similar Pages"

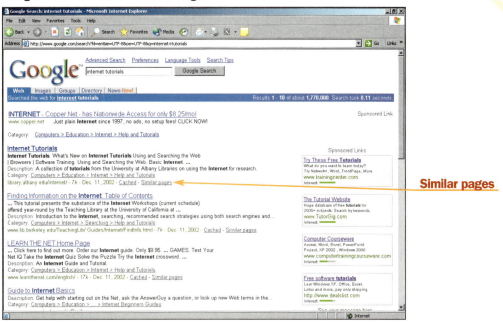

As you learn more about Internet searching, keep in mind that no single organization indexes the Internet the way the Library of Congress catalogs books. So how many ways can you search? There are dozens of primary search engines and hundreds of specialty search engines. New ones are added on a continual basis. It is almost like looking for the needle in the haystack. With a little effort, however, you probably will find that special Web page that contains the information for which you are searching.

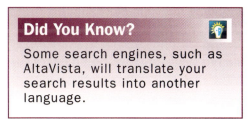

Did You Know?

Some search engines, such as AltaVista, will translate your search results into another language.

SUMMARY

In this lesson, you learned:

- Two basic tools that you can use for finding information are search engines and directories.
- People assemble directories and search engines are automated.
- A search engine is a software program.
- Most search engines support keyword searches.
- Concept-based searching occurs when the search engine returns hits that relate to keywords.
- Stemming relates to the search engine's finding variations of the word.
- Meta tags are special tags embedded in a Web page; many search engines use the tags to create their indexes.
- Keywords describe the information you are trying to locate.

- Search engines contain a database of organized information.
- Some search engines use natural language.
- A search engine has three main parts: the search engine software, a spider that searches for keywords, and an index.
- Stop words, such as *www, but, or*, and so forth, are not indexed by many search engines.
- The URL is the same as the Web site address.
- A search engine uses an algorithm to index Web sites.
- Specialized search engines focus on a particular topic.
- Multimedia search engines focus on video, animation, graphics, and music.
- Subject directories are organized by subject categories.
- Subject experts check the Web sites that are part of the subject directory's database.
- Use double quotation marks around a set of words for phrase searching.
- Use the plus and minus signs for inclusion and exclusion of words within a search.
- Boolean searching uses the three logical operators OR, AND, and NOT.
- The * symbol is used for wildcard searching.
- Some search engines support title searching.
- A related search is a preprogrammed question suggested by the search engine.
- No single organization indexes the entire Internet.

VOCABULARY *Review*

Define the following terms:		
Algorithm	Math symbols	Subject Directories
Boolean Logic	Meta tags	Uniform Resource Locator
Database	Related search	(URL)
Hits	Search engine	Wildcard character
Keywords	Spider	

REVIEW Questions

MULTIPLE CHOICE

Select the best response for the following statements.

1. There are _____ basic tools that you can use for finding information on the Internet.
   A. one
   B. two
   C. three
   D. four

2. _____ occurs when the search engine includes other variations of the keyword.
   A. Concepts
   B. Stemming
   C. Meta tags
   D. Natural language

3. The _____ is a search engine robot that roams the Internet looking for keywords.
   A. index
   B. searcher
   C. spider
   D. wart hog

4. The _____ is the same as the Web site address.
   A. search box
   B. hits
   C. indexer
   D. URL

5. If you were looking for video and music resources, you might use a _____ search engine.
   A. multimedia
   B. sports
   C. phrase
   D. spider

TRUE/FALSE

Circle T if the statement is true or F if the statement is false.

T F 1. It is easy to find information on the Internet.

T F 2. Keywords describe the information you are trying to locate.

T F 3. The lower the relevant percentage, the more likely that your search terms are included.

T F 4. The Britannica Web site is a search engine.

T F 5. Boolean searches and math symbol searches are identical.

FILL IN THE BLANK

Complete the following sentences by writing the correct word or words in the blanks provided.

1. The _____ is a symbol for a wildcard character.

2. A preprogrammed query is a(n) _____.

3. Web pages for _____ directories are reviewed by people.

4. The AskJeeves search engine uses _____ language.

5. A Web author uses _____ to specify keywords within a Web page document.

CROSS-CURRICULAR *Projects*

MATH

1. Use search engine math and math symbols and create searches for the following:
    A. Carnivals and circuses in Canada, but not in Vancouver.
    B. Skateboards and roller blades in Florida.

2. Create searches for A. and B. above using Boolean logic.

SCIENCE

Your teacher has assigned a research project. You are to select a type of insect and provide information about the life and habits of the insect. Create a Search Strategy form that your fellow classmates can use to search the Internet. Within the form, list possible search tools and ways in which to search. Include the URLs for any suggested search engines or directory Web sites.

SOCIAL STUDIES/SCIENCE

One infamous question that most of us have heard throughout our lives is "Why did the chicken cross the road?" Use the search engine AskJeeves located at *www.askjeeves.com* to find the answer to this question. How many links did you find? Prepare a report on your findings and present it to your class.

LANGUAGE ARTS

Create a Boolean search on your favorite search engine to locate information about your two favorite bands. Create a one-page report. Include within the report what search engine you used and why; how many sites you found; and how you were able to narrow the search.

 ## WEB PROJECT

You and members of your class want to know more about how search engines work. Your teacher thinks this is a great idea and has asked your group to prepare a report and share your findings with the class. Your report should include Web searching methodologies and Web-based resources.

TEAMWORK PROJECT

Ms. Perez would like more information on MP3. Downloading and selling music from the Internet could be a possible additional item for Vista Multimedia. Ms. Perez would like to have a detailed description of how MP3 works, how to download this music, what the copyright issues are for downloading music, what kind of MP3 hardware is available, and what type of player and encoder she should use. She has requested that you and a group of your fellow employees put together a two-page report with this information and other any relevant information you may find. A good place to start searching is at *www.music.lycos.com/downloads*.

LESSON 13

Evaluating Electronic Information

OBJECTIVES

Upon completion of this lesson, you should be able to:

- Identify reasons for evaluating Internet resources.
- Identify criteria for evaluating electronic information.
- Describe software piracy.
- Identify Internet resources.
- Understand the rules of copyright.
- Cite Internet resources appropriately.
- Explore other legal and ethical issues concerning information you obtain from the Internet.

Estimated Time: 1.5 hours

VOCABULARY

Copyright
Currency
Navigation
Public domain
Shareware

Information is only as good as the source. Anyone, anywhere, can put anything on the Internet. It may be true; it may not be true. How can you determine if the information is legitimate? Developing the ability to evaluate information critically on the Internet is a very important skill today in this information age!

Evaluating Information Found on the Internet

The Internet provides opportunities for students, teachers, scholars, and anyone needing information to find it from all over the world. It is fairly easy to locate information and to publish it electronically. However, because anyone can put information on the Internet, it is not always accurate or reliable. Anyone using information obtained from the Internet needs to develop skills to evaluate what they find.

> **Hot Tip**
>
> The Internet epitomizes the concept of *caveat lector:* Let the reader beware.

Viewing a Page

The pages on the Web have so many different looks. Some pages are filled with pictures, sounds, animations, links, and information. Some are very exciting; others may be just plain. Sometimes the appearance of the page alone may draw you to a site and, after reading it, you realize it is not the site you need.

Following are some questions you may want to ask when you open a Web page:

- Did the page take a long time to load?
- Are the graphics on the page related to the site?
- Are the sections on the page labeled?
- Who wrote the information on this page?
- How can you communicate with the author?
- When was the page last updated?
- Are there appropriate links to other Web pages?
- Is it easy to follow links?
- Can you tell what the page is about from its title?
- Is the information useful to you?
- How old is the information?
- Does any of the information contradict information you found someplace else?
- Did the author use words like *always, never, best, worst*?
- Do you think the author knows the information he or she is sharing?

These questions represent just a start at evaluating electronic information.

> **Did You Know?**
>
> Links that are no longer active are called *dead links*.

Ethics in Technology

RESTRICTING INTERNET ACCESS

In various situations, people might want to block access to specific Internet sites or to sites that contain certain content. For instance, parents often want to prevent their children from visiting sites with adult-oriented material. Or companies might want to deny their employees access to online shopping and entertainment sites that are not business-related.

There are several tools to restrict site access. A low-tech solution is to simply have someone oversee computer users and what is on their monitors. At the other end of the spectrum, there are software programs that can be installed on a computer or network that will automatically block access to user-specified sites or to sites with specified content.

Determining Authorship

A well-developed resource identifies its author and/or producer. You will be given enough information to be able to determine whether the originator is a reliable source. What expertise or authority does the author have that qualifies him or her to distribute this information? If you don't see this information, use the Back button to see whether another part of the file contains this information. Look especially for a name and e-mail address of the person who created or maintains the information. You can always contact him or her for information regarding credentials and expertise.

If the information regarding the author is not visible, a search by the author's name using a search engine may provide the information regarding the author. It may also lead to other information by the same author. If an e-mail address is visible, use it to request information regarding the author.

The domain portion of the URL will also give you information concerning the appropriateness of the site for your area of study. Examples:

- .edu for educational or research information
- .gov for government resources
- .com for commercial products or commercially sponsored sites
- .org for nonprofit organizations
- .mil for military branches

Ethics in Technology

SOFTWARE PIRACY

One of the biggest problems facing the computer industry today is software piracy, the illegal copying or use of programs. Copying software is very easy. Some people believe it is all right to copy software and use it for free. They think software is too expensive. And it can be. Some low-level software costs less than $25, but more specialized software can cost hundreds, even thousands of dollars! When users copy the software, they are only giving up access to documentation and tech support; so they decide it is worth it to copy it illegally.

You, too, may ask, "What is the big deal about copying software?" Remember, developing a software program is an expensive process that takes highly trained programmers hundreds of hours to develop.

Shareware, free software that can be used for a given period of time, is also being abused. Many people use it with no intention of purchasing it. You will probably be surprised to know that not only individual users copy software illegally—so do businesses. Billions of dollars are lost every year as a result of pirated software.

Software can be pirated in many ways. Of course, the easiest is to copy from the original disks. Software can also be copied from the server of a network and over an e-mail system.

The Copyright Act of 1976 was passed to govern software piracy. In 1983, a Software Piracy and Counterfeiting Amendment was added. It is no longer a misdemeanor to copy software illegally—it is a felony.

Evaluating Content

Is the purpose of this Web site stated? Is the information accurate? Is the information in-depth enough? Has the information been reviewed? Don't take any information presented on the Internet at face value. The source of the information should be clearly stated whether it is original or borrowed from somewhere else. Make sure you understand the agenda of the site's owner. Is it trying to sell a product or service? Is it trying to influence public opinion? As you read through the information, pay close attention to determine whether the content covers a specific time period or an aspect of a topic or whether it is more broad. Check other resources, such as books or journals at the local library, that contain similar information.

Is Content Timely?

A very important consideration of an effective site is its *currency*, which refers to the age of the information, how long it has been posted, and how often it is updated. Some sites need to be updated more often than others to reflect changes in the kind of information. Medical or technological information needs to be updated more often than historical information. Out-of-date information may not give you the results you need.

Most sites on the Internet have numerous links that will take you to additional sites of similar information. Sometimes, however, it is not information you can use. Decide whether the site you plan to use has useful information or whether it is just a site that links you to more and more sites. Does the site contain dead links—links that are no longer active? Also, determine whether the links go only to other pages within the site. This will help you assess the objectivity of the information on the site.

The style of writing and the language used can reveal information about the quality of the site. If the style is objective, the chances are the information is worthy of your attention. However, if it is opinionated and subjective, you may want to give second thought to using it. Ideas and opinions supported by references are additional signs of the value of the site.

The overall layout of the page is also important. The page should be free of spelling and grammatical errors. Even if the page appears to contain valuable information, misspelled words and incorrect grammar usage tend to bias a reader regarding the validity of the information.

Navigating the Site

Navigation is the ability to move through a site. Being able to move quickly through the links on a Web site is a very important element. Having the information laid out in a logical design so you can locate what you need easily adds to the efficiency of the site. The consistency of the layout from page to page adds to the ability to navigate easily. The first page of a Web site indicates how the site is organized and the options available.

Moving through a site is done by clicking on the links on the page. Some pages consist of many links; others may only contain a few. Regardless, the links should

- Be easy to identify.
- Be grouped logically.
- Be pertinent to the subject of the original page.

There should be a link on each page that will take you back to the home page and one that will allow you to e-mail the author.

Types of Internet Resources

The types of electronic resources include the following:

- Journals and journal articles
- Magazines and magazine articles
- Newspapers and newspaper articles
- E-mail
- Mailing lists
- Commercial sites
- Organizational sites
- Subject-based sites

Some of these are presented in complete form; others are only portions of the document. Regardless of the type, the site should give information concerning

- The identification of the publisher
- Article reviewer information
- Special hardware requirements
- Availability of older copies of the article, newspaper, or journal
- The currency of the site

Search Engines

Search engines are programs written to query and retrieve information stored in a database. They differ from database to database and depend on the information stored in the database itself. Examples of search engines are AltaVista, Excite, Yahoo, and Google. If you used one of the many search engines available to locate information on the Internet, you need to know

- how the search engine decides the order in which it returns information requested. The top spaces (the first sites listed) are sold to advertisers by the search engines. Therefore, the first sites listed are not always the best sites or the most accurate and reliable.
- how the search engine searches for information and how often the information is updated.

Understanding Rules of Copyright

For the most part, information displayed on an Internet site is easy to copy. Often you can highlight whatever text or graphics that you want to copy, hit the "copy" command, and then paste it into another document. Or you can print out an entire page that's displayed on the monitor. The ease with which information can be copied, however, does not mean that users have a legal right to do so. Internet publications can claim the same legal protection as books, newspapers, CDs, movies, and other forms that are protected by copyright rules.

Most sites have copyright information. *Copyright* is the exclusive right, granted by law for a certain number of years, to make and dispose of literary, musical, or artistic work. Even if the copyright notice isn't displayed prominently on the page, someone wrote or is responsible for the creation of whatever appears on a page. This means that you cannot use the information as your own. You must give credit to the person who created the work.

If Internet content, such as music files, is copyrighted, it cannot be copied without the copyright holder's permission. To do so is a violation of copyright laws. It can lead to criminal charges for theft as well as civil lawsuits for monetary damages.

Copyright law does provide certain exceptions to the general prohibition against copying. If copyright protection has lapsed on certain material, then it is deemed to be in the *public domain* and is available for anyone to copy. Also, the law allows for the fair use of properly identified copyrighted material that is merely a small part of a larger research project, for instance, or cited as part of a critique or review.

 Technology Careers

INTERNET WEB DESIGNER/WEBMASTER

Every page on the Internet was designed by someone. Today, that someone is called a Web designer. The way a page looks on the Internet is the responsibility of the Web designer. The overall goal of the Web designer is to design and create a page that is efficient and appealing.

Each page on the Internet has to be maintained and kept up-to-date. The Webmaster is responsible for this task. A typical Webmaster manages a Web site. That usually includes creating content, adapting existing content in a user-friendly format, creating and maintaining a logical structure, and running the Web server software.

Not so long ago, both of these functions were the responsibility of the Webmaster. However, with today's growing technology in hardware and software, these tasks are becoming more and more specialized and therefore performed by more than one person. Webmasters and Web designers can work in any organization that has a Web site. Such organizations include educational institutions, museums, libraries, government agencies, and of course, businesses.

A person working in either of these capacities needs to have skills in graphic design, HTML language, Web design software programs, general programming, and the ability to adapt to new Web technology as it evolves.

An associate or bachelor's degree in computer science or graphic design is usually required. However, because the field is relatively new, many employers will accept persons with extensive experience in graphic design combined with computer skills.

The starting salary for a Webmaster or Web designer will vary depending on location and experience. The average salary can vary from $20,000 to $36,000.

Citing Internet Resources

Internet resources used in reports must be cited. You must give proper credit to any information you include in your report that is not your original thought. This will also provide the reader of the document with choices for additional research. It will also allow the information to be retrieved again. You can find general guidelines for citing electronic sources in the *MLA Handbook for Writers of Research Papers*, published by the Modern Language Association. *The Chicago Manual of Style* is another source for this information.

Here are some samples of citing Internet resources as suggested in the *MLA Handbook for Writers of Research Papers*:

- *Online journal article:* Author's last name, first initial. (date of publication or "NO DATE" if unavailable). Title of article or section used [Number of paragraphs]. Title of complete work. [Form, such as HTTP, CD-ROM, E-MAIL]. Available: complete URL [date of access].

Internet
For information concerning using MLA style for citing sources, visit *www.mla.org*.

- *Online magazine article:* Author's last name, first initial. (date of publication). Title of article. [Number of paragraphs]. Title of work. [Form] Available: complete URL [date of access].

- *Web sites:* Name of site [date]. Title of document [Form] Available: complete URL [date of access].

- *E-mail:* Author's last name, first name (author's e-mail address) (date). Subject. Receiver of e-mail (receiver's e-mail address).

Remember, anyone can put information on the Internet. Evaluate any resources that you choose to use carefully to ensure you have a high-quality resource that could really be of value to you.

Internet Detective

There is an online tutorial on evaluating the quality of the information you locate on the Internet. It gives specific information regarding evaluating electronic resources. You can access the Internet Detective by visiting *www.sosig.ac.uk/desire/internet-detective.html*. You can surf though the pages of this site. Your instructor may give you additional directions for using this site.

Evaluation Survey

You can use the information discussed in this lesson to construct a survey to evaluate electronic resources. See Figure 13-1.

FIGURE 13-1
Survey form

CRITERIA FOR EVALUATING ELECTRONIC RESOURCES

1. Can you identify the author of the page?   Yes _____ No _____
2. Is an e-mail address listed?   Yes _____ No _____
3. Can you access the site in a reasonable time?   Yes _____ No _____
4. Is the text on the screen legible?   Yes _____ No _____
5. Are the commands and directions easy to follow?   Yes _____ No _____
6. Is the information current?   Yes _____ No _____
7. When you perform a search, do you get what you expect?   Yes _____ No _____
8. Are instructions clearly visible?   Yes _____ No _____
9. Is the information updated regularly?   Yes _____ No _____
10. Make any comment here you would like concerning the site.

   _____

   _____

Identify a site on the Internet and use the survey to evaluate it. You may select a site such as a magazine article of interest to you, the White House, or any topic on which you may want to gather information.

Other Legal and Ethical Issues

The ease of obtaining information from the Internet and of publishing information on it can contribute to other legal problems as well. Just because information is obtained from an Internet site does not mean that someone can copy it and claim it as their own, even non-copyrighted information. That's plagiarism. The Internet does not relieve an author of responsibility for acknowledging and identifying the source of borrowed material.

Likewise, the Internet does not relieve anyone of the burden of ensuring that information they publish is true. If someone publishes information about another person or organization and it is not true, they can be sued for libel and forced to pay compensation for any damage they caused. The Internet makes widespread publication of information easy. It also creates the potential for huge damages if the information turns out to be false.

The free flow of information via the Internet also creates opportunities for criminals to gather personal information, acquire credit, and conduct transactions using false identities. Identity theft, as it is called, is a growing problem that can cause big headaches for unsuspecting victims. Other criminal problems that the Internet has been feeding include making sexual advances to minors, posting anonymous threats, and circulating rumors to manipulate stock prices. All are made easier by the Internet, but they are just as illegal and just as wrong.

And not all improper activities that make use of the Internet are necessarily illegal. Pranks, hoaxes, and making unfair use of free-trial "shareware" software may not be against the law, but they can still cause harm to innocent people—often more harm than their perpetrators might realize. The Internet is a powerful tool, for good and ill, which needs to be handled with care.

SUMMARY

In this lesson, you learned:

- The criteria for evaluating Internet resources include authorship, content, copyright information, navigation, and quality control.
- There are various types of Internet resources including electronic journals, magazines, newspapers, Web sites, and e-mail messages.
- Internet publications and Web site content can claim the same legal protection as books, newspapers, CDs, movies, and other forms that are protected by copyright law.
- It is very important to cite any information that you use from the Internet. The MLA style is widely used for citing electronic resources.

VOCABULARY *Review*

Define the following terms:

Copyright	Navigation	Shareware
Currency	Public domain	

REVIEW *Questions*

MULTIPLE CHOICE

Select the best response for the following statements.

1. _____ is the illegal copying or use of software.
   A. Piracy
   B. Webmastering
   C. Counterfeiting
   D. Surfing

2. _____ refers to the age of information.
   A. Date
   B. Infancy
   C. Currency
   D. Dead link

3. .Edu, .gov, .org, and .com are examples of the _____ portion of an URL.
   A. name
   B. domain
   C. ending
   D. handle

4. _____ is the exclusive right, granted by law for a certain number of years, to make and dispose of literary, musical, or artistic work.
   A. Copyright
   B. Security
   C. Privacy
   D. Resource

5. _____ is the ability to move through a site.
   A. Linking
   B. Grouping
   C. Citing
   D. Navigation

TRUE/FALSE

Circle T if the statement is true or F if the statement is false.

T F 1. It can be assumed that all information found on the Internet is accurate.

T F 2. The age of an article will affect its usefulness to a user.

T F 3. Everyone who puts information on the Internet is an authority on the particular subject.

T F 4. Shareware is free software that can be used for a given period of time.

T F 5. Spelling and grammatical errors on a Web page may affect a user's opinion of a site.

FILL IN THE BLANK

Complete the following sentences by writing the correct word or words in the blanks provided.

1. _____ refers to the age of the article.

2. All sites should have the _____ address of the author so the user can make contact.

3. Some information on the Internet is classified as _____, which means it can be used without citation.

4. _____ refers to the ability to move through a site.

5. A(n) _____ is responsible for managing and maintaining a Web site.

CROSS-CURRICULAR *Projects*

SOCIAL STUDIES/LANGUAGE ARTS

Search the Internet for Web sites containing information on Olympic gold medalists. In the results list, pick at least two sites that you think might contain useful information. Using the survey form shown in Figure 13-1, evaluate each site. Write a 100-word report on your evaluation of the sites. Be sure to include the URL of the site and elaborate on what you found in answer to each of the survey questions.

SOCIAL STUDIES/LANGUAGE ARTS

Go to the Web site for the White House (*www.whitehouse.gov*). Review the section in the lesson on navigation, and then evaluate the navigation system and tools at the White House Web site. You'll want to click links on various pages. Write a 100-word report that explains the site's system for navigating. Be sure to mention any problems you had in getting around the site.

WEB PROJECT

Choose a topic to research on the Internet. Print the first two sites that you find. Using the information you studied in this lesson, critique the two sites and write a report of your findings.

TEAMWORK PROJECT

Your supervisor, Ms. Perez, has informed you that she has contracted the services of a Web designer to create a Web page for the store. However, she would like to be able to talk intelligently with the Web designer when telling him or her exactly what she wants on the Web page. She has asked you and the other part-time employee to work together to provide her with samples of Web pages for five video/multimedia stores. She also wants you to provide her with a critique of each page.

CRITICAL *Thinking*

ACTIVITY 13-1

You want to design a Web site on a topic of your choice. Sketch out a design for the home page of the Web site. Review the evaluation criteria discussed in this lesson and make sure your Web site follows the criteria.

LESSON 14

Desktop Publishing

OBJECTIVES

Upon completion of this lesson, you should be able to:

- Define desktop publishing.
- Identify the stages in desktop publishing.
- Identify layout and design techniques.
- Identify the parts of a font and select appropriate fonts.
- Insert graphics into documents.
- Create an effective publication.

Estimated Time: 1.5 hours

VOCABULARY

Ascenders
Balance
Cap height
Coherence
Descenders
Desktop publishing
Focus
Font
Layout and design
Point
Sans serif
Scanners
Serif
Simplicity
Templates
Thumbnail sketch
Typeface
Wizards
WYSIWYG
X-height

Vista Multimedia is having a sale on discontinued CDs and videos! Hundreds will be sold at great savings. Ms. Perez, your supervisor, has asked you to prepare a flyer. She had thought about sending the job out to a printing company, but she heard you talking about preparing flyers in one of the classes you are taking at school. After discussing this with her, you assure her that the flyer will look very professional when you are finished with it. It will even be in color because the store has a color printer. See Figure 14-1.

FIGURE 14-1
A flyer created using desktop publishing looks more professional

What Is Desktop Publishing?

Desktop publishing is the process of producing professional-looking documents such as flyers, brochures, reports, newsletters, and pamphlets using a personal computer and a color printer. Years ago, the preparation of these documents involved many participants including a copywriter, an editor, a designer, a typesetter, and a paste-up artist. Today, the tasks performed by these persons have merged and can be completed by one person.

The advantages of desktop publishing over traditional publishing include (1) substantial savings in production costs, (2) time saved in sending copy and proofs back and forth between the printer and the author, and (3) greater author control of the entire production process.

Before the mid-1980s, publishing meant taking your work to a professional typesetter. Four inventions changed this:

- In 1984 the Apple Macintosh was introduced. It used pictures and the mouse to communicate.
- In 1985 the first laser printer was invented. The LaserWriter, as it was called, could deliver professional output at a cost the general public could afford.
- A dedicated desktop publishing software program called PageMaker was developed.
- **WYSIWYG** capability, which means "What You See Is What You Get", became available. This software feature allows you to see on your computer screen how the publication will look when it is printed.

There are several types of desktop publishing software. Some are called dedicated desktop publishing software. These are page layout or composition software programs such as PageMaker or Quark Xpress. Another type is word processing software with desktop publishing capabilities, such as Microsoft Word. So now almost anyone can be a publisher. However, in addition to obtaining the necessary software, a good understanding of design theory is invaluable. Although many of the software programs are very sophisticated, the user must be familiar with page layout and design and the use of graphics, as well as have some degree of creativity.

> **Did You Know?**
> Many individuals have gone into business for themselves providing desktop publishing services.

Stages in the Desktop Publishing Process

In order to produce our sales flyer, two steps must be followed: planning the publication and creating the content. Careful thought must be given to the purpose of the publication and the audience that the publication is being designed for, as well as how the final document will look.

Planning

Planning is the most important stage in the desktop publishing process. The flyer must contain all the information prospective customers will need to make the decision to purchase products.

- Identify the purpose of the publication.
- Identify the audience.
- What format should be used to deliver the message?
- What response do you want from your audience?

Creating the Content

The content must be exact. It must say what we want to say in a way that will appeal to prospective customers. It must be visually attractive.

- Decide what information needs to be included.
- Prepare a *thumbnail sketch*, a rough draft drawing used to explore layout options of the document you are creating. A thumbnail sketch is shown in Figure 14-2.

Ethics in Technology

HACKERS/PIRATES

The most popular definition of a computer hacker is a person who has gained unauthorized access to computer systems. Hackers are part of the computer underground that engages in illicit and/or illegal behavior. Modern hackers are skilled at invading computer systems and concealing the fact that they have been there. They range from teenagers to computer professionals.

Hacking activity falls into four categories: searching for systems, attempting to gain entry into unauthorized systems, exploring systems, and bragging about getting into systems.

A software pirate is a person who copies and distributes commercial software in violation of copyright laws. A pirate is very organized and uses the Internet for distribution of this illegal software.

Follow Appropriate Design Guidelines

- Create *focus* on the main element to pull the reader's eye to it. This can be a graphic or large headlines or titles.
- Create *balance* by distributing the weight of all of the various elements that make up the page. This includes graphics, text, lines, and white space.
- Maintain *simplicity*. The simpler the design, the more likely the reader will understand the publication's message.
- Create *coherence*. Documents, especially multipage documents, should follow a consistent format.
- Use white space appropriately. Do not fill every inch of space with text, graphics, and other elements. See Figure 14-2.

FIGURE 14-2
Focus, balance, simplicity, and coherence in a thumbnail sketch

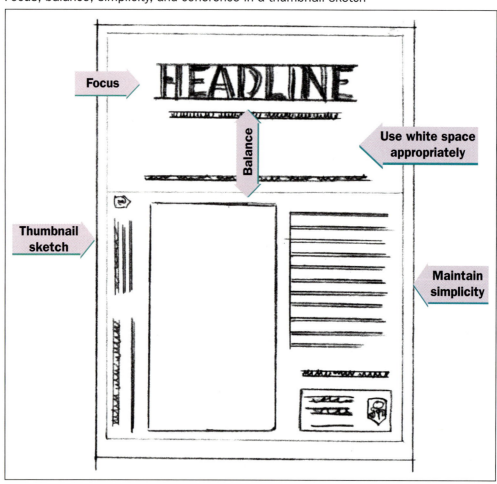

Layout and Design

The microcomputer and desktop publishing software alone will not ensure a well-designed publication. A very important element in the desktop publishing process is *layout and design*: the way graphics and text are used to produce a quality document.

Using Text

The text used in a document is very important. It must be readable and must clearly communicate the message to your audience. The content of the document sometimes will influence the style of text that is used. A *typeface* is a set of characters with a common design and shape. Typefaces can add mood or "feeling" to a document. An elementary school teacher may use a comical or childish typeface to create a flyer about an upcoming fair at the school, a hostess may use an elegant typeface to create invitations to a dinner party, and so on. A *font* is a typeface of a certain size and style, such as 12-point Times New Roman bold.

Typefaces have design elements that distinguish them from each other. However, they all have characteristics in common. These characteristics are shown in Figure 14-3.

FIGURE 14-3
Anatomy of a typeface

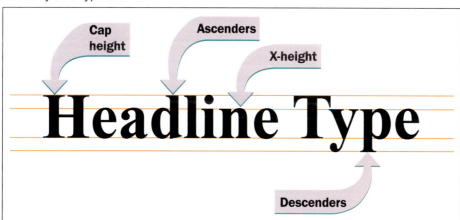

Each typeface rests on an imaginary baseline located at the bottom of the character.

- *X-height* is the height of the main body of the lowercase characters.
- *Cap height* is the distance between the baseline and the top of the capital letters.
- *Ascenders* are the parts of the lowercase characters that extend above the x-height.
- *Descenders* are the parts of the lowercase characters that extend below the baseline.

Types of Typefaces

Serif typefaces are font types in which the letters have small strokes at their ends. Times New Roman is an example of a serif typeface. *Sans serif* typefaces are those font types in which the ends of the letters are plain (without serifs). Technical is an example of a sans serif typeface. Ornamental typefaces are those font types used for special effects and headlines. Engravers is an example of an ornamental typeface.

The font size determines how large or how small the font will appear when printed. The standard measurement unit is the *point,* approximately 1/72 of an inch. The higher the point size, the larger the font. However, a 14-point character in one typeface may not be the same size as a 14-point character in another. A popular size for text in the body of a document is 12 points. Attributes like bold, italic, and color can also be added to any font. See Figure 14-4.

FIGURE 14-4
Font sizes and styles

> Times New Roman is a serif font. This is font size 10.
> Palatino is a serif font. This is font size 14.
> **Helvetica Bold is a sans serif font. This is font size 16.**
> Avant Garde is a sans serif font. This is font size 18.
> *Isadora is a decorative font. This is font size 20.*
> Tekton is a sans serif font, point size 24.

To select various fonts and font sizes, click Fonts on the Format command on the menu bar. You may also select attributes to enhance the font. See Figure 14-5.

FIGURE 14-5
Font attributes

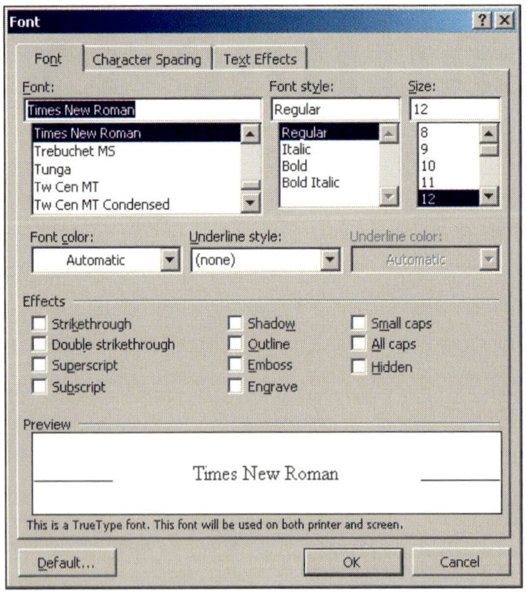

Using Graphics

Graphics are used to add focus, interest, and excitement to a publication. To be used effectively, they should relate to the subject of the document.

Word-processing software programs come with a fairly adequate number of graphic images. These are sometimes referred to as clip art. In addition to using the graphics included in the software, free clip art can be found on the Internet. Additional graphics can be purchased and installed on the computer.

Pictures that have been scanned may also be used. Scanners are used often in desktop publishing. **Scanners** create digital copies of pictures so they can be used in publications. Pictures taken with digital cameras are also a good source of graphics for your publication.

Inserting a Graphic Into a Document

1. Click the Insert command from the menu bar. From there, click Picture, and then Clip Art if you are using clip art provided with the software. If you are using a graphic other than one provided with the software, click on From File and indicate the graphic's location. See Figure 14-6.

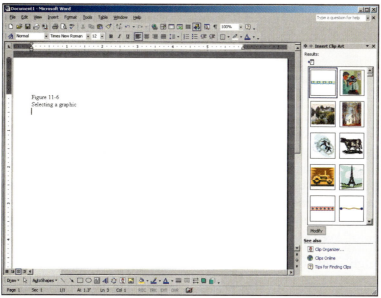

FIGURE 14-6
Inserting a graphic

2. Once a graphic has been inserted into the document, it can be cropped, rotated, sized, or moved.

- *Cropping* a graphic means cutting out a part of the graphic that you do not want to use.
- *Rotating* a graphic means changing the direction of the graphic.
- *Sizing* a graphic means changing the size of the graphic.
- *Moving* a graphic means changing the location of the graphic on the page.

Using WordArt

Some word-processing software programs have a feature that changes normal text into graphic objects. These can be used for headlines or instead of clip art. This feature may have a different name in different programs. It is called WordArt in Microsoft Word and Textart in Corel WordPerfect. See Figure 14-7.

FIGURE 14-7
Text as a graphic object

Using Color

Color can be used to organize ideas and highlight important facts, create focus, and add emphasis. You can add color to your text, lines, borders, symbols, bullets, and shapes. You can even change the color of some graphics. If you do not have access to a color printer, you can print your document on colored paper. Choose colors that complement the contents of the document if possible. When using color, keep these guidelines in mind:

> **Hot Tip**
>
> To find clip art on the Internet, use "free clip art" or the name of the clip art you want as the keywords for your search.

- Use color sparingly—less is best. Use only two or three colors per page.
- Use color to communicate, not to decorate!
- Color can be used to identify a consistent element.
- Do not let color overpower the words!
- Light-colored text is difficult to read, even on a dark background. Black type on a light background is usually best.

Using Lines

Lines can be used in a document to create a focal point, add emphasis, separate columns, or add visual impact. Both horizontal and vertical lines can be created. Lines can be created in various lengths, thicknesses, and shadings.

Using Other Elements

Other elements available to enhance documents include page borders, color, drawing objects, watermarks, and even text boxes.

Many word-processing software programs have features that assist in the creation of documents. These are wizards and templates. *Wizards* walk you through a series of steps in completing a document. You respond to questions as you supply information related to the document you are creating. *Templates* are predesigned documents that already have formatting for margins, tabs, fonts, and some objects included. They save time in creating basic documents such as letters, memos, and reports.

Technology Careers

DESKTOP PUBLISHER/GRAPHIC DESIGNER

What is a desktop publisher? It is anyone whose job or business involves using desktop publishing systems to produce documents. Often, graphic designers are also desktop publishers. Their background and education give them many of the skills needed to perform desktop publishing.

Graphic designers use visual media to convey a message. They create art for corporations, stores, publishing houses, and advertising agencies. They use the computer for designing, sketching, and manipulating images.

Graphic designers still create printed flyers, brochures, newsletters, and pamphlets; however, their work has expanded to include multidimensional work including graphics for screen displays such as television and World Wide Web pages. Graphic designers also work on the design and layout of magazines, newspapers, and other print publications.

The likely employers for a graphic designer would be advertising agencies, design firms, and commercial art houses. Still others are employed by manufacturing firms, retail and department stores. They can also work for themselves, deciding on their own set of clients who contract their services. This is called freelancing.

Graphic designers usually maintain a portfolio of their work to demonstrate their abilities. A bachelor's degree in fine art, graphic design, or visual communications is helpful. Many companies require demonstrated skill in scanning and image correction, the ability to manage multiple simultaneous projects, and demonstrated experience using HTML to develop pages.

Entry-level graphic designers earn between $21,000 and $24,000 annually. Experienced designers can earn much more; up to approximately $55,000, depending on location, level of experience, and type of work.

STEP-BY-STEP 14.1

We are ready to begin to create our sales flyer. Before we begin using the computer, we need to create a thumbnail sketch of how the flyer might look. We will include at least one graphic or WordArt object, various font sizes, color, and possibly a border. Once the thumbnail is completed, we are ready to begin the flyer. Refer again to Figure 14-1 on page 326.

1. Launch your word-processing program and open a blank document.

2. Set the document's margins at .5 inch.

3. Key the text for the flyer. Use font types, sizes, and color that will add to the appearance and message of the flyer. You may center each line of text. (Do not key the word "Sale"; you will use WordArt to create this object.)

4. Insert an appropriate clip art in the flyer. Search for video-related clip art. You may need to size and place the graphic appropriately on the page. Copy the graphic several times so that you will have several on the flyer.

5. Place a border around the page by selecting Borders and Shading on the Format menu. Select a style and color that will be appropriate for the flyer. You may also choose to format with a full-color background by selecting Background on the Format menu.

6. Save the flyer with the filename **Sale**.

7. Print the flyer and close your word-processing software.

Using Microsoft Publisher

If you do not want to take the time to design and lay out a publication, you can use the templates provided in a desktop publishing software program to create business cards, flyers, newsletters, and other such documents easily. Microsoft Publisher is one of these programs. Publisher uses templates for producing these professional-looking documents. You only need to insert the desired information.

Creating a Document Using Publisher

1. Launch Microsoft Publisher. You will see the Publisher screen. See Figure 14-8.

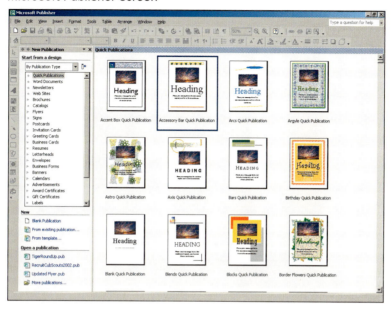

FIGURE 14-8
Microsoft Publisher screen

2. At the left portion of the screen is the task pane. Within the task pane is a list of the various wizards available to create documents using the predesigned templates in Publisher. Scroll through these to see the various available publications.

3. Select the type of publication you want to create. You should see various formats for the type you chose. Select the one you want.

4. You may be prompted for personal information. This information is stored and will be automatically inserted in later publications. You can also update the personal information on the Edit menu. See Figure 14-9.

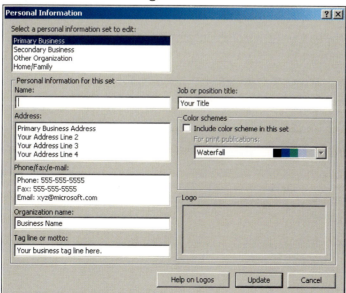

FIGURE 14-9
Personal Information dialog box

5. You will see a screen with an enlarged view of the type of publication you chose. In the task pane, you will see additional options for this publication. See Figure 14-10.

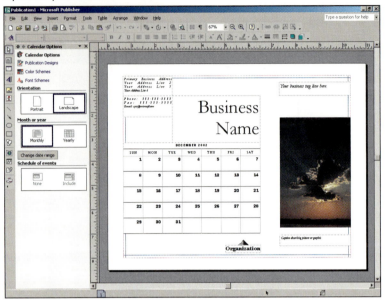

FIGURE 14-10
Specific publication

6. Click in the areas where information is to be added. If you click an area, such as the logo box, a wizard icon will appear. Click it and you will be given additional choices such as various styles of logos. Click the style you prefer.

7. Once you have included all information, save the file.

STEP-BY-STEP 14.2

Let's create a calendar using Microsoft Publisher.

1. Launch Publisher.

2. Select the Calendar Wizard.

3. Scroll through the various styles of calendars and select the one you want. It should appear on the screen. See Figure 14-11.

STEP-BY-STEP 14.2 Continued

FIGURE 14-11
Selected Calendar format

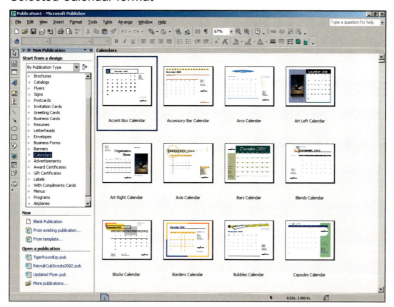

4. Click in the logo area, and then click the wizard icon. Select the style of logo you want to use. Key the desired information in the box.

5. If you did not fill in all of the needed information on the Personal Information screen, you may click in the area where information is still needed and add it. If the text is too small to read, press **F9** to enlarge. Once you have keyed the information, press **F9** again to return the box to its original size.

> **Hot Tip**
>
> If you are preparing a series of documents such as letterhead, business cards, envelopes, etc., for one company or group, you can use the By Design Sets option. This option allows you to maintain consistency throughout all of the documents.

6. Once you have completed the calendar, save it as **Calendar**. Close Microsoft Publisher.

Desktop Publishing Tips

Here are some guidelines that will help you to design and create professional-looking documents.

- Collect ideas that appeal to you from other print publications.
- Use no more than two typefaces per page. Use a serif typeface for the body of the document and a sans serif typeface for the headings.
- Use plenty of white space so the pages do not look overcrowded.
- Use good contrast between the background and the text that appears on it.

- Keep the design simple so the reader gets the message immediately. Limit the number of objects on a page.
- Make the design consistent within a multipage publication.

> **Hot Tip**
> Desktop publishing publications can be converted to HTML documents so they can be uploaded to the Web.

SUMMARY

- Desktop publishing is the process of producing professional-looking documents such as flyers, brochures, reports, newsletters, and pamphlets.
- The advantages of desktop publishing over traditional publishing include savings in production costs, time saved, and greater control.
- The two stages in the desktop publishing process are planning and creating the content.
- Follow these guidelines in designing the publication:

    Focus

    Balance

    Coherence

    Appropriate white space

- Layout and design refer to the way graphics and text are used to produce a high-quality document.
- The text, font style, font size, and typeface used in a document are very important.
- Serif fonts have small strokes at the ends of the letters. Sans serif fonts do not have small strokes at the ends of letters.
- Font size is measured in points. Seventy-two points equal 1 inch.
- Graphics are used to add focus, interest, and excitement to a publication.
- Color can be used to organize ideas and highlight important facts, create focus, and add emphasis.
- Lines can be used in a document to create a focal point, add emphasis, separate columns, or add visual impact.
- Other elements available in most desktop publishing software include wizards and templates.

VOCABULARY Review

Define the following terms:

Ascenders	Font	Templates
Balance	Layout and design	Thumbnail sketch
Cap height	Point	Typeface
Coherence	Sans serif	Wizards
Descenders	Scanners	WYSIWYG
Desktop publishing	Serif	X-height
Focus	Simplicity	

REVIEW Questions

MULTIPLE CHOICE

Select the best response for the following statements.

1. To save time in creating basic documents, _____ may be used.
   A. Thumbnail sketches
   B. Fonts
   C. Templates
   D. DTP

2. In terms of font size, _____ points equal 1 inch.
   A. 36
   B. 24
   C. 18
   D. 72

3. The invention of the _____ computer was the beginning of desktop publishing.
   A. IBM Selectric
   B. Windows 95
   C. Apple Macintosh
   D. Gateway

4. _____ is the element that pulls the reader's eye to it.
   A. Coherence
   B. Consistency
   C. Balance
   D. Focus

5. _____ is/are used to add focus, interest, and excitement to a publication.
   A. Color
   B. WordArt
   C. Lines
   D. Graphics

TRUE/FALSE

Circle T if the statement is true or F if the statement is false.

T   F   1. The Apple Macintosh computer was introduced in 1984. This was the beginning of desktop publishing.

T   F   2. Planning is the first step in designing and creating a professional-looking document.

T   F   3. Serif fonts have small strokes at the ends of each part of the letters.

T   F   4. Graphics downloaded from the Internet may be inserted into a document.

T   F   5. Using color in a document will make the document more effective.

FILL IN THE BLANK

Complete the following sentences by writing the correct word or words in the blanks provided.

1. _____ is the first step in the desktop publishing process.

2. The ability to see on the screen how the document will look when printed is called _____.

3. A _____ is a rough draft drawing used to explore layout options of a document you are creating.

4. A _____ is a set of characters with a common design and shape.

5. _____ are used to add focus, interest, and excitement to a publication.

CROSS-CURRICULAR *Projects*

MATH

Seldom are the measurements used in desktop publishing and typesetting in inches. The most popular measurement is points. Use the Internet and any other resources to identify other measurements used for desktop publishing and typesetting. Create a flyer that will display each measurement, convert it to inches, and give a brief description. Use the keywords *desktop publishing* and *desktop publishing measurements* with your favorite search engine such as *www.AskJeeves.com, www.mamma.com,* or *www.dogpile.com.*

SCIENCE

Use the Internet to locate information on the first typewriter. Look for specifics on the design of the keyboard, how it was supposed to work, and reactions and responses to this new tool (during that time). Design and prepare a flyer announcing this new phenomenon using the desktop publishing features of your word-processing software or your dedicated desktop publishing software. (*Hint:* Christopher Sholes invented the typewriter.) Use the following keywords with search engines: *early typewriters, typewriters, Christopher Sholes,* and *typewriter keyboards.*

SOCIAL STUDIES

Research the Internet and other sources to find information on a place you would like to visit. Gather all the important information you would need to make a decision to visit this place and create a travel brochure. List exciting places to see, historical information, tourist attractions, and any other information you think would enhance your brochure.

LANGUAGE ARTS

Select a book that you have read in class. Design and create a new cover for the book. Use the desktop publishing features of your software program.

WEB PROJECT

You and a friend are very interested in sports and have followed the careers of many athletes for years. Your friend has expressed an interest in becoming an agent for sports personalities. Sports figures make big salaries, and their agents make impressive salaries also. Your friend is not exactly sure just what sports agents do to earn their salaries. You have decided to do some research on this topic and prepare a brochure on a career as a sports agent.

TEAMWORK PROJECT

The store manager has asked you and the other part-time employees to work together to develop a brochure on the services and products that Vista Multimedia offers. You are to work together on all aspects of the brochure: development, writing, editing of the text, page layout, and any graphics that will be incorporated. You will need to make individual assignments. Remember to create a thumbnail sketch first.

LESSON 15

CREATING A WEB PAGE

OBJECTIVES

Upon completion of this lesson, you should be able to:

- Understand how a Web page works.
- Plan a document.
- Understand and explain basic HTML syntax.
- Understand and apply headings.
- Understand and apply bold and italics.
- Understand and apply lists.
- Understand and add links.
- Understand and add graphics.
- Publish a Web page.

Estimated Time: 1.5 hours

VOCABULARY

Absolute link
Attribute
Background
Body
Character entities
E-mail link
Font
Head
Headings
Home page
HTML
Hyperlinks
Images
Links
Lists
Relative link
Title
Web page
Web server

Ms. Perez is very excited about the possibilities of advertising Vista Multimedia on the Web. She also would like to have her own personal Web page. She has one or two ideas about what she would like to do, but she still does not fully understand what is involved. You explain to Ms. Perez that the process of creating a Web page is not difficult. You further explain that several Web page authoring programs are available that will create the underlying code. To fully understand Web page creation and to better use the authoring programs, however, it is important to have an understanding of hypertext markup language (HTML). The basic HTML tags are covered in this lesson. Many other tags and methods are available that you can use to develop and enhance Web pages.

How a Web Page Works

Have you ever wondered how a Web page works? When you consider the billions of Web pages on the Internet, you might make the assumption that it is not that difficult to create a Web page. In fact, not only is it incredibly easy to create a Web page, it also is a lot of fun.

Before beginning the process of creating a Web page, you need an understanding of some basic terminology:

- *Web page*: This is a plain text document on a server connected to the World Wide Web. Every Web page is identified by a uniform resource locator (URL), or unique Web address.

- *HTML*: HTML, or hypertext markup language, is the language of the Web. HTML is a series of tags that are integrated into a text document. These tags describe how the text should be formatted when a Web browser displays it on the screen.

- *Web browser*: A Web browser is an application program that interprets the HTML tags within the page and then displays the text on the computer screen. Two of the most popular Web browsers are Microsoft Internet Explorer and Netscape Navigator.

- *Web server*: A Web server displays Web pages and renders them into final form so they can be viewed by anyone with an Internet connection and a Web browser. Every Web server has a unique Web address or URL.

You may infer from these basic terminology definitions that you need a Web server before you can create your Web page. This is not true. The only tools you need are your Web browser and a text-editing program. A Web browser easily can display your Web page from a personal computer. Once you create a Web page and have it in final format, most likely you will want to publish it to a Web server. Publishing a Web page is covered later in the lesson.

Plan a Document

Many times when people start a project, they have a tendency to jump right in without any planning. Sometimes this works, but more often than not, they find themselves having to back up and redo some of the work. Planning may take a small amount of extra time in the beginning, but it will save time in the long run. Before you start creating your personal Web page, consider some of the elements you may want to include. See Figure 15-1.

FIGURE 15-1
Sample Web page outline

Sample Web page outline
Title: A title for your Web page

Page Content:
    Hobbies
    School Favorites
    Family
    Favorite Vacation destination
    What I did last summer

Hyperlinks:
    Sony PlayStation
    My School
    Skateboarding.com
    My favorite sports team

Closing:
    My e-mail address
    My favorite quote

- *Title:* This can be anything you choose, but should be relevant to the content contained on the page. An example title is "Joe Smith's Personal Web Page." (You would substitute your name for Joe Smith.) When someone accesses your Web page on the Internet, the title displays on the browser's title bar.

- *Page content:* Determine what you want to include in your Web page. Do you want to share information about your family, your hobbies, your school, or sports? Make a list of what features you would like to include. Limit the content to one topic per Web page.

- *Links:* To what other Web sites would you like to link? Make a note of these. You will need the URL, or Web site address, for each link.

- *Closing comments:* Do you want to include any closing comments? Perhaps you want to add your e-mail address so that someone accessing your Web page can contact you.

A Basic Page

An HTML page has two components—page content and HTML tags. The page content is that part of the document that displays in the browser. This could be, for example, a list of your hobbies or other information about yourself or your school. HTML tags are easily identifiable because they are enclosed in brackets: <HTML>. The tags do not display in the browser. The HTML tags define the structure and layout of the Web page. The main page or index page of most Web sites is referred to as the *home page*.

- Many tags come in pairs with a start tag and an end tag. For instance, <TITLE> is a start tag and </TITLE> is an end tag. You identify an end tag by including the slash (</>) character before the name of the tag. The start and end tag identify the content between them as being HTML formatted. These sometimes are called *container tags*.

- Some tags are a single entity—that is, they do not have an end tag. An example is the <BR> tag, which indicates a line break.

- Tags are not case sensitive, but it is best to select a format and stay with it. In this lesson, uppercase letters are used for all HTML tags.

- Some tags can contain *attributes*. For example, the <BODY> tag is required for all HTML documents. But if you wanted the background color of your Web page to be blue, you can add an attribute so your <BODY> tag would look like this: <BODY bgcolor = "Blue">.

> **Net Tip**
> You can view the HTML code for documents on the Web. Surf the Internet and find a Web page that you like. On your browser's menu, click View and then click Source to display the HTML code.

Every new page you create requires a set of tags structured in a particular format. See Figure 15-2. The structure of the tags always remains the same. In Figure 15-2, each tag is on a separate line. In HTML, you could key everything on one continuous line because the tags determine how the page displays. For readability and editing purposes within the HTML document, however, typing each command on a separate line is a better procedure.

- **HTML:** In Figure 15-2 the first line in the document is <HTML>, a start tag, and the last line is </HTML>, an end tag. All other tags and page content are contained within these two tags.

- **HEAD:** Contained within the start and end <HEAD> tags is the <TITLE> tag.

- **TITLE:** The title tag (<TITLE>) gives the page its official title. The content entered between the start and end title tags is displayed on the browser's title bar.
- **BODY:** All Web page content is contained between the start and end <BODY> tags.

In the examples in this book, Windows Notepad is used to create the HTML documents. As previously mentioned, however, you can use any text-editing program to create a Web page. You can use a word-processing program, for instance, but you must save your document in text format.

The tags contained in Figure 15-2 are required for all HTML documents; therefore, your first goal is to create a template containing these tags.

FIGURE 15-2
Required HTML tags

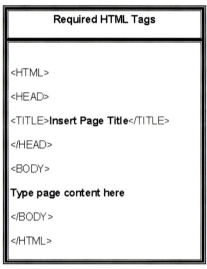

STEP-BY-STEP 15.1

1. Launch your text-editing program.

2. Create the template shown in Figure 15-3.

3. Save your text file with the filename **template.htm**. (You may want to change Save As type from the default, which is Text Document, to All Files.)

4. Keep your text editor open for the next Step-by-Step.

When you create any future HTML document, you can open this template file, save it with a different filename, and add your page content.

Your next task is to add a title and a line of page content, and then view your Web page in your browser.

FIGURE 15-3
HTML template

STEP-BY-STEP 15.2

1. If necessary, launch your text-editing program and open the template document **template.htm**.

Note that most programs save with a particular file type or extension. To display this document name and to open the document, you may have to change Types of files to All files (*.*).

STEP-BY-STEP 15.2 Continued

2. Click **File** on the menu bar and then click the **Save As** command. Save the document using your first and last name and the .htm extension. Use an underscore (_) between your first and last names.

In the example in Figure 15-4, we create a Web page for Joe Smith, a student who works part time for Vista Multimedia. We save the page as Joe_Smith.htm using Joe's first and last names.

3. Between the start and end <TITLE> tags, key **[Your name]'s Web page**.

4. Between the two BODY tags, key **Welcome to my Web page**.

5. Click **File** on the menu bar and then click the **Save** command.

6. Launch your browser.

7. Click **File** on the menu bar and then click the **Open** command.

8. Click **Browse**, locate your file, click **Open**, and then click **OK**.

9. Close your browser.

Congratulations! You have just created and displayed your first Web page.

FIGURE 15-4A
HTML source page

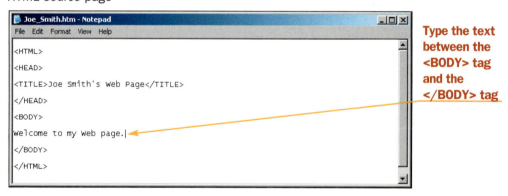

Type the text between the <BODY> tag and the </BODY> tag

FIGURE 15-4B
Web page displayed in Internet Explorer

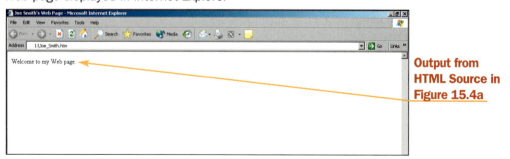

Output from HTML Source in Figure 15.4a

Review your Web page as it displays in the browser and compare it to your HTML document. Notice that none of the HTML tags display. The text you keyed between the start and end <TITLE> tags displays in the browser's title bar. This text does not display as part of the document itself. The only text that displays as part of the document is the text you keyed between the start and end <BODY> tags: *Welcome to my Web page.*

Page Formatting

One of the first things you will discover when creating a Web page is that pressing the keyboard's Enter key has no effect on how a Web page displays in a browser. You can press Enter a dozen times or more, but it will not make a difference when the page displays. The browser ignores any blank lines you attempt to enter from the keyboard. Instead, you use HTML tags to start a new line and/or to leave spaces between lines.

Line Breaks

If you want to start a new line but not leave a space between lines, you use the break tag: <BR>. The break tag is a single entity. That is, you do not need a start and end tag. You can use the break tag to start a new line or you can use two line break tags to insert a blank line. See Figure 15-5.

FIGURE 15-5
Adding the break tag

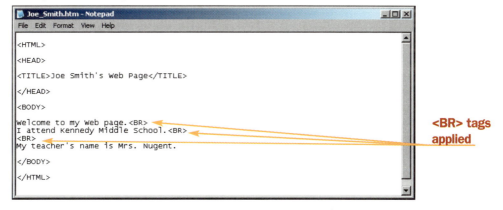

Paragraph Breaks

A second way to insert a blank line is with the paragraph tag: <P>. An end tag </P> is not required, but many Web programmers include it as a matter of style. When the Web page displays in a browser, a paragraph tag shows a blank line between two paragraphs—basically the same thing as two line break tags <BR> entered consecutively. See Figure 15-6A and B.

FIGURE 15-6A
Adding the paragraph tag

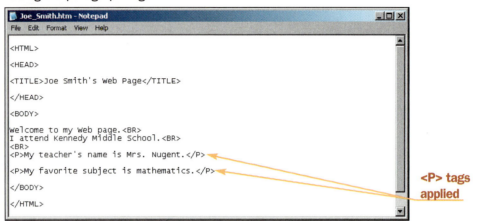

<P> tags applied

FIGURE 15-6B
Output from the HTML source

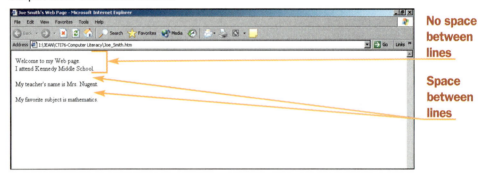

No space between lines

Space between lines

 Technology Careers

CONSULTANT

Consultants provide professional advice or services. They have specialized knowledge that they can sell to their clients. Many consultants work on short-term projects for companies that may not have employees with the required skills for a particular job. Consultants may telecommute or work from home.

Successful consultants can be found in just about every field imaginable. There are garage-sale consultants and consultants who will help you arrange your closets. However, the information technology field has created an entire new line of consultants. There are programming consultants, database consultants, and even Web designer and Web development consultants. If you enjoy working with computers and, in particular, developing Web pages, consulting may be a job field that you would want to investigate.

STEP-BY-STEP 15.3

1. If necessary, launch your text-editing program and open your Web page .htm document.

2. At the end of the *Welcome to My Web page* line, key **
**.

3. Press **Enter** two times. (Remember that pressing Enter does not affect the way in which the Web page displays in a browser. You press Enter for readability purposes within your HTML document. Adding blank lines when creating your Web page makes it easier to read and edit your document.)

4. Key **<P>I attend Kennedy Middle School.</P>**. Key **
** and then press **Enter**.

5. Key **<P>My teacher's name is Ms. Nugent.</P>**. Press **Enter** two times.

6. Key **<P>My favorite subject is mathematics.</P>**. Press **Enter**.

7. Click **File** on the menu bar and then click **Save**.

8. Launch your browser.

9. Click **File** on the menu bar and then click **Open**.

10. Click the **Browse** button, locate your Web page file, click **Open**, and then click **OK** to display your page in the browser.

11. Close your browser.

Lists

Lists are a popular way to arrange and organize text on a Web page. Within HTML, there are three types of lists:

- **Ordered list:** This is generally a numbered list and requires a start <OL> and an end </OL> tag. Each item in the list begins with <LI>.

- **Unordered list:** This is generally a bulleted list and requires a start <UL> and an end </UL> tag. Each item in the list begins with <LI>.

- **Definition list**: This is a list of terms with indented definitions, generally used for glossary items or other definitions. This list requires a start tag <DL> and an end tag </DL>. Additionally, the tag <DT> is required for the term and <DD> is required for the definition. See Figures 15-7A and 15-7B. In Figure 15-7A, the entire template is not displayed—only the text that is between the start and end <BODY> tags.

FIGURE 15-7A
Ordered, unordered, and definition lists

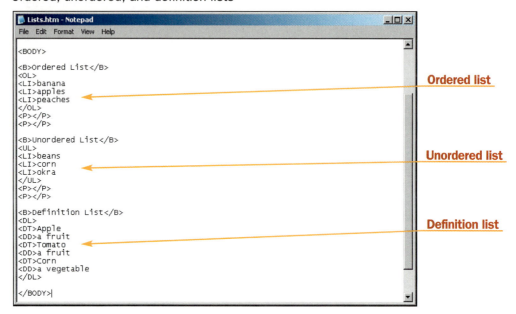

FIGURE 15-7B
Lists displayed in browser

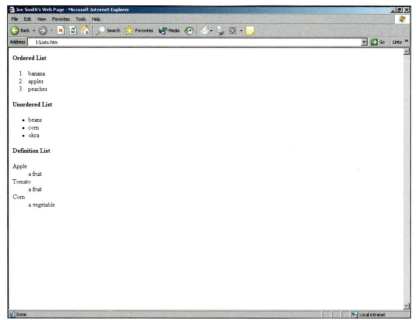

Center

Another way to organize text on the page is to use the <CENTER> tag. This tag requires both a start and end tag. Simply enclose the text between the start tag and the end tag and the text will be centered when displayed in a browser. You can center a single word, a sentence, a paragraph, a series of paragraphs, a table, or even an image. See Figures 15-8A and 15-8B.

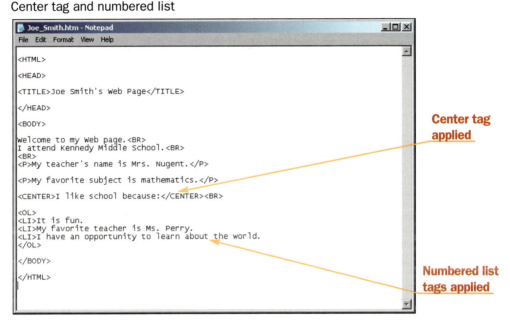

FIGURE 15-8A
Center tag and numbered list

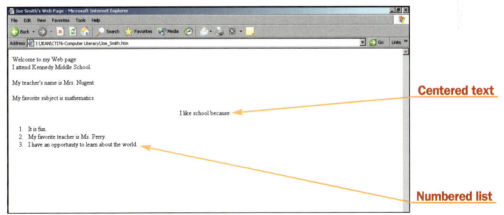

FIGURE 15-8B
Text centered in browser

STEP-BY-STEP 15.4

1. If necessary, launch your text-editing program and open your Web page document.

2. Position the insertion point below the last sentence you entered in the previous Step-by-Step (*My favorite subject is mathematics.*) and key **<CENTER> I like school because: </CENTER>**.

STEP-BY-STEP 15.4 Continued

3. Key a Break **
** tag and press **Enter** two times.

4. Key **<OL>** to begin your ordered list. Press **Enter**.

5. Key **<LI>** to begin the first item in the list.

6. Key **It is fun.** Press **Enter**.

7. Key **<LI>** and then key **My favorite teacher is [add teacher's name].** Press **Enter**.

8. Key **<LI>** and then key **I have an opportunity to learn about the world.** Press **Enter**.

9. Key **</OL>** to end the list.

10. Save your file.

11. Display the file in your browser.

12. Close your browser.

Text Formatting

Now that you have learned some ways in which you can control the placement of text in the browser, it is time to learn how to format the text. Just like formatting text within your word processing program, you also can apply formatting to text that is displayed in a Web browser. Some of the text formatting attributes you can apply are as follows:

- **Bold:** To bold text requires start <B> and end </B> tags. Surround the text with these tags and your text displays as bold in your browser.

- **Italics:** To display italicized text, use the start <I> and end </I> tags.

- **Underline:** To underline text, use the start <U> and end </U> tags.

You can apply one attribute such as bold to a word, sentence, or paragraph, or you can apply two or all three attributes at one time. See Figures 15-9A and 15-9B.

FIGURE 15-9A
HTML for bold, italics, and underline

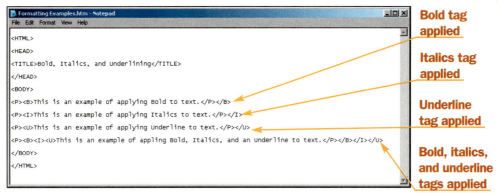

FIGURE 15-9B
Text formatting attributes in browser

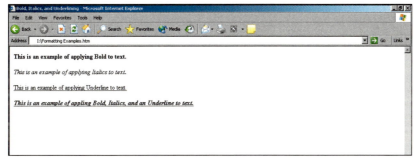

Changing Font Size and Color

When you browse the Internet, your browser displays the text based on a default *font* size, type, and color. The font size, type, and color, however, can be changed. This is done through the start <FONT> and end </FONT> tags.

If you have used a word-processing program, you know it is easy to change the font or text size. You can make the text very small or very large. Your options within HTML are not as flexible as they are within a word-processing program. Most browsers support and display seven different font or text sizes. The sizes range from 1, which is the smallest, to 7, which is the largest. The default font size is 3. To change the font size, you add the SIZE attribute to the FONT tag, for example: <FONT SIZE = 5>. Figure 15-10A shows the HTML tags and Figure 15-10B displays a list of how the various font sizes display within a browser.

FIGURE 15-10A
HTML tags for changing font sizes

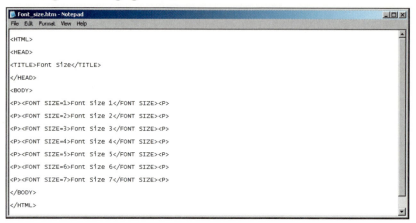

FIGURE 15-10B
Font tags displayed in browser

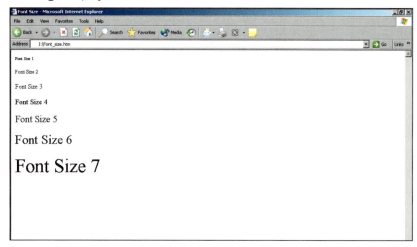

Changing the font color is just as easy as changing the font size. This is accomplished by using the COLOR attribute, for example: <FONT COLOR = RED>. Another option is to combine the font size and font color within one tag. Example: <FONT SIZE = 1 COLOR = RED>. See Figures 15-11A for the HTML tags and Figure 15-11B for an example of how the font color and size display in a browser.

FIGURE 15-11A
HTML tags for changing font sizes and font color

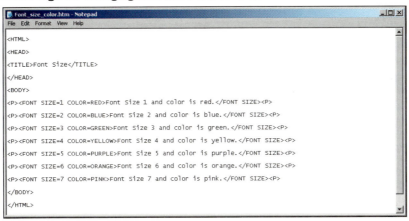

FIGURE 15-11B
Font sizes and colors in browser

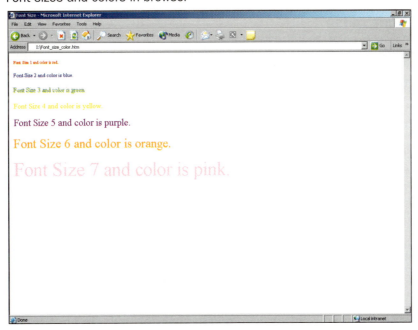

A third font attribute you can add is the font type, for example: <FONT FACE = ARIAL>. If you wish, you can even specify color, size, and type all within one start and end tag. See Figures 15-12A and 15-12B.

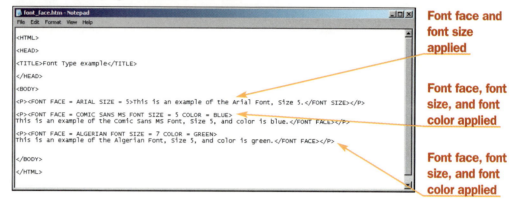

FIGURE 15-12A
Font tags specifying face, color, and size

Font face and font size applied

Font face, font size, and font color applied

Font face, font size, and font color applied

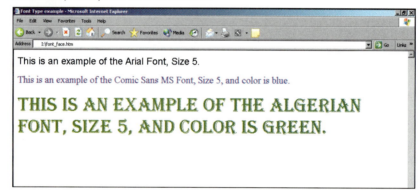

FIGURE 15-12B
Font face, color, and size in browser

Headings

If you are familiar with word processing, you may have used styles. A style is a set of formatting characteristics that you can apply to text in your document to quickly change its appearance. HTML does support styles, but only through stylesheets. Stylesheets are not covered in this book. The HTML heading tags, however, do provide some formatting options. The characteristics of *headings* include the typeface, size, and the extra space above or below the heading. The browser you use, however, determines the final appearance.

Seven levels of HTML headings are available. The start tag for the first level is <H1> and the end tag is </H1>. For the other six levels, just substitute the desired number within the start and end tags. Level 1 is the largest and level 7 is the smallest. In Figure 15-13A, no break <BR> or paragraph <P> tags are added following each line. In Figure 15-13B, however, in which the Web page is displayed in the browser, blank lines appear between each of the headings. This is a characteristic of the heading tag.

FIGURE 15-13A
Heading tags

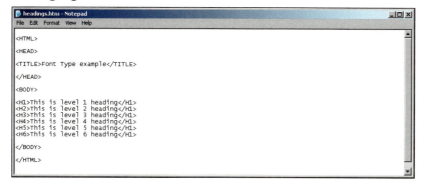

FIGURE 15-13B
Heading tags displayed in browser

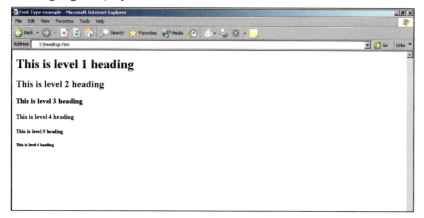

Links

A defining feature of any Web document is *links* or *hyperlinks*, which are active references to other parts of the same document or to other documents. The other documents can be on the same computer, on a local network server (intranet), or stored on a computer in another country. If you know the address or URL of the document and the address of the computer on which it resides, you can link to it.

Providing links between documents gives the user easy access to related information. Links are relative or absolute.

Relative Links

When all the files, including the graphics and images, are saved in one folder or will be published on the same Web server, you should use relative links. A *relative link*, also called an *internal link*, gives the file location in relation to the current document. When you use relative links, you can move the folder and files that contain the hyperlink and maintain the destination of the link without breaking the path of the relative link.

The tags for a relative link are <A HREF = "FILE-NAME"> </A>. The <A> within this tag represents *Anchor* and the HREF represents *hyperlink reference*. Assume that Joe Smith's Web page is located in a folder titled Personal. Joe Smith creates a second Web page titled Hobbies and saves it in the Personal folder. He would like to link to this second Web page from his Joe Smith's Web page. To do this, he creates a relative link. The link would look like the following: <A HREF = "HOBBIES.HTM"> </A>.

> **Did You Know?**
>
> One of the greatest problems on the Web is that users do not know where they are going when they follow links. Most browsers support the capability to pop up a short description of the link. When the user moves the cursor over the link, the description is displayed. To create a title within the link, you would key <A HREF="ROCKCLIMBING.COM" TITLE="Good information at this site">Rock Climbing </A>.

STEP-BY-STEP 15.5

1. Launch your text-editing program and open your Web page document.
2. Click at the end of the last line you keyed (the ending tag for the ordered list </OL>) and press **Enter** two times.

 Ethics in Technology

UNDERSTANDING E-MAIL ENCRYPTION

When you send an e-mail message, you may not realize that it can literally bounce all over the world before it reaches its final destination. As your e-mail message travels from computer to computer, it may encounter "sniffers," or software programs that are waiting to alter or tamper with your e-mail. Most of the time, the e-mail that you send may not be that important. It could be a note to a friend or a request for information. On the other hand, it could contain your computer network login and password and or maybe even a credit card number.

Several companies have made available programs to encrypt your e-mail. In fact, there are literally hundreds of e-mail encryption programs. If you are using recent versions of Netscape Communicator or Internet Explorer, you have encryption options. Internet Explorer, for example, has two different types of certificates to protect your privacy: a personal certificate and a Web site certificate.

Encryption programs work with cryptographic keys. The user provides a password and the program turns the password into a key. There is both a public key and a private key. The user retains the private key for decryption purposes.

STEP-BY-STEP 15.5 Continued

3. Key **<A HREF="Hobbies.htm">Click here for a list of my favorite hobbies.</A>**. See Figure 15-14A.

4. Save your document and then close it.

5. Open the **template.htm** file.

6. Click **File** on the menu bar and then click **Save As**. Key **Hobbies.htm** for the filename. (You may want to change Save as type, which is Text Document, to All Files.)

7. In between the start and end <BODY> tags, key **<CENTER><H1>My Favorite Hobbies </CENTER></H1>** and then press **Enter**.

8. Key **<P>My favorite hobbies are [list two or three of your favorite hobbies] </P>**. See Figure 15-14B.

FIGURE 15-14A
Relative link added to HTML document

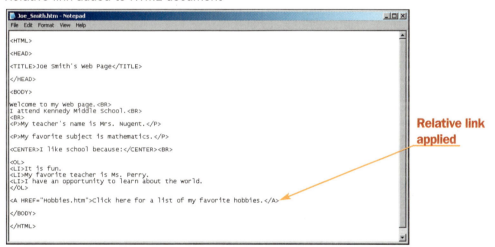

FIGURE 15-14B
HTML for Hobbies page

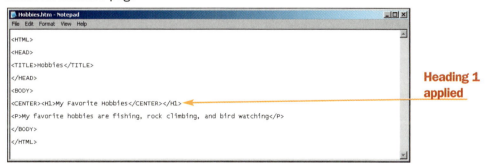

STEP-BY-STEP 15.5 Continued

9. Key **Hobbies** between the two <TITLE> tags for the new title.

10. Save and close your Hobbies.htm document.

11. Launch your browser and open your Web page document. You should see the link to the Hobbies page as shown in Figure 15-14C.

12. Click the **Hobbies** link to display the Hobbies page in your Web browser. It should appear similar to Figure 15-14D.

13. Close the browser.

FIGURE 15-14C
Link to Hobbies page

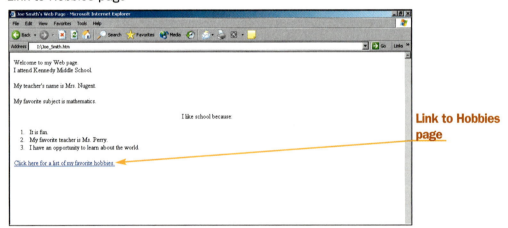

FIGURE 15-14D
Hobbies Web page displayed in browser

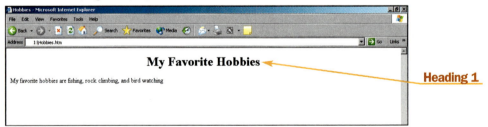

Absolute Link

Absolute links are links to Web pages on other servers. If you want to link to a list of your favorite places on the Web, you would use an absolute link. These links use a fixed file location or Web address. The fixed location identifies the destination by its full address. An example of an absolute link is <A HREF = HTTP://WWW.ROCKCLIMBING.COM> Rock Climbing </A>. See Figures 15-15A and 15-15B for the HTML example and browser display.

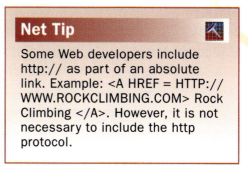

Net Tip

Some Web developers include http:// as part of an absolute link. Example: <A HREF = HTTP://WWW.ROCKCLIMBING.COM> Rock Climbing </A>. However, it is not necessary to include the http protocol.

FIGURE 15-15A
Absolute links

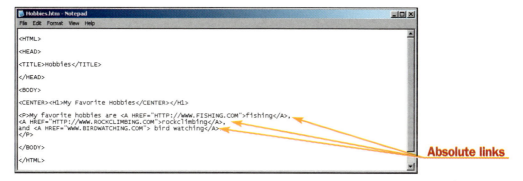

FIGURE 15-15B
Absolute links displayed in browser

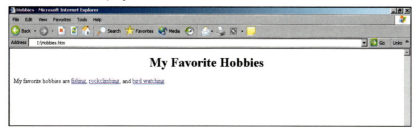

E-Mail

Another type of link is an e-mail link. An *e-mail link* displays a blank e-mail form containing the recipient's address. It is a good idea to include your e-mail address on every page of your site. When the user clicks the e-mail address, the browser starts a mail program, and the e-mail address automatically is inserted into the address line. You use the <A> tag to create the link. Example: <A HREF="mailto:joesmith@hotmail.com">Joe Smith</A>. See Figure 15-16 for an example of an e-mail link displayed in a browser.

FIGURE 15-16
E-mail link displayed in browser

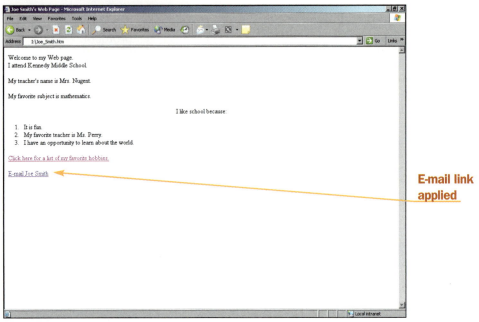

Images

Images (also called *graphics*) add life to your Web site and make it exciting and fun. As much as they can add to a page, however, they also can slow the downloading of your file, especially for someone with slow access to the Internet. Many times when it takes too long to download a page, the person browsing the Web clicks the browser's Stop button and moves on to another site. Keep this in mind when you are creating your pages.

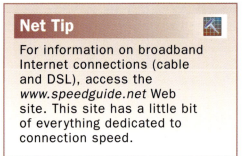

Net Tip

For information on broadband Internet connections (cable and DSL), access the *www.speedguide.net* Web site. This site has a little bit of everything dedicated to connection speed.

Image Formats

Three different image types are supported by most browsers and are displayed on the Web:

- **GIF:** This is the most commonly used file type. It stands for graphic interchange format and is pronounced "jif."

- **JPG or JPEG:** This is another commonly used file format that results in smaller file sizes than GIF. This format is best used for photographs and other photo-quality images. JPEG stands for joint photographic experts group.

- **PNG:** This is a more recent format. It has the advantages of both JPEG and GIF. It is native to Macromedia Fireworks® and is not widely used. PNG stands for portable network graphics.

To add an image to your Web page, use the <IMG> tag. This is a single tag; that is, there is no end tag. However, many attributes are available that you can use within this tag. Table 15-1 contains a list of image attributes. Three of the most popular are as follows:

- The first is SRC and is mandatory. Example: <IMG SRC = "Joe.gif">. SRC stands for *source*.

- The second attribute that you can use with this tag is <ALT>. Use this attribute to provide alternative text. Some people with slow Internet access turn off automatic image loading. Using the ALT (alternate) attribute provides them with an indication of the nature of the picture. For visually impaired users who use speech synthesizers with text-only browsers, the text in the ALT tag is spoken out loud. In some browsers, this text also appears when the pointer is over the image. Example: <IMG SRC = "Joe.gif" ALT = "Joe Smith's picture">.

> **Internet**
>
> If you are looking for a Web site with free graphics and information on creating graphics, try Laurie McCanna, author of the "Creating Great Web Graphics" Web site located at *www.mccannas.com/*.

- A third attribute is ALIGN. Using this attribute, you can align the image in relation to the location of the image and the text. This is an optional attribute. Example: <IMG SRC = "Joe.gif" ALT = "Joe Smith's picture" ALIGN = LEFT>.

TABLE 15-1
Image attributes

ATTRIBUTE	FUNCTION
ALIGN	Controls alignment; options include bottom, middle, top, left, right
BORDER	Defines the border width
HEIGHT	Defines the height of the image
HSPACE	Defines the horizontal space that separates the text from the image
SRC	Defines the location or URL of the image
VSPACE	Defines the vertical space that separates the text from the image
WIDTH	Defines the width of the image

When you look at a Web page with images, the images appear to be part of the page. In reality, however, if the browser displays three images, you have four separate files—the HTML file and the three image files. When the browser encounters the <IMG> tag, it knows to look for the SRC or source. The image could be located in the same folder as your HTML document, or it could be located on a totally different computer on the other side of the world. If it is an external link, you would specify the address of the image, just like you specify the address of the absolute link. Example: <IMG SRC = "www.rockclimbing.com/Joe.gif" ALT = "Joe Smith's picture" ALIGN = LEFT>.

You might wonder how the browser knows where to display the image on the page. You can place images almost anywhere within the body of your Web page. They can be on a line by themselves, at the end of a paragraph, at the beginning of a line, in the middle of a line, and so forth.

Using the <ALIGN> tag and other attributes listed in Table 15-1, you can control to an extent where they are placed. See Figures 15-17A and 15-17B.

FIGURE 15-17A
Image tags

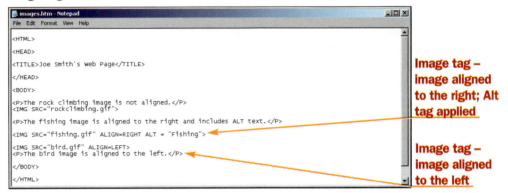

FIGURE 15-17B
Alignment of images in browser

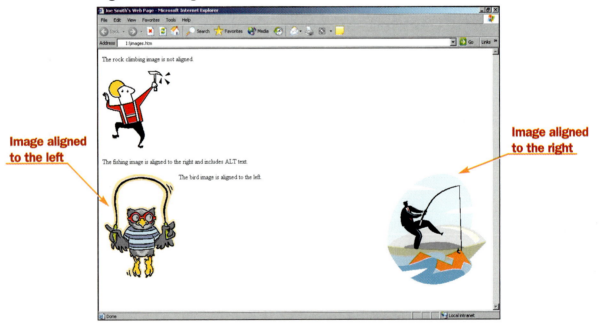

Horizontal Rules and Bulleted Lists

Many Web designers use horizontal rules (also called lines) to separate blocks of text. The horizontal rule <HR> is a single-entry tag that renders a thin line that extends across the width of the browser window. Simply enter the code and the line displays.

Another option for separating blocks of text is to use some type of graphical divider. Many graphical dividers are available for download on the Web, or you can create your own with a paint or draw program such as Jasc® Paint Shop Pro or Adobe® PhotoShop®. To add a graphical horizontal line to your Web page, simply go to the location within the document where you would like it to display. Then use the <IMG SRC> tag to insert it into your page, for example: <IMG SRC = "graphical_line.gif">.

Earlier in this lesson you learned how to create and display bulleted lists. Suppose you prefer graphical bullets instead of the standard bullets. This also is accomplished easily with the <IMG SRC> tag. Simply place the tag and the image name before the line of text. See Figures 15-18A and 15-18B.

FIGURE 15-18A
Horizontal rule, graphical line, and graphical bullets

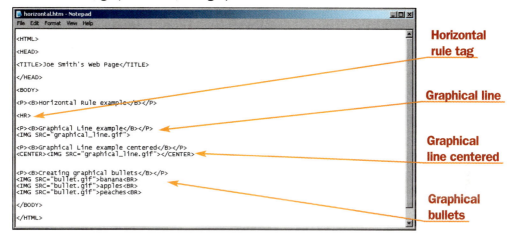

FIGURE 15-18B
Horizontal rule, graphical line, and graphical bullets displayed in browser

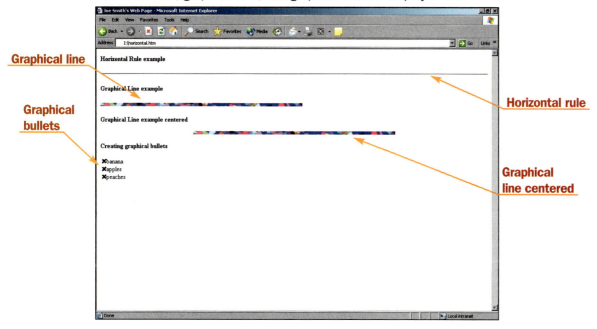

Character Entities

Some characters have a special meaning in HTML, such as the less than sign (<) that defines the start of an HTML tag. To have the browser display these characters requires that the *character entities* be inserted in the HTML document. A character entity has three parts: an ampersand (&), a # and an entity number, and a semicolon (;). The most common character entity in HTML is the nonbreaking space. If you key five spaces, for example, in your HTML document, the browser only recognizes one. Table 15-2 contains a list of the more common character entities. See Figure 15-19 for an example of a nonbreaking space.

> **Internet**
> Many places on the Web provide free images. Access the AskJeeves natural language search engine at *www.aj.com* and ask Jeeves "Where can I find free graphics?"

TABLE 15-2
Character Entities

CHARACTERS	DESCRIPTION	NAME
&	ampersand	&amp;
'	apostrophe	&#39;
>	greater than	&gt;
<	less than	&lt;
	nonbreaking space	
"	quotation mark	&quot;

Backgrounds

As you surf the Web, you may notice the background color of many Web pages is either white or gray. Generally, the browser you are using determines the background color. You also may have noticed that many Web pages have color or an image for the *background*. You, too, can add color or images to the background of your Web pages. To add a background color, include the BGCOLOR attribute in the <BODY> tag, for example: <BODY BGCOLOR = "PINK">. See Figures 15-19A and B.

> **Internet**
> If you are looking for backgrounds for your Web site, then one of the first places you should visit is Yahoo's Background for Web Pages. Here you will find an extensive list of links to many Web sites. Just go to *www.yahoo.com* and search for Web Page backgrounds.

FIGURE 15-19A
Background color tag

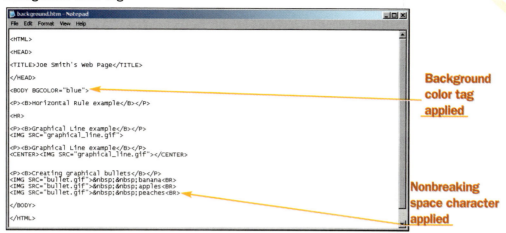

FIGURE 15-19B
Background color displayed in browser

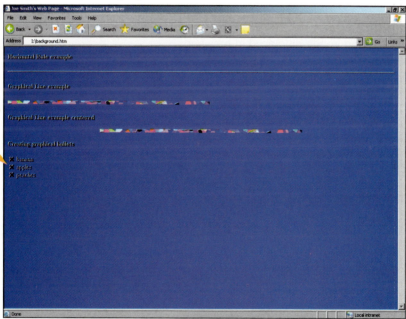

To add a background image to your Web page, specify the image name within the <BODY> tag. Example: <BODY BGGROUND = "IMAGE.GIF">. See Figures 15-20A and B.

FIGURE 15-20A
Background image tag

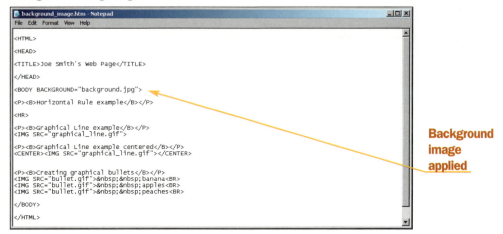

FIGURE 15-20B
Background image displayed in browser

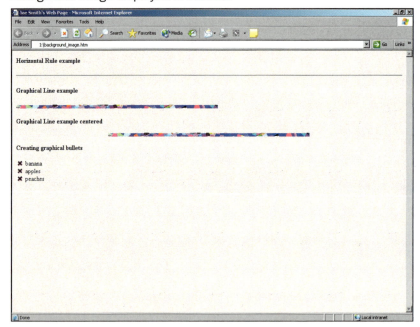

Publishing Your Web Page

Your school may have its own Web server that you can use to publish your Web page creations. If not, do not be dismayed. A dozen or more Web sites on the Internet offer free space.

Two of the more popular of these are Tripod, located at *http://www.tripod.lycos.com/*, and Yahoo's GeoCities, located at *geocities.yahoo.com/home/*. See Figures 15-21 and 15-22.

FIGURE 15-21
Yahoo! Geocities free Web space

FIGURE 15-22
Tripod free Web space

Most of the sites that provide free space also provide step-by-step instructions on how to upload your page. Just locate and click on the Sign up link or the link indicating free home page or free space on their server. If you wonder how someone can offer free space for you to save your Web pages, check out the advertising on the Web site. These companies generate their income by selling banners and other advertising space.

> **Did You Know?**
>
> There are many free hosting sites on the Web. Some of them even offer several MB of free disk space. One of the most popular of these is *http://www.freeservers.com/*. This site advertises 12 MB of storage space for your files and free e-mail forwarding.

SUMMARY

In this lesson, you learned:

- A Web page is a document on the World Wide Web and is defined by a unique URL.
- HTML is the language of the Web.
- A Web browser is an application program that interprets the HTML tags within the page and then displays the text on the computer screen.
- A basic Web page has both page content and HTML tags.
- Some tags come in pairs and others are single entities.
- Every Web page requires a particular set of tags structured in a particular format.
- Pressing the keyboard Enter key has no effect on how a Web page displays.
- To start a new line in a Web page, use the break <BR> tag.
- To insert a blank line in a Web page, use the paragraph <P> tag.
- HTML supports three types of lists that you can use to organize text on a Web page.
- The Center <Center> tag is used to center text or graphics.
- HTML supports bold, italics, and underline text formatting.
- HTML supports changing of font size and font color.
- Seven different font sizes are supported by most browsers.
- Six levels of HTML headings are supported by most browsers.
- A hyperlink is an active reference to another part of the same document or to another document.
- A relative link gives the file location in relation to the current document.
- Absolute links are hyperlinks to other Web sites.
- One of the most common types of non-Web links is e-mail.
- Three different image types are supported by browsers—GIF, JPEG, and PNG.
- HTML supports the use of horizontal lines to separate blocks of text.
- HTML supports adding a background color to a Web page.

- HTML supports adding a background image to a Web page.
- Many Web sites provide free space online for publishing your Web page.

VOCABULARY Review

Define the following terms:

Absolute links	Head	Links
Attribute	Headings	Lists
Background	Home page	Relative link
Body	HTML	Title
Character entities	Hyperlinks	Web page
E-mail link	Images	Web server
Font		

REVIEW Questions

MULTIPLE CHOICE

Select the best response for the following statements.

1. _____ is the language of the Web.
   - A. Image
   - B. BGCOLOR
   - C. HTML
   - D. HTTP

2. The _____ of your Web page is what appears on the browser title bar.
   - A. Body
   - B. Heading
   - C. Title
   - D. Closing

3. All Web page content is contained between the start and end _____ tags.
   - A. Title
   - B. Head
   - C. IMG
   - D. Body

4. To leave a blank line on a Web page document, use the _____ tag.
   - A.
   - B. <P>
   - C. <END>
   - D. <START>

5. There are _____ different font sizes.
   A. One
   B. Three
   C. Seven
   D. Twelve

TRUE/FALSE

Circle T if the statement is true or F if the statement is false.

T F 1. The only way you can view your Web page is to log on to a Web server.

T F 2. Within a Web page, you can change the color of text.

T F 3. All Web page backgrounds are either white or gray.

T F 4. A relative link would link to another Web site.

T F 5. Use the ALT attribute to display a text description of an image.

FILL IN THE BLANK

Complete the following sentences by writing the correct word or words in the blanks provided.

1. A _____ is a thin line that extends across the width of the browser.
2. Use the _____ attribute to display a background color.
3. Use the _____ tag to create bold text.
4. An _____ list generally is a numbered list.
5. To center text or an image on a Web page, use the _____ tag.

CROSS-CURRICULAR *Projects*

MATH

Create a Web page document for your math class. Include within this document a heading, a numbered list, a background color, and absolute links to two other mathematics Web sites.

SCIENCE

Select a special science project you may be working on. Create two Web pages for this project. Include somewhere within these two pages an H1 heading, a definition list, a background color, relative links from one of the Web pages to the other, and absolute links to at least one other Web site on your selected topic. Include at least two images in your Web page.

SOCIAL STUDIES

Ask your social studies teacher for a list of topics that you will study in the next month. Create a Web page on one of the topics, using a heading and a background color. Use "Links to (topics as provided by your teacher)" for the heading. Search the Web for Web sites related to the topics. Create a list of absolute links to the Web sites. Include at least ten Web sites and include a short description of what can be found at each Web site.

LANGUAGE ARTS

Your teacher has asked you to write an article about your last vacation. After you write the article, convert it to a Web page document. Illustrate the page with images and graphical dividers.

WEB PROJECT

You are a member of a group learning about HTML and how to create and publish Web pages. Your teacher has asked you to put together a presentation on HTML commands not covered in this lesson. You are to research, report, and present an example of at least two linked Web pages and display the HTML code used to create the Web pages.

TEAMWORK PROJECT

Now that you have the basic skills necessary to create a Web page, Ms. Perez would like to have a Web site of at least three pages for Vista Multimedia. Create the Web site for Ms. Perez. Use as many tags as possible that were introduced in this lesson. To extend your HTML knowledge, use *www.AskJeeves.com* for HTML tutorial links. Include some additional HTML tags that you may find in one of these tutorials.

LESSON 16

HOW TECHNOLOGY IS CHANGING THE WORKPLACE AND SOCIETY

OBJECTIVES

When you complete this lesson, you will be able to:

- Describe the impact of technology on education.
- Describe the impact of technology on science and medicine.
- Describe the impact of technology on work and play.
- Identify types of computer crimes.
- Identify computer viruses.
- Identify various security measures.
- Identify computer-related laws.
- Identify the "work" of hackers.
- Describe how privacy is invaded with computer use.

Estimated Time: 2.5 hours

VOCABULARY

Artificial intelligence (AI)
Biometric security measures
Computer-based learning
Computer crime
Computer fraud
Computer hacking
Copyright
Data diddling
Digital cash
Distance learning
Electronic commerce
Genetic engineering
Groupware
Plagiarism
Shareware
Simulation
Software piracy
Time bomb
Virtual reality (VR)
Virus
WebQuest
Worm

As the age of innovation blazes its way into the world of technology, changes are taking place in every aspect of life—from home to school to the workplace. And the changes are swift and dramatic. Just as soon as we settle in and become comfortable with a new technological change, along comes something more innovative and different. As things look now, the world is in for a lot more of this type of change. Some of these changes have, unfortunately, also brought about concerns such as computer crimes, computer health-related issues, and even the need for laws to protect those injured by computer crimes and offenses.

Ms. Perez is very interested in how all of these changes could affect Vista Multimedia, her personal life, and the lives of her employees. She has asked you to provide some insight into some of the changes taking place.

Education

There are many similarities between today's schools and those of 40 or 50 years ago. In many classrooms, the students still sit in rows and the teacher stands at the front of the class, lecturing and using a chalkboard. However, in other classrooms, a technological revolution is taking place.

Many people predict that technology will change the entire structure of education. Others believe the way in which most students receive education today—students and teacher in a traditional classroom—will remain for many years. Regardless of who is right, one thing is certain: Technology is having a tremendous impact on education in general and in more and more classrooms around the world.

Internet

The Internet and the World Wide Web are the biggest factors affecting education today. For instance, not so long ago, if a science teacher gave the class a project to find out how a television works, the students would go to the library and do the research. In many of today's classrooms, the students most likely go to the Internet, and maybe to the How Stuff Works Web site to find this information. See Figure 16-1. Using the Internet, it is fast and easy to find the information you need.

FIGURE 16-1
How Stuff Works Web site

Perhaps you're having a geography test next week, and you would like to pretest your geography knowledge. You can again use the Internet as your resource. One site you might visit is the CIA Geography Quiz Page. See Figure 16-2.

FIGURE 16-2
CIA Geography Quiz Page

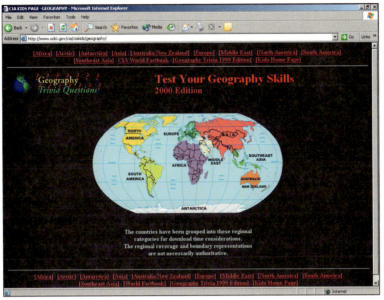

You may have had an opportunity to participate in or work with a *WebQuest*. Bernie Dodge developed the WebQuest Model March at San Diego State University. This type of activity uses the Internet for investigation and problem solving. Hundreds of WebQuests have been developed by schools all over the country. Example WebQuests include countries around the world, politics, learning about money, and so forth. You can find a list and a link to some of these at *www.macomb.k12.mi.us/wq/webqindx.htm*. One of the more popular of these is about clouds. See Figure 16-3.

FIGURE 16-3
Clouds WebQuest

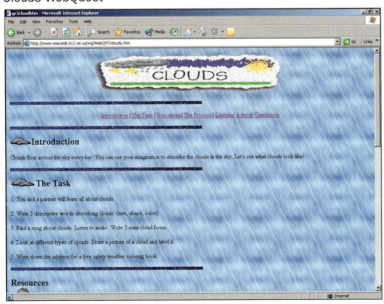

You may be given an assignment to read a book or an article in a journal. Instead of having to check a book or journal out of the library, you can access and read it on the computer.

Distance Learning

For years many people have been receiving their education via distance learning methods. These methods include television and correspondence courses that are completed through the mail. In the last few years, however, the Internet has become a way to deliver *distance learning*. At the elementary and secondary school levels, the Department of Education supports an initiative called the Star Schools Program. This program provides distance education learning to millions of learners annually.

Imagine, if you will, being able to complete high school from home. This is possible in some states. For instance, any high school student who is a Florida resident can attend the Florida High School Online for free. This is a certified diploma-granting school, open any time—night or day. Students enroll, log on, and complete their work through the guidance of a certified Florida high school teacher. See Figure 16-4. Other states are developing similar models.

> **Did You Know?**
>
> According to the National Center for Education Statistics, 93% of public schools are connected to the Internet.

FIGURE 16-4
Florida Online High School

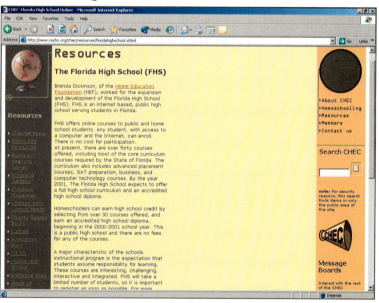

New types of programs are on the market that help teachers develop online courses. These programs are an integrated set of Web-based teaching tools that provide guidance and testing for the student. Two of the most popular of these are Blackboard and WebCT. See Figure 16-5.

FIGURE 16-5
WebCT example

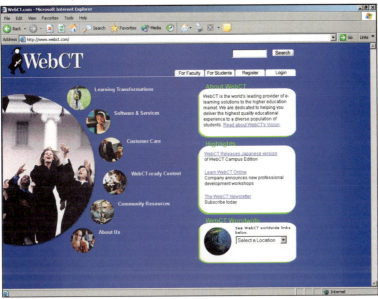

Computer-Based Learning

There are probably 20 or 30 other students in your class. And all of these students, including you, learn in different ways and at different rates. Likewise, information can be presented in many formats and at different levels. This could be through lecture, homework, group projects, movies, and so forth. The more ways in which information can be presented, the more opportunities everyone has to use their own learning styles so they can master the particular topic.

You may have heard the terms *computer-based learning* or computer-assisted instruction (CAI). These are examples of ways your teacher can use the computer for instruction. It is basically using a computer as a tutor. For many students this is one of the most effective ways to learn. For example, you may have difficulty understanding a specific mathematics concept, such as how to calculate percentages. Your teacher may suggest a special computer program to help reinforce that difficult concept. Using such a program provides you with the opportunity to master the idea by reviewing the concept as many times as necessary. See Figure 16-6. Or you may be taking a biology class and instead of using live specimens for experiments, you may complete all of your lab assignments using computer software. These types of labs are called dry labs.

FIGURE 16-6
Students at work in computer lab

Simulations

Learning doesn't have to be dull, boring work. Learning can be fun for everyone, especially if it is done through computer simulation. *Simulations* are models of real-world activities. They are designed to allow you to experiment and explore environments that may be dangerous or unavailable. Using simulations, you can explore other worlds and settings without leaving your classroom. With this type of model, you learn by doing. You can find simulations on the Internet, or the simulations may come on a CD-ROM disk that you run from a local computer.

Some example simulations are as follows:

Many of you have probably heard about fortunes being made and lost in the stock market. If you would like to see how good your investing skills are, you might want to try The Stock Market game located at *www.smgww.org*. This simulation is for students of all ages—from middle school to adults. By playing this game, you learn about finance and the American economic system. To participate in this game, you invest a hypothetical $100,000 in the stock market and follow your investments over a 10-week time period. See Figure 16-7.

FIGURE 16-7
Stock Market simulation game

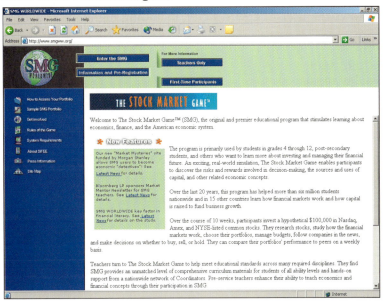

Maybe you are interested in outer space and would like to explore Mars. You can do this through simulation. Try the Mars 2200 simulation located at *www.inworldvr.com/Mars2200/*. Several options and versions are available. You can even select screen size and processor speed. See Figure 16-8.

FIGURE 16-8
Mars 2200 simulation

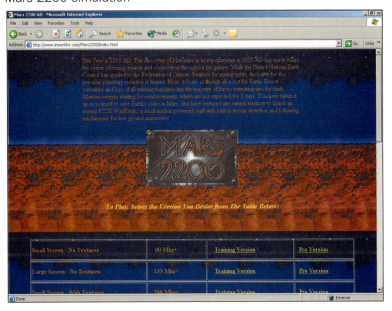

One of the earliest and still most popular simulations is SimCity. Several versions of this program have been released. It is used extensively in schools throughout the world. This problem-solving software program allows the user to create a city, including highways, buildings, homes, and so forth. See Figure 16-9.

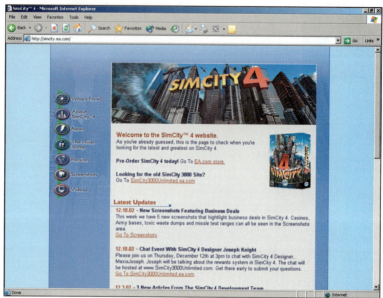

FIGURE 16-9
SimCity simulation

Scientific Discovery and Technological Innovations

Our world is changing at an ever-increasing pace. Currently, people around the world are able to communicate with each other almost instantaneously. The amount of available information is increasing each and every day. In fact it is continuing to increase faster than we can process it. On the positive side, the information and discoveries are contributing to a better lifestyle for many people. Predictions are that we will learn to cure illnesses and continue to increase our life span.

But there's another aspect to all of this. Within all of this change, other predictions are that an antitechnology backlash is possible. Many people feel technology is creating a world out of control. Moral and cultural dilemmas are becoming more and more common, and many people want to return to a simpler, slower way of life.

Whether society could and would return to something simpler is highly debatable. Even today, there are very few places in the world one can live that are not affected by technology. And many scientists say we're "only at the Model-T stage" of what's to come. Let's take a brief look at some of the predicted and possible scientific changes on the horizon. See Figure 16-10.

FIGURE 16-10
The future

Artificial Intelligence

Some of you who enjoy science fiction may have read the book or seen the movie *2001: A Space Odyssey*. In this movie, originally released in the late 1960s and re-released in 2000, a computer referred to as HAL controls the spaceship on its way to Mars. This computer has artificial intelligence, so it never makes a mistake. No computer such as HAL yet exists, but the concept of artificial intelligence is still a branch of computer science. Computer scientists have made many advancements in this area.

The concept of *artificial intelligence* (AI) has been around for many years. In fact the term was coined in 1956 by John McCarthy at the Massachusetts Institute of Technology. The goal for this software is to process information on its own without human intervention. There are many ways in which artificial intelligence applications are being developed and are being used today. Some examples are as follows:

- *Game playing:* The most advances have been made in this area.
- *Natural language:* This offers the greatest potential rewards by allowing people to interact easily with computers by talking to them.
- *Expert systems:* These are computer programs that help us make decisions. For instance, an expert system may help your parents determine the best type of insurance for their particular needs.

- ***Robotics:*** When we think of robotics, we may think of humanoid robots like those in *Star Wars*. In real life, however, we do not see this type of robot in our society. Robots, mostly used in assembly plants, are only capable of limited tasks. One of the newest types of robots is called a *bot*, commonly used by search engines.

Genetic Engineering

The human life span has almost tripled in the last 200 years. We can now expect to live almost 80 years. Implications are that the average life span in the twenty-first century will continue to increase, possibly dramatically. One of the major factors contributing to this increase is ***genetic engineering***, which refers to changing the DNA in a living organism. There are groups of people who argue against this technology. The supporters, however, point out many benefits. Here are some examples:

- Increasing resistance to disease
- Enabling a plant or animal to do something it would not typically do
- Enabling a fruit to ripen without getting squashy

One of the most widely known projects ever developed within this area was the Human Genome Project. Its goal was to identify all of the approximately 100,000 genes in human DNA, store and analyze this data, and address the ethical, legal, and social issues surrounding the project. The project was coordinated by the Department of Energy and the National Institute of Health. Because of the data and resources resulting from this project, some observers such as Bill Gates and former President Bill Clinton predict the twenty-first century will be the "biology century."

Ethics in Technology

WHO IS RESPONSIBLE?

Increasingly, computers participate in decisions that affect human lives. Consider medical safety, for instance, and consider that just about everything in a hospital is tied to a computer. So what happens if these machines don't produce the expected results? What happens if they have been incorrectly programmed?

When programmers write a program, they check for as many conditions as possible. But there is always the chance they might miss one. So what happens if a computer malfunctions and applies a high dosage of radiation? Or what happens if two medications are prescribed to an individual and the computer doesn't indicate the medications are incompatible? Or what happens when someone calls for an ambulance and the system doesn't work and there is no backup?

Then the question becomes, *Who is responsible for these mishaps?* Is it the programmer? Is it the company? Is it the person who administered the radiation treatment?

The incidents described here actually happened. These are ethical issues that are being decided in court.

Virtual Reality

The term *virtual reality (VR)* means different things to different people. A general definition is an artificial environment that feels like a real environment. This environment is created with computer hardware and software. Virtual reality and simulation share some common characteristics. Simulation is sometimes referred to as desktop VR. However, with virtual reality, there is more of a feeling of being in the actual environment—of using all or almost all of the five senses. The user is completely immersed inside the virtual world, generally through some head-mounted display. This helmet contains the virtual and auditory displays. Virtual reality is used in many different ways and areas. Some examples are as follows:

- *Education*: The creation of virtual environments so students may have a better understanding of history is one example. Imagine experiencing World War II as though you were really there. Or maybe you would like to experience what it would be like to live during the age of dinosaurs. With a virtual world, you feel as though you are really there.

- *Training:* You may have had an opportunity to play Doom or Torok: Dinosaur Hunter or some of the other virtual games. If so, you may have felt you were part of the action. You could control much of the environment and make choices as to what your next move would be. A variation of this type of virtual reality is being used to train pilots, navigators, and even astronauts. These individuals are put into virtual life and death situations where they must make decisions. This helps prepare them in the event a similar situation occurs in real life.

- *Medicine:* One example of a medical VR application is the "Anatomic VisualizeR" being developed at the University of California, San Diego. This project is a virtual reality–based learning environment that will enable medical students to actively learn human anatomy. Or, at a university in Germany, a VR system allows student surgeons to practice operations.

- *Miniaturized chips:* Researchers at Texas Instruments have developed an advanced semiconductor manufacturing technology. The transistors are so small that more than 400 million of them will fit onto a single chip the size of a fingernail. And we can expect this type of technological advance will continue.

These are just a few examples of activities taking place today. As in the past, it is fairly certain that scientific discovery and technological innovation will greatly affect our economic and military developments in the future. Predictions are that science and technology will continue to advance and become more widely available and utilized around the world. Some people have forecast, however, that the benefits derived from these advancements will not be evenly distributed.

Work and Play

How will technology affect us as individuals in our work and social life? Although no one knows what the future will bring, predictions are numerous. Many people predict that with high-skilled work more in demand, semi-skilled work will start to disappear. We've already discussed some of the changes taking place in education and how genetic engineering is helping increase life expectancy. As a result of these advances, what types of changes can we expect in the economy and in our personal lives?

Global Economy

One thing is for certain about the new economy: Knowledge is the greatest asset. However, knowledge will be limited by time—it can be incredibly valuable one moment and worthless the next. The spread and sharing of knowledge, the development of new technologies, and an increased recognition of common world problems present unlimited opportunities for economic growth.

Consider banking, finance, and commerce. Electronic technology is having a dramatic effect on these industries. Think about currency. Will it become obsolete? Most likely it will. Already, huge amounts of money zip around the globe at the speed of light. Technology is affecting the way information and money are transmitted. See Figure 16-11. You no longer have to go to the bank to do your banking; you can do it in the comfort of your home using online banking. Online banking allows you to transfer money electronically, which makes it possible for you to pay your bills online and check your account balances. This can all be done from anywhere in the world!

> **Hot Tip**
>
> The economy created by the Internet is generating enormous environmental benefits by reducing the amount of energy and materials consumed by businesses. It is predicted that the Internet will revolutionize the relationship between growth and the environment.

FIGURE 16-11
Transmitting data

Electronic Commerce

You have probably read about the Industrial Revolution and how it affected our world. The Internet economy is being compared to the Industrial Revolution. *Electronic commerce*, or e-commerce, which means having an online business, is changing the way our world does business.

We find e-commerce in every corner of the modern business world. Predictions are that over a billion people will be connected to the Internet by the year 2005. Internet speed will increase as more people add cable modems or digital subscriber lines (DSL). All of this activity and high-speed connections indicate more online businesses. Some analysts predict that within the next 10 years the value of Internet-based business will account for up to 10% of the world's consumer sales. And the Center for Research in Electronic Commerce at the University of Texas indicates that out of the thousands of online companies, over two-thirds of them are not the big Fortune 500 companies—they are smaller companies.

Within this electronic business, one can buy and sell products through the Internet. When it comes to buying online, many people hesitate because they fear someone will steal their credit card numbers. However, *digital cash* is a technology that may ease some of those fears. The digital cash system allows someone to pay by transmitting a number from one computer to another. The digital cash numbers are issued by a bank and represent a specified sum of real money; each number is unique. When one uses digital cash, there is no way to obtain information about the user.

As you read about electronic commerce, you may wonder about what effects it will have on you personally. You or someone in your family may have already made a purchase online. Buying online will become much more common in the future, and you may find it becomes a way of life.

Rarely a day goes by that you or someone in your family doesn't receive junk mail. In the future, much of the postal junk mail will be replaced by SPAM, junk mail sent to your e-mail address. Several states are already looking at ways to legislate this new junk mail.

> **Hot Tip**
>
> Want to find out more about the Internet and electronic commerce? The Internet Economy Indicators Web site located at *www.internetindicators.com* provides lots of statistics and links to other sites on how to start your own online business.

Ethics in Technology

THE TEN COMMANDMENTS FOR COMPUTER ETHICS

1. Thou shalt not use a computer to harm other people.
2. Thou shalt not interfere with other people's computer work.
3. Thou shalt not snoop around in other people's files.
4. Thou shalt not use a computer to steal.
5. Thou shalt not use a computer to bear false witness.
6. Thou shalt not use or copy software for which you have not paid.
7. Thou shalt not use other people's computer resources without authorization.
8. Thou shalt not appropriate other people's intellectual output.
9. Thou shalt think about the social consequences of the programs you write.
10. Thou shalt use a computer in ways that show consideration and respect.

Another aspect you might consider is the increasing number of jobs and the new categories of jobs being generated due to electronic commerce. This might be something you want to consider as you look toward a future career. Some examples include Webmasters, programmers, network managers, graphic designers, Web developers, and so forth. You may also think about going into an online business for yourself. Individuals with imagination and ambition will discover that the greatest source of wealth is their ideas.

The Workplace

The computer has caused many changes in the workplace. The way information is managed has changed. Instead of file cabinets and paper file folders, electronic copies of documents can be created and stored.

Computers also can be used to improve communication in a business. A computer network can be a vital tool helping work run more smoothly. One category of software that assists in communicating over a network is called *groupware*. Groupware refers to programs and software that help people work together even if they are located far from each other. One of the most common types of groupware is e-mail. E-mail is an easy and cost-effective way for users to communicate across short or long distances. E-mail allows users to keep documentation of correspondence about a particular topic, something that is lacking with telephone communication.

Groupware also includes electronic calendars and daily/monthly planners. With this software, users enter their own individual appointments that are then available across the network. All meetings are scheduled in the electronic calendar system, which then checks to see that everyone invited can attend. This software can also check the electronic room scheduling system and find a conference room for the meeting.

Collaborative writing software is another form of groupware. This software allows different users to add their own parts, comments and changes to a single common document, such as a report. The software keeps track of the additions from each user. The changes can be accepted or rejected in the final document. Database software can also be used collaboratively, with different departments providing their own data, such as product specifications or due dates, in the database for the whole company to see and use.

A related type of groupware is project management software. This software allows users to track time lines and processes for complicated projects that involve many workers and departments. Every department can contribute to the information and track their own parts of the project, ensuring that everything is accomplished correctly and on time.

Another type of groupware is video conferencing. This allows users at different locations to hold a virtual meeting without traveling to a central location. Cameras and microphones connected to each person's computer allow users to see and talk to each other.

Many employers allow their employees to work from home. This arrangement is called telecommuting. It involves using communications technology to keep the employee connected to the office. Telecommuting has many advantages for both the employer and the employee. It saves traveling time and expense, and it allows the employee to work at a time that is convenient.

Personal Lives

Computers play such an important part in our lives that sometimes we take for granted the role they play because they work "behind the scenes." When you order a pizza, the order is transmitted through a computer. When you get money out of an ATM, the transaction is completed by a computer. And let's not forget the latest model cars. Many have features such as wipers that turn on automatically, directions available at a moment's notice, and even a feature that will slow the car down if it gets too close to an object in front of it!

Will our personal lives become almost like *Star Trek*? Many people predict they will. Just as technology is affecting our work environment, it is also affecting our personal lives.

In the twentieth century, society witnessed all types of changes in the places people lived. They moved from the farms to the cities and then to the suburbs. The twenty-first century will also witness changes as the home becomes the center for work, entertainment, learning, and possibly even health care. More and more people will telecommute or run businesses from their homes. As a result, they will have to manage their own lives in a world of uncertainty. This will be a great change for many people. They will have to make decisions about how to separate their business and personal lives.

Some examples of potential technological advances that could affect our personal lives are as follows:

- *Clothes that fight odor and bacteria:* Some clothing companies are manufacturing clothes that keep you comfortable and smelling good. For example, when the temperature drops, jackets grow warmer and sweat socks resist bacteria and odors. Or how about clothing that kills mosquitoes on contact?

- *The flying car:* This has long been a fantasy of the American public, but the question is how long will it be before we all have flying cars? It will probably be a few more years before we're flying around like the Jetsons, but there are possibilities on the horizon. Moller International has developed a personal vertical takeoff and landing vehicle (VTOL). The Skycar is able to operate in a much less restrictive area than a helicopter or airplane and is less expensive and safer. These factors allow this type of future transportation to be addressed and investigated for the first time. See Figure 16-12.

FIGURE 16-12
Moller Web site—Skycar

- *Nonlethal weapons:* A company in San Diego is working on a nonlethal weapon that uses two ultraviolet laser beams. These two beams of UV radiation ionize paths in the air to create "wires" in the atmosphere. This device is harmless, but it can immobilize people and animals at a distance.

- *Space travel:* Would you like to take a trip around the world—that is, by low-earth orbit? You may be able to do so in the near future. The Rotary Rocket Company is developing a fleet of commercial vehicles to provide the public the opportunity to access space. See Figure 16-13.

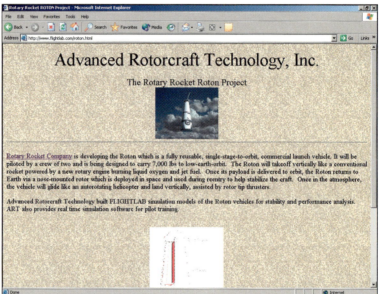

FIGURE 16-13
Rotary Rocket Space Flight

- *Smart shoes and smart seats:* When we think of technology, not too many of us consider our shoes. No matter how expensive our shoes are, they can still become uncomfortable after wearing them for long hours. A technology called expansive polymer gel uses a micro voltage to expand or contract the gel. Weight can be evenly distributed and heat dissipated. This technology is also being applied to car seats.

Technological Issues

It is true that computers have made a positive impact in our lives. They have made our daily lives much easier, our work more efficient, learning more interesting and convenient, and even made our game playing more exciting. However, problems exist such as misuse of information, computer crimes, risks of using hardware and software, health issues, privacy, and security.

Misuse of Information

Use of the Internet has grown at an astounding rate. Users are able to access a multitude of information in a very short amount of time. Putting together a report is a snap with the ability to access information on almost any topic with just a few clicks. This is causing a rise in plagiarism and violation of copyright laws. ***Plagiarism*** is presenting someone else's ideas or work as your own, without authorization. *Copyright* is the legal protection for authors of creative works. It guards against the unlawful copying or using of someone else's original work. Some specific examples of plagiarism include:

- Buying a report from a "free term paper" Web site.
- Paraphrasing information from a source, but not indicating that the information is taken directly from that source.
- Having someone else write a report for you.

Types of Computer Crimes

What is *computer crime*? It is a criminal act committed through the use of a computer; for example, getting into someone else's system and changing information or creating a computer virus and causing damage to information on others' computers. Computer crime is a bigger problem than most people realize. Billions of dollars every year are lost to corporations because of this often undetected, and therefore unpunished, crime. Computer crimes have increased since data communications and computer networks have become popular. Many computer crimes consist of stealing and damaging information and stealing actual computer equipment. Other types of computer crimes include:

- Unauthorized use of a computer
- Infection of a computer by a malicious program (a virus)
- Harassment and stalking on the computer
- Theft of computer equipment
- Copyright violations of software
- Copyright violations of information found on the Internet

Computer Fraud

Computer fraud is conduct that involves the manipulation of a computer or computer data in order to obtain money, property, or value dishonestly or to cause loss. Examples of computer fraud include stealing money from bank accounts or stealing information from other people's computers for gain.

Computer Hacking

Computer hacking involves invading someone else's computer, usually for personal gain or just the satisfaction of invading someone else's computer. Hackers are usually computer experts who enjoy having the power to invade someone else's privacy. They can steal money or change or damage data stored on a computer.

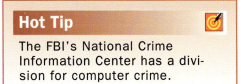

Hot Tip

The FBI's National Crime Information Center has a division for computer crime.

Computer Viruses

A *virus* is a program that has been written, usually by a hacker, to cause the corruption of data on a computer. The virus is attached to an executable file (like a program file) and spreads from one file to another once the program is executed. A virus can cause major damage to a computer's data or it can do something as minor as display messages on your screen. There are different variations of viruses:

- A *worm* makes many copies of itself, resulting in the consumption of system resources that slows down or actually halts tasks. Worms don't have to attach themselves to other files.

- A *time bomb* is a virus that does not cause its damage until a certain date or until the system has been booted a certain number of times.

- A Trojan horse is a virus that does something different from what it is expected to do. It may look like it is doing one thing while in actuality it is doing something quite different (usually something disastrous).

In order to protect your computer against virus damage:

- Use antivirus software. This software should always run on your computer and should be updated regularly.

- Be careful in opening e-mail attachments. It is a good idea to save them to disk before reading them so that you can scan them. It is also a good idea to open messages only from people you know.

- Don't access files copied from disks or downloaded from the Internet without scanning them first. See Figure 16-14.

FIGURE 16-14
Scanning a file for a potential virus

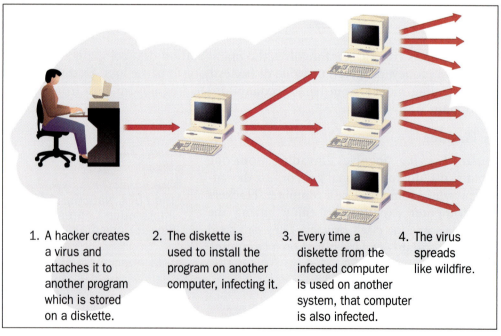

Other Computer Crimes

Theft of computer time is also a crime committed regularly in the workplace. This crime is committed when an employee uses a company's computer for personal use such as running a small side business, keeping records of an outside organization, or keeping personal records. When you are engaged in these types of activities on the job, you are not being as productive as you could be for your employer.

Using the information you see on someone else's computer screen or on a printout to profit unfairly is theft of output.

Changing data before it is entered into the computer or after it has been entered into the computer is called *data diddling*. Anyone who is involved with creating, recording, encoding, and checking data can change data.

> **Did You Know?**
> The first computer crime, electronic embezzlement, was committed in 1958.

Risks of Using Computer Hardware and Software

Computer equipment as well as data stored on computers are subject to various types of hazards. These include damage caused by improper use by employees, damage caused by improper configurations, fire, flood, and even electrical outages or storms. Many of these conditions can be prevented by proper planning such as providing employees with appropriate training to use and safeguard the equipment. Computers should be equipped with surge protectors and other types of protection to prevent outages. When flooding is a possibility, it is a good idea to locate computers above the first floor of a building.

Illegally copying and using software is called *software piracy*. It has become a big problem because it is so easy to copy software. It has cost software companies millions of dollars in sales each year. Many persons are misusing shareware as well. *Shareware* is software you can use for free for a specified period of time to try it out. If you decide you like the software and it meets your needs, you are supposed to pay for it.

> **Did You Know?**
> The penalty for copying software can be up to $250,000, five years in prison, or both.

Health Issues

Working on computers for long periods of time can cause various types of health problems and concerns. These are referred to as ergonomics-related concerns and are usually caused by repetitive motions that result in wear and tear on the body, such as rapid hand and wrist movement. A very common disorder caused by using a keyboard on a consistent basis is carpal tunnel syndrome. One remedy to reduce this condition is to replace a regular keyboard with an ergonomic keyboard. See Figure 16-15. This type of keyboard will take the stress off of the wrists and reduce injury. Problems can also occur because of poor lighting or inappropriate furniture and equipment such as the type of monitor used. It is the responsibility of the employer to provide a safe working environment for its employees, which will result in a healthy and productive workforce.

FIGURE 16-15
Top: a traditional keyboard; Bottom: an ergonomic keyboard

Privacy

The amount of personal information electronically available on each of us is astonishing. You would probably be very upset to know the extent to which this information is available and to whom it is available. There are many companies that gather information to create databases and sell or trade this information to others.

Any time you submit information on the Internet, it is possible for this information to be gathered by many persons and used for various situations. Information can also be gathered from online data regarding school, banking, hospitals, insurance companies, and any other information supplied for such everyday activities.

Much of the information gathered and sold can result in your name being added to mailing lists. Companies use these lists for marketing purposes. Information regarding one's credit history is also available for purchase. Using credit cards to purchase merchandise on the Internet can be risky. Some sites are advertised as being secure. If the sites are not secure, your credit card number can be released and used.

Security

Computer security is necessary to keep hardware, software, and data safe from harm or destruction. Some risks to computers are natural causes, some are accidents, and some are intentional. It is not always evident that some type of computer crime or intrusion has occurred. Therefore, it is necessary that safeguards for each type of risk be put into place. It is the responsibility of companies or individuals to protect their data.

The best way to protect data is to control access to the data. The most common form of restricting access to data is the use of passwords. Passwords are used to protect against unauthorized use. Users must have a password in order to log into a system. Companies sometimes restrict access to certain computers. Passwords are usually changed periodically.

Other security measures include the following:

- Making security a priority; maintaining and enforcing security measures.
- Using electronic identification cards to gain access to certain areas within a building or department.
- Protecting individual companies' networks from external networks by using firewalls, which consist of special hardware and software. A firewall allows users inside the organization the ability to access computers outside of their organization while keeping outside users from accessing their computers.
- Using antivirus software to protect data.
- Instituting a very selective hiring process that includes careful screening of potential employees. Do not keep employees on staff who refuse to follow security rules. This measure will prevent internal theft or sabotage.
- Regularly backing up data and storing it offsite.
- Employing *biometric security measures*, which examine a fingerprint, a voice pattern, or the iris or retina of the eye. These must match the entry that was originally stored in the system for an employee. This method of security is usually used when high-level security is required. See Figure 16-16.

FIGURE 16-16
Biometric security measures

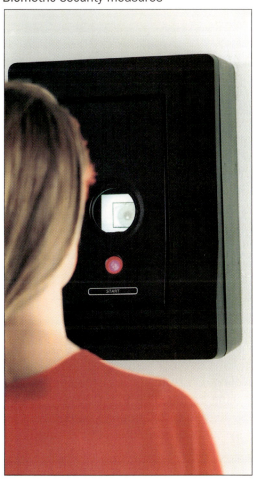
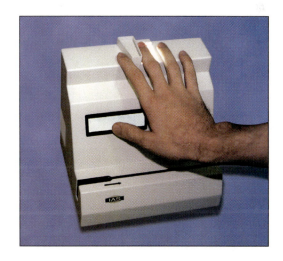

Protection for Technology Injuries

Many laws have been passed in an effort to assist those injured by computer crimes and other technology issues. However, many of the offenses are difficult to prove. Below is a list of some of the laws that protect users.

- Copyright Act of 1976 protects the developers of software.
- Electronic Communication Privacy Act of 1986 prohibits the interception of data communications.
- Computer Fraud and Abuse Act of 1986 prohibits individuals without authorization from knowingly accessing a company computer to obtain records from financial communications.
- Software Piracy and Counterfeiting Amendment of 1983.
- Many states have individual laws governing computer crimes in their states.

Technology Careers

SIMULATION ANALYSTS

Simulation analysts work with large and small companies. Their primary job is to investigate different options to determine which would be the best for a particular situation. For instance, health care company administrators might want to implement a new system for filing and processing insurance claims. Before spending a huge amount of money, they may hire a simulation analyst to determine which system would best meet their needs. Or a bank is going to bring in a new system to process checks. It hires an analyst to do simulation modeling of what the system might and might not do.

Simulation analysts work with all types of companies and industries. Some necessary skills include the ability to see detail in a system and to be a good technical writer. The person should be a logical thinker and have good analytical skills. A good memory is an additional asset.

Opportunities and the need for simulation analysts are increasing. One of the reasons for the increase is that more and more companies are applying simulation to a larger variety of problems.

As a consultant, you would probably do some traveling. Consulting fees are generally quite generous, with some simulation analysts making as much as $75,000 or more. You may find some analysts with only a two-year degree, but generally you need at least a bachelor's degree in computer information systems or computer engineering.

SUMMARY

In this lesson, you learned:

- Many people predict that technology will change the entire structure of education.
- Technology is having a tremendous impact on education.
- The Internet and the World Wide Web are the biggest factors affecting education today.
- Some people predict an antitechnology backlash.
- In the new global economy, knowledge is the greatest asset.
- Electronic commerce is the buying and selling of goods and services using the Internet.
- Digital cash allows someone to pay online by transmitting a number from one computer to another.
- New jobs and new job categories are being developed because of the Internet and electronic commerce.
- Some technological advances are clothes that fight odors, flying cars, voice recognition, nonlethal weapons, space travel, smart shoes and smart seats, and electronic shopping.
- Computer crime has become a major problem, costing companies billions of dollars annually.
- Computer fraud is conduct that involves the manipulation of a computer or computer data for dishonest profit.
- Computer hacking involves invading someone else's computer. Sometimes it is done for financial gain and sometimes just as a prank.
- A computer virus is a program that has been written to cause corruption of data on a computer.
- To protect against viruses, install and keep an antivirus program running on your computer. Be sure to update regularly.
- Computer security is necessary in order to keep hardware, software, and data safe from harm or destruction.
- The most common way to control access to data is to use passwords.
- Illegally copying and using software is called software piracy. It has cost companies millions of dollars in lost sales.
- Laws have been passed in an effort to assist those who have been injured by computer crimes and offenses. Many computer crimes are difficult to prove and prosecute.

VOCABULARY Review

Define the following terms:

Artificial intelligence (AI)	Digital cash	Simulation
Biometric security measures	Distance learning	Software piracy
Computer-based learning	Electronic commerce	Time bomb
Computer crime	Genetic engineering	Virtual reality (VR)
Computer fraud	Groupware	Virus
Computer hacking	Plagiarism	WebQuest
Copyright	Shareware	Worm
Data diddling		

REVIEW Questions

MULTIPLE CHOICE

Select the best response for the following statements.

1. _____ invade other people's computers.
   A. Hackers
   B. Programmers
   C. Trojan horses
   D. System analysts

2. Software that users may use on a trial basis is called _____.
   A. freeware
   B. shareware
   C. antivirus software
   D. Microsoft Office

3. _____ is the delivery of education over the Internet.
   A. Simulation
   B. Distance learning
   C. Virtual reality
   D. None of the above

4. _____ is a criminal act that is committed through the use of a computer.
   A. Hacking
   B. Piracy
   C. Copyright
   D. Computer crime

5. The buying and selling of goods on the Internet is called _____.
   A. economic commerce
   B. electronic commerce
   C. on-hand business
   D. local commerce

TRUE/FALSE

Circle T if the statement is true or F if the statement is false.

T F 1. With digital cash, you can pay someone by transmitting a number from one computer to another.

T F 2. Worms, time bombs, and Trojan horses are variations of viruses.

T F 3. Hackers only invade other people's computers for fun.

T F 4. Submitting a report to your teacher that you obtained from a "free term paper" Web site is an example of plagiarism.

T F 5. Simulations are models of real-world activities.

FILL IN THE BLANK

Complete the following sentences by writing the correct word or words in the blanks provided.

1. _____ is necessary in order to keep hardware, software, and data safe from harm or destruction.

2. Using _____ you learn by doing.

3. SimCity is a popular _____ activity.

4. _____ security measures involve examining a fingerprint, a voice pattern, or the iris or retina of the eye.

5. _____ is software that works without human intervention.

CROSS-CURRICULAR *Projects*

MATH

Computer crimes have been responsible for the loss of millions of dollars. Some crimes result in more loss than others. Use the Internet and other resources to locate information on lost revenue due to computer crimes. If you have access to spreadsheet software, prepare this information in a spreadsheet and perform formulas that will not only add the totals, but also display the percentage of each crime's portion of the total. Some keywords that may be helpful are *computer crime, computer crime costs, hackers, viruses,* and *software piracy*. Use various search engines to research each term.

SCIENCE

Use the Internet and other resources to identify early security measures that were used to protect computers and computer data. Describe how these measures counteracted the intrusions made. Write a report on your findings to share with your classmates. You may find helpful information at *www.looksmart.com*.

SOCIAL STUDIES

Viruses have been around for quite a while. Use the Internet and other resources to research the history of early viruses. Prepare a report to share with your classmates on the types of viruses and the damage they caused. Also include any information you may find on the person who programmed the virus if possible. Use a search engine and the keywords *computer viruses* or *early computer viruses*.

LANGUAGE ARTS

The year is 2070. You were born in 2055. Use your word processing program to write a letter to someone who lived 50 years ago and tell him or her about your life and your community.

WEB PROJECT

It is probably impossible to go through an entire day without being involved in some way with technology. Prepare a poster indicating each technology/computer use you encounter/use during an entire day. Describe the technology/computer activity as well as how you use it.

TEAMWORK PROJECT

Ms. Perez is interested in other information pertaining to the global economy and electronic commerce. She would like you to prepare a report for her on what information she would need to know before setting up an e-commerce Web site.

ADVANCED COMPUTER CONCEPTS

UNIT 3 REVIEW

REVIEW Questions

FILL IN THE BLANK

Complete the following sentences by writing the correct word or words in the blanks provided.

1. _____ are the number of Web sites returned based on keywords used for a search.
2. A(n) _____ is a formula or set of steps for solving a particular problem.
3. Links that are no longer active are called _____.
4. _____ refers to the age of the information on a Web site, how long it has been posted, and how often it is updated.
5. _____ is a software feature that allows you to see on your computer screen how the publication will look when it is printed.
6. A(n) _____ is a person who has gained unauthorized access to computer systems.
7. The main page or index page of most Web sites is referred to as the _____.
8. _____ are popular ways to arrange and organize text on a Web page.
9. _____ are models of real-world activities.
10. An artificial environment that feels like a real environment is _____ _____.

MULTIPLE CHOICE

Select the best response for the following statements.

1. A(n) _____ is a collection of organized information.
   A. meta tag
   B. database
   C. spider
   D. algorithm

2. The _____ symbol is considered a wildcard character.
   A. &
   B. "
   C. #
   D. *

3. AltaVista, Excite, Yahoo, and Google are examples of _____.
   A. domains
   B. search engines
   C. electronic resources
   D. shareware

4. _____ is the ability to move through a site.
   A. surfing
   B. navigation
   C. citing
   D. sharing

5. _____ is the way graphics and text are used to produce a quality document.
   A. layout and design
   B. balance
   C. focus
   D. coherence

6. The standard measurement unit in desktop publishing is a(n) _____.
   A. ascender
   B. serif
   C. sans serif
   D. point

7. _____ add life to your Web site and make it exciting and fun.
   A. Images
   B. Links
   C. Bullets
   D. Characters

8. _____ are active references to other parts of the same document or to other documents.
   A. Headings
   B. Hyperlinks
   C. Tags
   D. Images

9. Game playing, expert systems, and robotics are examples of _____.
   A. simulations
   B. artificial intelligence
   C. e-commerce
   D. distance learning

10. Worms, time bombs, and Trojan horses are examples of _____.
    A. computer crimes
    B. data diddling
    C. viruses
    D. Web quests

TRUE/FALSE

Circle the T if the statement is true or F if the statement is false.

T F 1. A related search can dramatically improve your odds of finding the information you are seeking.

T F 2. You can use math symbols to enter a formula to filter out unwanted listings.

T F 3. The domain portion of a URL will give you information concerning the company's name.

T F 4. Links that are no longer active are called outdated links.

T F 5. The font size determines how large or how small the font will appear when printed.

T F 6. Color should be used extensively to make publications lively.

T F 7. A Web browser is an application program that interprets the HTML tags within the page and then displays the text on the computer screen.

T F 8. A Web server displays Web pages and renders them into final form so they can be viewed by anyone with an Internet connection and a Web browser.

T F 9. One category of software that assists in communicating over a network is called groupware.

T F 10. A computer crime is a criminal act committed through the use of a computer.

CROSS-CURRICULAR Projects

MATH

Use the Internet and other resources to identify at least five antivirus software programs. Create a spreadsheet to record the name of the programs, the costs of programs, and special features of the programs. Determine the average cost of the antivirus programs. Create a chart (type of your choice) to visually show the cost of the programs.

SCIENCE

Use the Internet and other resources to research new technology that will affect our lives in the future. Report the information in a table format. Include the name of the "new technology," a picture if possible, and an explanation of the technology.

LANGUAGE ARTS

Prepare a handout that identifies electronic sources and how to cite these sources when using in a report or other research. Include samples in your handout. Use desktop publishing skills learned earlier to make your handout attractive.

HISTORY

Prepare a presentation on the history of desktop publishing. Include at least five slides. Enhance the presentation by including graphics, sound, animation, etc.

 ## TEAMWORK PROJECT

Your FBLA advisor has asked a group of the members to get together and create a Web site for the school's FBLA chapter. Include at least three pages. These may include the Home page, an officer's page, an activities page, and so forth. Make the pages attractive and interesting.

 ## WEB PROJECT

Technology has changed considerably the way education is delivered in recent years. Use the Internet and other resources to research how technology will continue to change education. Prepare a report identifying and describing at least two new educational technologies that will affect education in the future.

SIMULATION

JOB 3-1

Mr. Randolph thinks it would help advertise his business if he had a Web site. He has asked you to create a Web site for Ground Works. Include two to three pages. Be sure to include elements that will make the page appealing.

JOB 3-2

A quarterly newsletter would be an excellent benefit to Ground Works' customers. Create a one-page, two-column newsletter that contains information that would be useful and of interest to Mr. Randolph's customers. Include appropriate graphics, lines, color, etc.

PORTFOLIO *Checklist*

Include the following files from this unit in your portfolio.

_____ Simulation Job 3-1

_____ Simulation Job 3-2

Glossary

A

Absolute cell reference Spreadsheet cell contents will not change when copied or moved to another cell.

Absolute link Hyperlink to another Web site.

Active cell Cell on which the cell pointer is located.

Address bar Part of the browser window; contains the URL, or address, of the active Web page.

Animated GIF A series of GIF images that appear in sequence to give the illusion of movement.

Animation Special visual or sound effects that you can add to text or to an object on a slide.

Applications software Software that helps you perform a specific task, such as word processing, spreadsheets, and so forth; also called productivity software.

Arithmetic/logic unit Part of the CPU where all calculations and comparisons take place.

Artificial intelligence (AI) Software that processes information on its own without human intervention.

Ascenders The parts of the lowercase character above the x-height.

Ascending sort Sort that arranges records from A to Z, or smallest to largest.

Attribute A format such as bold, underline, italic, or color that can be applied to text.

Audience handouts Printouts representing your presentation that can be given to your audience.

AutoFormat Predesigned formats that add a professional look to spreadsheets.

AutoSearch Browser feature that gives you Web search results when you type part of an URL in the address bar.

B

Balance Element of good design that is created by distributing the weight of various elements in a document.

Biometric security measures Examining a fingerprint, a voice pattern, or the iris or retina of the eye for identification purposes.

Bit In the binary system, a bit represents a zero or one.

Body Element on a Web page that contains information identifying the intended audience and purpose of the information; required tag for all HTML documents.

Bookmark Browser feature that allows users to store shortcuts to most frequently visited Web sites.

Boolean logic A method of searching; makes use of three logical operators—AND, NOT, OR.

Browser Software program used to retrieve documents from the World Wide Web (WWW, or Web) and to display them in a readable format.

Bus topology A type of network arrangement.

Byte Another word for character; generally represented by 8 bits.

C

Cap height Height of a capital letter in a font.

Cell Point at which a column and a row meet in a spreadsheet.

Cell range A group of cells in a spreadsheet.

Central processing unit Also known as the microprocessor; the brains of the computer.

Charts Visual representations that show statistical information and simplify complex sets of data.

Client/server network Type of network in which one computer acts as the server, managing resources, and the rest are clients, using the resources.

Clients Computers on a network that are not acting as a server.

Coherence A consistent format.

Column Vertical arrangement of cells in a spreadsheet; identified by letters.

Computer Electronic device that receives data, processes data, stores data, and produces a result.

Computer crime A criminal act that is committed through the use of a computer, such as getting into someone else's system and changing information or creating a computer virus. It can also involve the theft of computer equipment.

Computer fraud Manipulation of a computer or computer data in order to obtain money, property, or value dishonestly or to cause loss.

Computer hacking Invading someone else's computer, usually for personal gain or just for the satisfaction of invading someone else's computer.

Computer-based learning Using the computer as a tutor.

Content Advisor Browser tool that provides control over what kinds of Web content can be viewed.

Control unit That part of the central processing unit (CPU) that coordinates all CPU activities.

Copyright The exclusive right, granted by law for a certain number of years, to make and dispose of literary, musical, or artistic work.

Currency Refers to the age of information found on a Web page.

Cursor Blinking line that appears on a blank screen that indicates where typing will begin.

D

Data Information entered into the computer to be processed. Consists of text, numbers, sounds, and images.

Data diddling Changing data before or after it has been entered into the computer.

Data source Consists of individual information that will appear in every merged document.

Database A collection of files and related data.

Datasheet View In a database, displays a row-and-column view of data in tables, forms, and queries.

Descenders The parts of the lowercase characters that extend below the baseline.

Descending sort Arranges records from Z to A, or largest to smallest.

Design templates Professionally designed formats that contain color schemes with custom formatting and styled fonts, all designed to create a special unified look.

Design View In a database, the view used to create a table, form, query, and report.

Desktop computer Computer that fits on a desktop.

Desktop publishing The process of producing professional-looking documents such as flyers, brochures, reports, and newsletters using a personal computer and a color printer.

Digital cash Allows someone to pay by transmitting a number from one computer to another.

Disk cache Temporary folders on the hard drive in which Web sites you visit are stored.

Distance learning Taking a course online over the Internet without having to meet in a traditional classroom.

Domain name Identifies a site on the Internet.

DOS Disk Operating System; an operating system originally introduced on the IBM PC in 1981.

E

Editing Changing an existing document.

Efficiency The logical layout of information on a Web page.

Electronic commerce Business conducted over the Internet.

Electronic communications Communication using computers.

Electronic presentation Using a presentation graphic software program to make a presentation using a projector or computer.

E-mail link A link on a Web page that allows the user to send an e-mail message.

Ergonomic keyboard A keyboard designed to relieve stress on the hands and wrists that can result from repeated and/or longtime keying.

Ethernet A network protocol for a LAN.

Extranet Applications that allow outside organizations such as suppliers or vendors to access internal company Web sites and information.

F

Fair use Refers to short, cited excerpts, usually as an example of research.

Favorites Browser feature that allows users to store shortcuts to most frequently visited Web sites.

Field In a database, an individual piece or item of information.

File menu Menu in many programs that contains such file-manipulation commands as New, Open, Close, Save, and Print.

Focus The element that attracts the reader's eye. Can be a graphic or large headlines or titles.

Font A typeface, size, and style.

Font style The way a character or letter looks.

Footer Portion of a Web page that contains the author or contact person and date of revision; information keyed at the bottom of every page in a report.

Form Object used to maintain, view, and print records in a database.

Form letters A letter prepared using word processing software and importing name and address information from a database file.

Format Painter Word processing feature that allows you to copy the format of one section of text and apply it to another section.

Formatting Process of preparing a disk so you can write data to and read data from the disk; applying certain attributes to text, specifying margins, spacing, and so on; enhancing the text in a document.

Formula In a spreadsheet, a statement that performs a calculation.

Formula bar The area on the spreadsheet that displays formulas that have been entered.

Function In a spreadsheet, a built-in formula that is a shortcut for common calculations such as addition and average.

G

Genetic engineering Using technology to alter genetic makeup.

Graphical user interface (GUI) Operating system with graphical symbols representing files, programs, and documents; type of interface that lets the user interact with the computer using pictures and symbols rather than text.

Groupware Software that can be used for working and communication within a group.

H

Handheld or palmtop computer Computer that can be held in the hand.

Hard disk drives Drives used to store data inside of a computer.

Hard return Moves the cursor to the next line of type.

Hardware The tangible, physical computer equipment that can be seen and touched.

Head Required tag for all HTML documents; contains the title tag between the starting and ending <HEAD> tags.

Header Portion of a Web page that contains a link to the sponsoring institution (this information may also be in the footer); information keyed at the top of every page.

Headings HTML tags that include the typeface, size, and the extra space above or below the heading; there are six levels.

Hits In a search, any time a piece of data matches search words you specify.

Home page First page that is displayed when the browser is launched.

Home row keys Keys on the keyboard from which all keystrokes are made. These keys are a, s, d, f, j, k, l, and ;.

Host computer Computer that is accessed remotely from a user's computer and links it to the Internet.

Host node Any computer that is directly connected to the network.

Hyperlinks Text or graphics in a Web document that reference another place in the same document or an entirely different document.

Hypertext markup language (HTML) Protocol that controls how Web pages are formatted and displayed; language used to create documents so they display in a browser.

Hypertext transfer protocol (HTTP) Protocol used on the Web that defines how pages are transmitted.

I

Images Pictures that add interest to publications.

Information Data that has been organized into a useful format.

Input Information fed into a computer to be processed.

Input devices Devices that enable the user to get data and commands into the computer.

Insertion point A vertical line that shows your current position on the screen.

Integrated software Software that combines applications such as word processing, spreadsheet, database, and others into a single package.

Internet The largest network, used as a communication tool.

Internet Keywords A browser feature that gives you Web search results when you type part of an URL in the address bar.

Internet service provider (ISP) A company that provides Internet connections for a fee.

Interoperability The ability of all brands, models, and makes of computers to communicate with each other.

Intranet A network used exclusively by the members of an organization for distributing company information.

J

Justification The placement of text between the left and right margins; text can be justified at the left, at the right, or in the center.

K

Keyboarding The ability to key text by using the correct fingers without looking at the keys.

Keywords In a search, the words that describe the information the user is trying to locate.

L

Label Alphabetical text in a spreadsheet.

Layout and design The way graphics and text are used to produce a high-quality document.

Line spacing Controls the amount of space between lines of text in a document.

Links Text or graphics in a Web document that reference another place in the same document or an entirely different document.

Lists A method used to organize and display information within a document; can be bulleted, numbered, or definition.

Local area network (LAN) A network generally confined to one geographical area.

Location bar Part of the browser window; contains the URL, or address, of the active Web page.

M

Magnetic tape drives A type of storage media that is used for making backup copies of large volumes of data.

Mail merge Joining a word processing document, such as a letter, and information from a database file, such as names and addresses.

Main document In a merge, it contains the information that is the same for all copies.

Main memory Another word for RAM or primary memory; volatile memory.

Mainframe computers Large and powerful computers used for centralized storage, processing, and management of large amounts of data.

Margins White space around the edge of the page where text ends.

Math symbols In a search, the plus and minus signs are used to filter out unwanted hits.

Menu bar Displays the commands that will be used in creating documents.

Mid-range server A computer on a network that manages network resources.

MLA Handbook for writers; gives rules for citing research information.

Modem A device connected between the computer and telephone line that converts analog signals to digital and vice versa.

Modifier keys Keyboard keys that are used in conjunction with other keys; CTRL, ALT, and Shift.

Monitor Video display screen that displays images.

Motherboard Circuit board that contains all of the computer system's main components.

Multimedia The use of text, graphics, audio, and video in combination to create an effective means of communication and interaction.

N

Name box The area on the spreadsheet that identifies the cell reference of the active cell.

Navigation The ability to move easily through a Web page.

NetWatch A browser tool that provides control over what kinds of Web content can be viewed.

Network A group of two or more computers linked together; connects one computer to other computers and to peripheral devices such as printers.

Network operating system The operating system software that runs on the server.

Nodes Computers on a network.

Notebook computer A computer that is smaller than a desktop model; it can be folded closed and easily carried.

Notes pane In presentation graphics software, the area available to allow the entering of notes for each slide.

O

Online service provider (OSP) A company that provides Internet connections for a fee.

Operating systems Provide an interface between the user or application program and the computer hardware.

Optical storage devices Devices that use laser technology to read and write data on magnetic-coated platters.

Outline pane In presentation graphics software, it shows an outline of the presentation's text. This view organizes the content of the presentation.

Output devices Devices that enable the computer to give the user the results of the processed data.

P

Parallel ports Ports used to connect input and output devices physically to the computer. Parallel ports transmit data eight bits at a time.

Peer-to-peer network A type of LAN, usually used in a small office or classroom.

Personal computer A computer used on a desktop, designed for use by an individual.

Plagiarism Using the work of someone else without crediting the source; presenting an idea as new and original that was derived from the work of another person.

Plug-ins Small software programs designed to work with a Web browser to perform a specific function that the browser cannot do by itself.

Point The standard measurement unit for fonts, approximately 1/72 of an inch. The higher the point size, the larger the font.

Presentation graphics program Software used to create graphical electronic presentations; examples are Microsoft PowerPoint, Corel Presentations, and Lotus Freelance.

Primary key In a database, the key that uniquely identifies a field for each record.

Printers Devices used to produce a paper or hard copy of the processing results.

Protocol A set of standards for exchanging data between computers.

Q

Query A question you ask about the data stored in a database.

QWERTY The arrangement of the alphanumeric keys on a standard keyboard; refers to the first six keys on the top row of letters.

R

Random access memory (RAM) Memory location where instructions and data are stored on a temporary basis; volatile memory.

Read-only memory (ROM) Permanent computer storage; instructions are burned onto chips by the manufacturer.

Record In a database, a collection of fields.

Related search Preprogrammed queries or questions suggested by the search engine.

Relative cell reference The contents of the cell will not change when copied or moved to another cell in a spreadsheet.

Relative link On a Web page, gives the file location in relation to the current document.

Report Contains the contents of the database in customized formats.

Ring topology A type of network arrangement.

Row In a spreadsheet, a horizontal arrangement of cells; identified by numbers.

Ruler The area on the screen that is used to change paragraph indentations and margin settings.

S

Sans serif Fonts that do not have little lines at the ends of the strokes of each letter.

Scanners Input devices used to make digital copies of pictures so they can be used in preparing publications.

Search engine A tool to help the user locate information on the Internet; software program used to search the Internet by using keywords.

Serial ports Ports used to connect input and output devices physically to the computer. Serial ports transmit data one bit at a time.

Serif Fonts that have little lines at the ends of the strokes of each letter.

Server A computer on a network that manages the network resources.

Shareware Software that can be used for free for a specified period to try it out.

Simplicity Design principle that promotes clarity rather than clutter.

Simulation Models of real-world activities.

Sizing handles A box with eight small squares surrounding a piece of clip art; by dragging the sizing handles, the dimensions of the clip art can be altered.

Slide Sorter A view in a presentation graphics program that displays thumbnails or miniature images of all slides in the presentation.

Software Intangible set of instructions that tells the computer what to do; program or instructions that give directions to the computer.

Software piracy Illegal copying and using of software.

Software suites Similar to integrated software packages, except they contain the full versions of the application software.

Sorting Arranging data according to some particular order, such as alphabetical or numerical.

Spell Checker A word processing feature that checks documents for correct spellings.

Spider A program that searches the Web; called a spider because it crawls all over the Web.

Spreadsheet Software designed to store and manipulate numeric data; row and column arrangement of data used to enter, calculate, manipulate, and analyze numbers.

Star topology A geometric arrangement of a network.

Status bar Area on the screen that displays information about the document including current page number, total pages in the document, location of the cursor, and the status of some of the specialized keys.

Storage Refers to some type of electronic storage device such as floppy disk, hard disk, and so forth.

Styles Predesigned formatting options that have been saved.

Subject directories Type of search engine in which the information is organized by subjects.

Supercomputer Fastest type of computer; used for specialized applications requiring immense amounts of mathematical calculations.

Symbols Characters that are not numbers or letters, such as the copyright symbol or ampersand.

Systems software Group of programs that coordinate and control the resources and operations of a computer system.

T

Tab stops Locations on the horizontal ruler that tell the insertion point to stop when the Tab key is pressed.

Table A group of records; an arrangement of information in rows and columns.

Task pane In many software applications, a separate pane to the right of the main window that displays commonly used commands.

TCP/IP A type of computer protocol; the main protocol used on the Internet.

Templates Predesigned documents that already have formatting for margins, tabs, fonts, and some objects included.

Text area The area on the screen that will contain the information that you type.

Thumbnail sketch A rough draft drawing used to explore layout options of a document being created.

Time bomb A computer virus that does not cause its damage until a certain date or until the system has been booted a certain number of times.

Timed writings Keyboarding drills used to develop speed and accuracy.

Title Information that appears on the browser title bar; inserted between the <TITLE> and </TITLE> tags.

Title bar Area of the screen that displays the name of the document you are working on as well as the name of the software program you are using.

Token ring A type of network topology.

Toolbar Row of buttons at the top of the browser; area of the screen that displays icons (little pictures) of commonly used commands.

Topology The geometric arrangement of how the network is set up and connected.

Touch typing Entering text by using the correct fingers without looking at the keys.

Transitions Special effects that display when you move from slide to slide in a presentation.

Transmission control protocol and Internet protocol (TCP/IP) Protocol used between computers on the Internet to establish a connection and transmit data.

Transmission media Media used to transmit data from one device to another; may be wireless or physical.

Typeface A set of characters with a common design and shape.

U

Universal Resource Locator (URL) Web site address; address that tells the browser where to locate the page.

Users The people who use computers.

V

Value Numeric text in a spreadsheet.

Virtual reality (VR) An artificial environment used in education, medicine, training, research, and other fields.

Virus A program that has been written, usually by a hacker, to cause the corruption of data on a computer.

Voice recognition Software and hardware used to "speak" commands into the computer and to enter text.

W

Web page A plain text document on the World Wide Web.

Web server A computer that houses and delivers Web pages.

WebQuest An educational method that uses the Internet for problem solving and investigation.

What-if analysis The process of using a spreadsheet to test different scenarios or to apply a certain condition if a certain condition exists.

Wide area network (WAN) A number of connected networks that cover a large geographical area. The Internet is an example.

Wildcard character The * (asterisk) symbol; used to search for words that the user is not sure how to spell or for word variations.

Wizards A software feature that walks the user through a series of steps in completing a task.

Word processing Using a computer to create text documents such as letters, reports, and so on.

Word-processing software Software that allows the user to create and modify documents.

Word wrap A word processing feature that wraps text around the right margin and continues it on the next line.

Workbook A group of related spreadsheets.

Worksheet A grid with columns and rows. The term worksheet is used interchangeably with spreadsheet.

World Wide Web A text and graphical subset of the Internet.

Worm A type of computer virus that makes many copies of itself, resulting in the consumption of system resources which slows down or halts tasks. Worms do not have to attach themselves to other files.

WYSIWYG "What you see is what you get." The capability of word processing software to show the document on the screen the way it will look when printed.

X

X-height The height of the main body of a lowercase character.

INDEX

A

Absolute cell reference, in spreadsheets, 186
Absolute links, 363
Accessing the Internet
 with cable modem, 27–28
 by direct connection, 27–28
Active cells, in spreadsheets, 180
Advanced Research Project Agency (ARPANET), 11–12, 22
Algorithm, used by search engines, 296
Alignment, HTML tags for, 365–366
<ALIGN> tag, in Web pages, 365–366
<ALT> tag, in Web pages, 365
Andreessen, Marc, 24–25
Animated movies, 250
Animation, in presentations, 250
Apple Computer, 8
Arguments, of spreadsheet functions, 184
Arithmetic/logic units (ALU), 54
Artificial intelligence, 385–386
Ascenders, of typefaces, 329
ASCII, 59
AskJeeves, 292–293
Attributes
 HTML tags, 345
 images, 365–366
Audio files, in presentations, 250, 252–253
Authorship, of Web pages, 315
Autocorrect, in word processors, 150
Autoformat, in spreadsheets, 193–194
Autosearch, Internet Explorer, 35–36

B

Backgrounds
 HTML tag for, 368–370
 in Web pages, 368–339
Backspace key, in word processors, 149
Balance, in desktop publishing, 328
Beaucoup Web site, 297
<BGCOLOR>, in Web pages, 368–370
Biometric security measures, for providing security, 397
<BODY> tag
 in creating a Web page, 346
 in Web pages, 368, 370
Bold
 HTML tag for, 354
 in Web pages, 354
Boolean logic, 304
Boolean searching, 304–305
Borders
 in spreadsheets, 192
 in word processors, 164
Bridges, for networks, 104
Browser software, 28–44. *See also* Web browser software
 accessing history with, 36–37
 address bar, 33–34
 basics of, 30–40
 location bar, 33–34
 menu bar, 35
 searching with, 35–36
 setting home pages with, 31–33
 terminology of, 30–40
 toolbar, 35

 tag, in Web pages, 345
<B> tag, in Web pages, 354
Bulleted lists, in Web pages, 366–367
Bus topology, 107
Bytes, 59

C

Cable modem
 for Internet connection, 27–29
 for transmitting data, 103
Cache memory, 57
Cap height, of typefaces, 329
CD-R, 97
CD-ROM, 96
Center, in Web pages, 353
Central processing unit (CPU)
 execution and instruction cycles of, 56–57
 in motherboard, 54–55
Channel, in data communications, 12
Character entities, in Web pages, 368
CIA Geography Quiz page, 379
Citing Internet resources
 with *Chicago Manual of Style*, 319
 with *MLA Handbook*, 319
Clients, in networks, 12, 105
Clip art, free, 168
Closing comments, of Web pages, 345
Clothing, impact of technology on, 391
Coaxial cable, for transmission of data, 100
Code of Ethics, 127
Coherence, in desktop publishing, 328
Color
 HTML tag for, 356
 in Web pages, 355
<COLOR> tag, in Web pages, 356
Columns,
 changing width of, 190–191
 deleting from spreadsheets, 193–194
 inserting into spreadsheets, 193–194

Index

Communications, Internet beginnings and, 11
Communications hardware, 103
Communications media, 99–103
Computer, 4–6
    advantages of using a, 6
    categories of, 9–11
    history of, 7–8
    literacy, 7
Computer-based learning, impact of technology on, 381
Computer crime, 393
    types of, 393–395
Computer ethics, 127. *See also* Ethics, of technology
Computer fraud, 393
Computer hacking, 393. *See also* Hackers
Computer programs, exiting, 74
Computers
    in future, 14
    impact of, 3–4, 9
    risks of using, 395–398
Computer system, 4–6
    components of, 51–59
    hardware, 4
Computer viruses, 95, 394
Consultant, 350
Content advisor, 39
Controllers, in motherboard, 58–59
Control unit, 54–55
Copyright, 244, 317–319, 393
Currency, of Web page, 316

D

Data, on computers, 4–6
Databases, 205
    creating, 206–211
    creating forms from, 220–222
    creating reports from, 223–227
    editing tables in, 211–212
    entering data into, 212
    modifying table structure of, 211
    printing, 213
    querying, 214–219
    structure of, 206
Database software, 205
Data diddling, as computer crime, 395
Data representation, 59
Data source, 260

Definition lists, in Web pages, 352
Delete key, in word processors, 149
Descenders, of typefaces, 329
Design template, in presentation software, 237
Desktop computers, 10–11
Desktop publisher, 333
Desktop publishing, 326–338
    color in, 332
    graphics in, 330–332
    layout and design in, 329
    lines in, 332
    text in, 329
    tips in, 337–338
    typefaces in, 329–330
    Wordart and, 332
Desktop publishing process, 327–328
    creating content, 327
    design guidelines in, 328
    planning, 327
Desktop publishing software, 326–327
Dial-up modem, Internet connection via, 27–29
Digital cameras, 89
Digital cash, in electronic commerce, 389
Digital signatures, 166
Direct connection, to Internet, 27–29
Director of information technology, 186
Disk cache, cleaning up, 40–42
Distance learning, impact of technology on, 380–381
Document, inserting graphic into, 331
Documents, formatting, 76
Domain name
    abbreviations, 25–26
    on the World Wide Web (WWW), 25
DOS (Disk Operating System), 123
Downloading files, from the Internet, 44–45
DSL (digital subscriber line), Internet connection via, 27–28
DVD media, 97

E

EBCDIC (Extended Binary Coded Decimal Interchange Code), 59
E-commerce, 21

Education
    impact of technology on, 378–384
    virtual reality with, 387
Electronic commerce, 389–390
Electronic communication, 11–12
Electronic presentations, 235
E-mail encryption, 360
E-mail links, in Web pages, 363–364
En dash, 76–77
ENIAC, 7
Ergonomic keyboards, 67
Ethernet, 108
Ethical issues, 320–321. *See also* Ethics in Technology feature
Ethics in Technology feature
    code of ethics, 127
    computer viruses, 95
    copyright, 244
    digital signatures, 166
    e-mail encryption, 360
    hackers, 327
    hackers, 39
    Internet security, 37
    junk e-mail, 215
    physical security, 196
    pirates, 327
    plagiarism, 72
    restricting Internet access, 314
    software piracy, 315
    Ten Commandments for computer ethics, 389,
    what is computer ethics?, 127
    who is responsible?, 386
Evaluating Web page content, 316
Evaluation survey, 320
Expansion slots, in motherboard, 58–59
Expert systems, and artificial intelligence, 385
Extranet, 13, 106

F

FBI (Federal Bureau of Investigation) National Crime Center, 393
Fiber-optic cable, 101
Fields, in databases, 206
File menu, for word processors, 144–145
Files
    importing, 269–275
    printing, 74
    retrieving, 75

Floppy diskettes, 94
Florida Online High School, 380
Flying car, 391
Focus, in desktop publishing, 328
Fonts,
    in desktop publishing, 329
    HTML tag for, 355
    point size of, 152
    sans serif, 152–153
    serif, 152
    in Web pages, 355
Font size
    HTML tag for, 355
    in Web pages, 355
<FONT SIZE> tag, in Web pages, 355–358
<FONT> tag, in Web pages, 355–358
Footers
    in spreadsheets, 196
    for word processors, 162–163
Format painter, 153–154
Formatting
    character, 152–154
    documents, 159–163
    lines, 154–159
    paragraphs, 154–159
    text in Web pages, 354–355
    in word processors, 151–168
Form letter, 260–265
Formulas, as spreadsheet data, 182–185
Form wizard, in databases, 220–222
404-Not Found, error message, 29
Functions, in spreadsheets, 182–185

G

Game playing, 385
Gates, Bill, 8
Gateway, network, 104
Genetic engineering, technology of, 386
GIF (Graphic Interchange Format),
    in presentations, 250
    in Web pages, 365
Global economy, impact of technology on, 388
Google, searching the Internet with, 295
Graphic designer, 333

Graphics in Web pages
    in desktop publishing, 331–332
    in word processors, 168–171
    See also Images
Graphics tablet, 87
Groupware, in the workplace, 390

H

Hackers, 39, 327
Handheld computer, 10–11
Hard disk drives, 95
Hardware, 4
    vs. software, 117–118
Headers
    in spreadsheets, 196
    in word processors, 162–163
Headings
    HTML tag for, 359
    in Web pages, 358–359
<HEAD> tag, in Web pages, 345–346
Health issues, when using computers, 395–398
History button, 36
Hits, when searching the Internet, 291
Hoff, Dr. Ted, 8
Home pages, 31, 345
Home row keys, on keyboard, 70
Horizontal rules, in Web pages, 366–367
Host computer, on the Internet, 23
Host node, in networks, 22
How Stuff Works Web site, 378
HTML (Hypertext Markup Language), 24, 344
    headings, 359
    tags, of Web pages, 345–346
    as World Wide Web protocol, 26–27
<HTML> tag, in Web pages, 345–346
HTTP (Hypertext Transfer Protocol), as World Wide Web protocol, 25–26
Hubs, in networks, 104
Hyperlinks. *See* Hypertext links
Hypertext, 26
Hypertext links, 359–364

I

IBM, 8
Images
    HTML tags for, 365–366
    in Web pages, 364–366
<IMG IRC> tag, in Web pages, 367
<IMG> tag, in Web pages, 365
Import
    files, 269–276
    PowerPoint file into Word file, 273
    Word file into a PowerPoint file, 274–275
Indenting, with word processors, 156–157
Information
    from computers, 4–5
    misuse of, 392–393
Information highway, 21. *See also* World Wide Web (WWW)
Input devices, 83–89
    connecting computers to, 93
Insert key, in word processors, 149
Installing files from the Internet, 44–45
Integrated software, 259
Interfaces
    command line, 121
    graphical user, 121
Internal links, 360
Internet, 22–27, 13
    evaluating information on, 313
    evolution of, 22
    features of, 24–27
    getting connected to, 28–29
    restricting access to, 314
    See also World Wide Web (WWW)
Internet detective, 319
Internet Explorer
    adding favorites with, 37–39
    cleaning caches of, 40–42
    controlling Web access with, 39
    History feature with, 36
Internet Explorer browser, 25, 29–45. *See also* Browser software
Internet keywords, with Netscape Navigator, 35
Internet resources
    citing, 319
    types of, 317
Internet security, 37

Internet service providers (ISPs), 28
Internet Web designer, 318
Interoperability, of computers, 23
Intranets, 13, 106
<I> tag, in Web pages, 354
Italics
    HTML tag for, 354
    in Web pages, 354

J

Jaz drives, 96
Jobs, Steve, 8, 122
Joystick, 85
JPEG (Joint Photographic Experts Group) files, in Web pages, 364
JPG (Joint Photographic Experts Group) files, in Web pages, 364
Junk e-mail, 215
Justification, with word processors, 155

K

Keyboard
    as input device, 84
    keystroking, 70–72
    layout of, 66–67
    QWERTY layout of, 66
Keyboarding, 65–66
    "hunt and peck" method, 65
    position, 70
    skills, 72–73, 78–79
    software, 77
    techniques, 69–72
    touch typing and, 66
Keyword searches, 291–292

L

Labels, as spreadsheet data, 182
Landscape orientation, in spreadsheets, 187
Legal issues, 320–321
Line breaks
    HTML tag for, 345
    in Web pages, 349
Line spacing, with word processors, 155
Link, data, 270–272
Links. *See* Hypertext links, 359–364
Lists, in Web pages, 351–354
Local area networks (LANs), 97
    client/server, 105
    Internet connection via, 27
    peer-to-peer, 106
    types of, 105–106

M

Macros, in spreadsheets, 184
Magnetic tape drives, 96
Mail labels, creating, 265–269
Mail merge, 260
Main document, 260
Mainframe computer, 10–11
Main memory, 56
Manager of information systems, 68
Margins, for word processors, 159
Medicine, virtual reality with, 387
Memory
    cache, 57
    main, 56
    in motherboard, 55–57
    random access (RAM), 55
    read-only (ROM), 57
Meta tags, in Web pages, 291
Microsoft Publisher, 334–337
Microwaves, for transmission of data, 102
MIDI port, connecting a device to, 93
Mid-range server, 10–11
Modems, 58
    Internet connection via, 27–29
    for transmitting data, 103
Mollar Web site-Skycar, 391
Monitors, 89–90
    resolution of, 90
    screen size of, 89
Mosaic browser, 24–25
Mosaic Web page, 24
Motherboards, 53–59
Mouse, 84–85
Multimedia, Web-based, 250–253
Multimedia presentations, 251–255
Multitasking, in Windows, 124

N

Natural language, 385
Navigation, of Web site, 316
Netscape Communications, founding of, 25
Netscape Navigator, 25, 28–45
    bookmarking with, 37–39
    cleaning caches of, 40–42
    controlling Web access with, 39
    History feature with, 36–37
Netscape Navigator browser, 25, 29–45. *See also* Browser software
Netwatch, 39

Network interface cards (NICs),
    Internet connections via, 27
    for transmitting data across networks, 104
Networks, 12–13, 97–99
    benefits of, 98–99
    types of, 105–106
    See also Internet; World Wide Web (WWW)
Network topologies, 107–108
Network transmission hardware, 104–105
Nodes, in networks, 12
Nonlethal weapons, impact of technology on, 392
Notebook computers, 10–11

O

Online Service Provider (OSP), for Internet connection, 28–29
Operating systems
    DOS (Disk Operating System), 123
    Macintosh, 122
    microcomputer, 122–126
    network, 126
    sharing files on different, 126
    Windows, 123–125
Optical storage devices, 96–97
Ordered lists, in Web pages, 351
Output devices, 83, 89–93
    connecting computers to, 93

P

Page, viewing, 314
Page content, of Web pages, 345
PageMaker, 326
Page numbers, for word processors, 162–163
Palmtop computer, 10–11
Paragraph breaks, in Web pages, 349–352
Parallel ports, connecting a device to, 93
PC cards, connecting a device to, 93
PC support specialist, 86
Personal computers, 10–11
Personal lives, impact of technology on, 390–392
PhotoCD, 97
Physical media, for networks, 100–101
Physical security, of computers, 196
Pictures, resizing, 197

Pirates, 327. *See also* Software piracy
Plagiarism, 72, 392–391
Play, impact of technology on, 387–392
PNG (Portable Network Graphics) files, in Web pages, 364
Practice work, saving, 74
Presentation expert, 245
Presentation graphics program, 234
Presentations
    charts in, 242–244
    clip art in, 241–242
    creating, 235–240
    delivering, 249
    multimedia in, 250–253
    playing, 247
    preparing effective, 248–249
    printing, 247
    visuals in, 234–235
    WordArt in, 244–246
Presentation software, different views in, 240–241
Primary key, in databases, 209–210
Printers, 90–93
    dot matrix, 93
    inkjet, 92
    laser, 91
Privacy, when using computers, 396
Program. *See* Computer programs
Protocol
    in data communications, 12, 108–109
    for Internet, 23

Q

Quark Xpress, 326
Querying, databases, 214–219

R

Radio signals, for transmission of data, 101
Read-only memory, 57
Receiver, in data communications, 12
Records, in databases, 206
Related search, 306
Relative cell reference, in spreadsheets, 186
Relative links, 360
Removable storage media, caring for, 97

Reports, in databases, 223
Ring topology, 107
Robotics and artificial intelligence, 386
Router, for networks, 104–105
Rows
    deleting from spreadsheets, 193–194
    inserting into spreadsheets, 193–194
    in spreadsheets, 190–191

S

Sans serif, 329
Satellites, for transmission of data, 102
Scanners, 88
Scientific discovery, 384–387
Screens
    Beaucoup Web site, 297
    CIA Geography Quiz page, 379
    Clouds WebQuest, 379
    copying a shortcut, 43
    for databases, 206–209, 211–213, 215–226
    for desktop publishing, 330–331, 335–337
    Florida Online High School, 380
    for global Internet map, 22
    for graphics, 168–169
    for interfaces, 121, 124–125
    How Stuff Works Web site, 378
    for HTML tags, 27, 346–348, 349, 350, 352, 353, 355, 356, 357, 358, 359, 361–363, 364, 366, 367, 369, 370,
    for importing files, 270–273
    for Internet Explorer, 29, 30, 32, 34–35, 38, 40
    for mail merge, 261, 263, 264, 265, 266, 267, 268, 269
    Mollar Web site-Skycar, 391
    Mosaic Web page, 24
    for Netscape Navigator, 33, 35–36, 38, 40–43
    for PowerPoint, 236–243, 247
    Search Engine Watch Web site, 293
    Smithsonian Institute Web page, 25
    for spelling and grammar checker, 150
    for spreadsheets, 180–182, 187–193, 195–197

    Tripod free Web space, 371–372
    for utility software, 120
    WebCT example, 381
    for Web pages, 292–293, 295, 298, 300–302, 305–307, 383–384, 392
    for WordArt, 245–246
    for word processors, 68, 76, 143–147, 151, 153, 156, 158, 160–164, 167, 173
Yahoo!
    directory, 299
    Geocities free Web space, 371
SCSI (small computer interface) ports, connecting a device to, 93
Search
    Boolean, 304–305
    features, 306
    keyword, 291–296
    phrase, 303
    reasons for, 290
    subject directory, 299–303
    title, 305–306
    tools and techniques, 303–307
    wildcard, 305
Search engines, 291
    as Internet resource, 317
    math, 304
    meta-, 298, 303
    multimedia, 298
    popular, 296
    specialty, 296–299
Search Engine Watch Web site, 293
Security
    Internet, 37
    when using computers, 396–397
Sender, in data communications, 12
Serial ports, connecting a device to, 93
Serif, 329
Servers, in networks, 12
Shading
    in spreadsheets, 192
    in word processors, 164
Shareware, 395
Simcity simulation, 384
Simplicity, in desktop publishing, 328
Simulation analysts, 398
Simulations, in education, 382–384

Sizing handles, in graphics, 169
Smart quotes, in documents, 77
Smart seats, 392
Smart shoes, 392
Smithsonian Institute Web page, 25
Software, 4
   applications, 118
   vs. hardware, 117–188
   language translators, 120
   operating systems, 118–119
   types of, 118–120
   utilities, 119–120
Software developer, 123
Software integration, 259–260
Software piracy, 315, 395
Software suites, 259–260
Sorting
   in databases, 213
   in spreadsheets, 194
Space travel, 392
Spacing, in documents, 76–77
Special characters, in documents, 76–77
Speech recognition software, 77
Spell checking, 75, 150
Spider, for Internet searching, 294
Spreadsheets, 179–180
   adding objects to, 197–198
   anatomy of, 180–181
   creating charts in, 199
   editing, 185–187
   entering data into, 182–183
   filling cells in, 185–187
   formatting, 187–194,
   hiding data in, 195
   linking with an Access table, 270–272
   moving around in, 182–182
   printing, 187–189
   purpose of, 180
<SRC> tag, in Web pages, 365
Star topology, 108
Storage devices, 93–97
Styles, for word processors, 163
Subject directories, 299, 303
Supercomputer, 10–11
Symbols, in graphics, 169

T

T1 line, 28
T3 line, 28
Tables
   creating simple, 172–173
   in databases, 206
   formatting, 173–174
   modifying, 173–174
   in word processors, 172
Tab stops, in word processors, 165–168
TCP/IP (Transmission Control Protocol and Internet Protocol), 23, 109
Technological discoveries, 384–387
Technology
   impact of, 3–4
   issues raised by, 392–395
Technology careers
   consultant, 350
   desktop publisher/graphic designer, 333
   director, information technology, 186
   Internet Web designer/Webmaster, 318
   manager of information systems, 68
   PC support specialist, 86
   presentation expert, 245
   simulation analysts, 398
   video game programmer, 274
   word-processing operator, 148
Technology injuries, protection from, 398
Templates
   in desktop publishing, 333
   in spreadsheets, 188
Ten Commandments for computer ethics, 389
Thumbnail sketches, in desktop publishing, 327
Time bombs, as computer viruses, 394
Timed writings, and keyboarding skills, 73
Timeliness of Web page content, 316
Titles
   HTML tag for, 346
   in Web pages, 345
<TITLE> tag, in creating a Web page, 346
Token ring topology, 108
Touch display screen, 87
Trackball, 86
Training, virtual reality with, 387
Transitions, presentation, 239
Transmission media, 99
Tripod free Web space, 371–372
Twisted-pair cable, for transmission of data, 100
Typeface, in desktop publishing, 329

U

Underline
   HTML tag for, 354
   in Web pages, 354
UNIVAC, 7
Unordered lists, in Web pages, 351–352
URLs (Uniform Resource Locators), 294. *See also* Web page address.
USB (Universal Serial Bus) ports, connecting devices to, 93
   in motherboard, 58
Users, of computers, 5
<U> tag, in Web pages, 354

V

Values, as spreadsheet data, 182
Video files, in presentations, 250, 252–253
Video game producer, 274
Video input, 89
Virtual reality, 387
Voice recognition devices, as input devices, 87–88

W

Web browsers, 344
Web browser software, 22, 28–44. *See also* Internet Explorer; Netscape Navigator
Webmaster, 318
Web page address, 25
Web pages, 26–27, 344–349
   copying and saving from, 43–44
   formatting, 349–359
   how it works, 343–344
   planning a, 344–345
   publishing, 370–372
WebQuest Web site, 379
Web server, 344
What-if-analysis, in spreadsheets, 199
White space, in desktop publishing, 328

Who is responsible, 386
Wide area networks (WANs), 97, 106
Wildcard character, 305
Windows operating system, 123
Windows CE, 124
Wireless media, for transmission of data, 101–103
Wizards, in desktop publishing, 333
Word processing operator, 148
Word processing software, 142–143
Word processor
 checking spelling, 150
 editing text in, 145–151
 insertion point in, 145
 menu options, 144–145
 opening file in, 146–147
 printing file with, 147–149
 saving file in, 146
 screen, 143–144
  display, 68–69
  title bar, 69
Word wrap, 69
Work, impact of technology on, 387–392
Workbooks, 195
Workplace, impact of technology on, 390
Worksheets. *See* Spreadsheets
Workstation, organization, 72
World Wide Web (WWW), 24–27. *See also* Internet
WORM disks, 96
Worms, as computer viruses, 394
Wozniak, Steve, 8, 122
WWW (World Wide Web) Virtual Library, 299
WYSIWYG (What You See Is What You Get), 326

X

X-height, of typefaces, 329

Y

Yahoo!
 Geocities free Web space, 371–372
 directory, 299

Z

Zip drives, 96